SHAKESPEARE AND THE NATURE OF WOMEN

- chaste marriage
- equality of women / and freedom
(B) marriage as partnership
   liberty and equality in marriage
M marriage as mystical union p 98
   2 in 1
subordination in equality p 110
- - marriage of minds 113
   Marriage of true minds 117
- friendship in marriage p 128
- reciprocal idolatry p 157

Also by Juliet Dusinberre

ALICE TO THE LIGHTHOUSE: Children's Books and
Radical Experiments in Art (1987)

Shakespeare and the Nature of Women

Juliet Dusinberre

Second Edition

St. Martin's Press
New York

St. Martin's Press, Scholarly and Reference Division,
175 Fifth Avenue, New York, N.Y. 10010

First published in the United States of America in 1996

Printed in Great Britain

ISBN 0–312–15972–2 (cloth)
ISBN 0–312–15973–0 (paper)

Library of Congress Cataloging-in-Publication Data
Dusinberre, Juliet.
Shakespeare and the nature of women / Juliet Dusinberre. — 2nd
ed.
p. cm.
Includes bibliographical references and index.
ISBN 0–312–15972–2 (cloth). — ISBN 0–312–15973–0 (paper)
1. Shakespeare, William, 1564–1616—Characters—Women. 2. Women
and literature—England—History—16th century. 3. Women—England–
–Social conditions. I. Title.
PR2991.D8 1996
822.3'3—dc20   95–26256
                                                          CIP

FOR
THEA AND JOHN STAINER,
MY PARENTS
and
FOR BILL

Contents

Acknowledgements

I am deeply indebted to the impeccable scholarship of Professor G. K. Hunter, who first directed my attention to Humanist and Puritan sources for the treatment of women and who required improvements at many different stages in the work. His readiness to make his own ideas and learning available has been invaluable to me.

Professors Inga-Stina Ewbank, D. J. Palmer and Patrick Collinson all read the complete manuscript and suggested corrections. I am grateful not only for their detailed advice but also for their generous encouragement. Needless to say, the imperfections which remain are my own.

Dr Robin Clifton gave me essential bibliography and access to his own extensive knowledge of the Puritans. Professors Harold Brooks and Bernard Harris spurred me to extend and develop my original study of women in late Elizabethan drama. Professor John Russell Brown gave me stringent and constructive criticism of Chapter I. Professor Kenneth Muir introduced me to Emilia Lanyer's poetry. Dr Stanley Wells kindly advised me on preparing the manuscript for the press. I received unstinting support and goodwill from the Staff and Fellows of the Radcliffe Institute.

I would like to thank Dr Gareth Lloyd Evans for many Shakespeare Summer Schools at Stratford; Mrs D. Bednarowska, Miss D. Cooper and the late H. V. D. Dyson; the staffs of the University of Warwick library, the British Library, the Widener and Houghton libraries and the Hilles library at Radcliffe College; Professor Bernard Bergonzi, Mrs V. Cutler, Mrs M. Caswell, Mrs E. Newlands; and William Dusinberre.

Juliet Dusinberre

Preface to the Second Edition

Beyond the Battle?

Shakespeare and the Nature of Women begins with a battle-cry. With its publication in 1975 I certainly embarked on a battle in which I – and others – shed blood. My generation of feminist scholars and critics will probably never completely emerge from that conflict. We might all have asked each other in the early 1970s, 'When shall we three meet again?/ In thunder, lightning, or in rain?' and we might equally have answered, 'When the hurlyburly's done,/ When the battle's lost and won.' In the 1970s feminism was inseparable from anger, expressed in my case in a particularly British mode of coruscating jokes, which even those who hadn't read Freud on jokes (which included myself) could recognise for aggression. It was an unconventional mode of writing, and the controversy the book immediately aroused astonished me. Not totally, however. The role of the book in culture is, after all, to *provoke* thought.

What was the battle about, and has it been lost, or won, or both? In the simplest terms, it was about the asking of questions. The educated world, with its cherished traditions of free speech, operates its own censors, sometimes overt, as in the present dispute about political correctness, but more often closely concealed. Scholars can hide even from themselves their own inner censorship, a process familiar to all students of literature in the late sixteenth and early seventeenth centuries.[1] What can and cannot be said. One of the things I felt unable to say was that the questions other people asked about literature bored me. For in my education, if you found things dull, it was because you yourself were unintelligent, ill-read and narrow-minded. Many students still feel a similar frustration with the academic world and the way it reads and writes. But the options open to them are now wider because in the last twenty-five years that dominant critical mode has been consistently challenged.[2]

Shakespeare and the Nature of Women participated in a battle about ownership.[3] Who determines the questions we ask and the answers we give? Who owns the literary text? Who owns the authoritative critical voice? Who owns the past? When I began in 1965 the work on women in Jacobean drama which subsequently became *Shakespeare and the Nature of Women*, there seemed no way to articulate these questions.[4] At the end of 'The Leaning Tower', an essay which Virginia Woolf published in 1940 just months before her suicide, she wrote: 'Literature is no one's private ground; literature is common ground. . . . Let us trespass freely and fearlessly and find our own way for ourselves.'[5] The injunction is written from the urgency of its own particular moment when Woolf felt that war would destroy writing and reading, but it speaks, as so much of her writing does, to that sense of exclusion shared by all first-generation feminist scholars. Keep off the grass (or at least only walk on it in respectable company). Literature doesn't belong to you. It didn't belong to us because we seemed to have no way of asking our own questions about it.

When I wrote *Shakespeare and the Nature of Women* I hoped to prise open the Shakespearean text and make it accessible to investigations about women's place in culture, history, religion, society, the family. I wanted to ask those questions from my own particular perspective, not from the impersonal one which I had been trained to adopt. My Shakespeare, not someone else's. Critics now accept that there is no single authoritative and authentic way of reading Shakespeare. The idea of plural Shakespeares gives the reader – for serious Shakespeare scholarship took place twenty years ago in the study not in the theatre – a new power over the text, the words that he or she reads. (In the 1970s women were always subsumed into 'he'; the male pronoun was *common* ground. Stop laughing in the back row.) Shakespeare then, as now, had the status of the Bible in

British culture. No one, and especially no woman (or artisan, child, mad person, Montaigne's category of *le vulgaire*) must make free with the sacred text. I wrote from the classic position of an outsider, because I didn't have an academic job and I was looking after a baby full-time. You can now get by in the professional world with a husband, but if you have a baby it is still wise for her or him to be more or less invisible. A baby makes a woman look like an amateur unless she can demonstrate that someone else is doing the domestic work. This is hardly ever said; but that it remains true most professional women would not deny.

My work on Shakespeare and his period grew out of my own negotiations between that way of life and my fascination with the literary, theological, historical and theatrical world of the early modern period. How could these two extremely disparate and apparently incompatible worlds be brought into any meaningful connection with each other? That was itself a question which women were not supposed to ask, because it blurs the distinction between the public and the private, the amateur and the professional, on which male-dominated culture is founded.[6] When I studied the culture which had nurtured Shakespeare and his theatre, it was plain that in the early modern period the boundaries between public and private were different from ours. Shakespeare's contemporaries asked questions about women in their own society which permeated the literary text, and could be recovered by women in the late twentieth century.

The lives of women in the postwar period in Britain were governed by a belief in the fixed inviolable natural givens of 'femininity' (*never* used with inverted commas) which could be invoked at any time, in any place, to prevent women stepping out of their allegedly preordained roles. Could a women ever be Prime Minister, was a question we asked our female teachers at school, and they replied firmly that woman's nature would make her unsuitable for such pre-eminence. Could a woman be an engineer, go to the moon, play the tuba, become a member of the Oxford Union, or write the plays of Shakespeare? No, certainly not. Nor could cats go to heaven. It is a fearful indictment of myself and my education that I graduated from university without having read *A Room of One's Own*, which burst on me, as on many women since, like the new planet which swam into Keats's vision when he read Homer in Chapman's translation. When I contemplated the enormous variety of men and women in the plays of Shakespeare and his contemporaries it seemed to me that ideas about a preordained feminine or masculine nature, though constantly talked about by characters on stage, were in fact often criticised, ridiculed, and discredited in the dramatic actions witnessed by the theatre audience.

Today one would start work on women from a recognisable political position. In 1961 I wrote an essay on chastity in Jacobean drama, and when I returned to graduate school I chose to write on women largely because I couldn't think of anything else to write about. It was only when I encountered the weight of traditional male wisdom (enshrined in medieval and Renaissance texts) which had over the centuries created the conditions under which I was seriously required to conduct my life in the mid-twentieth century, that I became a feminist. Was Eve inferior to Adam because she was created second, or was she superior to him because she was God's final effort? Hélène Cixous never said a truer word than when in a famous essay she urged women in to blow up the whole male edifice with laughter.[7] Or as Helena says to Parolles in *All's Well that Ends Well*, when he suggests bawdily that men will blow up virgins: 'Is there no military policy how virgins might blow up men?' (I.i.121–2).[8] I was not a virgin but a married woman, and I had no particular desire to blow up individual men. I did want to blow up some of the structures of thought created by centuries of male tradition, within which we were all, men and women, expected to operate.

The book's assertion of Shakespeare's feminism trespassed on sacred ground by suggesting a political frame of reference for a work of art, this polluting it with propaganda. Nowadays there is nothing particularly startling about this position. Work on the intersections between politics and literature in the early modern period has made the statement of the political, social and historical contexts of Shakespeare's plays seem rudimentary to an understanding of them.[9] *Shakespeare and the Nature of Women* approaches the literary work from the perspective of the history of ideas, combining close reading with as comprehensive a recovery of contextual material as is possible. Intertwined with this procedure is a political feminist argument about the relevance of Elizabethan and Jacobean material to the feminist debates of the late twentieth century.

My book is an ambitious enterprise, spanning an entire period, involving some discussion of Restoration drama when women actresses supplanted boys, containing a considerable comparative element in its contrasting of Molière and Lope de Vega with English drama, and drawing on feminist writing from later periods, as well as on the novel. It compares Jacobean and Elizabethan drama both with Caroline theatre[10] and with the Restoration, finding in both periods increased conservatism in relation to women.[11] The book needs to be taken as a whole, which is how it was written. I urge my kind readers, as Donne urged the readers of *Pseudo-martyr* (1610), to read to the bitter end: 'I thought not that any man might well and properly be called a Reader, till he were come to the end of the Booke.'[12] Donne also exhorted his readers to take up their pens and correct the printing errors. I hope this will not be necessary, but I can assure my readers that they may safely read to the end without fear of martyrdom.

To my surprise and fascination, Puritan writings on marriage and the family in domestic conduct books in the late sixteenth and early seventeenth centuries revealed a patriarchal world under pressure to change. To that extent, the early modern world looked in the mid-sixties like mine; for I began my work in 1965 at the just-opened University of Warwick which soon leapt to fame in student protests, a place where new questions were asked all the time. Without that heady sense that anything was possible, and the freedom given to me in that environment, I probably would not have had the courage or the determination to build a bridge between Shakespeare's world and my own. The Puritan domestic conduct books preached domestic harmony through the model of the ideal household, man and wife, children, servants, a little commonwealth which mirrored the order of the state with the king as its overlord. Puritan writers ratified patriarchal authority and demonstrated the ways in which it could successfully be maintained. It is perfectly true that there is nothing remotely feminist about the genre described in this way, and many scholars are happy to accept that description.[13] But one of the excitements of the study of literature in the late twentieth century is that reading itself has changed and is now understood as a complex transaction between writer, text and reader. In 1975 I read Puritan writings on marriage for the breaches in that patriarchal wall, and found a fabric ruptured by questions which could not be answered by the pious pronouncements of patriarchal discourse. Some historians are now also convinced that these books cannot be read as straight endorsements of orthodox patriarchy.[14]

One source of tension was the Puritan insistence on the spiritual equality of man and wife, and on a concept of relationship which stressed equal fellowship in preference to the subjection of the woman. The reconciling of an authoritarian model with egalitarian practice was obviously fraught with difficulty.[15] It would in due course have its own repercussions on ideas of government, that the political as well as the domestic state should be run by mutual consent.[16] The writers of Puritan conduct books, drawing on the writings of sixteenth-century Protestant and Humanist reformers, often gave traditional answers about the position of woman, but they asked new questions about the limits of authority, equality, freedom of conscience, sexuality, property, and the legacy of inherited ecclesiastical wisdom about the inherently frail nature of woman. That wisdom, derived from the Church Fathers' teaching on the Fall and endorsed in popular culture, was at odds with the radical Protestant and Puritan determination to reassess the role of marriage in society, and as a corollary, the role of Eve in relation to Adam. Under the Puritan redefinition of Eve's place in God's creation, sexuality was seen as a prelapsarian source of mutual joy, and the woman as the equal partner whose presence confirms man's blessedness in the eyes of his Creator.[17] There is no doubt that the Puritan preachers did not want to change social structures. But social structures do eventually change if enough questions are asked, and the subtle shifts in emphasis which the conduct books display created a leaning tower even while the men on top of it continued to think it was straight.

Puritan domestic ideals were forged in a society in which marriage seems to have been under extreme pressure and women themselves far from subservient, as new historical research demonstrates. Women were not even prepared to listen quietly while William Gouge preached their domestic duties from his Blackfriars pulpit.[18] They had their own networks and their own spheres of power – Alice Clark's pioneering work on the working life of women in the seventeenth century has still not been superseded as an account of a society in which many women had financial and business responsibilities outside the home quite apart from their indispensable roles in running the household.[19] The great advances in women's history in the past twenty years have fleshed out a picture which complicates the simple reading of early modern patriarchy as a society in which women were subject to male authority.[20] Of course they were, but they also had their own modes of challenging that authority. Haven't we all?

What then was the place of the theatre in this culture in which new ideas and structures, religious, social, educational, fired questions under the bows of patriarchy, much as the little English ships of the Armada peppered the great Spanish galleons stuck in the sand of the English Channel by their own weight? Did the theatre fulfil a conservative and establishment role in confirming the domestic authority which Puritan preachers and writers of conduct books proclaimed? Or did the dramatists read behind the lines to the tensions and discontinuities in the patriarchal text, and dramatise not a stable world, but one in flux?[21] Did the drama in the main confirm the orthodoxies of its time, or did it subvert them?

Critical debate still centres on these problems, and Stephen

Greenblatt's containment theory is one answer to them, maintaining that subversion was a calculated licence controlled by authority,[22] an *allowed* fooling, such as Viola identifies for Feste in *Twelfth Night*. It is questionable, however, whether the carnivalesque – Mikhail Bakhtin's formulation – can be totally exorcised by a resumption of authority. In the famous essay 'Women on Top' Natalie Zemon Davis includes Rosalind among unruly women whose impact is not contained by the authority structures which the end of *As You Like It* – in replacing the Forest of Arden with the court – invokes. The charge of disorder has been too great to be completely dispersed.[23] In comparable fashion the trial-scene in Webster's *The White Devil*, in which Vittoria repudiates the judgements of the male court against her, releases into the auditorium an energy incapable of being dissipated by the play's conventional retributive ending.

It would not be possible now to discuss any of Shakespeare's plays without reference to theatrical performance. Twenty years ago the emphasis in the academy on reading rather than seeing Shakespeare's plays allowed a sense of stability to surround his texts which cannot now survive either an awareness of the infinite variety of theatrical performances, or an awareness of the unstable nature of the texts themselves. The notion of an authoritative edition has given way to an understanding of texts modified by performances and by other material considerations.[24] *Shakespeare and the Nature of Women* considers the theatre in Shakespeare's period as a space in which the dramatist interacted with a known audience, often using a language which would be intelligible to an audience in more complex ways than that of simple exhortation or endorsement of current orthodoxies. The book argues that the dynamic instability of the theatre and the theatrical text undermines and rewrites the discourses of womanhood available to both author, actors and audience. Plays, the central concern of my study, do not simply underwrite cultural codes; they query them, from the centre of their own vitality within the social arena of the theatre.

Elizabethan and Jacobean plays dramatise precisely the problems, inconsistencies and cracks in the fabric of patriarchal discourse, which are evident in Puritan writings. Moreover, the attempts in the drama to resolve some of those conflicts – between authority and conscience, equality and submission – often move Puritan thinking into a more radical and subversive territory, because a play means a performance to a crowd of people, not a book read privately in a study. Insofar as the theatre itself was under attack in the period for potential political and social disruption, not least in its employment of boy actors for women's parts, the dramatists had a special interest in the new questions, which allied them with the women in their audiences. The playwrights shared with the many women in Elizabethan and Jacobean society who expressed their discontent through cross-dressing, gossip and slander, or writing pamphlets or even poems, an often tempestuous relation to the authoritarian structures of a patriarchal culture.[25]

Attacks in Elizabethan and Jacobean drama on literary constructions of women, both populist, satirical and Petrarchan, can be read as part of a self-identification, on the part of the dramatists, with a world outside the court. Plays released into the theatre dissent from the literary discourses about women current in that inside world of the court, because the dramatists recognised a shared outsider status with the women in the audience. The class orientation of the playwrights themselves, and the composition of the audience in the public theatre, made Puritan sympathies an important element in the political and social frame of reference of the drama,[26] in a period when plays could express with comparative freedom ideas not tolerated anywhere else. Shakespeare was not a bourgeois city dramatist, but his immensely subtle negotiations of courts and courtiers in his plays were in part the consequence of his own distance from the court. The men and women who attended Shakespeare's theatre – and research into the composition of that audience has expanded fruitfully since the book was published – would, through their hearing of Puritan preachers (in the early seventeenth century often still members of the Anglican church) have been exposed to that shift in values, particularly in the domestic sphere, which had its origins in the writings of Luther and Erasmus on marriage.[27]

The theatre was not considered in this period as part of the
literary world. Plays were not literature, with the lamentable
consequence that many men and women who must have seen
and heard Shakespeare's plays – Donne, Sir John Harington, Lucy
Countess of Bedford, Lady Anne Clifford – never mention
them.[28] Literary convention, whether Petrarchan idealisation of
women or its corollary, conventional satire, comes under fire in
numbers of plays for a literariness taken seriously within a social
context. 'I'll write against them,' cries Posthumus in *Cymbeline*
after rehearsing a long list of recognisable complaints about
women, applying them all to his wife, and wishing men could
procreate like trees. Posthumus is a victim of his own reading
habits. Shakespeare's audience, made up of men and women not
in the main identified with a 'literary' culture, would have been
able to assess the distance between the dramatist, and his
characters' use of a misogynist discourse for dramatic purposes.
Shakespeare's contemporary playwrights share with him
techniques for dismantling the views on woman expressed by
characters on stage. The effect of this process is to highlight, as
theatrical performance itself does, the artificial construction of a
creature called 'woman', a being who can be set into dialogue
with a figure on stage, another woman – albeit impersonated by a
boy – who undermines and contradicts those presuppositions.
This person constitutes some different idea of the 'real', of
individual women capable of testifying against a generic
definition of womankind.

Shakespeare and the Nature of Women claims that this revision of
traditional thinking about women, together with the actual
activities of women in society, not least those of Elizabeth herself
in the manipulation of gender roles, created a ferment of new
questions which animated the drama of Shakespeare and his
contemporaries, and deserves the name feminist. The subject of
the feminism of this period continues to engage some of the
liveliest debate in both history and literature, and in contemporary
debate the word 'feminist' has acquired for both historians and
literary scholars a legitimacy with reference to the early modern
period, which earlier writers were unwilling to accord it.[29]

If I were rewriting the book I would have to address the theoretical problems surrounding the relation of history to the play as fiction, itself often drawing on fictional sources. The 'real' world is now considered by many historians, as well as literary critics, to be as much an artificially constructed model as the plays themselves. I don't totally regret, however, the simplicity of the book's critical language, which was not the consequence of lack of thought about these connections, but rather of the absence of a theoretical discourse in which to analyse them. That simplicity, whatever its intellectual disadvantages, made the work accessible to a wide readership, not least in secondary schools. That Shakespeare's plays, all of them and not just the comedies, reveal to audiences multiple instances of power structures under pressure, which can be paralleled in Elizabethan and Jacobean society, politics and culture, remains central to the book's original conception, and to my own view of the relations in this period between plays, audiences and the world outside the theatre.

Despite the fact that my book was written before Foucault's language of competing discourses was available to scholars, I wanted to demonstrate in it that individuals within Shakespeare's plays are often acutely aware of the discourses within which they and others conduct their lives. 'Is she not a modest young lady?' enquires Claudio to Benedick, of Hero in *Much Ado About Nothing*. Benedick replies: 'Do you question me, as an honest man should do, for my simple true judgement? or would you have me speak after my custom, as being a profess'd tyrant to their sex?' (I.i.165–9). Benedick stands outside the gender roles he invokes, and asserts his freedom from them as Rosalind does when she declares on entering the forest of Arden disguised as a boy: 'I could find in my heart to disgrace my man's apparel and to cry like a woman; but I must comfort the weaker vessel, as doublet and hose ought to show itself courageous to petticoat' (II.iv. 4–8). A consciousness of masculinity and femininity as acting is implicit in both these speeches.[30] Men and women perform on stage the gender roles which they are required to perform in society, thus highlighting the theatricality inherent in social behaviour. In doing so they unsettle those social roles by demonstrating that they play parts which have been learnt, rather than determined by innate characteristics.

Implicit in my suggestion that both Benedick and Rosalind offer a critique of their own discourse is the critical question of the unified self.[31] I do not believe that all we hear in the plays of Shakespeare and his contemporaries – and the book places Shakespeare deliberately within a company of dramatists – are different discourses skilfully arranged. We hear that in some of the plays of his contemporaries – *The Miseries of Enforced Marriage*, perhaps – but in surprisingly few, and never all the time. Foucault's theory of the individual as the site on which competing discourses play suggests that we are none of us free to do anything except unwittingly bear witness to that condition. But the study of literature, as of history, demonstrates that we can all create new discourses. Whether the consciousness which makes that possible, which decrees a capacity for independence from inherited culture, is rightly described as a 'self' I would hesitate to proclaim, preferring the model of continually dissolving and reconstituting selves presented in those texts of which Shakespeare himself shows cognisance, the *Essais* ('trials') of Michel de Montaigne. But discourses can be resisted even within a predominantly patriarchal world, as Ann More demonstrated when she defied the marriage arrangements of her society in secretly marrying John Donne, just four years after they might both have witnessed in the theatre a comparable defiance in Shakespeare's Juliet. If those acts of resistance carried in their wake various disasters they nevertheless had the capacity to threaten the stability of the worlds in which they were perpetrated.

Allied to the problems surrounding the concept of the autonomous 'self' are the difficulties of discussing the author's intentions. I wouldn't now use the language of authorial intention; if I had to choose the most important essay written for modern criticism it would still be Roland Barthes' 'The Death of the Author' (English translation 1977). But recent challenges to Barthes's argument – with which I concur – have gone a long way towards reinstating a concept of authorial intention.[32]

Allowing Shakespeare into his own texts as an informing authorial presence has always been a dubious critical procedure. As Richard Helgerson has argued, Hal, not Shakespeare, rejects Falstaff: 'Shakespeare is simply not there.'[33] My readings of many key moments surrounding women in Shakespeare's plays discover in the plays an ethic of dissent from established orthodoxies about women in general, current in writings outside the theatre. That dissent is certainly my own, but it is also often representative of a dissent experienced by the audience in the theatre. Furthermore, it is reflected back from the protagonists in the plays themselves. 'Frailty, thy name is woman.' The sentiment is instantly identifiable as a key myth of Western culture. But the play invites the audience to condemn that sentiment as a source of destructiveness for both Ophelia and Hamlet. How is that invitation constituted? It is apparently produced by some kinetic energy generated between author, audience, text and action.

The same question can be pursued in relation to *The Duchess of Malfi*, or any number of other plays written by Shakespeare's contemporaries. The Duchess's sexuality is condemned by her brothers and their society, with blatant hypocrisy, but, in contrast to the reader's reaction to the source novella in Painter's *Palace of Pleasure*, the theatre audience remains convinced of her innocence and the perverse wickedness of her brothers. Her sexuality is condemned by a corrupt environment which destroys her. Does the dramatist endorse the values of that society? If he intended to do so, his failure is palpable.[34] Some of the most interesting recent research both from feminists and others, has been in the field of audience response,[35] which has been stimulated by the much closer connections in the last decade between the academic world and the theatre.

The women's movement, of which 1970s feminist criticism was one offshoot, gave theatrical performance of Shakespeare a much-needed shot in the arm; some of the plays now receive interpretations which would have been inconceivable twenty years ago. Productions breaking new ground have in recent years been mounted by female directors – among them Deborah Warner and the late Buzz Goodbody.[36] Classic interpretations have been undermined, as in the case of *Troilus and Cressida*, where Cressida's role is now dissociated from Ulysses's judgement of her in the Greek camp as a 'daughter of the game.' Ulysses' speech used to have the status of authorial instruction as to how Cressida was to be played. A parallel could be drawn with the same character's famous speech on degree, which was upheld as the final statement of Elizabethan ideas on order, derived from the *Book of Homilies*. The Homily 'Concerning Good Order and Obedience to Magistrates and Rulers' formed part of an Elizabethan enunciation of the rhetoric of a social control which that society was far from possessing. In Shakespeare's play it was equally in the Greek commanders' interests to declare Cressida a camp whore, because if she were not, what were they? The scene in the Greek camp now forces the audience to encounter its own horror at the passing from hand to hand of a young and defenceless woman with the multiple images such actions conjure up in modern society.

Similar changes in theatrical presentation spring to mind in relation to the feminist reconstitution of female desire. In the first scene of Adrian Noble's RSC production of *A Midsummer Night's Dream* at the main theatre in Stratford-upon-Avon in 1994, when Theseus had finished his diatribe to Hermia on the alternatives open to her – to marry Demetrius (her father's choice) or to enter a nunnery – he graciously extended his hand to his betrothed, Hippolyta, Queen of the Amazons, to escort her from the room. She glared at him, seized her long skirt with the hand she should have joined to his, and flounced off the stage, slamming the stage door behind her. The second example relates to the acting of Gertrude, always previously presented to audiences in the impenetrable packaging of Hamlet's disgust at her middle-aged sexuality. To recognise in Gertrude a woman pursuing her own desires in a world which denies her the right to do so enriches the play by complicating the relationship with Hamlet.

The variety of readings given to Kate's obedience speech in *The Taming of the Shrew* in the last ten years provides evidence of the interaction between criticism and theatrical practice.[37] I first saw an ironic rendering of that speech at a student production at

Harvard early in 1972, where the wager was played as collusion between Kate and Petruchio. Petruchio rewarded his bride's performance with the purse he might have given Lucentio if Bianca had obliged her husband with the performance of obedience which he requested from her. If the apprentice playing Bianca had been capable of such a performance. The heady sense of stage mastery generated in the theatre by Kate's speech in defiance of its ideology of subjection, draws its impetus from the stage reality of the boy apprentice's carrying the climax of the play. He can make or break its culminating moment by his performance. The apprentice who plays the leading lady acknowledges in this play – as in many others – a natural affinity with women in the audience, who enjoy fantasies of power in the theatre, before returning to subordinate status in the workaday world. What is the relation between those fantasies and the instinct to acquire real power in a social context? Women in Shakespeare's audience, as in later audiences, may have drawn from the play an energy which they took back with them into the social world outside the theatre. To teach and delight. All for your delight we are not here. Yes. No. Sixpence a day for playing Pyramus.

When I wrote *Shakespeare and the Nature of Women* I considered the chapter on 'Disguise and the Boy Actor' to be the most original in the book. The intersection of the boy actor with the woman he must represent, and what this meant for representations of gender in Elizabethan society – what I called the 'masculine' and the 'feminine' – was a new field. The shift from feminism to the study of gender which is a controversial aspect of today's scholarly activity, was implicit in the shift in my book from the history of ideas about women in the first two sections, to the representation of them in the theatre in the remaining chapters. These focus on how the 'feminine' and the 'masculine' were socially constructed. I encountered within the plays an awareness of the performing of gender roles as an inevitable constituent in social behaviour, stimulated by the special circumstances of a theatre in which boys represented women. The role of the boy actor in Shakespeare's theatre has become the site of intense scholarly activity.

In the light of contemporary scholarship *Shakespeare and the Nature of Women* underplays the issue of homoerotic relationships, illuminated by many scholars investigating homosocial and homoerotic desire both in the plays and in Elizabethan and Jacobean society.[38] I still see the boy actor as the source of a performative energy which focuses attention on the theatricality implicit in all gender roles. The theatre creates a congruence between the social role of the apprentice and the subordinate role of women in the audience, both of whom within the theatre usurp power, whether theatrical or social.[39]

The book also underplays the question of desire,[40] and its relation to reason. In Mary Wollstonecraft's *A Vindication of the Rights of Women* the battle is to prove women rational beings. Historically this was the case in Renaissance thought, which put such a high price on reason as the characteristic which distinguished men from beasts. But the binary opposition of reason and passion now seems to me as much in need of dissolution as all the other oppositions in that Aristotelian system. *Shakespeare and the Nature of Women* criticises Puritan thought for underestimating passion, especially when illicit, but it doesn't consider sufficiently whether reason itself ought to be under attack, or indeed is under attack in those plays, something it would not be hard to demonstrate from almost any work from *A Midsummer Night's Dream* to *Hamlet* and *King Lear*.[41]

Shakespeare and the Nature of Women was written before the impact of French feminist psychoanalytic theory on Anglo-American feminists. Work is still in progress from various scholars negotiating this field. Freudian psychoanalysis is a significant influence in a number of books written in the early 1980s, but the most provocative and original theoretical writing has been in the field of what Irigaray and Cixous both describe as 'writing the body.' This approach seems to me a fruitful one for Shakespearean studies, not only because the body of the actor is a constant presence in the mediation of the play to the audience, but because the body itself was in the process of being put into discourse in the Renaissance in the works of Rabelais, and some of his English imitators: Sir John Harington's *The Metaphorphosis of Ajax*, Donne's poetry, and Ben Jonson's plays. Shakespeare certainly knew Rabelais, and his own awareness of the body as a socially constructed counter in the discourses of his time – political, sexual, theological, poetic – are inseparable from his constructions of gender. Elizabeth used metaphors of androgyny for her own manipulation of cultural images of male power and female weakness. The theatre was the territory in which the body was socially constructed for the audience.[42] If I had written another chapter to the book, it would have been on Elizabeth I and the discourses surrounding the woman ruler, subjects canvassed in my chapter on women and politics, with its analysis of Elizabeth's manipulation of her own womanhood in the interests of power.[43]

The figure and utterances of Elizabeth I have become increasingly dominant in discussions of Shakespeare's plays. Elizabethan society is distinguished by the powerful presence of a woman's voice in public life. Contemporary feminist scholars are concerned to trace intersections between the voices of women in society and the female voices represented on stage. One of the most absorbing questions raised by new research into women's writing in this period is about the nature of that interaction. Did Shakespeare's women provide the same spur to female thinking and writing that has been demonstrated in later periods? Or did his women reflect activities already present in his audiences?[44]

This is where the question of women's relation to language becomes pressing.[45] In Shakespeare's plays men are conscious of being effeminised if their only weapons are words, historically the weapons of powerless women. There is a new awareness of women not just as users of language, but as born into language structures. This derives both from Irigaray's battle with Lacan – with her exhorting of women to mimic male language – and from Cixous's insistence on women's seizing a language of their own. There is still research to be done on women's historic relation to rhetoric, and to oral tradition. These concerns prompt us to ask whether women are trapped into language in Shakespeare's plays. Do they have a language of their own, forged from their own difference in history, culture and their relation to literacy?[46]

If women have their own history in the history of language itself, how does this affect their positioning in Shakespeare's period as readers and writers? The recovery both of women's history in the Renaissance period and of female-authored texts – often in manuscript – allows women in the early modern period to speak in newly audible voices of their own.[47] Shakespeare wrote his plays for a society in which rhetorical models were under challenge. Work on women as readers, and on the extent to which that reading was part of the author's process of writing[48] – in Sidney, Harington, Donne, Montaigne – can be fed into our understanding of voices of difference in Shakespeare's plays. In *Shakespeare and the Nature of Women* I discussed some women's writing available in print – *The Letters of Dorothy Osborne to William Temple,* Lady Brilliana Harley's letters to her son Edward during the Civil War, and the diaries of Lady Anne Clifford and Lady Margaret Hoby – because I wanted the voices of women outside the theatre to intersect with the voices of women speaking on stage. That those voices were physically the voices of boys, does not seem to me to invalidate the fact that they reached audiences as the voices of women, any more than Daniel's 'Letter from Octavia to Marcus Antonius' seems to me to be less interesting for the woman reader because it was in fact written by a man. Daniel wrote it from his knowledge of his patron's, the Countess of Cumberland's, unhappiness with her philandering husband,[49] and offered his voice in her support, urging in his letter of dedication that she should herself use her own voice. What Octavia at one point says in the letter, is that women have desires like men. What do we hear? We hear Emilia's speech in *Othello* IV. iii: 'But I do think it is their husbands' faults/ If wives do fall. . . . Have not we affections,/ Desires for sport, and frailty, as men have?' Frailty, they name is woman. Like hell it is.

Feminist scholarship not only recovers female-authored texts, but also demands whether women want to read male-authored texts. Elaine Showalter identified this distinction as the difference between 'gynocritics' (women's reading of texts by women) and revision (women's searching within a male-authored tradition for texts open to new readings from the perspective of women).

Feminist scholarship and feminist publishing have, in the last twenty years, encompassed both aims. The ways in which Shakespeare's women have been used as models within culture have established a two-way process between women on stage and women in society.[50] The rewriting of Shakespeare by women, and the revising of his women's roles by actresses able to comment on their own performances – the latter a largely late-twentieth-century phenomenon stimulated by the women's movement – have enriched our understanding of the agency of Shakespeare's plays in transforming culture.[51]

The writings of many feminists on the intersections of gender with race and class are as central to feminist scholarship as is a recovery of men excluded by race and class from dominant male cultural models. My own anger can be very quickly revived when I hear, as I still do from the most respectable academic sources, statements about feminism being mainly concerned with the comic heroines, as if no other class of woman existed in Shakespeare, and as if the discourses of feminism were narrowly centred on character study, which was not the case in my book, nor in most works since then. Feminist scholarship is rooted in the far-reaching theoretical debates surrounding the whole study of English, and feminist Shakespeare scholars work within, and extend, these debates. It's too easy for an old prejudice to be perpetuated, that Shakespeare only creates female heroines, and any women who isn't a heroine isn't really a woman. *Shakespeare and the Nature of Women* was at pains to point out the ways in which class structure determined, within the fictions of the plays, attitudes to chastity, from *The Winter's Tale* to Middleton's *The Changeling*. Important new work is now being done on racist discourse in Shakespeare's plays, on prostitutes, on servants, and on women whose access to another culture and another language gives them the potential to challenge dominant discourse.[52]

Feminist scholars have expressed concern that the shift from feminist criticism to the study of gender depoliticises the enterprise of feminist scholarship by dissociating it from women's authorship and women's lives, making it instead just another academic discipline which anyone can learn and apply. Feminist activity is now more confident, easier with itself, less angry and more cooperative than it was for any of us in the first decade of its existence. The early days witnessed on occasion the spectacle of women fighting each other for rights to a new territory, and exhibiting the well-known phenomenon (which I describe in the book in relation to the women in Shakespeare's histories)[53] of the oppressed turning on each other rather than on their oppressors. The rather daunting and distancing rhetoric of sisterhood has been replaced by a rich network of support and of collaborative work.[54] When I look back twenty years one of the most important changes has been the one prophesied by Virginia Woolf when she said that if Chloe liked Olivia (with whom she shared a laboratory) the novelist would 'light a torch in that vast chamber where nobody has yet been.'[55] I believe that most women are more comfortable and more capable of working well in the present atmosphere than in the more aggressive one of earlier days, despite the overwhelming excitement of those times, lit by a pioneering spirit which is perhaps, inevitably, not quite so bright now as it used to be. The whole enterprise is now established so solidly that an era of outstanding work is only just beginning. There is no danger of feminist work being subsumed in gender studies, to the exclusion of women's interaction with the literary world from their own position in culture.[56] Feminism's political agenda operates on a broad base which is inclusive rather than exclusive, involving many different kinds of study rather than being focused on a single objective.[57]

The question of women's celebration of difference would now modify the terms in which I tried in *Shakespeare and the Nature of Women* to understand confrontations of the 'masculine' and the 'feminine' within the plays, and to argue for a category of 'humanity' which exposed the dangerous and corrupting artificiality of those gender divisions. Twenty years on, I am not, alas, quite so sold on 'humanity'. My arguments were good Emily Davies and Girton College stuff – women the same as, and equal to, men. But feminism has moved on from that bargaining base. For me, as for Davies, that position was a bargaining base. I wanted my book to be read, and considered, not cast aside as the ravings of the dispossessed, nor misunderstood in a climate which in the 1970s saw 'separate but different' as the inevitable route to second-class citizenship. It is because so much has been achieved that women can afford to celebrate difference.

I argued in *Shakespeare and the Nature of Women*, in relation to the feminising of culture by Christianity, that the radical impulse too often over the passage of time becomes conservative,[58] a transformation often in evidence in nineteenth-century recreations of Shakespeare's women. Flower's editions in the Shakespeare Centre Library in Stratford show how much cutting of the texts used by actors in production involved a clear concept of propriety, of what refined women ought and ought not to say on stage.[59] Dialogues with the past can be created out of investigations into women's acting of Shakespeare, out of the theory and practice of performance, out of rewritings, parodies and burlesques.[60] The work of scholars in trying to localise particular performances in Shakespeare's own time, and on the relation between the quartos and the First Folio with regard to performance, all aims at the recovery of a specific moment in the theatre, and a specific audience, which brings us closer to an understanding of the dynamics of a theatre in which women were important as audiences.

How far can one describe these immensely varied activities as 'feminist'? Is it more appropriate to speak of the study of gender and writing? If so, has one excised from the record the feminist drive which animated all first-generation writers on women in literature? Some saw in those texts works misrepresented and distorted by centuries of male-dominated criticism; others believed them to be replications by male authors of the oppressive structures of their own societies. There is now also the question of the male feminist critic, whether 'reading as a woman' can be learned in the way that my generation learnt to read as a man.[61] Behind this debate is the problem of experience, whether the experience of being a woman is a significant element in the enterprise of feminist scholarship, or whether that empirical base ought to be totally subsumed in deeper investigations of psychoanalytic and linguistic study. The divide here, as many will recognise, can roughly be drawn between Anglo-American feminism, in which women's experience has been given high priority, and French feminism, with its analysis of psychoanalytic and linguistic structures.

When I wrote *Shakespeare and the Nature of Women* there was no question in my mind but that being a woman created the feminist work, not from a preordained essentialist view of a feminine nature, but from a position marked out for women in culture, history, society, language. As Adrienne Rich declared in an address to the women of Smith College on 1979: 'Much of the first four decades of my life was spent in a continuous tension between the world the Fathers taught me to see, and had rewarded me for seeing, and the flashes of insight that came through the eye of the outsider. . . . It was only when I could finally affirm the outsider's eye as the source of legitimate and coherent vision, that I began to be able to do the work I truly wanted to do, live the kind of life I truly wanted to live.'[62] 1970s feminists drew energy from a passionate sense of being outsiders, even when attached to various institutions.[63] It was a psychological state created by culture, which women were supposed to inhabit in order to secure the state of insider for male authority: a structure everywhere in evidence in Virginia Woolf's diaries. Nevertheless some of us had the power of the pen at our disposal, and that itself bespoke privilege. We fought with what we had for what we could; but the flaw in that position is its monolithic classing together of all men and women, when culture, history and the modern world demonstrate the overwhelming divisions of those two categories into class, race and diverse sexualities. The original claim of being an outsider now sounds simplistic and could hardly be voiced by an articulate woman on behalf of her sex without sounding complacent, and even downright foolish. But that is partly because some of that original battle has been won.

What has been won has been the fight to make the marginal central, although there is still a good way to go. Feminist scholarship is here to stay, and the new freedom it has created to remap the territories of literary study has benefited all readers who sense the hidden barbed wire which demarcates the boundaries of traditional literary study. *Shakespeare and the Nature of Women* saw the beginning of a protest against the enclosure of common land, enclosed, ironically enough, by the very movement which had set out to open that land to more people. Literature in the vernacular belonged historically to women within an oral tradition. The Renaissance saw one of the most significant changes in relation to gender with the shift from oral to print culture.[64] In the nineteenth century the study of English literature was pursued by women and working-class men who had no access to classical education in the public schools.[65] There is still a violent backlash against feminist scholarship from some members of the establishment, in proportion to their sense of being ousted from intellectual pre-eminence, not least by the popular voice of readers who find the new approaches to literature more exciting than the old. The attempt to ghettoise feminist scholarship, and the women who take part in it, is strong in proportion to the success of the whole feminist enterprise. Women only know about women, has been one of the least reputable ways in which the challenged establishment has continued to exclude from its centres of power the new scholarship and its practitioners. The steady advance of feminist scholarship into an unassailable position within culture has been one of the great gains of the last twenty years, in Shakespeare and Renaissance studies, as everywhere else.

Elaine Showalter has identified some of the problems that advance causes for first-generation feminists, who spoke from the margins of that world.[66] That dynamic is transformed by a movement to the centre. One would be tempted to say that the danger is a new conservatism. The pioneer spirit in any movement cannot last for ever. What will it become? Are there new battle-lines to be staked out? Or is the battle won?

I would say that it is at present lost and won. It has been won in Britain for a very small number of privileged women, who discuss gender issues in further education. For the vast majority, the slippers are still by the fire. For ethnic minority groups, and many others outside European or American culture, the battle

has hardly begun. The enormous gap between the professional
'new' man and his counterpart in society as a whole makes the
enterprise of feminist scholarship a drop in a huge ocean. This, as
the struggle recedes in high places, it is easy to forget. The battle
is, for women at the end of the twentieth century, by no means
over, as current concern over under-achievement by women in
every aspect of society demonstrates. Where should we, and the
new generation of feminist scholars, take it in the new century?

First of all, the female signature of the woman writer mustn't
be obliterated. If we take seriously Barthes' 'The Death of the
Author', we ought logically to declare that the text is free of its
author, and whether that person is a man or a woman is of no
significance.[67] This Preface cites many works by men which have
been vitally important to me in my own feminist enterprise. But
that this particular book could ever have been written by a man I
strenuously deny. *Shakespeare and the Nature of Women* is written
from beginning to end not in ink – no, Hélène Cixous, not even
in white ink – but in blood, my blood, a woman's blood.
Secondly, the question of how to define feminism remains as vital
as it was when I wrote that original battle-cry: Shakespeare the
feminist. For me feminism is about having a voice; it is about
women's voices, but also about voices with whom women have
always been able to claim allegiance across the divide of gender:
the voices of the dispossessed, many of whom are male artists,
often homosexual, often working-class. My feminism encounters
those groups as much as it encounters other ethnic groups. Some
of the nonsense which is currently talked about that loathsome
and anti-educational concept, the 'canon' of literary works,
ignores the fact that some of its chief protagonists – as, for
example, the poet Milton or John Bunyan[68] – wrote their
greatest works from positions as culturally marginal as any
occupied by women. In some respects this was also true of
Shakespeare and most of his fellow dramatists. What were they?
Hack playwrights in a London where people who counted were
courtiers and if they wrote, amateurs. In those days money did
not dignify what was frivolous if unpaid. The reverse. Thirdly,
feminism is about the pursuit of happiness. The inalienable right

of all men. Don't tell me that that word means women too. Because it never has.

Many battles are still to be fought in all these arenas: for voice, choice, and the pursuit of happiness. The next battle I want to see waged is about how to write.[69] I wanted both in *Shakespeare and the Nature of Women* and in *Alice to the Lighthouse: Children's Books and Radical Experiments in Art* (1987), to write for a readership outside the academy as well as within it. I always wrote *Shakespeare and the Nature of Women* with a reader in my head, almost always a particular reader. One was the Shakespearean scholar, the late H. V. D. Dyson, Fellow of Merton College, Oxford. He had a special way of criticising pretension. He used to call out, when one was in mid-sentence, 'O my eye!' and if there is rather less 'my eye' in this book than there might have been, it is because Dyson sat in my head while I was writing it. The second reader was George Hunter, Foundation Professor of English at the University of Warwick, whom I always heard saying, in satirical Scots tones: '*Some* might say so.' The other two readers were my uncle and my late aunt, whom I could hear quietly protesting: 'Didn't understand a word of it.' The rather limpid text which emerges was gobbled up by many readers, as I intended that it should be, but it took some time for the academy to take it seriously.

Women must stand out for their own way of writing and be willing to maintain that that way is different from the way men write, and that men will have to accept it, along with the writings of men who want to write in alternative modes. Feminist scholarship is now a recognised and completely respectable academic discipline. But the whole apparatus of how work is valued is still vested overwhelmingly in the almost entirely male establishment of the media, journal and newspaper editors, even the universities themselves. The way I write, the way I construct an argument, the tone of voice I adopt which if often light-hearted when I intend seriousness (yes, I do intend things when I write), that way of writing is itself a political statement, and always has been. I don't believe that the mode of writing at present preferred in the academy, which has its origins in a long history of male education in rhetoric and the classics, is the way most women either want to write, or write best. Women – and men also if they want to develop more various and vital cultural models – should resist a single dominant mode of writing, reading and speaking. But at present, if one does, and this is an important aspect of women's under-performance in competitive examinations, one will be assessed and found wanting according to that dominant standard. For me feminism is nothing to do with separatism. We occupy this planet together, and it will go down with all of us together. It is to do with writing, having a voice, just being there speaking from my own place in women's history and culture. The battle for how to write has only just begun, and *Shakespeare and the Nature of Women* sets out recklessly along that path, as along many others. Go, little book.

Shakespeare and the Nature of Women is issued in a corrected new edition although the main lines of its original argument remain unaltered, as this would seem the most useful policy for students of 1970s feminist scholarship, as well as for those studying the book's main areas of interest. I am grateful to Tim Farmiloe and Macmillan for their support of this book over a twenty-year period.

I would like to thank David Bevington, Dympna Callaghan, Bernard Capp, Steve Hindle and Ann Thompson for generous help with this essay, and my colleague Anne Fernihough for many stimulating discussions of issues in gender and writing. Girton College kindly gave me study leave, and has for many years supported me in the innumerable ways in which it has always nurtured women's scholarship, for which I remain its lifelong advocate.

Juliet Dusinberre
Cambridge

Notes

1. Annabel M. Patterson, *Censorship and interpretation: The conditions of writing and reading in early modern England* (Madison, Wisconsin, 1984); Jonathan Goldberg, *James I and the Politics of Literature* (Baltimore, 1983).

2. I have concentrated here on works specifically relevant to the topics raised in the Preface, and to scholarship since 1988, in the hope that this will be useful to students. I decided not to attempt to survey in this Preface the field of either feminist scholarship or related schools of thought (New Historicism, Cultural Materialism, and related interminglings of all three). Inevitably many important works of feminist scholarship and criticism in the 1980s which are not here mentioned by name have influenced my thinking. In the field of Shakespeare studies they are fully documented up to 1988 in Philip C. Kolin, *Shakespeare and Feminist Criticism: An Annotated Bibliography and Commentary* (New York and London, 1991); see also Ann Thompson, ' "The Warrant of Womanhood": Shakespeare and Feminist Criticism', in Graham Holderness (ed.), *The Shakespeare Myth* (Manchester, 1988), and Thompson's essay, 'Shakespeare and Sexuality', *Shakespeare Survey 46* (Cambridge, 1994): 1–8.

3. Jonathan Dollimore and Alan Sinfield (eds.), *Political Shakespeare: New Essays in Cultural Materialism* (Manchester, 1985); John Drakakis (ed.), *Alternative Shakespeares* (1985); Patricia Parker and Geoffrey Hartman (eds.), *Shakespeare and the Question of Theory* (New York, 1985).

4. The early pioneering works on women in literature and society were Mary Ellmann, *Thinking about Women* (1968); Germaine Greer, *The Female Eunuch* (1970); Kate Millett, *Sexual Politics* (1972); Patricia Meyer Spacks, *The Female Imagination* (1976); Ellen Moers, *Literary Women* (1977); Elaine Showalter, *A Literature of Their Own* (1977). For pioneer theoretical essays on feminist scholarship, see Gayle Green and Coppélia Kahn, *Making a Difference: Feminist Literary Criticism* (1986); Elaine Showalter (ed.), *The New Feminist Criticism* (1986); Shari Benstock (ed.), *Feminist Issues in Literary Scholarship* (Bloomington, 1987).

5. Virginia Woolf, *The Moment and Other Essays* (Hogarth Press, 1949), p.125.

6. Jean B. Elshtain, *Public Man, Private Woman: Women in Social and Political Thought* (Princeton, 1981); Alan Grafton and Lisa Jardine, *From Humanism to the Humanities* (1986); Merry E. Wiesner, 'Women's Defense of Their Public Role', in Mary Beth Rose (ed.), *Women in the Middle Ages and the Renaissance; Literary and Historical Perspectives* (Syracuse, 1986): 1–27; Juliet Dusinberre, *Virginia Woolf's Renaissance: Woman Reader or Common Reader?* (Macmillan, forthcoming 1996).

7. Hélène Cixous, 'The Laugh of Medusa', in Elaine Marks and Isabelle de Courtivron, *New French Feminisms* (Hemel Hempstead, 1981), pp. 245–64.

8. *All's Well That Ends Well*, I.i. 121–2, *The Riverside Shakespeare*, ed. G. Blakemore Evans (Boston, 1974). All quotations in the Preface are from this edition.

9. In addition to works already noted I would include David Norbrook, *Poetry and Politics in the English Renaissance* (1984); Jonathan Dollimore, *Radical Tragedy: Religious Ideology and Power in the Drama of Shakespeare and His Contemporaries* (2nd edn Hemel Hempstead, 1989); Steven Mullaney, *The Place of the Stage* (Chicago and London, 1988); Jean Howard, *The Stage and Social Struggle* (1994).

10. See Martin Butler, *Theatre and Crisis 1632-1642* (Cambridge, 1984), for the political subversiveness of Caroline drama.

11. Jean I. Marsden, 'Rewritten Women: Shakespearean Heroines in the Restoration', in Jean I. Marsden (ed.), *The Appropriation of Shakespeare: Post-Renaissance Reconstructions of the Works and the Myth* (Hemel Hempstead, 1991), pp.43–56.

12. John Donne, *Pseudo-martyr* (1610), p. 393.

13. See, for example, Patrick Collinson, *The Birthpangs of Protestant England: Religious and Cultural Change in the Sixteenth and Seventeenth Centuries* (London, 1986).

14. Anthony Fletcher, 'The Protestant idea of marriage in early modern England,' in Anthony Fletcher and Peter Roberts (eds), *Religion, Culture and Society in Early Modern Britain* (Cambridge, 1994), pp.161–81; S. D. Amussen, 'Gender, Family and the Social Order, 1560–1725', in Anthony Fletcher and John Stevenson, *Order and Disorder in Early Modern England* (Cambridge, 1985): 196–218, pp. 199–201; in the same volume D. E. Underdown, 'The Taming of the Scold: the Enforcement of Patriarchal Authority in Early Modern England', pp. 116–136.

15. Patricia Crawford, *Women and Religion in England 1500–1720* (1993), p. 68; Phyllis Mack, 'The Prophet and Her Audience: Gender and Knowledge in The World Turned Upside Down,' in Geoff Eley and William Hunt (eds), *Reviving the English Revolution* (1988): 139–52, p. 148.

16. James T. Johnson, 'The Covenant Idea and the Puritan View of Marriage,' *Journal of the History of Ideas,* xxxii (1971): 107–18.

17. The sources of my information were the sermons of Protestant reformers collected in the multiple volumes published by the Parker Society; the writings of Erasmus, and of a number of sixteenth-century reformers, of which the most important was Heinrich Bullinger, *The Christen State of Matrimonye*, translated by Miles Coverdale (1541). This work was imitated throughout the later part of the century, as for instance in Henry Smith, *A Preparative to Marriage* (1591). The secondary interpretations I followed were Christopher Hill's argument for the spiritualisation of marriage under the Puritans in *Society and Puritanism* (New York, 1964) and *Puritanism and Revolution* (1958); two key essays by Keith Thomas, 'The Double Standard', *Journal of the History of Ideas*, XX (1959): 195–216, and 'Women and the Civil War Sects', *Past and Present*, XIII (1958): 42–62; and William and Malleville Haller, 'The Puritan Art of Love', *Huntington Library Quarterly*, V (1942): 235–72. Fletcher, 'The Protestant idea of marriage' (*op. cit.*, 1994) writes that the Hallers' 'enthusiastic account' of the Puritan domestic conduct book 'has been too much neglected' and endorses their view that the Puritans radically rethought Christian ideas of love, marriage and sexuality (p. 180 and n. 90). See also Mary Beth Rose, *The Expense of Spirit: Love and Sexuality in English Renaissance Drama* (Ithaca, 1988); Sarup Singh, *The Double Standard in Shakespeare and Related Essays: Changing Status of Women in 16th and 17th Century England* (Delhi, 1988).

18. Fletcher, 'The Protestant idea of marriage', p. 167.

19. Alice Clark, *The Working Life of Women in the Seventeenth Century*, ed. Amy Erickson (1992 [1919]).

20. Bernard Capp, 'Women and Authority in Early Modern England', in Adam Fox, Paul Griffiths and Steve Hindle (eds), *The Experience of Authority in Early Modern England* (Macmillan, forthcoming 1995); Steve Hindle, 'The shaming of Margaret Knowsley: Gossip, gender and the experience of authority in early modern England,'

Continuity & Change 9 (1994): 1–29; Susan Dwyer Amussen, *An Ordered Society: Gender and Class in Early Modern England* (Oxford, 1988). Theoretical issues in women's history useful to this topic are discussed in Lilian S. Robinson, 'Sometimes, Always, Never: Their Women's History and Ours', *New Literary History,* 21 (1990): 377–93; Ann-Louise Shapiro, 'History and Feminist Theory, or Talking Back to the Beadle', in *History and Theory,* 31 (volume entitled *History and Feminist Theory*), (Wesleyan University Press, 1992): 1–14.

21. See Karen Newman, *Fashioning Femininity and English Renaissance Drama* (Chicago, 1991), especially pp. 15–31.

22. Stephen Greenblatt, *Shakespearean Negotiations: The Circulation of Social Energy in Renaissance England* (Oxford, 1988).

23. This position has been brilliantly argued by Maik Hamburger in a paper on East German theatre delivered at the 1994 International Shakespeare Association at Stratford-upon-Avon, forthcoming in *Shakespeare Survey 48* (1996). For the carnivalesque, see Mikhail Bakhtin, *Rabelais and His World,* trans. Helen Iswolsky (Bloomington, 1984); Natalie Zemon Davis, 'Women on Top: Symbolic Sexual Inversion and Political Disorder in Early Modern Europe', in Barbara A. Babcock (ed.), *The Reversible World* (Ithaca and London, 1978): 147–89, p. 158; for criticism of New Historicist theories of containment, see Lynda E. Boose, 'The Family in Shakespeare Studies; or – Studies in the Family of Shakespeareans; or – The Politics of Politics', *Renaissance Quarterly,* 40 (1987): 707–42.

24. Douglas Bruster, *Drama and the Market in the Age of Shakespeare* (Cambridge, 1992); Leah Marcus, *Puzzling Shakespeare: Local Reading and Its Discontents* (Berkeley, 1988); Margreta De Grazia and Peter Stallybrass, 'The Materiality of the Shakespearean Text', *Shakespeare Quarterly,* 44 (1993): 255–83; see also Janette Dillon, 'Is There a Performance in this Text?' *Shakespeare Quarterly,* 45 (1994): 74–86.

25. Jean Howard, *The Stage and Social Struggle in Early Modern England* (1994), especially pp. 73–128.

26. Margot Heineman, *Thomas Middleton and Opposition Drama under the Early Stuarts* (Cambridge, 1980); Richard Dutton, *Mastering the Revels: The regulation and censorship of English Renaissance drama* (1991); Janet Clare, ' "Greater Themes for Insurrection's Arguing":

Political Censorship of the Elizabethan and Jacobean Stage', *Review of English Studies New Series*, XXXVIII (1987): 169–83; Andrew Gurr, *Playgoing in Shakespeare's London* (Cambridge, 1987); for a different view, see Ann Jenalie Cook, *The Privileged Playgoers of Shakespeare's London*, 1576–1642 (Princeton, 1981).

27. The continuity which I saw between Erasmian Humanism and Puritan writers is endorsed by Margo Todd, *Christian Humanism and the Puritan Social Order* (Cambridge, 1987), see particularly Chapter 4, 'The spiritualized household'.

28. Harington possessed, according to an autograph note written in 1609, eighteen quartos of Shakespeare (three in duplicate) and many more of other dramatists including most of Jonson, but he never comments on a performance although he stated that he had 'assisted' at the performance of plays at Elizabeth's court. See F. J. Furnivall, 'Sir John Harington's Shakespeare Quartos', *Notes and Queries*, 7th Series 9 (17 May 1890): 382–3; *Nugae Antiquae*, vol. 2 (1779), p. 129, letter to Mr Secretary Barlow, 1606; see Juliet Dusinberre, 'As *Who* Liked it?' *Shakespeare Survey 46* (Cambridge, 1994): 9–21, p. 14.

29. Constance Jordan, *Renaissance Feminism: Literary Texts and Political Models* (Ithaca and London, 1990), reads Renaissance defences of women for the rupturing of inherited discourses, a method central to my research; Linda Woodbridge's founding work in this area, *Women and the English Renaissance* (Hemel Hempstead, 1984), proposed models of change which I call feminist even though she herself was reluctant to use the word. Although some of her conclusions seemed to contradict mine, the areas of agreement between us are considerable (see particularly p. 181, and her conclusion, pp. 323–8). Ian MacLean, *The Renaissance Notion of Woman* (Cambridge, 1980), pp. 82–92, points, albeit cautiously, to areas where feminist thought might develop.

30. What Judith Butler calls, in *Gender Trouble: Feminism and the Subversion of Identity* (1990), the 'performance' of gender.

31. See Catherine Belsey, *The Subject of Tragedy* (1985); Alice Jardine, *Gynesis: Configurations of Woman and Modernity* (Ithaca, 1980); Dollimore, *Radical Tragedy*.

32. Roland Barthes, 'The Death of the Author', *Image, Music, Text,* trans. Stephen Heath, (1977), pp. 142–8; D. F. McKenzie, *Bibliography and the Sociology of Texts* (The British Library, 1986);

Seán Burke, *The Death and Return of the Author* (Edinburgh, 1992); Patterson, *Censorship and Interpretation*; Juliet Dusinberre, 'Much Ado About Lying: the Dialogue with Harington's *Orlando Furioso*', in *The Italian World of English Renaissance Drama: Cultural Exchange and Intertextuality* (forthcoming 1997).

33. Richard Helgerson, *Self-Crowned Laureates* (Berkeley, Los Angeles and London, 1983), p. 10.

34. Lisa Jardine, *Still Harping on Daughters: Women and Drama in the Age of Shakespeare* (Sussex, 1983), p. 72, argues that the 'obsessive insistence' of the brothers on the Duchess's lust represents authorial intention; 'That male interpretation of female action must colour the audience's own response: only men surround the Duchess; the audience can do little more than accept their version of her behaviour and motives' (p. 72).

35. Barbara Freedman, *Staging the Gaze* (Ithaca, 1991); Kent Cartwright, *Shakespearean Tragedy and Its Double: The Rhythms of Audience Response* (Pennsylvania, 1991); Katherine Eisaman Maus, 'Horns of Dilemma: Jealousy, Gender and Spectatorship in English Renaissance Drama', *ELH*, 54 (1987): 561–83.

36. Dympna Callaghan, 'Buzz Goodbody: Directing for Change', in Marsden (ed.), *The Appropriation of Shakespeare*, pp. 163–81; Lorraine Helms, 'Acts of Resistance: The Feminist Player', in Dympna C. Callaghan, Lorraine Helms and Jyotsina Singh, *The Weyward Sisters* (Oxford, 1994), pp. 102–56.

37. See Ann Thompson (ed.), *The Taming of the Shrew* (Cambridge, 1984) for a full account of the feminist critical debate on *The Taming of the Shrew*; H. R. Coursen, *Shakespearean Performance as Interpretation* (Delaware, 1992), pp. 49–73; Lynda Boose, 'Scolding Brides and Bridling Scolds: Taming the Woman's Unruly Member', *Shakespeare Quarterly*, 42 (1991): 179–213; Graham Holderness, The Taming of the Shrew: *Shakespeare in Performance* (Manchester, 1989).

38. Bruce R. Smith, *Homosexual Desire in Renaissance England* (Chicago, 1991); Eve Kosofsky Sedgwick, *Between Men: English Literature and Male Homosocial Desire* (1985); for further analysis of this distinction see Alan Bray, 'Homosexuality and the Signs of Male Friendship in Elizabethan England', *History Workshop*, 29 (Spring, 1990): 1–19; Joseph A. Porter, *Shakespeare's Mercutio* (Chapel Hill, 1988); Valerie Traub, *Desire and Anxiety* (1992); see also Adrienne Rich,

'Compulsory Heterosexuality and Lesbian Existence' (1980), in *Blood, Bread and Poetry: Selected Prose 1979-85* (Virago, 1987), pp. 23–75; James M. Saslow, *Ganymede in the Renaissance* (Yale, 1986); Jonathan Goldberg, *Sodometries: Renaissance Texts, Modern Sexualities* (Stanford, 1992) especially pp. 105–43; Stephen Greenblatt, 'Fiction and Friction', in Thomas Heller, Morton Sosna, and David E. Wellbery (eds), *Reconstructing Individualism* (Stanford, 1986). Other crucial discussions of the boy actor are contained in Jardine, *Still Harping on Daughters*, pp. 9–36; Kathleen McLuskie, 'The Act, the Role and the Actor: Boy Actresses on the Elizabethan Stage', *New Theatre Quarterly*, 3:10 (1987): 120–30; Stephen Orgel, 'Nobody's Perfect: Or Why Did the English Stage Take Boys for Women?', *The South Atlantic Quarterly*, 88 (Winter, 1989): 7–29; Jonathan Dollimore, *Sexual Dissidence* (Oxford, 1991), pp. 284–306; Marjorie Garber, *Vested Interests: Cross-Dressing and Cultural Anxiety* (1992); Howard, *The Stage and Social Struggle in Early Modern England*, pp. 93–128; Laura Levine, *Men in Women's Clothing: Anti-theatricality and effeminization 1579–1642* (Cambridge, 1994); Richard Rastall, 'Female Roles in All-Male Casts', *Medieval English Theatre*, 7 (1985): 21–51; Jyotsna Singh, 'Renaissance Antitheatricality, Antifeminism, and Shakespeare's *Antony and Cleopatra*', *Renaissance Drama*, NS, XX (1989): 99–121; Madelon Sprengnether, 'The Boy Actor and Femininity in *Antony and Cleopatra*', in Norman N. Holland, Sidney Homan and Bernard J. Paris (eds), *Shakespeare's Personality* (Berkeley, Los Angeles and London, 1989), pp. 191–205; Phyllis Rackin, 'Androgyny, Mimesis and the Marriage of the Boy Heroine on the English Renaissance Stage', *PMLA*, 102 (1987): 113–33.

39. Juliet Dusinberre, '*King John* and Embarrassing Women', *Shakespeare Survey 42* (1990): 37–52; '*The Taming of the Shrew*: Women, Acting and Power', *Studies in the Literary Imagination*, XXVI (Spring, 1993): 67–84; '"Squeaking Cleopatras": Gender and Performance in *Antony and Cleopatra*', in James Bulman (ed.), *Shakespeare, Theory and Performance* (Routledge, forthcoming 1995).

40. See Susan Zimmerman (ed.), *Erotic Politics: Desire on the Renaissance Stage* (1992); Dympna C. Callaghan, 'The Ideology of Romantic Love: The Case of *Romeo and Juliet*', in Callaghan *et al*, *The Weyward Sisters*, pp. 59–101.

41. See Margaret Whitford, 'Luce Irigaray's Critique of Rationality', in

Morwenna Griffiths and Margaret Whitford (eds), *Feminist Perspectives in Philosophy* (1988); Genevieve Lloyd, *The Man of Reason: 'Male' and 'Female' in Western Philosophy* (1984); Jean Grimshaw, *Feminist Philosophers* (Brighton, 1986). Hilda L. Smith, 'Intellectual Bases for Feminist Analyses in the Seventeenth and Eighteenth Centuries', in Elizabeth D. Harvey and Kathleen Okruhlick, *Women and Reason* (Ann Arbor, 1992), and Smith's earlier study, *Reason's Disciples: Seventeenth-Century Feminists* (Urbana, 1982); Carol McMillan, *Women, Reason and Nature* (Oxford, 1982); for the Puritans and desire see Edmund Leites, 'The Duty to Desire: Love, Friendship and Sexuality in some Puritan Theories of Marriage', *Journal of Social History*, 15 (1982); 383–408.

42. The best single introduction to French feminist theory in this context is Ann Rosalind Jones, 'Writing the Body; Towards an Understanding of l'écriture féminine', in Showalter (ed.), *The New Feminist Criticism*, pp. 361–77; see also Helen Wilcox *et al.* (eds), *The Body and the Text* (New York, 1990); Susan Rubin Suleiman (ed.), *The Female Body in Western Culture* (Cambridge, Mass., 1986); Jane Gallop, *Thinking Through the Body* (New York, 1988); Manfred Pfister, 'Reading the body: the corporeality of Shakespeare's text', in Hanna Scolnicow and Peter Holland (eds), *Reading Plays: Interpretation and reception* (Cambridge, 1991); Thomas Laqueur, *Making Sex: Body and Gender from the Greeks to Freud* (Cambridge, Mass., 1990); Julia Epstein and Kristina Straub (eds), *Bodyguards: The Cultural Contexts of Gender Ambiguity* (1991); Gail Kern Paster, *Body Embarrassed: Drama and the Disciplines of Shame in Early Modern England* (Ithaca. 1993).

43. Louis Adrian Montrose, ' "Eliza, Queen of shepheardes," and the Pastoral of Power', *English Literary Renaissance*, 10 (1980): 153–82, and ' "Shaping Fantasies": Figurations of Gender and Power in Elizabethan Culture', *Representations*, 2 (1983): 61–94, also in Margaret W. Ferguson, Maureen Quilligan, and Nancy J. Vickers (eds) *Rewriting the Renaissance* (Chicago, 1986); Philippa Berry, *Of Chastity and Power: Elizabethan Literature and the Unmarried Queen* (1989); Marcus, *Puzzling Shakespeare: Local Reading and its Discontents*; Theodora A. Jankowski, ' "As I Am Egypt's Queen': Cleopatra, Elizabeth I, and the Female Body Politic', *Assays: Critical Approaches to Medieval and Renaissance Texts*, 5 (1989): 91–111; Maureen Quilligan, 'The Comedy of Female Authority in *The*

Faerie Queene', *English Literary Renaissance*, 17 (1987): 156–71; Helen Hackett, *Virgin Mother, Maiden Queen*, (1994); Grafton and Jardine, *From Humanism to the Humanities*, with its important chapter on women's education, 'Education for what?' (a subject discussed in *Shakespeare and the Nature of Women*, pp. 199–231, especially p. 210), underestimates Elizabeth's impact on Elizabethan politics and culture; see also Margaret Christian, 'Elizabeth's Preachers and the Government of Women: Defining and Correcting a Queen', *The Sixteenth-Century Journal* XXIV (1993): 561–76.

44. Barbara Lewalski, *Writing Women in Jacobean England* (Cambridge, Mass., 1993), pp. 9–11: 'If we admit the power of literary and dramatic images to affect the imagination, we might expect the very presence of such a galaxy of vigorous and rebellious female characters to undermine any monolithic social construct of woman's nature and role. There is some evidence that women took the oppositional support they needed or wanted from books and plays. Women of all social classes went to the theater, and the Queen herself was passionate about it.'

45. See Deborah Cameron, *Feminism and Linguistic Theory* (1985); Sally McConnell-Ginet, Ruth Borker and Nelly Furman (eds), *Women and Language in Literature and Society* (New York, 1980); see Nelly Furman, 'The politics of language: beyond the gender principle?' in *Making a Difference*, pp. 59–79, and 'Textual Feminism', in McConnell-Ginet, *et al., op. cit.*

46. Walter J. Ong, *Orality and Literacy: the technologizing of the word* (1982), and 'Latin language study as a Renaissance puberty rite', in *Rhetoric, Romance and Technology* (Ithaca and London, 1971), pp. 113–41; Ong's model of the oral and the written is challenged in Jonathan Goldberg, *Writing Matter: From the hands of the English Renaissance* (Stanford, 1990); on Shakespeare see Eve Horwitz, '"The Truth of Your Own Seeming": Women and Language in *The Winter's Tale*', *Unisa English Studies*, 26 (1988): 7–13; Edward Snow, 'Language and Sexual Difference in *Romeo and Juliet*', in Peter Erickson and Coppélia Kahn (eds), *Shakespeare's 'Rough Magic': Renaissance Essays in Honor of C. L. Barber* (Newark, 1985), pp. 168–92; Patricia Parker, 'On the Tongue: Cross Gendering, Effeminacy, and the Art of Words', *Style*, 23 (1989): 445–65 and *Literary Fat Ladies* (1987); Lorraine Helms, 'The Saint in the

Brothel: Or, Eloquence Rewarded', *Shakespeare Quarterly*, 41 (1990): 319–32; Douglas Bruster, 'In a Woman's Key: Women's Speech and Women's Language in Renaissance Drama', *Exemplaria* 4 (1992): 235–66.

47. Valuable collections of primary sources include Margaret L. King and Albert Rabil Jr (eds), *Her Immaculate Hand* (Binghamton, NY, 1983); Elspeth Graham *et al.*, *Her Own Life: Autobiographical writings by seventeenth-century English Women* (1989); Germaine Greer *et al.*, *Kissing the Rod* (1988); Charlotte F. Otten (ed.), *English Women's Voices, 1540-1700* (Miami, 1990); multiple secondary studies include Patricia H. Labalme, *Beyond Their Sex: Learned Women of the European Renaissance* (New York, 1980); Margaret Hannay (ed.), *Silent but for the Word: Tudor Women as Patrons, Translators, and Writers of Religious Works* (Kent, Ohio, 1985); Rose, *Women in the Middle Ages and the Renaissance; Literary and Historical Perspectives*; Elaine V. Beilin, *Redeeming Eve: Women Writers of the English Renaissance* (Princeton, 1987); Richard Greaves (ed.), *Triumph over Silence: Women in Protestant History* (Westport, Conn., 1985); see also Ann Rosalind Jones, 'Surprising Fame: Renaissance Gender Ideologies and Women's Lyric', in Nancy K. Miller, *The Poetics of Gender* (New York, 1986), pp. 74–95, and Jones's subsequent book, *The Currency of Eros: Women's love lyric in Europe, 1540-1620* (Bloomington, 1990). See for women's writings and manuscript circulation, Margaret J. Ezell, *The Patriarch's Wife: Literary Evidence and the History of the Family* (Chapel Hill, 1987); Stephanie H. Jed, *Chaste Thinking: The Rape of Lucretia and the Birth of Humanism* (Bloomington, 1989); Harold Love, *Scribal Publication in Seventeenth-Century England* (Oxford, 1993).

48. Juliet Fleming, 'The French Garden: An Introduction to Women's French', *English Literary History*, 56 (1989): 19–51.

49. Joan Rees, *Samuel Daniel* (Liverpool, 1964), p. 76.

50. Elaine Showalter, 'Towards a Feminist Poetics', in Showalter (ed.), *The New Feminist Criticism* (1986), pp. 125–43; 'Representing Ophelia: Women, Madness, and the Responsibilities of Feminist Criticism', in Parker and Hartman, *Shakespeare and the Question of Theory*, pp. 77–94; 'Miranda's Story', in Showalter, *Sister's Choice: Tradition and Change in American Women's Writing* (Oxford, 1991); see also for a negotiation of some of the central questions surrounding the male imagining of women, Jeanne Addison

Roberts, *The Shakespearean Wild* (Lincoln, Nebraska, 1991).

51. For pre-twentieth-century accounts by women actresses of their performances of Shakespeare, see Ann Thompson and Sasha Roberts, *Women Reading Shakespeare, 1600–1900* (forthcoming, Manchester, 1996); see also classic accounts by Helena Faucit, Lady Martin, *On Some of Shakespeare's Female Characters* (Edinburgh, 1891), and Ellen Terry, *Four Lectures on Shakespeare*, ed. Christopher St John (1931); for modern actresses see Penny Gay, *As She Likes It: Shakespeare's Unruly Women* (1994); Carol Rutter, *Clamorous Voices: Shakespeare's Women Today* (1988); Judith Cook, *Women in Shakespeare* (1980); for women's rewriting of Shakespeare, see Marianne Novy, *Women's Re-Visions of Shakespeare* (Chicago, 1990).

52. Patricia Yaeger, *Honey-Mad Women: Emancipatory Strategies in Women's Writing* (New York, 1988); Ania Loomba, *Gender, Race, Renaissance Drama* (Manchester, 1989); Margo Hendricks and Patricia Parker (eds), *Women, 'Race' and Writing in the Early Modern Period* (1994); *Renaissance Drama*, XXIII (1992), special issue, 'Renaissance Drama in the Age of Colonization'; Jyotsna Singh, 'The Interventions of History: Narratives of Sexuality,' in Callaghan *et al.*, *The Weyward Sisters*, pp. 7–58; in the same volume, for Joan of Arc, see Helms, 'Acts of Resistance: The Feminist Player,' pp. 102–56; Tina Krontiris, *Oppositional Voices: Women as Writers and Translators of Literature in the English Renaissance*, especially pp. 27–62, 'Servant Girls Claiming Male Domain'.

53. See Phyllis Rackin in 'Anti-Historians: Women's Roles in Shakespeare's Histories', *Theatre Journal* 37 (1985): 329–44, and her subsequent book, *Stages of History* (1990); Carole Levin, '"I trust I may not trust thee": Women's Visions of the World in Shakespeare's *King John*', in Carole Levin and Jeanie Watson (eds), *Ambiguous Realities: Women in the Middle Ages and Renaissance* (Detroit, 1987).

54. See Carol Thomas Neely, 'Constructing the Subject: Feminist Practice and the New Renaissance Discourses', *English Literary Renaissance*, 18 (1988); *ELR* has been consistently hospitable to feminist scholarship. See also Neely's later article, 'History and Literature: "after the new historicism"', *New Literary History*, 21 (1990); 253–81.

55. *A Room of One's Own* (Harmondsworth, 1945), p. 84.

56. See Margaret Waller, 'The Empire's New Clothes: Refashioning the Renaissance', in Sheila Fisher and Janet E. Halley (eds), *Seeking*

the Woman in Late Medieval and Renaissance Writings (Knoxville, 1989), pp. 160–83, for an attack on New Historicist scholars for reading from an exclusively male standpoint.

57. See Valerie Wayne, *The Matter of Difference: Materialist Feminist Criticism of Shakespeare* (Hemel Hempstead, 1991), p .5: 'Many feminists in Renaissance studies actively resist tendencies towards exclusivity'.

58. See Terence Hawkes, *That Shakespeherian Rag* (1986), for the ways in which Shakespeare has become a monument to cultural conservatism; Isobel Armstrong, 'Thatcher's Shakespeare?', *Textual Practice* 3 (1989): 1–14.

59. A subject discussed in a different context in Ann Thompson, 'Sexuality and Textuality in the Editing of Shakespeare', Inaugural lecture at the Roehampton Institute, 6 June 1994.

60. Jonathan Bate, *Shakespearean Constitutions* (Oxford, 1989); Jane Moody, 'Writing for the Metropolis: Illegitimate Performances of Shakespeare in Early Nineteenth-Century London', *Shakespeare Survey* 47 (Cambridge, 1995, forthcoming): 61–69.

61. The terms of this debate are set out in the essays collected in Alice Jardine and Paul Smith (eds), *Men in Feminism* (New York and London, 1987); see also Mary Jacobus, *Reading Woman* (1986), pp. 3–24; see also Peter Erickson, *Patriarchal Structures in Shakespeare's Drama* (1985), and *Rereading Shakespeare, Rewriting Ourselves* (1991); Ian Donaldson, *The Rapes of Lucretia* (Oxford, 1982).

62. Rich 'What Does a Woman Need to Know?', in *Blood, Bread and Poetry: Selected Prose 1979-85*, pp. 3–4.

63. See Annette Kolodny, 'Dancing Through the Minefield: Some Observations on the Theory, Practice, and Politics of a Feminist Literary Criticism', in Showalter, *The New Feminist Criticism*, pp. 144–67; Adrienne Munich, 'Notorious signs, feminist criticism and literary tradition', in Greene and Kahn, *Making a Difference: Feminist Literary Criticism*, pp. 238–59.

64. Ong, *Orality and Literacy*, pp. 111–12.

65. Chris Baldick, *The Social Mission of English Studies 1848-1932* (Oxford, 1983); David Palmer, *The Rise of English Studies* (1965); Juliet Dusinberre, 'Virginia Woolf and Montaigne', *Textual Practice*, 5 (1991), 219–41; Stephen Foley, 'Nostalgia and the "Rise of English": Rhetorical Questions', in Wayne, *The Matter of Difference*, pp. 237–55.

66. 'Towards a Feminist Poetics', p. 141.
67. A subject brilliantly debated in Nancy K. Miller, *Subject to Change: Reading Feminist Writing* (New York, 1988).
68. Juliet Dusinberre, 'Bunyan and Virginia Woolf: A history and a language of their own', *Bunyan Studies*, 5 (1994): 53–84.
69. See Gallop, *Thinking Through the Body*; Catherine Belsey, 'A Future for Materialist Feminist Criticism', in Wayne, *The Matter of Difference*, pp. 257–70; Alan Sinfield, *Faultlines: Cultural Materialism and the Politics of Dissident Reading* (Berkeley, 1992); Jane Moore, 'An other space: a future for feminism?' in Isobel Armstrong (ed.), *New Feminist Discourses* (1992), pp. 65–79.

Introduction

The feminism of Shakespeare's time is still largely unrecognised. The struggle for women's rights is thought of as primarily a nineteenth century phenomenon which has been intermittently resurgent ever since. The modern women's movement claims to be new in working from a wider context of deeply ingrained attitudes to women, instead of fixing itself to a limited political goal as earlier militants like Mrs Pankhurst did. But this striking at cultural assumptions about women is not new. The ideology, the literature, the social reform, the activism, and the increased awareness necessary to all of them dominated the society for which Shakespeare and his contemporaries wrote their plays.

This is hardly surprising; it is a cliché to say that the Renaissance was a period of intense questioning of many orthodoxies – from Copernicus, to Luther, to Machiavelli. It would have been strange if attitudes to women had escaped, especially as the way societies think about and treat women is often considered a means of measuring how civilised they are. One would expect the astonishing cultural impetus of the Renaissance to encompass ideas about women, as indeed it did. What is surprising is that the popular ramifications of changed attitudes to women in the Renaissance have received so little attention. What became a real issue in late Elizabethan and Jacobean London is ignored in favour of studying the women of the sixteenth century court.

Shakespeare was born at the height of the English Renaissance when the English were stimulated by identifying themselves as a Protestant nation, and when the intellectual and artistic prestige of the English court was unmatched. The Protestant ideology inaugurated new attitudes to women and coalesced with the practical concern of Humanists like More and Erasmus to reform women's education. Aristocratic women round the court certainly evinced constant proof of More's contention that women were the intellectual equals of men. Henry VIII's queens, in particular Catherine of Aragon and later Catherine Parr, were notable for their own scholarship, for their generosity in endowing scholars, and for their education of the young women around them, among them the Princess Elizabeth. The remarkable women of Elizabeth's court – Lady Anne Bacon, the Countess of Pembroke, Lady Anne Clifford – stood in a line which stretched from Lady Margaret Beaufort to Margaret Roper and Elizabeth Cooke. Aristocratic women in England in the sixteenth century and into the seventeenth enjoyed an emancipation comparable to that of aristocrats like Vittoria Colonna in Renaissance Italy. For them the battle for recognised equality with men had been fought and won. Shakespeare knew that the tough intellect behind the raillery of the court ladies in *Love's Labour's Lost*, or of Beatrice and Rosalind, or behind the self-awareness of Helena in *All's Well That Ends Well* had plenty of basis in real life.

But ideas confined to the circle of the court, like the fad of Platonic love fostered by Henrietta Maria and her supporters in the court of Charles I, tend to be a scholar's playground rather than a significant influence in society as a whole. What is important about Jacobean feminism is that it was not courtly but popular. James ran a homosexual court which was hostile to women; the pioneer movements which in the previous century had been primarily courtly, moved down into the middle class. The Puritans, preaching to a largely middle-class congregation, were at least in part responsible for a new interest, evident outside the court, in the nature and position of women.

In many ways Puritanism is at its most exciting during Shakespeare's lifetime. By the time that Hooker wrote his statement in 1596 of the beliefs of the Anglican church, the Puritans represented a body of opinion in England sufficiently strong and influential to be worth opposing. The Anglican church contemplated sects like the Anabaptists, the Family of Love, the Brownists, contemptuously but calmly. They were too eccentric to enlist widespread support, and many of their members left England for the more congenial climate of Amsterdam. But Puritanism was not the same as sectarianism. Puritanism was a movement within the Church of England for closer identification with the principles of the early Protestants, which meant, in effect, with Calvin. Many of the best known Puritans remained Anglicans – men such as Henry Smith or William Perkins. Puritanism in the early part of the seventeenth century was neither the fanatical sectarianism which James I labelled 'puritan' when he described the Family of Love in *Basilicon Doron*,[1] nor the political institution which it became under Cromwell. The cultural changes of diverse origin with which the Puritans were identified, particularly in the early days of Puritan activity at the end of Elizabeth's reign, included ideas about the nature of women. Many men not explicitly connected with the Puritans – Spenser, Bacon, Sidney, Shakespeare himself – demonstrated in their writing a sympathy with attitudes to life espoused by Puritan preachers.

Puritan attitudes to women are born with the doctrine of chaste marriage which Calvin took from Luther: the insistence that virginity and chastity are not synonymous and that a married person has as much right to be called chaste as a celibate. Luther reported that 'when I was a boy, the wicked and impure practice of celibacy had made marriage so disreputable that I believed I could not even think about the life of married people without sinning.'[2] The reformers insisted that chaste marriage was a condition of equal spiritual prestige with celibacy. The influence of this doctrine on attitudes to women is two-fold. In the first place it initiated an enquiry which led ultimately to the Puritan assertion of spiritual equality between men and women with its significant implications for the relation of man and wife. Secondly, it precipitated the necessity for reforming marriage practices. The arranged marriage in the sixteenth century was only tolerable through adultery, but it was plain to the reformers that theoretical idealism about marriage was lamentably out of step with the practice. The early Protestant

[1] Basil Hall, 'Puritanism: The Problem of Definition', *Studies in Church History*, II, 294, 285.

[2] *Luther's Works*, 1, 135.

reformers, and notably Calvin himself, were not interested in changing attitudes to women; if anything, they wanted to entrench existing attitudes – the Pauline insistence on the subjection and inferiority of women – in order not to seem to undermine the existing social order along with its theology. But if every nobleman could produce in effect two wives, the doctrine of chaste marriage was founded on sand. So it became imperative to attack customs such as forced marriage, marriage for money, child marriage, marriages between very old men and very young women in order to make the ideal viable by making adultery unnecessary. The reformers' pressure on the aristocracy in the sixteenth century produced results: noticeable reticence about bastards in wills after the middle of the century, and ironically, a marked increase in the divorce rate among peers in the years between 1595 and 1620 when Puritanism was at the height of its influence.[3] A high divorce rate in this case seems to have been a yardstick for higher expectations from married life. The order of change is interesting; in modern times it would be possible to argue either that ideas about women changed, and this changed ideas about marriage, or that ideas about marriage changed, and this inevitably changed attitudes to women. In the sixteenth century ideas about marriage changed first, and the consequence, whether the reformers liked it or no, was changed attitudes to women.

The Puritans absorbed both Calvin's idealism about marriage, and the concern of Humanists like More for liberal attitudes to women. But the Puritans addressed themselves to a middle-class urban environment, which meant that they disapproved of an unstable marriage situation not only for spiritual reasons, but also for economic ones: middle-class men cannot afford to run two establishments.[4] Puritanism in its treatment of women as in many other areas represents a curious marrying of ideals and social expediency. But whatever the mixture of motives involved, the Puritans exerted a widespread influence on attitudes to women by popularising, with their multifarious oratorical and literary talents, the

[3] Lawrence Stone, *The Crisis of the Aristocracy 1558–1641*, pp. 663, 664, 661.

[4] Keith Thomas, 'The Double Standard', *Journal of the History of Ideas*, XX (1959) no. 2, 204.

new ideals about marriage, and by pressing for reform of inhumane marriage customs in a middle-class context and refusing to tolerate the double standard for adultery. Their reforms were aimed at men and women equally, but their effect was greater for women because they alleviated the exploitation made possible by the economic dependence of the woman. Thus the agitation for women's rights and for changed attitudes to women which was a vital aspect of the society for which Shakespeare wrote was to a large extent set in motion and furthered by the most powerful pressure group, both numerically and morally, of the time, and one which had the moral support of the most talented and creative of Shakespeare's contemporaries. This was the climate into which Milton was born, and in which Shakespeare took root as a dramatist.

The drama from 1590 to 1625 is feminist in sympathy. Shakespeare's modernity in his treatment of women has always attracted attention, but it is not nearly so well known that his attitudes to women are part of a common stock to be found in the plays of almost all of his contemporaries – in Marston, Middleton, Dekker, Webster, Heywood, Jonson, Massinger, and to some extent even in Chapman and Beaumont and Fletcher. These dramatists ask the same questions about women as Shakespeare, about their natures, about men's attitudes to them, about the stereotypes society imposes on them; in many cases they find the same answers, and these are essentially the Puritan answers: that the old Pauline orthodoxies about women and about marriage must give way to a treatment of women as individuals. Like the Puritans the dramatists reject or ridicule the old pieties, and struggle to realise, and then to test, the new. Shakespeare's women are not an isolated phenomenon in their emancipation, their self-sufficiency, and their evasion of stereotypes. The women in Marston's plays share many of their characteristics. Shakespeare's are different only in the degree of Shakespeare's artistry. Hazlitt called Shakespeare's contemporary playwrights 'the scale by which we can best ascend to the true knowledge and love of him', and claimed that admiration of them increased and confirmed 'our relish for him.'[5] This is

[5] 'General View of the Subject', in D. Nichol Smith, *Shakespeare Criticism: A Selection*, p. 322.

true of Shakespeare's attitudes to women. To observe their evolution from the popular thinking of his time, to see that thinking incorporated into the drama of his fellows is to measure the use that he made of ideas about women in his own society at a time of intense interest in change. It is to measure at the same time his ability to go beyond his contemporaries in his understanding of change and in his transforming of dogma into drama.

The influence of Puritanism on Shakespeare and on his fellow dramatists has been grossly underestimated. Jacobean drama flourished in a period of concentrated moral energy which proved invigorating to the dramatists. Puritanism, however, was not the only factor in creating awareness of attitudes to women in Jacobean society and in arousing feminist propaganda.

The Jacobean period witnessed the climax of a controversy which had been growing right through the sixteenth century. It was triggered off by protests about satire on women in the medieval tradition, first by male defenders of the sex – theologians such as Bullinger, dabblers in popular literature like Edward More, or Humanists like Agrippa – and then by women themselves, starting with Jane Anger's pamphlet in 1589 protesting against the denigration of women in *Euphues*.[6] But this was only one aspect of a much wider protest against discrepancy between the portrayal of women in literature and the reality in life. Humanists such as More, Erasmus, Vives and Ascham, attacked bitterly the ethic of courtly love as set forth in medieval romance, as a false elevating of adulterous romance where the woman was a symbol of lust, depicted not as a rational being, but as a goddess. In essence this is the same complaint as that made against the medieval satirist. Women are people and individuals; the creature evoked both by the courtly lover and by the satirist bears no relation to woman as a social being, and yet the assertions of those writers influenced the treatment of women in society, and their stereotypes were considered valid.

The Humanists saw courtly love, like war, as the corrupt practice of an effete aristocracy. In Shakespeare's lifetime the Puritans'

[6] *Jane Anger her Protection for Women*. Cf. Helen Andrews Kahin, 'Jane Anger and John Lyly', *Modern Language Quarterly*, VIII (1947) no. I, 31–5.

own middle-class identity reinforced the opprobrium of upper-class adultery which they inherited from men like Ascham. Increasingly the rejection of stereotypes both of deifying the woman, and also of denigrating her, becomes the prerogative of the bourgeois, rejecting with them the profligacy and extravagance of the courtier which for Shakespeare's contemporaries was ever-present in the debauched court of James I. Shakespeare and his fellow dramatists write for an audience accustomed to reject the literary as false, accustomed to associating literary positions about woman the goddess or woman the devil with an alien and reprobate aristocratic tradition. Attitudes to women in the drama reflect the alignment of the dramatist with the middle class, and in a period when antagonism between the court and the city is marked, the attitudes which express differences between the two receive a good deal of attention. This is perhaps one reason why the successors of Jane Anger – the female protesters against male satirists in the decade following 1610 – receive such sympathetic notice in the theatre.

The controversy over satire reached its height in the early seventeenth century with the protests of these women against one Swetnam. A pamphlet war was waged in the popular press, partly a joke, but also partly serious, which ended in a play called *Swetnam the Woman-Hater Arraigned by Women* where Swetnam was brought to justice by his enraged accusers. The dramatists cashed in on the interest aroused in their audience, depicted satirists and their opponents and the fates of both; moralised on the art of satire, and on the artificialities of literary stereotypes. This dispute was another powerful stream through which enquiry into the nature of women was stimulated both in Shakespeare's society and in his plays.

Protests need militants. No amount of theory can make a movement without activists. Jacobean society found its activists for women's liberation in a group of London women who provoked uproar by wearing men's clothes, not only doublet and hose, and broad-brimmed hats, but also weapons. The phenomenon was not peculiar to the Jacobean period; women had been causing comment by wearing men's clothes from the 1580's onward. But in the

first two decades of the seventeenth century the fad was not only
inveighed against by the monarch, by the Bishop of London, and
by numerous preachers and moralists in the popular press, but it
stimulated its own dialogue in the press between the women who
wore men's clothes, and the men who condemned them. Inevitably many questions were raised by the debate: the custom of differentiating male and female in dress, and ultimately the whole
area of assumption about masculinity and femininity. For the
dramatists, not only interested in women, but also in the ethic of
dressing up, this was a golden opportunity to transpose the man-
woman controversy onto the stage. That they are basically sympathetic to the female protesters is congruent not only with their
Puritanism but with their own position as creators of an art which
demands that the sexes exchange clothes. But there can be no
doubt that Jacobean society saw some of the first active protests by
women against their dependence on, and subjection to, men, and
like the flappers, or like the unisex models, they expressed their indifference to social stereotypes about their role by adopting the
clothes of the opposite sex. This was yet another challenge to the
dramatists to explore assumptions about women in their plays.

The stage conditions for which Shakespeare and his contemporaries wrote were ideally suited to reflecting attitudes to women
current in his society. The Elizabethans reaped the advantages of
Burbage's first public commercial theatre which was built in
London in 1576. Its significance was twofold. In the first place the
building of a permanent public theatre in London guaranteed the
professional status of both the playwright and the acting companies. The strolling players of the sixteenth century had been out-
lawed as vagabonds. The companies which played in the new
theatre were nominally associated with a noble household,[7] but in
practice they were independent of patronage because they were
financed on a commercial basis by their own takings in the theatre.
The playwrights, instead of being wholly dependent on patronage, like Lyly, and on command performances at court, were now
employed by the acting companies, as Shakespeare was for the
Chamberlain's Men, and then the King's Men, and as Heywood

[7] M. C. Bradbrook, *The Rise of the Common Player*, pp. 33, 39–40, 53.

was for the Red Bull. This gave them security; they were not dependent on the vicissitudes of personal favour for making a living.

This is one of the marked differences between Lyly's plays and those of his successors who wrote for the public theatre. Lyly's plays were composed for the Children's companies attached to the Chapel Royal and St Paul's. In the period before 1600 these companies were strictly amateur; their performances were given at court about twice a year; even in the Blackfriars theatre performances other than those specifically requested by the court were billed as rehearsals.[8] Lyly always writes with an eye to the court performance. His plays are two-dimensional: they require the court audience for their completion,[9] the queen as the icon whom they acknowledge with devotion. Thus the plays never acquire their own life; their world cannot stand up on its own account. For the professional playwrights in the public theatre the situation is different. Their relation is not to a patron, nor to the favour of a capricious monarch. The new masters are the audience, but a different audience from a court audience.

This is the second significant change set in motion by the erecting of a public theatre. The plays had to appeal to an extremely diverse group of people – gallants and courtiers undoubtedly, but also a large following of tradesmen, citizens, merchants, artisans, and workers, and their wives and children, who came to the theatre as the most exciting popular entertainment. They could do this because it was cheap; the standing seats were a penny, the gallery seats twopence and threepence. Computing comparative prices is difficult, but it is certain that these prices were within the reach of the working man, and that the playwrights had to please a very mixed audience when they composed their plays.[10] For a modern critic 'commercial' is a dirty word, a bastardising of art to pander to the lowest forms of popular taste. Jonson would probably agree, but nevertheless the commercialism of the public theatre exercised a wholly salutary influence on the playwrights of the late Elizabethan and Jacobean period because it forced them to

[8] Irwin Smith, *Shakespeare's Blackfriars Playhouse*, p. 134.

[9] G. K. Hunter, *John Lyly*, pp. 307–8, 346, 348.

[10] Alfred Harbage, *Shakespeare's Audience*, pp. 56, 64, 68, 83.

leave the hothouse of academic school drama, and of elegant inter-
ludes for the court, and get in touch with the concerns of the
London world at a time when it was seething with new ideas and
activities. One of the important areas with which the audience was
concerned was ideas about women, and the dramatists could not
afford not to be concerned also in a very positive way. Their ability to reflect controversy, to comment on it, to provoke it, to
pioneer, was their guarantee for a livelihood.

The fact that they were dealing with adult actors where Lyly
had written exclusively for boys also enabled them to extend their
range of interest. The child actor had special talents of precocity,
wit, quickness in debate, the beguiling but also slightly gadfly
acuteness which Shakespeare gives to Moth in *Love's Labour's Lost*,
or to Falstaff's Page in *Henry IV* Part II; but he also had limitations.
Children tire more quickly than adults; their light voices are not
suitable for elaborate soliloquies involving complex psychological
development. Hamlet could not have been written for a boy; if
Shakespeare had not had the possibility of Burbage or an adult
actor of comparable stature the play would probably not have
been written at all, certainly not in its existing form.[11] An adult
company opened a new range of subjects to the dramatist: the
domestic drama both comic and tragic, the psychological analysis
of individual characters, the emergence of the hero and of the
heroine. Throughout the Tudor period the drama had become
steadily secular, from the purity of *Everyman* to the hybrid school
dramas and the heterogeneousness of romances like *Clyomon and
Clamydes*. The public theatre and the adult actor together dealt the
death blow to eschatological drama. Certainly Lyly continued to
write for the Children, as did Chapman and Marston and Jonson
when the Children were at Blackfriars. But the more important
role of these three was that of playwright for the public theatre,
and with the possible exception of Chapman their plays are not
specifically geared to the boy actor. It is also true, of course, that
women in Jacobean drama were always played by boys; but one
boy in a professional company of adults had a different status and a
different dramatic potential from what he would have had in a

[11] Harold Newcomb Hillebrand, *The Child Actors*, pp. 254, 271.

company consisting solely of boys. The presence of the boy actor in the secular drama of character and personal relations spurred the dramatists to look beyond a femininity susceptible of imitation, to ways of representing women which would be less superficial.

Nevertheless given both the social and theatrical conditions conducive to the dramatists being exceptionally interested in attitudes to women, the question still remains as to why their predisposition is towards feminism. There are perhaps three main reasons. The dramatists had a common concern with women in that both groups were constantly attacked by conservative moralists, and by fanatic Puritan-cum-failed-playwrights like Stephen Gosson, who saw the theatre in Zeal-of-the-Land-Busy terms as a sink of sin which sanctioned hypocrisy – the age-old shadow of the actor – and also inevitably unlimited sexual vice. The men who satirised and condemned women concentrated, as Gosson himself did, or Swetnam, on their sexual licence, their extravagance and their unsuitable uppishness, in particular their liberty in gadding about. And, of course, one of the places they gadded to with the greatest frequency and relish, was the theatre. The dramatists' adoption of radical attitudes to women's rights is consistent not only with their need to please their audience of whom a sizeable part was female, and obviously, if there at all, the more liberated female, but also consistent with their own status and their own need to repudiate conservative judgements on their calling. Like will to like, quoth the devil to the collier.

Secondly, the dramatists were in a unique position for condemning and exposing false literary attitudes to women, whether satirical or romantic. The drama was not considered a literary form in Shakespeare's time. His poems gained him acclaim before his plays. When Jonson's works were collected in 1616 it was suggested that his plays should not have been included as they were not literature. Plays were entertainment. A new play was good entertainment, an old one poor, whatever its artistic merit, so that there were demurs at the idea of putting on *Richard II* six years after its first performance.[12] Had novelty been less of a god, and permanent merit more prized, Shakespeare's originals might perhaps

[12] Harbage, *Shakespeare's Audience*, pp. 76–8, 10–11.

have survived. But the dramatists saw themselves as entertainers competing with bear-baiting, wrestling and fencing. They were not artists but craftsmen, the cooks of the Prologue to *Epicoene* engaged in pleasing palates, and if Shakespeare cast himself as Prospero this is not how his public, that rowdy, indiscriminate, voracious, robust and enthusiastic penny-paying crowd, saw him. Thus the dramatists were in an ideal situation for championing the images of life – the individual woman, the rational being insisted on by the Humanists against the fictions of medieval poetry – against the falsehood of poetry. Their prestige lay in their separation from the élitism of poetry, the aristocratic game of literature. Their reputation depended on their success in entertaining the people. To champion women against literary men who forced stereotypes upon them was to reinforce their own position and make it stand for positive values. Once again, it was really class identification. The drama was a popular form, and the protagonists for liberal attitudes to women in the crudest terms stood for the virtuous bourgeois against the corrupt aristocrat.

Thirdly, the drama provided a wonderful opportunity for the talents of men who were not courtiers, or who had not had a university education. Just as Shakespeare was a theatre man, so Jonson was a brick-layer's stepson and his apprentice, and Middleton, whose father was also a brick-layer, struggled through his studies in an Oxford stocked with courtiers. Scepticism about university men, indeed about professional men generally – lawyers, doctors, pedagogues – is as marked in Elizabethan and Jacobean drama as contempt for the prototype of the Jacobean effete courtier – the Osric figure. These were men who were not tied to the establishment, apart from the theatrical establishment, who would probably never have made their way if there had not been a public theatre able to develop and exploit and house their talents.[13] Spenser, after all, spent his whole life trying to acquire court favour, patronage and what these meant – that is, financial backing. But some of the dramatists in this period enjoyed the remarkable and democratic freedom of not being indebted to the establishment either for their upbringing, or for their means of support.

[13] Harbage, *Cavalier Drama*, pp. 21–2.

Indeed, even in Jonson's plays contempt for established institutions is a recurrent theme. Shakespeare himself had enormous fun at the expense of the academic, the schoolman, the lawyer, the cleric. Harbage is surely right in asserting that one of the chief, though often latent objections to the theatre at this time was that it was a form of highly democratic assembly in an autocratic age.[14] Many of the playwrights profited professionally from the democracy of the theatre in a period when everyone else, to be successful, had to be of the hierarchy. These men were not likely to be the quashers of protest, of new ideas, of rebellion against outdated orthodoxies. They stood quite as firmly as the Puritans did, for a kind of person who had not previously had much of a voice. If women too were taking advantage of rifts in the old fabric to make themselves heard, the dramatists from their own experience and position would be likely to give them a platform and encourage them in their bid for change.

However, the theatre itself was changing during the course of the Jacobean period, and it is interesting to consider whether changes in the theatre, and changes which took place outside but affected the theatre, also affected attitudes to women in the drama.

Two events influenced the theatre in the first thirty years of the seventeenth century. The first was Burbage's purchase of the private theatre at Blackfriars in 1609 and the subsequent gradual movement of significant drama into this arena from the public theatre. The second was the accession in 1625 of Charles I and of his French Catholic queen, Henrietta Maria.

When Burbage bought the indoor theatre at Blackfriars a long ambition was accomplished; the King's Men now had a permanent winter home, where previously winter performances had been given at the Cross Keys Inn as the Globe was outdoor; furthermore they now commanded a site within the city limit instead of in the suburbs with their unsavoury reputation for brothels, and thus within easy access of a court audience and a world of culture and fashion. It was a much smaller theatre, inevitably, than the Globe, which housed probably about three thousand people at a sitting. There was no standing room, and seats cost from sixpence to two

[14] *Shakespeare's Audience*, p. 11.

shillings and sixpence.[15]

Probably these circumstantial changes only gradually changed the type of plays written. Shakespeare's last plays show a change of direction easily predictable from the internal interest of the trage-dies, without the need for external stimulus from theatrical con-ditions. Fletcher's *The Faithful Shepherdess* was not liked by the Blackfriars audience any more than it would have been by the Globe crowd. It was a pastoral written too early for an audience used to enjoying at the theatre a mirror of the concerns of its own society. But the price of seats and the location of the Blackfriars squeezed out the artisan, craftsman, lower middle-class element from the audience because they could not afford to go to a theatre able to tap court resources. The playwrights became more con-cerned to please the court and its circle than to entertain the ex-tremely various cross-section of society which made up Shakespeare's audience at the Globe.

In the Jacobean period, despite Harbage's stimulating theory of the separateness of style apparent in the 'coterie' drama written for Blackfriars,[16] there is no clear line in technique, subject-matter or morals between the plays written for the public theatre and those for the private. In the first place most of the playwrights — Mar-ston, Middleton, Jonson, Shakespeare himself — wrote for both and expected their plays to be performed by both. Secondly, the tastes of James I were towards the popular; he liked the rough comedy with which Jonson prefaced his masques.[17] Although the masque was a form in the ascendant, patronised by James' Queen Anne and developed through the collaboration of artists as gifted as Jonson and Inigo Jones, it existed parallel to a popular drama which retained its prestige, partly because of its talented expon-ents, and partly because the king enjoyed it. To write with the Blackfriars audience in mind during the 1610 to 1625 period was still to write largely for the same interests and tastes that the public audience had evinced in the heyday of the Globe.

The change which really affected the theatre was the accession

[15] Irwin Smith, *Shakespeare's Blackfriars Playhouse*, pp. 297–301.

[16] *Shakespeare and the Rival Traditions*.

[17] Stephen Orgel, *The Jonsonian Masque*, pp. 80, 100.

of Charles I. It is traditional to state that after 1625 the Puritans withdrew in large numbers from the theatre audience, leading up to the eventual closing of the theatres in 1642. In fact probably the Puritan backbone of modest-incomed citizens ceased to go to the theatre which was to dictate taste in drama when that theatre became Blackfriars instead of the Globe, because they could not afford to pay sixpence a time instead of a penny. But their absence did not noticeably influence the dramatists until the change of monarch. Thereafter the more prosperous Puritans who had continued to patronize Blackfriars probably stopped going in protest first of all against the conservatism of Charles I both in politics and religion – a High Church Anglican – secondly against his Catholic consort, Henrietta Maria, and thirdly against the dramatic tastes of both of them and the extravagance with which they gratified those tastes. The removal of the Puritan element from the audience meant the loss of a receptive response to everything that Puritanism stood for in attitudes to women and to marriage, and also of a substantial body who stood for middle-class morality against court ethics.

The dramatists responded in two ways to this change in the composition of the audience. Playwrights like Montague, Davenant, Suckling, and Cartwright, men who in many cases are remembered more for their poetry than their plays, show no cognisance of Puritan ideas about women; when they write about women they do so from a viewpoint more in tune with court taste. On the other hand playwrights like Brome and Shirley find themselves in the difficult position of writing in a style which is akin to that of the Jacobean professional playwrights – Middleton, Massinger, Heywood, even sometimes Jonson – but for an audience deprived of the people who dictated that style – the Puritan citizenry. Shirley was a favourite with Henrietta Maria, but his best plays, like *The Lady of Pleasure*, read like a castrated form of Jacobean comedy because he, and Brome also, lacked the vital relation to the audience which stimulated a playwright like Middleton. Shirley and Brome never fully adapt to the art of writing for court tastes, and the consequence is that their plays seem not to be written for anyone, because the court in the Caroline period is the only

fashionable audience for the drama. The result in the plays of both
these dramatists demonstrates itself in an uneasy relation to the
audience and to the morality which appealed to the Puritans in
Shakespeare's theatre. They cannot thrive on the animus towards
the court which provided a constant spur to men like Marston because Charles' court is different from James' in not being li-
centious, largely due to the marital example of Charles and
Henrietta Maria – a fact often registered in the drama. Thus they
lack an important subject and also a significant element in estab-
lishing their own class identity. Their plays need the convention of
the corrupt courtier, but they are obliged to make him virtuous –
as for instance in Brome's *The Sparagus Garden* where some courtiers visit the brothel which is thinly disguised as a garden, but only
for curiosity, and go away without doing anything: a non-event
dramatically. This also takes away from them an important Jacobean theme: the triumph of the virtuous but sharp-witted citizen's
wife – or sometimes daughter – over the lewd aristocrat. Brome
and Shirley can no longer rely on the partisanship of a bourgeois
audience; they never acquire the confident touch of the Jacobean
playwrights. In their plays they always seem to be trying to have it
both ways – to jibe at the court, and simultaneously to propitiate
it. They would like to present Puritan ethics in the tradition of the
earlier playwrights, but fail to find a sympathetic audience.

The effect of this situation on attitudes to women in their plays is
that Puritan ideas about women, the new questions, the suggested
answers, the whole context of debate, have hardened into convention. What in late Elizabethan drama is still in the melting pot,
fought over, tested, proclaimed, sifted, in the plays of Brome and
Shirley is there like a shell – the framework of domestic relations
and a few simple ideological pieties, but not vital, not emerging
from the dust and heat of controversy, not risking anything, not
energetically presented either for approval or opposition from the
audience. The questions which Elizabethan and Jacobean dramatists harried over – what freedoms should women have from their
husbands, from their fathers, and the tricky area of the double standard – are not asked. There are some answers, but they do not
resolve a living debate. They are appliquéd to an unruffled surface.

This is what the loss of the Puritans to the theatre meant to the treatment of women in the drama. For other playwrights who were courtiers in the circle of Charles I and Henrietta Maria there was no dilemma, but there was equal loss. Shakespeare and his fellows belonged admittedly largely to one class – that of self-made professional men. But they had to please much more than their own class: they had to entertain the monarch, courtiers, men of letters, churchmen as critical as Donne, noble ladies as versatile and well-read as Lady Anne Clifford, young bloods, Inns of Court men, and the whole rank and file of the London citizenry from the wealthiest merchant to the shoe-maker's apprentice. The audience challenged invention. When play-going, play-making, and even play-acting, moved into the confined circle of the court the fashionable playwrights like Montague, Suckling – the whole undistinguished crew of Caroline noble dramatists – not only belonged to one class, they also wrote for one class. The effect on the drama was like the effect on democracy of a one party system. There was no opposition. Ideas needed no strength to survive because there were no inimical elements to be overcome. The result was an enervating pursuit of fashions in taste and a polite presentation of attitudes and ideas complimentary and acceptable to the monarch and his queen. Lacking the impetus of class struggle, of financial incentive, of competition, of contact with a society rapidly developing and changing, Caroline drama presents a wearisome and precious articulation of the intellectual diversions of a leisured class.

These diversions were, briefly, Platonic love, whose embryo Henrietta Maria brought with her from France, saluting spiritual love divorced from the flesh; secondly war, and primarily from war the conflicts familiarised by Lovelace in his poem *To Lucasta* between patriotic honour and romantic love; thirdly the fashion for the pastoral. In addition the royal pair prompted reverence for the Divine Right of the king, and respect for Roman Catholicism.

The dramatists who embraced these themes moved into literary fiction as surely as their predecessors rejected it. The result for the treatment of women is predictable: attitudes to women become part of a game played, like Lyly's games, to amuse an élite, but bearing no relation to actual attitudes to women in society. Caroline drama is frivolous where, beneath all the roistering, the Jacobeans were serious. Montague propounds Platonic love and plays at feminism; Cartwright shows a man's war (in *The Lady-Errant*) and fantasizes on an uprising of the women left at home and a women's commonwealth; everyone plays at shepherds and shepherdesses and sexlessness and innocence. Suckling writes two endings to *Aglaura*, one for the populace where the king gets killed, and one for the court where he does not. Women take the veil, men become monks, and Catholic ideas about virgins, wives, widows and subjection prevail without protest. Caroline drama has nothing to say except how to do nothing elegantly, and Time, the old justice of the Forest of Arden, in Montague's *The Shepherd's Paradise* is the god of boredom. The ferment about women in Shakespeare's society which provided such stimulus to the dramatists moves out of the drama when the drama moves out of that many-sided society. Charles and Henrietta Maria, particularly Henrietta Maria, loved plays, but loved the masque more, not the Jonsonian masque with the comedy dear to James, but the refined, laborious verse spectacle of the Catholic Montague. The Puritan closing of the theatres in 1642 was as much a protest against the expense of Henrietta's masque – one could cost as much as £3000 in the money of the time[18] – and against the licence of the queen's acting in it, thus setting a precedent for the vogue of women actors which was already developing, as against the art of acting itself. The public theatre could not finance masques to compete with those at Blackfriars; the middle classes, the backbone of Puritanism, were thus alienated from the theatre and alienated on the very grounds for which they felt the greatest bitterness towards the king – his inability to finance himself. The theatre in the Caroline period became the élitist entertainment which it continued to be in the Restoration, and which it still is. The motley multitude who demanded a drama which spoke to their condition lost its power over the dramatist for ever.

[18] *The Triumph of Peace*, of which Henrietta commissioned a repeat performance, cost, according to Harbage's computation, $1,000,000 in modern money (*Cavalier Drama*, p. 17).

Shakespeare and his contemporaries could rely on their audience's alertness to controversy about women. They shared with it an awareness to changing attitudes heightened by Puritan propaganda, by controversy in the popular press, and by women militants themselves. The richness, range and vitality of late Elizabethan and Jacobean drama grow out of its close relation to the concerns of its time. The unique quality of the dramatists of this period lies in their ability to grasp what were the really interesting questions of their time and to think creatively about them. Shakespeare was not alone in realising that many of the lastingly significant questions had to do with beliefs about the nature and position of women.

CHAPTER I

The Idea of Chastity

1 The Puritans and the Playwrights

Puritanism has acquired such a drear aspect in the modern world that it seems rash to associate Shakespeare with its withering influence. The prejudice is that with the Puritans English culture took a turn for the worse; cakes and ale went out and Bible-bashers came in. May Day merriment, Sunday ball-games and theatres were sacrificed to the ancestors of the Lord's Day Observance Society; God the Father taking family prayers, and sex as obligatory and hygienic as cleanliness. Shakespeare was surely a Falstaff to this world of Angelos.

Compared with this race of penny-pinchers and window-breakers, quaffing orange-juice and talking with Huntingdon accents, the Cavaliers mean Van Dyck's portrait of Charles I, long hair, lace, big hats, the non-utilitarian in life; patronage of the arts, the men who returned the merry monarch and the gay life to London; Purcell and Pepys and Congreve and Nell Gwyn and the reinstatement of upper-class values. This is what Matthew Arnold had in mind when he talked of the provincialism of the English Puritans, and called them 'mutilated men' who had divorced themselves from the fullness of life.[1] Puritanism nowadays stands for the burgher consciousness, the sober money-making and sexual prudery of the Victorian middle classes. The Cavalier spirit has moved into the Hippie world. Compared with both, Shakespeare comes from an integrated England, winning the Armada with one hand while it played bowls with the other, toasting Gloriana with a tankard on her progresses through the country, and sporting under the greenwood tree. The portrait is not of Charles I but of

[1] *Culture and Anarchy*, pp. 11, 14.

Sir Philip Sidney, scholar, statesman, soldier, poet – the emblem of the Renaissance. To annex Puritanism to this vision seems to cast an untimely frost on the sweetest flower of all the field.

In a world sated with bourgeois morality it is easy to blame the Puritans for being its first spokesmen. But the Puritans saw themselves not as a bourgeois establishment playing safe, but as the heralds of a new society, realising, at least to some extent, the values of More's *Utopia* in the face of a decadent aristocracy. They preached as torchbearers of the Renaissance and the Reformation, expounding for ordinary men and women new truths about themselves, their society, and their God. Where they sound cautious to a modern ear, in their own time they were audacious. They did not offer a cut-and-dried women's magazine morality; they challenged people to discover what freedom of conscience meant.

Puritanism in its widest sense attracted the support of the most talented men of the period, from Bacon to preachers like Henry Smith and William Perkins, to a man as precariously balanced between Anglicanism and Puritanism as Donne. The drama, presented to audiences accustomed to hearing the sermons in the London churches, was not likely to remain untouched.[2] The line between the pulpit and the stage was less distinct in the early seventeenth century than it is today. Donne's sermons are as much a dramatic performance as Hamlet's soliloquies. Exhortation played a large part in the hybrid morality play. Shakespeare and his contemporaries inherited from medieval drama a relation with the pulpit both in what was said and in how it was said.[3] The break with tradition would have lain in their imperviousness to Puritanism, not in their assimilation of it.

Reluctance to relate Shakespeare to Puritanism derives from the popular belief that all Puritans were Zeal-of-the-Land-Busies who attacked the stage and were derided throughout Elizabethan and Jacobean drama, from Middleton's *The Family of Love*, to Chapman's *An Humorous Day's Mirth*, to *Twelfth Night*. The dramatists were antagonistic to the sects, whom, like James I, they

[2] Harbage, *Shakespeare and the Rival Traditions*, p. 27. L. C. Knights, *Drama & Society in the Age of Jonson*, p. 156, n. 4.

[3] Cf. G. R. Owst, *Literature and Pulpit in Medieval England*, p. 485.

labelled 'puritan.' But they were sympathetic to the wider ideals of Puritanism, of which sectarianism was only one form of expression. Unfortunately sectarianism dominates the subsequent image of Puritanism, what one writer called 'the shriveled manifestation of the spirit of Puritanism.'[4] When Puritanism became embodied in a political institution it lost the breadth of appeal and the spirit of intellectual pioneering which it had had in the Jacobean period. The years between 1590 and 1625 – Shakespeare's years – were the most creative and fertile years for English Puritanism.

The dogmatic, kill-joy picture of the Puritans is a powerful example of the evil that men do living after them. Men unerringly perpetuate not the strengths but the weaknesses of the great. T. S. Eliot measured Milton by the damage he claimed that his use of English had inflicted on eighteenth century poetry.[5] The Pre-Raphaelites and later the Georgian poets soured the taste for Keats. Wesleyan Methodism stamped the Bulstrode character irrevocably on seventeenth century Puritanism. The judgement of posterity on a movement which set out to free men and women was that it had landed them everywhere in chains. To connect Shakespeare to the Puritans is not to detract from the dramatist but to restore to the idea of Puritanism the brilliance and energy which went into creating it.

The Protestant doctrine of married chastity attacked the theological basis for extolling virginity. The dramatists' treatment of chastity in women relates to their contact with the ideas of the early Protestants and of the Humanists through Puritan propaganda. The Puritan values of the dramatists of Shakespeare's theatre stand in marked contrast to the predilections of playwrights in the late 1620's. In Caroline drama the debate about marriage and celibacy expires without protest under the influence of a Catholic queen to whom, surrounded by her Capuchins, satire on nunneries and the call to single life would hardly be acceptable, who had herself an almost fanatical aversion to female unchastity.[6]

[4] Elbert N. S. Thompson, *The Controversy between the Puritans and the Stage*, p. 9.

[5] 'Milton I', *On Poetry and Poets*, pp. 138, 141.

[6] Carola Oman, *Henrietta Maria*, p. 116.

She brought with her from France a theory of Platonic love which idealised beauty in women and proclaimed love without sex. The Platonic lady in Suckling's *Aglaura* announces:

> Love's a chameleon, and would live on air,
> Physic for agues; starving is his food.[7]

There is plenty of scoffing at the Platonics in Caroline drama but no equilibrium emerges, as it does in Shakespeare's comedies, between the extravagancies of the spirit and the demands of the flesh. There is nowhere the sanity of Donne's reminder:

> Loves mysteries in soules doe grow,
> But yet the body is his booke.[8]

The Caroline idea of chastity in a relation between man and woman is, in all its unreality and absurdity, 'friendship-love,' as one of the characters in Killigrew's *The Parson's Wedding* designates the phenomenon. It is a literary game for polite society instead of the serious exploration of the actual relations between men and women offered by Shakespeare and his contemporaries. Even as a dramatic motif it offers little scope for invention or variation. The inevitable movement is away from the image of a love so refined as to be virtually non-existent to the contemplation of a more recognisable friendship – that between two men. Caroline drama is ostensibly the drama of sentiment, and the male friendships it salutes – Charalois and Remont in Massinger's *The Fatal Dowry*, Doria and Vitelli in Glapthorne's *The Ladies Privilege* – witness the Caroline escape from the complexity of heterosexual relations into a hot-house. The playwrights' depiction of friendship lacks the classical austerity of Chapman's Clermont who preferred 'friendship chaste and masculine'[9] to marriage, and lacks also the straightforward purity of the morality theme for boy actors apparent in Elizabethan friendship plays like *Damon and Pythias*. As far as Caroline drama is concerned the rich and complex enquiry by the earlier dramatists into attitudes to women sparked off by the

[7] I.v.61.
[8] *The Extasie.*
[9] *The Revenge of Bussy D'Ambois*, v.i.

Puritans might just as well not have taken place.

The Puritans embraced Calvin's doctrine of chaste marriage as an emancipation for men and women from the celibate ideal. Celibacy was hard because it was unnatural. The reformers' cry against the Roman priesthood was that they repudiated marriage but condoned whores. For women the effect of the celibate ideal was to undermine the status of wives, and to cast women in general in the role of temptress. Adam succumbed to Eve and was banished from Paradise. The popular interpretation of the Fall by the Church fathers was that Adam's sin was lust.[10] Homage to the Virgin Mary had little influence on attitudes to women generally because she had transcended nature. The ordinary Eve was still raring to go.

Calvin, who of all the reformers exerted the greatest influence on the Puritans, claimed for marriage the spiritual prestige which had previously been reserved for celibacy. He scoffed at 'rhapsodic praises of virginity,' and refused to call marriage a sacrament because copulation is not sinful and does not need special sanctification. The single life, in his view, was a special calling for the few rather than for the many.[11] The Puritans took their position on marriage from Calvin. Marriage was 'a state in it selfe, farre more excellent, then the condition of single life.'[12] They argued that chastity was for married people as well as for virgins. Donne protested in a marriage sermon that the Roman Church 'injure the whole state of Christianity, when they oppose mariage and chastity, as though they were incompatible.'[13]

The Puritan preachers concentrated on aspects of morals and behaviour which were directly affected by the theory of chaste marriage. They reassessed monastic life, talked about sex in marriage, sex outside marriage, the double standard and male attitudes to female virginity. They tried to define chastity in the wife both in terms of inherent virtues and of behaviour.

Many Puritan strictures are lifted wholesale into the drama.

[10] W. E. H. Lecky, *History of European Morals from Augustus to Charlemagne*, II, 281. C. H. and K. George, *The Protestant Mind of the English Reformation 1570–1640*, pp. 257–89.

[11] *Institutes of the Christian Religion*, II, 130, 1483; I, 406.

[12] William Perkins, *Christian Oeconomie*, p. 11.

[13] *The Sermons of John Donne*, II, 340.

Generally speaking, the less skilled the dramatist, the clearer the lines of Puritan thought because they have not been incorporated into a new artistic entity. The anonymous *How a Man May Choose a Good Wife from a Bad* sets up the same model of the chaste wife contrasted with the whore as Marston's *The Dutch Courtezan*, but Marston's play contains more full-bodied characters and a less linear conception of conflict than the uncompromisingly homiletic play. George Wilkins' *The Miseries of Enforced Marriage* is a bald blueprint for the concerns which govern most of Middleton's plays, of Heywood's and Dekker's, of some plays of Marston and Jonson, and of *The Merry Wives of Windsor*.

The same situations of forced marriage and usually consequent adultery are admittedly a staple part of Molière's comedy which was not influenced by Puritanism; whether in *L'École des Femmes*, or even more explicitly in *George Dandin ou Le Mari Confondu* where the heroine disclaims being bound to a marriage to which she had not consented in the first place. But Molière has no illusions about marriage, or about the treatment of women in his society. He observes the results of forced marriage dispassionately, with good humour, not taking sides with either the wronged husband, the fatuous parents or the rebel wife. His plays do not resolve into unambiguous ethical judgements derived from a theory of how society and men and women ought to be. Molière might say with Philinte in *Le Misanthrope* in protest against the rigour of Alceste's condemnation of human folly: 'Je prends tout doucement les hommes comme ils sont.'[14] Molière's comedy is corrective only in advocating tolerance in preference to the perfervid pursuit of ideals regardless of human weakness. Molière anticipates the Enlightenment in an attitude to life which was to inform the movement for religious toleration. By contrast the English Renaissance dramatists were concerned, like Erasmus, and like the Puritans, with the meaningful union of secular living with religious conviction.

Jonson was not alone in seeing his comedy as a reforming instrument. Marston in the Induction to *The Malcontent* claims for his play the vinegar asperity of satire. Dekker and Heywood write as

[14] I.i.

propagandists for a Puritan vision of bourgeois society. Middleton, despite a more ironic approach to ideals than either Dekker or Heywood, nevertheless ties his observations of human nature to a Puritan ethical structure. This identity with Puritan attitudes marks a major difference between his tragedies and Ford's where the conventional moral redress which takes place at the end of *'Tis Pity She's a Whore* is at war with the emotional magnetism of the play and with Ford's own sceptical cast of mind. Ford's plays witness the movement of Puritan influence out of the theatre as clearly as Marston's or Middleton's or Webster's reflect that influence. But Jonson, although the most explicit of the dramatists about his corrective aims,[15] stands equidistant between a playwright like Marston insistently exposing and haranguing, and Molière exposing and making a virtue out of not haranguing. Jonson defined his purpose as that of reformer but in fact he enjoyed the deftness of vice against the obtuseness of virtue and failed to condemn evil because he created good so much less attractively. His theory was with Marston but his heart was with Molière.

The dramatists of Shakespeare's theatre differ in the degree of their consciousness of having a specific moral purpose. With Heywood it is paramount, with Beaumont and Fletcher subordinated to entertainment value and what that means in terms of commercial success. Chapman is the only dramatist relatively unconcerned with Puritan ideals and propaganda because he reverts to classical models of virtue for his heroes, and adopts a handful of stereotypes by which to represent female character.[16] His women are of a different and less enquiring world than those of Middleton or Webster.

Shakespeare is the only dramatist of the period who writes with no explicit reforming purpose, and the nearest to him in this respect is Webster. Yet compared with Molière's, or with Congreve's, Shakespeare's plays propose attitudes to life, ideals, relations between people which have the effect of stimulating emulation: the married relation of Brutus and Portia, the way in

[15] Induction to *Every Man Out of His Humour*, Prologue to *Epicoene, or The Silent Woman*.

[16] Harbage, *Shakespeare and the Rival Traditions*, p. 242.

which Helena in *All's Well That Ends Well* sees and deals with her dilemma, the exuberant celebration in the comedies of married life against celibacy, of the madness of the lover in preference to the 'living humour of madness – which was, to forswear the full stream of the world and to live in a nook merely monastic.'[17] It is the same method by which Tolstoy declares for the creativity and capacity for growth of Kitty and Levin in *Anna Karenina* against the sterility and diminishing influence of Anna and Vronsky on each other. In Molière, as in Restoration drama, there is no convincing image to suggest the superiority of marriage to adultery. Marriage is a dreary end to an exciting chase, or a convenient mask for an exciting illicit passion. Even in *Le Misanthrope* where the flirt is discredited and the misanthrope shown his delusions, the final marriage of the well-balanced Éliante to the man who had always respected her as a companion fails utterly to provide an emotional lodestone, to make marriage anything other than the depressing condition rejected by Célimène. Molière's married couples are always dreadful people having a dreadful time. In Elizabethan drama the possibilities of married life are explored, whether in Adriana and Antipholus, warring and yet admitting a vitality in their relation which makes Adriana retort to her sister's question: 'Who would be jealous then of such a one?' with the words: 'Ah, but I think him better than I say,'[18] or in Posthumus and Imogen, or in the Duchess of Malfi and Antonio, or in the tension of closeness between Macbeth and Lady Macbeth. Shakespeare's concerns and ideals owe as much to Puritanism as Heywood's but the influence is less raw and crude because Shakespeare transforms it into drama.

The Puritan propaganda in plays acted between 1590 and 1625 is made more concrete by the fact that many of the comedies of this period are set in London and reproduce a strongly city way of life, whether in the booths of *Bartholomew Fair* or in the tavern presided over by Mistress Mulligrub in *The Dutch Courtezan* or the succession of merchants' shops which figure in the comedies of Middleton and Dekker. The life of the Blue Boar in Eastcheap in *Henry IV* is different from the tavern world of Jacobean city comedy only in

[17] *As You Like It*, III.ii.408.

[18] *The Comedy of Errors*, IV.ii.23.

being placed in a richer and more resonant context and frequented
by more fully realised and more varied kinds of people. But the
concreteness of London life is an essential part of both Mistress
Quickly and Falstaff, and Falstaff transplanted into Windsor is a
displaced person as much because of his lost city life as because of
his lost court life. Mistress Quickly is less muddied by city trivia
than Mistress Mulligrub, but her inn bears the traces of Puritan
London as firmly as Mistress Mulligrub's speech. The Blue Boar is
hung around with flea-bitten tapestries of the Prodigal Son,
Falstaff's favourite story which was to turn the tables on him at the
Coronation. Falstaff himself bears a likeness in which Shakespeare
delighted to his original, the fanatical Lollard, Sir John Oldcastle.
He has the Puritan jargon to a turn, accusing the rascally young
prince of being 'able to corrupt a saint' with the consequence that
he is now 'little better than one of the wicked.' Purse-taking is his
vocation, and ''tis no sin for a man to labour in his vocation.' Men
are to be saved by faith not merit, otherwise what hole in hell were
hot enough for Poins? He has lost his voice with singing of
anthems[19] and his knowledge of the Bible is what Coverdale and
Tyndale must have dreamed of for future generations of Protestants. It is one of Shakespeare's jokes at Puritanism that the character closest to Falstaff in exuberant living and confident easy
progress between disparate worlds is also connected to the Puritans, Bottom, the weaver, singing songs about cuckolds in the
wood outside Athens (when weavers were notorious as Puritans
and psalm-singers) among men not liking to hear tell of a paramour. Shakespeare rode on the tide of the Thames where his fellows let it engulf them, but the London setting of their plays
provides them with a frame of reference, a sense of an immediate,
relevant, working world. Middleton's Touchwood in *A Chaste
Maid in Cheapside* comments on the improved godliness of the city:

> There has been more religious wholesome laws
> In the half-circle of a year erected
> For common good than memory e'er knew of.[20]

[19] *Henry IV* Part I, I.ii.88; *Henry IV* Part II, I.ii.189.
[20] II.i.111.

Iago, glancing venomously over his shoulder at an audience of potential city cuckolds, retorts to Othello's: 'A hornèd man's a monster and a beast,' with:

> There's many a beast then in a populous city,
> And many a civil monster.[21]

The Caroline dramatists lifted their plays out of London into a no-man's-land, that weird, over-refined, over-articulate armchair world of court theatre in the thirties, leaving the old-style dramatists like Brome and Shirley mouthing city morality without the city setting which gives concreteness to many Elizabethan and Jacobean plays.

The relation between propaganda and art is difficult to plot. The critic's prejudice is to consign propaganda to the second-rate talent: a great artist is demeaned and sullied by being labelled propagandist. These are not the terms in which it seems either proper or illuminating to talk about Chaucer, Shakespeare, Milton, George Eliot, the Greek dramatists, the nineteenth century Russian novel or any artist of stature. The problem remains, nevertheless, that if propaganda is done well enough it becomes art, as in Milton's *Areopagitica*, or Mary Wollstonecraft's *The Rights of Woman*, or *Bleak House* and *Oliver Twist*, or almost any specifically religious writing from St Paul's Epistles to Donne's sermons and *The Pilgrim's Progress*. *Uncle Tom's Cabin* is propaganda not because it contains more propaganda than Dickens' novels, but because Harriet Beecher Stowe lacked Dickens' imagination. Nor is it obvious at what point the voicing of strongly held convictions becomes propaganda or if the question of propaganda is not primarily a question of how those convictions are voiced. The *Areopagitica* contains as much of the manipulation associated with propaganda as of the vision associated with art. Moreover the satirist's artistic purpose is not different from that of the propagandist although his methods — whether the poetry of Pope or the prose of Swift — require more virtuosity. The extent to which the greatest art is stimulated by propaganda and grows from it is everywhere demonstrable, whether in Shakespeare's history

[21] *Othello*, IV.i.62.

plays moving from the given of Tudor piety into an expansive
ironic vision of human vicissitude, or in *Paradise Lost* which in
inspiration is as strongly a child of its time as in creative power it
transcends that time. The greatest modern novels are probably
those which come from Russia, the reaction of the individual artist
to a propagandist culture, which is the dominant impulse behind *A
Day in the Life of Ivan Denisovitch* or *The First Circle*. Novels of distinction have come from the modern race issue. The modern
women's movement has yet to produce a creative talent comparable to Ibsen's or Virginia Woolf's. In the late Elizabethan period
the talents which focused on the debate about women fostered by
Puritanism varied from Shakespeare who concealed propaganda
in art and therefore, it is always claimed, had no relation to Puritanism, to Heywood, or a more extreme case, George Wilkins,
who professed and proclaimed and pioneered Puritan attitudes to
women, marriage and society without the interference of the
enlarging and humanising medium of art. In Shakespeare Puritan
attitudes to women undergo a sea change. In the plays of his contemporaries the transmutation of propaganda into art is in almost
every case, including Jonson's, less than complete. Shakespeare's
superiority as a dramatist is not dependent on his imperviousness to
propaganda but on what he did with it.

Puritanism pushed the dramatists into talking about women.
The preachers posed questions about attitudes to women which
provided the playwrights with raw material, and created an atmosphere which stimulated them to use it.

2 Chastity as Mystique

Donne declared: 'I call not that *Virginity a vertue*, which resideth
onely in the *Bodies integrity*.'[1] The Calvinist commitment to the
chastity of married people impelled its supporters to clarify the relation between chastity as a virtue and virginity as a physical state.

In the monastic vow of chastity, chastity implies virginity. But
in the sixteenth century many of the ideals of monastic living were
discredited, by men more disinterested than Henry VIII, at the

[1] 'That Virginity is a Vertue', *Complete Poetry and Selected Prose*, p. 346.

same time that the monasteries were destroyed. Erasmus attacked the notion of a spiritual élite separated from the world; it conflicted with his belief in lay spirituality. Each man was called, and therefore none could claim a special calling. The virgin averse to matrimony in one of Erasmus' Colloquies wants to espouse herself to Christ but is told: 'You have espoused him already, and so we have all. Where is the Woman that marries the same Man twice?' To Erasmus the chastity of the convent was merely formalism. 'They are not all Virgins that wear Vails, believe me,' remarks his critic of the nunnery. Chastity is not a question of obedience to externals which 'make no Body more acceptable in the Eyes of Christ, who only regards the Purity of the mind.'² The question which emerged to challenge and perplex the reformers was whether it was possible to be pure in mind, and thus chaste, without being physically a virgin. The theory of chaste marriage answered that it was if the virgin had exchanged her title for that of wife. But if chastity were more than virginity it seemed as if physical virginity must be less than chastity. The doubt prompted Vives to add to his admonitions to young women to protect their physical virginity the proviso that 'the virginity of the body is nought worth except the mind be pure withal.'³ Milton focused the issue in *Comus* where the Lady, imprisoned and seduced by Comus, claims proudly: 'Thou canst not touch the freedom of my mind.'⁴ This is the logical conclusion of Puritan attitudes to chastity, the ultimate supremacy of purity of intent over the physical state, which Richardson was to invoke for Clarissa, drugged and seduced by Lovelace.⁵ The tribunal which judges the individual is his own conscience not his obedience to an external authority exalting a physical condition.

The divorcing of chastity from physical virginity had important

² 'The Virgin Averse to Matrimony', *All the Familiar Colloquies of Desiderius Erasmus*, pp. 153–4.

³ *The Instruction of a Christian Woman*, in *Vives and the Renascence Education of Women*, p. 87.

⁴ ii. 663.

⁵ Christopher Hill, 'Clarissa Harlowe and her Times', *Essays in Criticism*, v (1955) no. 4, 331–2.

consequences for attitudes to women. The ideal of chastity in
women symbolised by the Virgin Mary, adulated by the medieval
Church and exalted in the literature of courtly love is a mystique
rather than a definable and limited attribute. The mystique flou-
rishes at times when there is a large disparity between the image
and the reality, the vision of how people would like themselves or
others to be, and the fact of how they really are. The medieval elevation of chastity in women is the counterpart to the conviction,
apparent in the writings of the Church fathers and of medieval satirists, that women are by nature inordinately lustful. In practical
terms a way of keeping the natural concupiscence of women under
control is to make the highest virtue of its antithesis: the state of
virginity. This protects women from themselves, and it protects
men from them. It is an almost Platonic vision of perfection made
piquant by the actual daily evidence of imperfection. To this
mystique the fact of physical virginity is essential; the intimacy, the
physical necessities and consequences of sexual contact, the implied
equality or, in the medieval ethic, inferiority of the woman in the
sexual relation, are inimical to the sense of remoteness and untouchability inherent in the image of chastity. This is the conflict
which Freud perceived in Victorian society in the impotence of
men with wives who would be violated by sex, and their capa-
bility with whores. The exaltation of chastity in women in medieval thought, or in the ethical mores of the Victorians, demands
virginity. To state, as the sixteenth century reformers did, that
chastity is compatible with sexual knowledge, is to destroy the
mystique by obliterating those associations which made it vital imaginatively. But on the other hand the disparity between image
and reality means that the mystique thrives in periods when ordinary women are thought of, and treated, as inferior. To demote the
chaste woman is to upgrade the whore, and this implies coming to
terms with the realities of what women are like and of what virtue
in women consists if it is not a label attendant on the physical condition of virginity. It is significant of attitudes to women that
virtue in women has nearly always meant sexual virtue, that is,
chastity. The contribution of the reformers to the emancipation of
women was to explode the idea that the highest spiritual qualities

were inseparable from virginity, and to make the concept of chastity embrace a whole range of attributes independent of virginity because they were to be found not in the nun but in the married woman.

The mystique of chastity in women suffered eclipse in the Renaissance to the same extent as the mystique of honour in men. In the ethic of courtly love honour is to a man as chastity is to a woman, a condition of life essential to his self-respect and his sense of identity as an individual, but intangible, and dependent not so much on innate virtue as on the reputation for virtue among other men. As Madame de Sotenville proclaims in Molière's *George Dandin ou Le Mari Confondu*, protesting the honour of her ancient family: 'La bravoure n'y est pas plus héréditaire aux mâles, que la chasteté aux femelles.'[6] The actual loss of honour in a man or of chastity in a woman is unimportant if unknown; the real loss is the loss of public esteem when private digression is made public. Hence the emphasis in the courtly love code on the secrecy of the lover. Honour provides a man, as chastity provides a woman, with an aura as vague but as unmistakable as the aura bestowed by high birth.

In the Renaissance the medieval concept of honour in men is analysed with a clear-headed matter-of-factness which no mystique can survive, based as it always is on an emotional rather than rational allegiance. The Humanists attacked honour as part of an aristocratic culture glorifying war.[7] In Renaissance drama honour has an old-fashioned ring; it is a mere scutcheon, a spurious justification by the rebel Hotspur for a betrayal of honour among thieves:

> By heaven, methinks it were an easy leap
> To pluck bright honour from the pale-fac'd moon.[8]

His colder companions sniff at the 'world of figures' without form conjured up by such braggardism. What Hotspur laments in this

[6] I.iv.

[7] Robert P. Adams, *The Better Part of Valor: More, Erasmus, Colet, and Vives, on Humanism, War, and Peace, 1496–1535*.

[8] *Henry IV* Part I, I.iii.199.

speech is the necessity for sharing the spoils of rebellion: this is hardly the old meaning of honour. Bacon might be describing Hotspur when he remarks in his Essay 'Of Honour and Reputation' that 'some in their Actions, doe Wooe and affect *Honour, and Reputation.* Which sort of Men, are commonly much Talked of, but inwardly little Admired.'[9] Brutus is the honourable man of Bacon's final category, he who puts his country before himself, 'aught toward the general good,'[10] yet throughout the play he is manipulated by men motivated by self-interest. At the last, despite Antony's tribute to his honesty, the impression printed on the audience is of the sardonic anatomising of honour after the death of Caesar 'For Brutus is an honourable man.' At Brutus' death Falstaff's sense of futility dominates:

> What is that honour? Air. A trim reckoning! Who hath it? He that died a-Wednesday. Doth he feel it? No. Doth he hear it? No. 'Tis insensible, then? Yea, to the dead. But will it not live with the living? No. Why? Detraction will not suffer it.[11]

The man who talks the most about honour in Shakespeare's plays is Henry V who claims that 'if it be a sin to covet honour, / I am the most offending soul alive.'[12] Henry V fulfils all Bacon's conditions for the honourable man, more talked of than inwardly admired, contenting 'euerie Faction,' gaining and breaking his honour over another, Hotspur, enlarging his country's territories and assigning all his successes to God which, Bacon advises with Machiavelli's Prince in mind,[13] is the best way of turning aside Envy. Yet Henry's triumphs seem ultimately clashing cymbals and sounding brass, an honour specifically related to military prowess, not promising any duration in a peaceful world, and prompted too explicitly by political expediency: 'To busy giddy minds / With foreign quarrels.'[14] Henry lives by a code of values attacked by

[9] p. 219.
[10] *Julius Caesar*, I.ii.85.
[11] *Henry IV* Part I, v.i.135.
[12] *Henry V*, IV.iii.28.
[13] Machiavelli, *The Prince*, p. 79.
[14] *Henry IV* Part II, IV.v.213.

More in *Utopia*, the aristocratic militaristic ideal of the medieval world. Prince Hal accuses himself of being a truant to chivalry. Shakespeare offers the mystique for what it is worth, but it is already tarnished in his time, out-of-date, the trappings of a particular social structure, an aristocratic culture by the side of which More's *Utopia* is unmistakably bourgeois. It is logical that an era which doubted and questioned the validity of the mystique of honour in men should also see in a different perspective the mystique of chastity in women.

The other mystique which the Renaissance Humanists criticised and undermined was that of birth. They attacked the notion that the physical accident of aristocratic birth conferred virtue, just as they attacked the conviction that the physical fact of virginity conferred chastity. In Castiglione it is a matter of debate whether the Courtier should be of noble birth or not, and one of the debaters declares that nobleness derived from birth is 'rather a praise of our ancestors than our owne' and expresses surprise to the speaker who supported hereditary nobility that 'those other good conditions which you have named shuld not be sufficient to bring him to the top of all perfection: that is to say, wit, beautie of phisnomy, disposition of person, and the grace which at the first sight shall make him most acceptable unto al men.'[15] Nobility of birth carries with it responsibility for acting virtuously and an incentive for avoiding slanders which must injure the whole line, but it is not itself a guarantee of virtue. In *All's Well That Ends Well* Bertram disdains Helena because 'She had her breeding at my father's charge.' He sees his own virtue as standing in his birth, and in the distinction he hopes to achieve in the wars, complaining at having to stay behind because he is young:

> Creaking my shoes on the plain masonry
> Till honour be bought up, and no sword worn
> But one to dance with.

But the play savagely exposes Bertram's idea of honour. His mother, hearing his rejection of the woman she had already accepted as a daughter-in-law, sends him word that 'his sword can

[15] *The Book of the Courtier*, p. 34.

never win / The honour that he loses.' The King expostulates with
Bertram on the illogicality of seeing virtue only in terms of birth:

> Strange is it that our bloods
> Of colour, weight, and heat, pour'd all together,
> Would quite confound distinction, yet stands off
> In differences so mighty.

If the only objection to Helena is her father's profession, then 'thou
dislik'st / Of virtue for the name.'

> Good alone
> Is good, without a name; vileness is so:
> The property by what it is should go,
> Not by the title.

The honour which Helena possesses through her own virtue, and
through her act of healing the king, weighs heavier than Bertram's
noble birth:

> Honours thrive
> When rather from our acts we them derive
> Than our foregoers.

This is Castiglione's comment on the praise of our ancestors rather
than ourselves. Bertram's actions in rejecting Helena and in
attempting to seduce Diana nullify the virtue of his birth.

The irony of Bertram's situation sharpens the seduction scene
with Diana. He refuses her his ring because it is the emblem of his
nobility:

> It is an honour 'longing to our house,
> Bequeathed down from many ancestors.

Diana counters by denying him her virginity, the emblem of
chastity. Bertram, who turned away his wife in dishonour in order
to obey a mystique, is outmanoeuvred on his own ground, the
authority of another mystique. But the bartering, the exchange of
the honourable house symbolised by the ring, for the chastity symbolised by virginity, is not one of equal weight. By casting off her
virginity Diana in Bertram's eyes becomes a stale, a common

gamester, a piece of property paid for and discarded:

> She got the ring
> And I had that which any inferior might
> At market-price have bought.[16]

Bertram himself remains the man of noble birth, his honour unsullied because the stain is unpublished, his chastity unmarred because he is a man. The exposing of Bertram attacks the mystique of birth, the aristocratic view of honour. The play points the relation between this way of looking at the world and attitudes to women which exalt chastity into a mystique, while making loss of virginity an irreparable injury which includes the loss of all other possibilities of virtue.

Shakespeare and his contemporaries wanted to do more than simply venerate chastity. They wanted to define and explain its nature. They inherited this preoccupation from the early Protestant reformers, and from the Humanists, and they could see it at work amongst the Puritans. In the other European drama of the period – the plays of Lope de Vega in Spain – the note of doubt about the mystiques of honour and chastity is strikingly absent. Lope criticises the rigidity of the ideal of honour, but his plays end without shattering its structure. To a certain extent the same is true of his treatment of chastity in women. In *El Perno del Hotelano* (*The Dog in the Manger*) the cult of chastity in the heroine, Diana, is as absurd and unreal as the notion of honour which forbids her from marrying her secretary while capriciously destroying his relation with a girl of his own class (Marcela). She constantly compromises her own virtue only to accuse him of presumption every time he takes her seriously. Diana has stage relations with Silvia in *The Two Gentlemen of Verona*, with Olivia in *Twelfth Night* and with the Duchess in Middleton's *More Dissemblers Besides Women*, but Lope's play does not expose the inconsistencies and indeed immorality of her behaviour. He allows a falsehood about Teodoro's (the secretary's) birth to remove her difficulties and she marries him, his forsaken bourgeois love making the best of it with an inferior suitor and a big dowry provided by Diana. Honour is satis-

[16] II.iii.114, II.i.31, III.ii.93, II.iii.118, IV.ii.42, V.iii.216.

fied by the falsehood, and chastity is satisfied by the honourable match.[17] But the play has no ethic to propose which would make these contrivances unnecessary; they are taken as seriously at the end of the play as at the beginning, and this is totally at variance with the practice and with the artistic and moral purpose of the English dramatists.

The double standard is written into a play like Lope's *El Castigo sin Venganza* (*Justice without Revenge*) and justified in its action. The only woman who questions it is eventually horribly murdered unknowingly by her lover, at the contrivance of her husband, who is motivated by a passion of self-righteousness on which Lope has no comment to make morally except that the husband was obliged to satisfy his honour. One of the reasons for the unquestioning acceptance of the double standard is the husband's rank – he is a Duke. In Lope's plays the class structure describes peasants and aristocracy. There is no articulate middle-class body of opinion to oppose aristocratic ethics. In *Peribanez* the hero, a peasant, can only avenge the Commander's attempt on his wife's honour when he has been given military rank. Peasants have no right to criticise the morals of the aristocracy: this is the message of *Fuenteovejuna*, even though in that play the peasants rebel against tyranny. The conclusion is their pardon, not the recognition of their right to rebel. Puritanism in Shakespeare's theatre stands not only for a body of Protestant opinion which is absent in Lope's plays, but for a class of interests which simply does not exist in his drama.

Criticism of the excesses of the aristocratic ideal of honour and chastity in Lope's plays is peripheral, usually voiced by all-knowing servant figures, such as Batin in *El Castigo sin Venganza*, commenting on the Lucretia story: 'Every time I hear her story it gives me nightmares. All that forced chastity and frantic retribution.'[18] This is the freedom allowed to the plebeian character who is in no danger of influencing the moral structure of society. It is through such characters that Lope satirises the Church. In *El Caballero de Olmedo* (*The Knight from Olmedo*) the heroine outwits her father, who wants her to marry the man of his choice, by feigning

[17] *Lope de Vega* (Five Plays), p. xxviii.

[18] I, p. 239.

a call to the nunnery, and hires a bawd, Fabia, to instruct her in devotion. Fabia gives Lope a marvellous opportunity to satirise the hypocrisies of the ecclesiastical establishment, as Batin does. She repulses an embrace from her pupil with the words: 'Careful, mind my hair shirt.'[19] But this is an extra. The play ends with the heroine contemplating her dead lover, learning the irony that her father would have let her marry him anyway, and vowing in seriousness to take the veil. There is a suggestion of retribution for her mockery of the nunnery. This is something possible in Caroline drama, as for instance in Massinger's *The Duke of Milan*, but inconceivable in Elizabethan and Jacobean drama. The criticism of single living is too integral a part of the dramatists' ethical framework.

Lope wrote in a climate for which the Catholic theology was still the accepted one and its attitudes to women had not been supplanted. The medieval mystiques are, in his plays, still firmly in place for both men and women, as is the class structure whereby the more aristocratic a man is, the more stringently he requires a virgin, and the less scrupulous he is about seducing women in a lower social rank than his own. The situation of Lady Faulconbridge in *King John*, forced to yield to a royal seducer, is in Shakespeare a cue for merciful treatment of loss of chastity because the relation of chastity and class has come under fire. In Lope the absurd, cruel, distorting, class-conscious, materialistic assertion that a woman's only virtue is virginity is still everywhere in evidence and accepted in the moral fabric of his plays. He lacked the impetus which the Puritans gave the Elizabethans and Jacobeans to explore what chastity might mean if, as Donne suggested, it meant more than physical virginity and a certain kind of emotional reaction to that virginity.

When chastity ceased to operate as a powerful mystique the ground was laid for enquiry into many attitudes which had been indispensable to the mystique, but which might be less central to a new interpretation of chastity.

---

[19] II, p. 204.

3 Virginity and Virtue

It is difficult to feel anything about virginity nowadays except that
it is beginning to be as unmentionable as sex was to the Victorians.
There is no modern ascetic parallel to the sixteenth century Catholic ideal of virginity. Christian asceticism for us means the great
medieval ascetics like St John of the Cross, Thomas à Kempis, St
Theresa or Julian of Norwich. Even Pascal is cast in a different,
more modern mould. Protestantism, despite its traditions of self-
flagellation, never inspired the imaginative passion which in-
formed the asceticism of a man like St Francis of Assisi. Protestant
asceticism is a watery, early-to-bed, early-to-rise phenomenon.

Sixteenth century Humanism was a movement away from asceticism. More and Erasmus both saw the Catholic ascetic ideal as a
denial of the fullness of life. To them monasticism seemed narrow,
corrupt and sterile. By the end of the Renaissance the secular battle
was won so conclusively that monasticism has never recovered as a
viable way of life. It is now what it was for the dramatists of
Shakespeare's theatre – a joke or an eccentricity – except that their
jokes had an edge because they commented on an issue that mat-
tered. Nor have any of the ascetic or mystical revivals of the twentieth century turned back to the Christian asceticism of the
monastery; they turn instead to the East. Thus in the modern
world it is hard to sense the significance of the sixteenth century
debate about the merits of single life. It seems too much like a
schoolmen's struggle: Calvin confronting the Council of Trent.
We do not feel their heat along the heart because we do not see life
in terms of a confrontation between the ascetic and the non-ascetic.
Our indifference is the measure of Erasmus' success in proclaiming
the wholeness of man's experience, the impossibility of segregating the life of the spirit from the life of the world.

For the reformers the debate about virginity and single life generated as much heat as population control, or contraception, or
abortion do today. These subjects arouse in their supporters the
same sense of engagement, of forging new values, which the reformers brought to the argument about celibacy. The issues at
stake are similar. The reformers wanted chastity to mean more
than virginity; to mean both a way of life and certain attitudes to

life. They wanted it to be a private virtue between the individual and his conscience. They wanted to extend the choices available to people in their moral lives, to move beyond the choice which Theseus offers Hermia of marriage to a man her father favours or the livery of a nun. The consequence of many of the reforms which they proposed was to bring the freedom of women in line with the freedom of men, either by making women more free to choose, or by making men less so. The Puritan attack on the double standard is an attack on traditional male freedoms. One of the reasons for the heat of the debate about virginity and marriage was that it demanded new attitudes to women and offered women choices which they had not previously had.

The extent to which a society holds that men should dictate women's moral life determines the degree of opposition to changes which give women a separate moral identity. The emergence of new attitudes exacerbates conflict between the generations. The young identify with the new, the old with the attitudes which determined their own moral development. In Elizabethan drama children assert the freedom claimed for them by the reformers against the authoritarianism of their parents – Capulet's impotent assertion to his daughter 'An you be mine, I'll give you to my friend.'[1] But attitudes change slower than the conditions which made them. Modern attitudes to women still halt behind the fact of a freedom not to have children. Women themselves are slow to found their lives on assumptions that were not bred into them. There is a time-lag between the fact of change and the dissemination of its effects.

The Puritans inherited from the sixteenth century reformers a world which had changed in principle but not in practice. Protestantism had triumphed, marriage had ousted celibacy, but the old attitudes to women remained in place. The double standard still operated, wives were still beaten, daughters forced to marry, and chaste marriage was still a dogma invented by theologians to accommodate a married clergy. The Puritans tried to spell out the new possibilities open to men and women.

When Donne claimed in one of his Paradoxes that virginity was

[1] *Romeo and Juliet*, III.v.191.

only a relative virtue, dependent on time in a way that no absolute virtue could be, he had major reformers – Luther, Erasmus, Thomas Becon, the Swiss Bullinger, Calvin – behind him. Erasmus dominated the argument because the monastic ideal conflicted with his whole philosophy of life. He did not believe in an institutionalised rejection of the world any more than he believed that the forms of the nunnery guaranteed virtue. He saw the discrimination between virtue and vice as a finer instrument than the choice of two different modes of life. In one of the Colloquies the young woman who plans to enter a nunnery, complaining of the salacious chat of married folks, is told: 'He that would avoid every Thing that offends him must go out of the World; we must accustom our Ears to hear every Thing, but let nothing enter the Mind but what is good.'[2] Isabella in *Measure for Measure*, who planned to enter the convent, finds the severer trials of virtue which she wants in the sisterhood, in the world around her. When she hears of Mariana's misfortunes she exclaims: 'What a merit were it in death to take this poor maid from the world.' The Duke, disguised as a Friar, finds that his cloth cannot protect him from contamination. Lucio tells him: 'By my troth, I'll go with thee to the lane's end. If bawdy talk offend you, we'll have very little of it. Nay, friar, I am a kind of burr, I shall stick.' Virtue is needed and tested not in the convent, nor in the privacy of a man's immunity to temptations to which he has not exposed himself:

> Heaven doth with us as we with torches do,
> Not light them for themselves; for if our virtues
> Did not go forth of us, 'twere all alike
> As if we had them not. Spirits are not finely touch'd
> But to fine issues, nor nature never lends
> The smallest scruple of her excellence
> But, like a thrifty goddess, she determines
> Herself the glory of a creditor,
> Both thanks and use.[3]

Middleton took up the theme in *More Dissemblers Besides Women*

[2] 'The Virgin Averse to Matrimony', pp. 149–50.
[3] III.i.231, IV.iii.175, I.i.32.

where his Duchess is faithful to her vow of perpetual chastity only so long as no temptation is offered. Those who argue against her seclusion echo Shakespeare's image, perhaps both drawn from the Biblical one of hiding a light under a bushel:

> 'Tis not enough for tapers to burn bright,
> But to be seen, so to lend others light.[4]

The drama at the turn of the century stands equidistant between Erasmus, repudiating seclusion from the world, and Milton, arguing in the *Areopagitica*: 'I cannot praise a fugitive and cloister'd vertue, unexercis'd & unbreath'd, that never sallies out and sees her adversary, but slinks out of the race, where that immortall garland is to be run for, not without dust and heat.'[5] Secular living acquired a new prestige.

The image of Nature as a thrifty goddess who wants a return on what she gives, 'Both thanks and use,' is congruous with Erasmus' conviction of the profitlessness of virginity. He held that marriage was natural and good where celibacy was perverse. Luther had preached that the sexual impulses of men and women were essential to Nature's good ordering of society. Without them society itself would perish.[6] Nature gives man nothing superfluous to his needs. 'Why (I pray you),' demanded Erasmus, 'Hath God geven us these membres? Why these pryckes and provocations? Why hath he added the power of begettynge, if bachelarshyp be taken for a prayse?'[7] This attitude to man's sexual nature separates Erasmus from the Church fathers who saw man's need to copulate as a consequence not of Nature's order, but of her disorder after the Fall. St Paul described marriage as a remedy for fornication. When the Clown in *All's Well That Ends Well* asks the Countess of Rossilion's permission to marry Isbel, he explains: 'My poor body, madam, requires it; I am driven on by the flesh, and he must needs go that the devil drives.'[8] Erasmus insisted, as Calvin did after him.

[4] I.iii.38.

[5] *Complete Prose Works of John Milton*, II, 515.

[6] *Luther's Works*, 1, 89, 117, 240.

[7] *In Laude and Prayse of Matrymony*, sig. Cviii[v].

[8] I.iii.26.

that sex in marriage predated sin. He argued testily: 'I here nat hym which wyll saye unto me that that foule ychynge and pryckes of carnall lust have come nat of nature, but of syn. What is more onlyke the trowth? As though matrimony (whose offyce can nat be executed without these pryckes) was nat before syn.'[9] Marriage was part of the good arrangement by Nature created for man in Paradise. Donne's image is compelling, and sums up the whole debate about the unnaturalness of single life:

> When God had made Adam and Eve in Paradise, though there were foure rivers in Paradise, God did not place Adam in a Monastery on one side, and Eve in a Nunnery on the other, and so a River between them. They that build wals and cloysters to frustrate Gods institution of mariage, advance the Doctrine of Devils in forbidding mariage.[10]

The Wife of Bath pointed out, to the irritation of the Clerk in *The Canterbury Tales*, that 'if ther were no seed ysowe,/Virginitee, thanne wherof shode it growe?'[11] Her logic carries only a kind of animal conviction. She recommends the easy way and, as the Clerk shows in the story of Griselda, Christian virtue can only be attained the hard way. The sixteenth century witnessed the remarkable change by which the Wife of Bath's view became central to the theology of a man like Erasmus who remained a cleric all his life. An irreverence became a new orthodoxy, and this was the Paradox which Donne exploited with such dexterity when he played with the premise 'That Virginity is a Vertue.' It has been said that paradoxes flourish on competing truths.[12] Donne circulated his Paradoxes in manuscript in the 1590's, and possibly Shakespeare saw them and had in mind the one on virginity when he made Parolles present Helena with that fabric of competing values which is a distinctive mark of Shakespeare's problem plays.

Parolles' arguments to Helena on the perversity of virginity

[9] *In Laude and Prayse of Matrymony*, sig. Bviii.

[10] *The Sermons of John Donne*, III, 242.

[11] Chaucer, *The Wife of Bath's Prologue*, 71.

[12] Rosalie L. Colie, *Paradoxica Epidemica: The Renaissance Tradition of Paradox*, pp. 37, 10.

keep pace with Donne's. Virginity wastes Nature's resources. Donne remarks: 'For surely nothing is more unprofitable in the Commonwealth of Nature, than they that dy old maids, because they refuse to be used, to that end for which they were only made.'[13] Parolles echoes him: 'It is not politic in the common-wealth of nature to preserve virginity. Loss of virginity is rational increase, and there was never virgin got till virginity was first lost.'[14] Shakespeare could have found this argument in Erasmus, but the community between his play and Donne's Paradox expresses the vitality which the issue had for its time. In a sense the whole of *All's Well That Ends Well* is founded on the Paradox. The play pinpoints Donne's perception of the relativity of the virtue of virginity. Helena as a married woman is possessed of a 'peevish' virginity, kept beyond its time. She resolves to exchange it for the 'farre more honorable name'[15] of wife. But in the course of the play this new-found orthodoxy encounters its own relativity by facing the justice of the old belief: for Diana virginity is a virtue which must be kept till marriage: 'Virginity is a vertue, and hath her Throne in the middle: The extreams are, in Excesse, to violate it before marriage; in Defect, not to marry.'[16] Parolles, like Donne, sees the virginity which is an end in itself as the fruit of pride and self-love, 'which is the most inhibited sin in the canon.'[17] Helena can claim to be a wife only when the child within her brags her loss of virginity.

Erasmus claimed that the celibate was 'no man but a playne stone:'[18] a comparison which may have been in Shakespeare's mind when he drew Angelo who

> scarce confesses
> That his blood flows; or that his appetite
> Is more to bread than stone.[19]

[13] 'That Virginity is a Vertue', p. 347.

[14] *All's Well That Ends Well*, I.i.123.

[15] 'That Virginity is a Vertue', p. 349.

[16] *Ibid.*, p. 347.

[17] *All's Well That Ends Well*, I.i.142.

[18] *In Laude and Prayse of Matrymony*, sig. Cviii ᵛ.

[19] *Measure for Measure*, I.iii.51.

Many Renaissance plays focus on the impossibility of suppressing man's nature. Marston's Malheureux in *The Dutch Courtezan* prides himself, like Angelo, on being a man of snow who can castigate the old Adam in others. Smitten with passion for his friend's whore he muses that Nature wars with virtue, and 'virtue's self is oft unnatural.' Like Angelo's, his lust demands surfeit in proportion to his previous abstinence. The moral of his state is pointed by Freevill, his friend, who controls his own passions not through ignoring them, but through recognising and ordering them:

> Of all the fools that would all man out-thrust
> He that 'gainst Nature would seeme wise is worst.[20]

Celibacy is suitable to clerics and old men. The Cardinal in Middleton's *More Dissemblers Besides Women*, urging perpetual chastity on the Duchess, boasts that he has 'ever been in youth an old man / To pleasures and to women.'[21] But to Erasmus – as to Luther – this was not a virtue but an abrogation of impulses which, if rightly ordered, might contribute to a fuller and more vital concept of virtue. Good counsel is not enough; most men follow it, like Pompey in *Measure for Measure* 'as the flesh and fortune shall better determine.'[22] The Church, in Erasmus' view, made the mistake of dividing a man's life so that to be virtuous he had to be less than a man. A constant conflict was set up between his principles and his practice. Portia pointed out in *The Merchant of Venice*:

> If to do were as easy as to know what were good to do, chapels had been churches, and poor men's cottages princes' palaces, – it is a good divine that follows his own instructions, – I can easier teach twenty what were good to be done, than be one of the twenty to follow mine own teaching: the brain may devise laws for the blood, but a hot temper leaps o'er a cold decree, – such a hare is madness the youth, to skip o'er the meshes of good counsel the cripple.[23]

[20] II.i.84, I.ii.271.
[21] I.ii.9.
[22] II.i.250.
[23] I.ii.12.

In *The Tempest* Prospero counsels restraint. The virtue of virginity depends on keeping it till marriage. Ferdinand promises:

> The strong'st suggestion
> Our worser genius can, shall never melt
> Mine honour into lust, to take away
> The edge of that day's celebration.

Juno and Ceres banish Cupid and Venus in the wedding masque. But the ideal of temperance is as demanding as the older idea of chastity. Prospero admonishes Ferdinand: 'The strongest oaths are straw / To th' fire in' th' blood.' The play reverberates with images of Eden, and Ferdinand, wondering at Prospero's creative power, muses:

> Let me live here ever;
> So rare a wonder'd father and a wise
> Make this place Paradise.[24]

The vision of chaste love and sinless passion in marriage, looks forward, like Middleton's eulogy of matrimony in *The Phoenix*,[25] to *Paradise Lost*.

Erasmus saw the sin of self-love in the pursuit of single life. He demanded: 'What is a more unkynde acte than to denye that to your yongers, which if ye toke nat of your elders, ye could nat be he that myght denye?'[26] Olivia in *Twelfth Night* upbraids Malvolio for his disaffection with the Fool: 'O, you are sick of self-love, Malvolio, and taste with a distempered appetite.' But in this play where the wise are fools and the fools are wise according to the doctrine of Erasmus' Stultitia, Olivia herself is guilty of self-love in mewing herself up in her chantry to mourn out her youth and beauty for her dead brother. Viola sees her as a miser, wasting the gifts of the thrifty goddess, 'for what is yours to bestow, is not yours to reserve.' The texture of the play is thick with references to

[24] IV.i.26, 52, 122.

[25] II.ii.164. R. B. Parker, 'Middleton's Experiments with Comedy and Judgement', in *Jacobean Theatre*, Stratford-Upon-Avon Studies, *1*, 181.

[26] *In Laude and Prayse of Matrymony*, sig. Av.

Olivia's folly. Sir Toby rebukes Sir Andrew for concealing his high capers from the world: 'Wherefore are these things hid? wherefore have these gifts a curtain before 'em? are they like to take dust, like Mistress Mall's picture?' The Fool calls Olivia, with mock-respect, Madonna – a veiled Mary. When Viola asks to see the lady of the house, Olivia lifts her veil, symbol of the nunnery, announcing: 'We will draw the curtain, and show you the picture.'[27] Mistress Mall is not any of those dark ladies of the Elizabethan court whom Shakespeare may or may not have known, but an ordinary Mistress Mary playing at Madonna and taking dust behind her veil.

Caroline drama reverts to adulation of virginity, partly from Catholicism, partly from an interest in Platonic love which elevated chastity – meaning virginity – almost as courtly love had done. Plays frequently end with heroes and heroines entering monasteries and nunneries as in Massinger's *The Maid of Honour*. Sometimes this solves the exigencies of Caroline plots, but it would not have been a feasible escape in the Elizabethan atmosphere of scoffing and scepticism towards the nunnery. Diminution of fervour about married life, and the horrible state of marriage in the plays of a dramatist like Ford, resuscitate enthusiasm for celibacy.

The Caroline fashion for the literary pastoral, moreover, revived an interest in the call away from the world. The pastoral romanticises retreat. Caroline pastoral is a Marie-Antoinette scene. The cultivation of a pagan classical seclusion from the world in Montague's *The Shepherd's Paradise* stems from the impulse which prompted religious seclusion. Montague's arcadia is a Catholic one; its initiates vow chastity for as long as they remain in the order. Its atmosphere would be other-worldly if its inmates were not so bored: 'The peace and setlednesse of this place is secured by natures inclosure of it on all sides by impregnablenesse, as if it were only for chastity to make a plantation here.' When Bellesa, played in the first performance by Henrietta Maria, is elected queen, she vows to uphold the laws of her community 'even as I hope to rise, /

---

[27] I.v.88, 188, I.iii.127, I.v.237.

From this, into another Paradise.'[28] The pastoral convention relates the shepherd both to Pan and to Christ. Montague exalts not the figure of the shepherd, but a way of life remote from the world as is the life of the religious. His play is to Elizabethan drama as Jacques is to Arden, hanging around in the pastoral world when everyone else has gone home. An audience who could stomach the Caroline pastoral would sympathise with the call to the cloister.

Late Elizabethan drama is full of jokes about virgins who have hung on to their virginity until its currency is devalued. However scurrilously voiced, this liberates women from the need for perpetual youth and beauty. In Dekker's *Westward Ho* the bawd advises her client:

> Strike whilst the iron is hot. A woman when there be roses in her cheekes, Cherries on her lippes, Ciuet in her breath, Iuory in her teeth, Lyllyes in her hand, and Lickorish in her heart, why shees like a play. If new, very good company, but if stale, like old Ieronimo: goe by, go by.[29]

A woman must know when to trade it in. Beaumont and Fletcher's Evadne scoffs at the husband who assumes her to be a virgin: 'A maidenhead, Amintor, / At my years.'[30] Donne pointed out, as all Shakespeare's Fools point out, that 'with long keeping it decayes and withers, and becomes corrupt and nothing worth.'[31]

Secondly, the argument that virginity denied life increased the value of fruitfulness. Fertility provided proof of the blessedness of marriage. 'The greatest good in married life . . . is that God grants offspring,'[32] declared Luther. The Cardinal in Middleton's *More Dissemblers Besides Women*, faced with the failure of his Catholic ideal of chastity, adopts the Puritan one:

> To be love-chaste, knowing but one man's bed;
> A mighty virtue: beside, fruitfulness

[28] II. pp. 26, 22.

[29] II.ii.181.

[30] *The Maid's Tragedy*, II.i.198.

[31] 'That Virginity is a Vertue', p. 349.

[32] *Luther's Works*, 45, 46.

Is part of the salvation of your sex;
And the true use of wedlock's time and space
Is woman's exercise of faith and grace.[33]

In Shakespeare's theatre the pregnant woman has status, whether Win-the-Fight in Jonson's *Bartholomew Fair* longing for sucking pig, or Lady Kix in Middleton's *A Chaste Maid in Cheapside*, tormenting her husband to the extent that he rejoices at her conceiving by a man other than himself. The curse on Goneril was the most horrific and far-reaching one that Lear could have devised: 'Into her womb convey sterility.'[34] The Clown in *All's Well That Ends Well* wants to marry because 'I think I shall never have the blessing of God till I have issue a' my body.'[35] The concept of celibacy suggested that man sacrificed nothing in his spiritual life by dispensing with woman. But the Puritans saw such a man as incomplete in the eyes of God, lacking the blessing of wife and children.

Thirdly, the suggestion that virginity was actually a less admirable state than marriage took away the stigma that a woman reduced a man's capacity for the life of the spirit. St Paul made no bones about marriage being a lesser calling. A man simultaneously demonstrated his strength and secured his spiritual status by repudiating women, and the minute monastic rules for the avoidance of contact with women demonstrate the extremes to which this principle was carried.[36] If marriage was the higher calling, the position of women immediately rose. A wife brought a man nearer God. Shakespeare glances at the argument in *The Winter's Tale* when Polixenes laughingly explains his sense of the lost innocence of his boyhood to Hermione:

> O my most sacred lady,
> Temptations have since then been born to's: for
> In those unfledg'd days was my wife a girl;

[33] IV.ii.30.
[34] *King Lear*, I.iv.287.
[35] I.iii.22.
[36] G. G. Coulton, *The Last Days of Medieval Monachism, Five Centuries of Religion*, IV, 648–62.

> Your precious self had then not cross'd the eyes
> Of my young play-fellow.

Hermione repudiates the role of seducer. A good wife protects a man's virtue rather than destroying it:

> Grace to boot!
> Of this make no conclusion, lest you say
> Your queen and I are devils. Yet go on;
> Th' offences we have made you do, we'll answer,
> If you first sinn'd with us, and that with us
> You did continue fault, and that you slipp'd not
> With any but with us.[37]

In the drama chastity is not the virtue of virginity, but the virtue of constancy.

Erasmus devalued virginity in the interests of marriage. The Puritans made his ideas familiar to a wider audience than he himself addressed. Shakespeare wrote at a time when the destruction of the ascetic ideal created, for better or worse, a new concept of marriage. For women in the early seventeenth century it was undoubtedly better.

4 *The Double Standard*

The elevation of chastity in women which had its origin in orthodox Catholic theology, and was ratified imaginatively by the poetry of courtly love, was a class ideal related to property. When the Puritans attacked the double standard they attacked a class system and a class-based morality. Shakespeare's theatre criticises the assumptions involved in the double standard. In *Measure for Measure* the Church sanctions the double standard. The Duke, as Friar, infers from Julietta: 'Then it seems your most offenceful act / Was mutually committed?' To her assent he assigns the ecclesiastical verdict that 'Then was your sin of heavier kind than his,' to which the Catholic response can only be the submission to all higher authority imposed on women by St Paul: 'I do confess it,

[37] I.ii.76.

and repent it, father.'[1] But neither in this play, nor in the drama generally, do the playwrights accept that chastity is mainly for women.

At the heart of the double standard lay the concept of virginity as a property asset. Virginity is more cherished among the upper classes who have more property to dispose of. Keith Thomas points out that 'an heiress who was demonstrated to have been unchaste was deprived of her inheritance' where an heir was not.[2] Fear of a bastard's intruding on the succession of property dictated virginity in brides and faithfulness in wives where a man like Gloucester might boast with impunity of a bastard son who had been 'out nine years'. The father's bastards presented no threat because they might be reared as a separate caste. Since virginity is essential where marriage is primarily a property transaction, virginity itself becomes a class symbol. Chastity in women has never been the shibboleth to the working classes that it is to the upper classes. In the drama waiting-women need not be so fastidious about their virtue as their mistresses. Diaphanta, maid to Beatrice in Middleton's *The Changeling*, suffers no loss of status by taking Beatrice's place in Alsemero's bed on the wedding-night. What is vital is that Beatrice's own whoredom should escape discovery because loss of virtue is loss of class. The Shepherd who finds the babe Perdita abandoned assumes her to be the bastard not of a great lady but of a working-woman: 'Sure, some scape: though I am not bookish, yet I can read waiting-gentlewoman in the scape. This has been some stair-work, some trunk-work, some behind-door-work.'[3]

A whore is always lower-class, a rake always upper-class. Claudio rejects in Hero, in *Much Ado About Nothing*, loss of caste as much as loss of virtue; he was a careful young man and had chosen Leonato's heir. To call a woman a whore, as Othello calls Desdemona, or Leontes Hermione, not only casts aspersions on her morals, but takes away her position in society. Hermione, hurried

[1] II.iii.26.

[2] 'The Double Standard', *Journal of the History of Ideas*, xx (1959) no. 2, 212, 202, 209, 206.

[3] *The Winter's Tale*, III.iii.71.

'to this place, i' th'open air,' like a common criminal to hear her husband's scurrility, remains regal; she loved Polixenes 'With such a kind of love as might become / A lady like me.' Her valediction recalls her state:

> The Emperor of Russia was my father:
> O that he were alive, and here beholding
> His daughter's trial.[4]

A man who is unchaste loses nothing in the eyes of the world. A woman who is unchaste is nothing.

Hermione suffers from an irrefutable way of assessing personal worth. A woman's chastity included all other virtues; loss of chastity meant the loss of virtues which in men existed independently of chastity. A man might sleep with a woman not his wife and remain courageous, generous, honest. A woman, on the other hand, in that one act registered her own worthlessness in every other sphere. For women honesty was not the plain-dealing of Kent in *King Lear*,[5] but chastity in sexual matters. 'To make an honest woman' of someone remains a cant phrase for restoring chastity through marriage. Hermione can offer no defence of her innocence because she has no identity apart from the chastity which has been discredited:

> What I am to say, must be but that
> Which contradicts my accusation, and
> The testimony on my part, no other
> But what comes from myself, it shall scarce boot me
> To say 'not guilty': mine integrity,
> Being counted falsehood, shall, as I express it,
> Be so receiv'd.[6]

In *Measure for Measure* Isabella's dilemma arises in part from her readiness to accept the judgement of society that without virginity a woman is nothing worth. Shakespeare creates situations in the

[4] *Ibid.*, III.ii.105, 64, 119.
[5] Rachel Trickett, *The Honest Muse*, pp. 9–10, discusses the concept of honesty only in relation to men.
[6] *The Winter's Tale*, III.ii.22.

problem plays where there can be no incontrovertibly right
action. Helena says of the deception of the bed-trick in *All's Well
That Ends Well* that it

> Is wicked meaning in a lawful deed,
> And lawful meaning in a lawful act,
> Where both not sin, and yet a sinful fact.[7]

If Isabella acquiesces in Angelo's proposal she sells her virginity for
tangible gain as the whore does. But the terms of her repudiation
of him underwrite the ethical assumption that a woman's only
virtue is her chastity. Isabella's virginity has a rateable value:
'More than our brother is our chastity.' Despite her indignant
purity, she assesses herself by the world's standards. Mariana, a
creature judged soiled by the world, is more independent of it, es-
pousing other-worldly values; the charity of the dispossessed:

> Sweet Isabel, do yet but kneel by me;
> Hold up your hands, say nothing: I'll speak all.
> They say best men are moulded out of faults,
> And, for the most, become much more the better
> For being a little bad. So may my husband.[8]

Generosity, compassion, tolerance are not present in Isabella's rig-
orous chastity. They develop in a woman who can see the limits of
the world's judgement of women.

Unchastity in one woman, moreover, jeopardises the chastity of
women in general. The tendency to judge women generically
rather than individually turns the behaviour of the individual into
a perpetual precedent. The capacity for virtue of men as a sex is not
threatened by specific examples of vice; in women it is. Antigonus
vouches for Hermione's chastity; the faith of his wife and daughters seems implicated in it:

> If it prove
> She's otherwise, I'll keep my stables where
> I lodge my wife: I'll go in couples with her;

---

[7] III.vii.45.
[8] *Measure for Measure*, II.iv.184, v.i.435.

Than when I feel and see her no farther trust her:
For every inch of woman in the world,
Ay, every dram of woman's flesh is false,
If she be.[9]

If Hermione is false he will geld his daughters to prevent them from bringing forth false issue. While his hyperbole is a mark of confidence in Hermione, it illustrates how the phenomenon of unchastity operates for women in general. It makes them all Eves. Emilia uses the same image to Othello of Desdemona:

If she be not honest, chaste and true,
There's no man happy: the purest of their wives
Is foul as slander.[10]

Unchaste women have a sense of betraying their own sex because they know that their weakness will be taken as female weakness rather than as an individual weakness. Anne Frankford in Heywood's *A Woman Killed with Kindness* calls herself a shame to womanhood.[11] The Puritan ideal of the chaste wife gave the chaste woman a power to influence ideas about her sex in general to the same extent as the unchaste woman had previously done. Imogen's chastity shows Iachimo in *Cymbeline* the limits of his own moral world.

Desdemona cannot believe that Emilia would wrong her husband; Emilia retorts that the world is 'a great price for a small vice.' She would do it 'and undo't when I had done it.'[12] Emilia challenges the judgement that loss of chastity is irreparable in a woman. In the marriage market a whore was soiled goods. 'Fallen' women in Renaissance drama confront attitudes inimical to their reform; a rake's frolic destroys a woman's hope of respectable marriage for ever. The Courtesan in Middleton's *A Trick to Catch the Old One* reminds her seducer:

I've been true unto your pleasure; and all your lands
Thrice rack'd was never worth the jewel which

---

[9] *The Winter's Tale*, II.i.133.   [10] IV.ii.17.

[11] xiii. 96.   [12] *Othello*, IV.iii.67.

> I prodigally gave you, my virginity:
> Lands mortgag'd may return, and more esteem'd,
> But honesty once pawn'd, is ne'er redeem'd.[13]

Dekker's Bellafront in *The Honest Whore* blames her first seducer, Maltheo, for her subsequent prostitution. No one wants to marry a whore, even if she vows fidelity; a man will not credit with loyalty a woman whose only sin may have been too much charity. The dramatists attack the double standard by criticising the convention of the reformed rake and the assumption that the whore is beyond reform. Society's prejudice is that an 'experienced man' makes a better husband than an inexperienced, but that an experienced woman does not make a better wife. But Luther, commenting on Mosaic law, had underlined a father's right to make the seducer either marry his daughter or provide her with a good dowry to buy a better husband. The Duke in *Measure for Measure* offers Mariana the same choice, implying that the cash in this instance might actually be a better bargain than Angelo. 'Would that this law were applied among us also,' proclaimed Luther, 'For the sake of the women, that pitiable sex.'[14] In Shakespeare's theatre rakes are forced to render account to the women they have injured. Lactantio in Middleton's *More Dissemblers Besides Women* finds that the presence of a 'page' whom he has made pregnant makes him as ineligible for marriage with a respectable woman as the 'page' is for marriage with a respectable man. His bitterness breaks out: 'Marry a quean for my labour.'[15] Middleton treats Lactantio as savagely as Lethe in *Michaelmas Term*, tidily married off to the Country Wench to whom he was both bawd and seducer:

> Who for his wife his harlot doth prefer,
> Good reason 'tis that he should marry her.[16]

The marriage prospects of the rake in Jacobean drama are no better than those of the whore. In *The Witch* Franceschina ('fruitful

[13] 1.i.36.
[14] *Luther's Works, 9*, 224.
[15] v.ii.257.
[16] v.iii.105.

wickedness') is married off to Aberzanes ('baseness and cowardice') by whom she has had a bastard. It is hardly an elevating beginning to Puritan marriage, but it serves the double purpose of
preventing the rake from enjoying further seductions of honest
women, and of removing him as firmly from the ranks of respectable suitors as society removes her from the ranks of respectable
brides. Nor is there any sense in the drama of pandering to a high-
class taste for loose life. Earl in *Westward Ho* is routed by middle-
class morals in his pursuit of Mrs Iustiniano. The traditional licence
of the rich to seduce the poor and marry another rich is not honoured by the Jacobeans. Fathers do not want their daughters to
marry rakes; the few who do, endure the miscarriage of their
ambitions.

When the dramatists make the rake a less romantic figure they
make the whore a less frightful one. They suggest that the *Cressida*
reformed whore will have a greater interest in becoming a faithful
wife. In *The Honest Whore* Maltheo is brought to account and married to Bellafront. The Duke assures him that 'its better/ To take a
common wench, and make her good.'[17] A good one will have
more temptation to become common, and many wives with
promising credentials – Anne Frankford in *A Woman Killed with
Kindness*, Bianca in *Women Beware Women* – end up as whores. The
Courtesan in Middleton's *A Trick to Catch the Old One* argues to the
reluctant Hoard who married her as a rich widow:

> Nor am I so deform'd, but I may challenge
> The utmost power of any old man's love,
>
> She that tastes not sin before twenty, twenty to one but she'll
> taste it after: most of you old men are content to marry young
> virgins, and take that which follows; where, marrying one of us,
> you both save a sinner and are quit from a cuckold for ever:
>
> . . . .
>
> She that knows sin, knows best how to hate sin.

She claims for herself the liberty of the rake to sow his wild oats:

[17] Dekker, *The Honest Whore*, Part I, v.ii.445.

> Lo, gentlemen, before you all
> In true reclaimed form I fall.[18]

Middleton, who endowed his courtesans with a wit he denied to his heroines, could not resist the pun on 'fall'.

In mocking an 'old man's love' Middleton's Courtesan hints at some of the motives which make a man's pursuit of a virgin for his wife less than noble. Virginity for some men titillates lust. De Flores aches to deflower Beatrice in *The Changeling*:

> Were I not resolv'd in my belief
> That thy virginity were perfect in thee,
> I should but take my recompense with grudging,
> As if I had but half my hopes I agreed for.[19]

Angelo is betrayed by Isabella's purity in *Measure for Measure*:

> Can it be
> That modesty may more betray our sense
> Than woman's lightness? Having waste ground enough,
> Shall we desire to raze the sanctuary
> And pitch our evils there?[20]

The Puritans would have approved of the notion that a man who courts a wife with the spirit of a whoremonger deserves a whore. In Middleton's morality Hoard's greed in pursuing a widow for her fortune weighs equal with her trickery of him into marriage. Hoard resents not her lack of virtue but her lack of land, but society allows him to harness his disappointment to her chastity instead of blaming it on his own avarice. The Courtesan remains cool:

> If error were committed, 'twas by you;
> Thank your own folly: nor has my sin been
> So odious, but worse has been forgiven.[21]

---

[18] v.ii.146, 167.

[19] Middleton, *The Changeling*, III.iv.117.

[20] II.ii.168.

[21] *A Trick to Catch the Old One*, v.ii.143.

It could be Moll Flanders speaking.

The dramatists are ironic about women who think that they can buy class with their virginity. Evadne in *The Maid's Tragedy* assures the king that she would never love 'A man of lower place.' She loves 'with my ambition / Not with my eyes.'[22] In a period of great mobility from city to court, from country to city, women are as eager as men to be children of the time. The Country Wench in *Michaelmas Term*, tricked up for prostitution, sighs: 'I am in a swoon till I be a gentlewoman.'[23] But these women discover their illusions. The Second Courtesan in Middleton's *Your Five Gallants* is not a real lady, she is only 'rustical insides and city flesh, the blood of yeomen, and the bum of gentlewomen.'[24] When Proditor in *The Phoenix* claims immunity from censure for the great lady: 'She's never lewd that is accounted great,' Phoenix emends his speech: 'She's never great that is accounted lewd.'[25] The curious paradox which presented itself to preachers and playwrights alike was that a woman might sell her virginity for class with impunity if that class was guaranteed by marriage. Allowing the whore to step back into line with the married woman suggested a painful parallel between the commerce of the backstreets and the transactions between parents in the parlour. Rejecting the morals of the market, the Puritans in talking about marriage had to decide what to put in their place. Anne Bullen in *Henry VIII* is a queen instead of a quean (prostitute) only because Henry marries her. Her avowal to the Old Lady – so often a title for bawd in the drama – that 'by my troth and maidenhead, / I would not be a queen,'[26] has an unmistakable jangle: Elizabeth fought the slur of bastardy all her life. Her mother's avoidance of the stigma of whore was part of a new way of thinking which was also emancipating to a whore's offspring.

The dramatists sympathise with women made pregnant by men who desert them. Taking spousals and precontract seriously

[22] Beaumont and Fletcher, *The Maid's Tragedy*, III.i.188.

[23] Middleton, *Michaelmas Term*, I.ii.58.

[24] v.i.27.

[25] Middleton, *The Phoenix*, v.i.27.

[26] II.iii.23.

benefits women like Julietta in *Measure for Measure* or Julia in
Heywood's *A Maidenhead Well Lost*, complaining to the Prince of
Parma:

> You haue dishonoured me, and by your flattery
> Haue rob'd me of my chaste Virginity:
> Yet ere I yeelded, we were man and wife,
> Sauing the Churches outward Ceremony.[27]

Men have to claim their bastards. The concern for women in this
condition was embodied in Cromwell's law of 1653 which made
spousals *de praesenti* the legal contract of marriage even without
church ceremony.[28] Angelo would have had no power to condemn
Claudio if he had lived fifty years later.

Attitudes to bastards change with attitudes to their mothers. The
drama reflects a dualism apparent in Puritanism in that the Puritans
saw bastardy as socially disruptive while creating an atmosphere of
greater tolerance towards the individual bastard. The Bastard in
King John, like Edmund, or like Don John in *Much Ado About
Nothing*, is a creature contemptuous of society's sacred cows, who
stands for a new freedom:

> Near or far off, well won is still well shot,
> And I am I, howe'er I was begot.

The bastard shares the classlessness of the whore. Unpropertied
themselves, they are the beneficiaries of an attack on the property
motive in sexual morality. The new world of the Henrys in
Shakespeare's history plays is opportunist, a world hospitable to a
queen dubiously conceived, where hereditary virtue was not the
only factor in making a man. The Bastard, knighted by Eleanor,
declares wryly: 'Well, now I can make any Joan a lady.'[29] The bastard has a claim on society, beautifully pleaded by Paulina in *The
Winter's Tale*:

> This child was prisoner to the womb, and is

---

[27] II.i.

[28] Chilton Latham Powell, *English Domestic Relations 1487–1653*, pp. 36, 37.

[29] *King John*, I.i.174, 184.

> By law and process of great nature, thence
> Free'd and enfranchis'd; not a party to
> The anger of the king, nor guilty of
> (If any be) the trespass of the queen.[30]

A doctrine of married chastity which made men reticent about their bastards made it easier for the bastard, like the whore, to take his place, as Edmund does at the end of *King Lear*, by the legitimate brother. The fact of birth, like the fact of virginity, is rendered insignificant by the presence of larger moral issues.

Caroline drama is conservative about the double standard. Rakes enjoy their old impunity. Wanton in Killigrew's *The Parson's Wedding* congratulates Wild that 'you wenchers make the best husbands.'[31] In Shirley's *Hyde Park* the unchastity of the suitor goes unscourged despite a prolonged trial of the heroine. Fowler in Shirley's *The Witty Fair One* vows a wedding-bed reform to his virgin bride which she – and the audience – must take on trust. In Ford's *The Fancies Chaste and Noble* Clarella interrogates a boastful rake:

> Spruce signior, if a man may love so many,
> Why may not a fair lady have like privilege
> Of several servants?

Both the men and the women know that the debate is a game, a flirtation with lawlessness which would be less titillating if it really challenged any social norm. Romanello evades her:

> The learnèd differ
> In that point; grand and famous scholars often
> Have argu'd *pro* and *con*, and left it doubtful.[32]

A Catholic reliance on the authoritative indecision of outside tribunals replaces Puritan faith in the individual conscience. The Restoration honoured the rake. Chastity in a man like Mirabell would lessen his charm. Nell Gwyn needed no Puritans.

[30] II.ii.59.
[31] IV.vii.
[32] III.iii.

The property and class values of virginity reassert themselves in
Caroline drama. The dowries which in Jacobean drama mend the
fortunes of fallen women, in Caroline drama are pay-offs. Brome's
A Mad Couple Well Match'd shows a wife with spirit enough to
charge her husband's whore for his services, but ends more conventionally. The husband confesses and is forgiven by his wife
who failed to commit adultery herself because her lover turned out
to be a woman. In Jacobean drama she would either have revenged
herself by really committing adultery, or reformed him with militant virtue. Keeping women chaste by accident is only important if
the playwright thinks the most important thing about women is
their chastity. Phoebe, Carelesse's whore who is faithful to him
and also with child by him, is married against her will to his servant, with a dowry. Gentlemen in Caroline drama do not mate
with whores even if they made them. Servants, on the other hand,
need no virgins for wives. In the earlier drama Carelesse would
have led Phoebe to the altar, willy-nilly. The lover who was really
a woman turns out to be a young gentlewoman previously seduced
by Lord Lovely whom she has followed faithfully in disguise. He
gives her £200 and commends her plan to enter the nunnery.
Shakespeare and his fellows would have forced the lord, in spite of,
and probably because of, his birth, to reward Amie with a good
middle-class marriage: no flummery about nunneries. The play
witnesses the decline of Puritan influence in the theatre; an
underwriting of the property and class value of virginity; concern
for class purity; indifference about justice to women in sexual matters. The double standard is back, ready to flower in Restoration
plays like Vanbrugh's *The Provoked Wife*.

The Puritan attack on the double standard implied that chastity
was as important in men as in women. But the image of chaste behaviour was uncompromisingly feminine. No one had ever
thought of putting a chaste man on a pedestal and adoring him
from afar. The new chastity, whatever that might mean, had to be
accessible to both men and women.

5 Chastity and Art

The enemy of chastity for sixteenth century writers was not Nature in the sense of man's fallen nature, but art. Viola's compliment to Olivia on her 'picture' queries the artist: 'Excellently done, if God did all.' Olivia assures her: ' 'Tis in grain, sir, 'twill endure wind and weather,' and Viola's praise is unqualified:

> 'Tis beauty truly blent, whose red and white
> Nature's own sweet and cunning hand laid on.[1]

Olivia is as aware as Viola that the question about paint is really a question about virtue. Disclaiming the arts of the whore, Olivia declares herself an honest woman. But there is a touch of irony in the assertion, because Olivia cultivates chastity in the same way that Orsino cultivates passion. In Shakespeare's theatre chastity demands artlessness. The concept of chastity thus expands to include virtues not specifically related to sexual conduct. The chastity of Cordelia wanting 'that glib and oily art / To speak and purpose not'[2] is nothing to do with virginity and yet it is an attitude to life which determines sexual behaviour. The promiscuity of Goneril and Regan is predictable from their self-selling in the opening scene of the play. When the dramatists defined chastity as a state of mind which abhorred art they took away its feminine connotations. Two centuries later Mary Wollstonecraft denied 'the existence of sexual virtues, not excepting modesty. For man and woman, truth, if I understand the meaning of the word, must be the same.'[3]

Elizabethan drama evinces a Renaissance fascination with the delusions of art. Duncan was as foxed by the second Thane of Cawdor as he had been by the first. He failed 'To find the mind's construction in the face.'[4] Viola risks trusting the Captain despite her awareness that 'nature with a beauteous wall / Doth oft close in pollution.'[5] In *The Merchant of Venice* the leaden casket appeals to Bassanio because it lacks the seductiveness and ostentation of art:

[1] *Twelfth Night*, I.v.237.   [2] *King Lear*, I.i.224.
[3] *The Rights of Woman*, p. 57.   [4] *Macbeth*, I.iv.12.
[5] *Twelfth Night*, I.ii.47.

> Look on beauty
> And you shall see 'tis purchas'd by the weight,
> Which therein works a miracle in nature,
> Making them lightest that wear most of it:
> So are those crisped snaky golden locks
> Which make such wanton gambols with the wind
> Upon supposed fairness, often known
> To be the dowry of a second head,
> The skull that bred them in the sepulchre.
> Thus ornament is but the guiled shore
> To a most dangerous sea: the beauteous scarf
> Veiling an Indian beauty; in a word
> The seeming truth which cunning times put on
> To entrap the wisest.[6]

The dramatists relished the piquancy of the actor's exposing the hypocrite's art.

The whore is an artist, calculating effects. When Franceschina in *The Dutch Courtezan* delays to satisfy her lover, he exclaims: 'What, you're a learn'd wanton, and proceed by art?'[7] Cressida has the Wife of Bath's attitude to love: 'For she koude of that art the olde daunce.'[8] Her suit to Troilus is carefully contrived: 'Men prize the thing ungained more than it is.' Dissimulation is her creed:

> Then, though my heart's content firm love doth bear,
> Nothing of that shall from mine eyes appear.

In her first encounter with Troilus she counterfeits the confusion of a lovesick girl, baffling Troilus who really feels that confusion. When the lark calls Troilus away her regret is for her own miscarriage of policy:

> You men will never tarry.
> O foolish Cressid! I might have still held off,
> And then you would have tarried.[9]

---

[6] III.ii.88.   [7] Marston, *The Dutch Courtezan*, v.i.35.
[8] Chaucer, *General Prologue* to *The Canterbury Tales*, 476.
[9] *Troilus and Cressida*, I.ii.275, IV.ii.16.

Juliet's persuading Romeo that the dawn has not come is poignant in its artless attempt at art:

> Wilt thou be gone? It is not yet near day.
> It was the nightingale, and not the lark,
> That pierced the fearful hollow of thine ear.
> Nightly she sings on yond pomegranate tree.
> Believe me, love, it was the nightingale.[10]

The parting scene in *Troilus and Cressida* reads like a sad parody of the earlier play.

For women like Cressida the forms of chaste behaviour usurp the fact. They follow the rules meticulously because they cannot afford not to. Cressida points out to Troilus that she never courted him:

> Though I loved you well, I wooed you not;
> And yet, good faith, I wished myself a man,
> Or that we women had men's privilege
> Of speaking first.[11]

The accomplished adulteress in Marston's *The Insatiate Countess* pretends reluctance to speak:

> Sir, though women do not woo, yet for your sake
> I am content to leave that civil custom.[12]

Evadne, whore to the king in Beaumont and Fletcher's *The Maid's Tragedy*, feigns squeamishness at the bawdy jokes of her maids on her wedding-night to another man: 'Thou think'st belike there is no modesty / When we're alone.'[13] The unchaste woman must be fastidious about her reputation for chastity. As the Duke observes in *Women Beware Women*:

> The ulcerous reputation feels the poise
> Of lightest wrongs, as sores are vex'd with flies.[14]

---

[10] *Romeo and Juliet*, III.v.1. [11] III.ii.119.

[12] II.iii.87. [13] II.i.13.

[14] Middleton, *Women Beware Women*, IV.i.140.

Chastity is thus debased into discretion. Any woman can be chaste who has the art to adopt certain recognised forms of behaviour. Spenser's Duessa in *The Faerie Queene*, the 'seeming simple maid' who 'Let fal her eien, as shamefast, to the earth,'[15] to the devastation of the Red Crosse Knight, has many daughters in the drama. Whores catch husbands by acting coy. Men, who judge women by externals, are easily duped by externals. In Chapman's *The Revenge of Bussy D'Ambois* Montsurry counsels Tamyra in the art of seeming chaste; for women:

> Modesty, the matter of their lives,
> Be it adulterate, should be painted true
> With modest out-parts; what they should do still
> Grac'd with good show, though deeds be ne'er so ill.[16]

Men who discover the disparity between the form and the reality are baffled and horrified. Alsemero in *The Changeling* brushes aside suspicions of the bride who is too full of virgin fears to come to his bed unveiled, protesting: 'Push! modesty's shrine is set in yonder forehead.' Faced with her faithlessness he cries: 'O cunning devils!/How should blind men know you from fair-fac'd saints?'[17] Lear's outburst in his madness is on a larger scale, but stems from the same source:

> Behold yond simp'ring dame,
> Whose face between her forks presages snow;
> That minces virtue, and does shake the head
> To hear of pleasure's name;
> The fitchew nor the soiled horse goes to't
> With a more riotous appetite.
> Down from the waist they are Centaurs,
> Though women all above.[18]

---

[15] Book I, Canto II, xxvii.   [16] I.i.
[17] Middleton, *The Changeling*, IV.ii.126, V.iii.109.
[18] *King Lear*, IV.vi.120.

A chastity which can be manufactured by art mocks morality, creating its own anarchy. Yet this is the only kind of chastity which has ever been required of men: not the reality of virtue but the fiction of virtuous behaviour. Luciana in *The Comedy of Errors* entreats Antipholus of Ephesus to dissemble fidelity to his wife:

> If you like elsewhere, do it by stealth;
> Muffle your false love with some show of blindness:
> Let not my sister read it in your eye;
> Be not thy tongue thy own shame's orator;
> Look sweet, speak fair, become disloyalty;
> Apparel vice like virtue's harbinger;
> Bear a fair presence, though your heart be tainted;
> Teach sin the carriage of a holy saint;
> Be secret-false; what need she be acquainted?
> What simple thief brags of his own attaint?
> 'Tis double wrong to truant with your bed,
> And let her read it in thy looks at board.
> Shame hath a bastard fame, well managèd;
> Ill deeds is doubled with an evil word.
> Alas, poor women! make us but believe,
> Being compact of credit, that you love us;
> Though others have the arm, show us the sleeve;
> We in your motion turn, and you may move us.[19]

Luciana, always the spokesman of the *status quo*, offers this advice in all seriousness. It is only when it is applied to women that men find it nefarious. The dramatists pointed out that if chastity meant the eschewing of art, men would have to eschew it as well as women.

When Ten Brink called Cleopatra a courtesan of genius[20] he referred to her virtuoso performance in those feminine arts which Dr Johnson found too low.[21] Bradley observed that 'the exercise of

[19] III.ii.7.

[20] Quoted in A. C. Bradley, 'Shakespeare's *Antony and Cleopatra*', *Oxford Lectures on Poetry*, p. 298.

[21] *Samuel Johnson on Shakespeare*, p. 107.

sexual attraction is the element of her life; and she has developed
nature into a consummate art.'[22] Coleridge defined the marriage of
the artful and the natural in Cleopatra:

> The art displayed in the character of Cleopatra is profound; in
> this, especially, that the sense of criminality in her passion is les-
> sened by our insight into its depth and energy, at the very
> moment that we cannot but perceive that the passion itself
> springs out of the habitual craving of a licentious nature, and
> that it is supported and reinforced by voluntary stimulus and
> sought-for associations, instead of blossoming out of spontan-
> eous emotion.[23]

Cleopatra feels that she needs art because she is not Antony's chaste
wife. Her policy is to sustain the infinite variety which custom
cannot stale; it is the guarantee of Antony's return to the East. Her
caprice is conscious:

> Say where he is, who's with him, what he does:
> I did not send you. If you find him sad,
> Say I am dancing; if in mirth, report
> That I am sudden sick.

Charmian protests: women should be more ductile. 'In each thing
give him way, cross him in nothing.' Cleopatra retorts, contempt
for the Octavias of the world flashing in her eye: 'Thou teachest
like a fool: the way to lose him.'[24] Cleopatra differs from Cressida
in that her natural emotions – grief, rage, tenderness – are heightened by art but not induced by art. Cleopatra is in Sidney's terms
the poet to her own nature, the actor and player 'as it were, of
what Nature will haue set foorth.' Like the poet who is 'lifted vp
with the vigor of his owne inuention,' Cleopatra disdains to be
enclosed within the narrow limits of Nature's gifts, choosing, like

[22] 'Shakespeare's *Antony and Cleopatra*', p. 300.
[23] 'Antony and Cleopatra', *Coleridge's Essays and Lectures on Shakspeare & Some
Other Old Poets & Dramatists*, p. 97.
[24] *Antony and Cleopatra*, I.iii.2.

him, to range freely 'within the Zodiack of his owne wit.'[25] At moments when she seems most natural – the scene when she arms Antony for battle – her art is greatest because it projects artlessness. Her reflection on the parting Antony has something of the weariness and relief of the player who has performed his part to perfection and in the privacy of his room can put aside his mask:

> He goes forth gallantly: that he and Caesar might
> Determine this great war in single fight!
> Then Antony – ; but now – Well, on.[26]

Chastity can be no yokefellow to Cleopatra. Cordelia and Helena and Juliet come from a moral universe alien to hers; to think of Cleopatra in a context of European Protestant ideas about chastity highlights Shakespeare's power of suggestion in creating an Empress of Egypt. Shakespeare gave Cleopatra her own moral law that in being always an artist she was in fact true to her own nature, and this constituted a kind of integrity, the integrity of the player who can only be true to himself by giving himself to his art. The player's distaste for his life surfaces in the sonnets:

> Alas, 'tis true I have gone here and there
> And made myself a motley to the view,
> Gored mine own thoughts, sold cheap what is most dear.[27]

Shakespeare in this sonnet felt prostituted to his art, but the art itself sets forth Nature.

In the shepherd scene in *The Winter's Tale* Perdita explains to the disguised Polixenes that she does not care to plant 'streak'd gillyvors / Which some call nature's bastards,' in her garden. They seem false to her:

> For I have heard it said
> There is an art which, in their piedness, shares
> With great creating nature.

He replies that Nature is the mother of all art. There can be

[25] Sidney, *An Apologie for Poetrie*, pp. 7, 8.

[26] IV.iv.36.

[27] *Sonnet* 110.

nothing adulterate in using art to enhance Nature:

> Say there be;
> Yet nature is made better by no mean
> But nature makes that mean: so, over that art,
> Which you say adds to nature, is an art
> That nature makes. You see, sweet maid, we marry
> A gentler scion to the noblest stock
> And make conceive a bark of baser kind
> By bud of nobler race. This is an art
> Which does mend nature – change it rather – but
> The art itself is nature.

He advises her: 'Make your garden rich in gillyvors, / And do not call them bastards.' But Perdita is resolute; artificiality offends her sense of purity:

> I'll not put
> The dibble in earth to set one slip of them;
> No more than, were I painted, I would wish
> This youth should say 'twere well, and only therefore
> Desire to breed by me.[28]

Her chastity dictates a fastidious rejection of art, reminding the audience of the innocence of her own birth.

The association of whore and witch in the drama comes from the fact that both employ art. Witches, like Erictho in Marston's *Sophonisba*, or the Wise-woman in Heywood's *The Wise-woman of Hogsdon*, are usually unchaste, and unchaste women take the risk of being labelled witches. Richard III, in a theatrical passion, blames his deformity on the arts of Mistress Shore:

> Look, how I am bewitch'd! behold! mine arm
> Is like a blasted sapling wither'd up:
> And this is Edward's wife, that monstrous witch,
> Consorted with that harlot, strumpet Shore,
> That by their witchcraft thus have marked me.[29]

---

[28] IV.iv.82.
[29] *Richard III*, III.iv.70.

Henry VIII claimed that he had been bewitched by Anne Boleyn. In *The Comedy of Errors* the Courtesan accosts the wrong Antipholus, and he concludes: 'It is the devil.' Dromio encourages him: 'Nay, she is worse, she is the devil's dam; And here she comes in the habit of a light wench.' Antipholus sets himself to exorcise her:

> Avoid then, fiend, what tell'st thou me of supping?
> Thou art, as you are all, a sorceress:
> I conjure thee to leave me and be gone.

He calls over his shoulder: 'Avaunt, thou witch.'[30] The arts of the unchaste were inspired by the devil figuratively if not literally.

Chaste women in the drama are not expert in the conventions of chaste behaviour. Juliet's openness and artlessness in declaring her love for Romeo is modest because honest:

> Fain would I dwell on form; fain, fain deny
> What I have spoke: but farewell compliment!
> Dost thou love me?
> . . . .
> I should have been more strange, I must confess,
> But that thou overheardst, ere I was ware,
> My true-love passion.[31]

Miranda, who is not educated in the art of courtship since she has never known other women, instinctively shies away from archness or timidity as a form of dissembling:

> Hence, bashful cunning!
> And prompt me plain and holy innocence!
> I am your wife if you will marry me.[32]

In *The Two Gentlemen of Verona* Julia is keenly aware of the conflict between the rules of modesty and the inclinations of honesty. When Lucetta brings her a letter from Proteus she refuses to look at it, only to feel pangs of regret: 'And yet I would I had o'erlook'd the letter.' Lucetta gives her another chance, but another fit of

[30] IV.iii.48.

[31] *Romeo and Juliet*, II.ii.88.

[32] *The Tempest*, III.i.81.

untimely modesty makes her tear it up without reading it, only to try and piece it together afterwards:

> Be calm, good wind, blow not a word away,
> Till I have found each letter in the letter.

Her love is strong enough to overcome her apprehension of seeming immodest in the eyes of the world. True modesty is in the mind, not in outward forms:

> It is the lesser blot modesty finds,
> Women to change their shapes than men their minds.[33]

Modesty is not a simpering feminine virtue. Virtue, in men or women, goes beyond form.

George Eliot wrote that 'it is remarkable that Shakespeare's women almost always *make love*, in opposition to the conventional notion of what is fitting for woman.'[34] Nineteenth century critics single out Helena in *All's Well That Ends Well* for comment. Coleridge demurred: 'It must be confessed that her character is not very delicate, and it required all Shakespeare's consummate skill to interest us for her.'[35] Hazlitt was more positive in his praise: 'She is placed in circumstances of the most critical kind, and has to court her husband both as a virgin and a wife: yet the most scrupulous nicety of female modesty is not once violated.'[36] Helena's modesty is more like the modesty shown by men than like that of women, involving self-respect: 'Who ever strove / To show her merit that did miss her love?' She is stringent with herself about her own responsibility for her happiness:

> Our remedies oft in ourselves do lie,
> Which we ascribe to heaven: the fated sky
> Gives us free scope; only doth backward pull
> Our slow designs when we ourselves are dull.[37]

[33] I.ii.50, 119, V.iv.107.
[34] Gordon S. Haight, *George Eliot*, p. 146.
[35] *Table Talk of Samuel Taylor Coleridge*, p. 217.
[36] *Characters of Shakespear's Plays*, p. 220.
[37] I.i.22, 212.

Helplessness and defeatism are too negative to masquerade as modesty. It is not surprising that nineteenth century men, nurtured on a more passive ideal of femininity, found Helena a little overpowering. But Helena is not isolated among Shakespeare's heroines. Desdemona, sometimes accused of lack of spirit, was 'half the wooer' of Othello. Viola arranged her own affairs as competently as her brother arranged his. Olivia woos first Cesario, and then Sebastian, without loss of chastity:

> If you mean well,
> Now go with me and with this holy man
> Into the chantry by.[38]

Shakespeare smiles at Olivia, wedding in the chapel she used for mourning, but he does not cast aspersions on her for her forthrightness. If anything she is more chaste proposing marriage to Sebastian than in flirting with the seclusion of the virgin. Silvia in *The Two Gentlemen of Verona* writes her own love-letter and persuades a somewhat slow-witted Valentine to deliver it to her. Shakespeare is consistently compassionate towards women who woo. Chastity is not a question of coyness of manner except to the unchaste. Chastity requires frankness.

Victorian inhibitions about sex are usually blamed on the Puritans on the grounds that they fomented feelings of sexual guilt in their followers. A modern critic observes of Vittoria in Webster's *The White Devil* that 'when we first see her with Brachiano the adultery is obviously right from any but a puritanical point of view.'[39] But the associations of the word 'puritanical' owe more to Methodism than to seventeenth century Puritanism which sought to liberate men and women from the oppression of sexual guilt. The real influence of Puritanism on Webster made him condemn Brachiano and Vittoria for the barrenness and antisocial nature of a passion conceived outside marriage: through Flamineo he controls the audience's reactions, never allowing the enjoyment of romance for its own sake which M. C. Bradbrook claims for Flamineo – a character who might take the prize for cynicism in a

[38] *Twelfth Night*, IV.iii.22.
[39] M. C. Bradbrook, *Themes and Conventions of Elizabethan Tragedy*, p. 187.

drama which bred cynics like flies. In Webster Puritanism leads to
the Duchess of Malfi, who is both sensuous and chaste, inquiring
light-heartedly: 'Alas, what pleasure can two lovers find in
sleep?'[40] The Puritans held, like Erasmus, that sex between man and
wife was sinless, and that what chaste marriage meant was in part
the joy of sexual freedom between man and wife. Erasmus' Eula-
lia declared that 'the wyfe ought to dyspose her selfe all that she
maye that lieing by her husband she shew him al the pleasure that
she can. Wherby the honest love of matrimony may revive and be
renewed.'[41] There is no compromise of chastity in Juliet's invoca-
tion to Night:

> Hood my unmanned blood, bating in my cheeks,
> With thy black mantle till strange love, grown bold,
> Think true love acted simple modesty.[42]

Desdemona sues without false shame for her wedding-night not to
be postponed:

> If I be left behind,
> A moth of peace, and he go to the war,
> The rites for which I love him are bereft me,
> And I a heavy interim shall support
> By his dear absence; let me go with him.[43]

To feel freely is also to speak freely. Flamineo scoffs sardonically
at women's squeamishness: 'Why should ladies blush to hear that
nam'd, which they do not fear to handle?'[44] Marston's Crispinella,
the emancipated heroine of *The Dutch Courtezan*, shocks her more
conventional sister with her contempt of false modesty:

> Now bashfulness seize you, we pronounce boldly, robbery,
> murder, treason, which deeds must needs be far more loathsome
> than an act which is so natural, just, and necessary, as that of pro-

[40] Webster, *The Duchess of Malfi*, III.ii.10.
[41] *A Mery Dialogue, declaringe the Propertyes of Shrowde Shrewes, and Honest Wyves*,
sig. Bvi[v].
[42] *Romeo and Juliet*, III.ii.14.
[43] *Othello*, I.iii.255.
[44] Webster, *The White Devil*, I.ii.19.

creation; you shall have an hypocritical vestal virgin speak that with close teeth publicly, which she will receive with open mouth privately; for my own part, I consider nature without apparel; without disguising of custom or compliment, I give thoughts words, and words truth, and truth boldness; she whose honest freeness makes it her virtue to speak what she thinks will make it her necessity to think what is good. I love no prohibited things, and yet I would have nothing prohibited by policy, but by virtue; for as in the fashion of time those books that are call'd in are most in sale and request, so in nature those actions that are most prohibited are most desired.[45]

Erasmus would have rejoiced.

The reformers saw chastity as a private ideal in which men and women adopted not the standards of social etiquette but standards of truthfulness dictated by their own consciences. Hamlet mocked Ophelia's chastity because she assumed 'devotion's visage' in her prayers, to deceive him, commanded by her father and Claudius. The harsh 'are you honest?'[46] – meaning chaste – represents a logical progression of thought in a period which saw art as the antithesis of chastity.

The attack on medieval ideas about chastity opened up a new world for women. It exposed the economic basis of chastity, its class affinity, its contribution to the double standard, the false values which it posed in relation to single life and to marriage. Out of the disarray of old forms arose the possibility of new attitudes. Chastity emerges as a private instead of a public virtue, in the same way that honesty comes to usurp the public honour of the chivalric ideal. The recognition that women as individuals have a right to regulate their own behaviour according to the demands of particular situations frees them from theological and social prejudice. The dramatists saw even more clearly than the Puritan preachers that married chastity created an almost endless nonconformity

45 III.i.31.
46 *Hamlet*, III.i.103.

in human relations just as Protestantism created nonconformity in relation to the Divine. Out of the ashes of Pauline orthodoxy rises the Phoenix of freedom for women.

CHAPTER II

The Problem of Equality

1 Women and Authority

There were many answers possible to Adriana's irascible demand in *The Comedy of Errors*: 'Why should their liberty than ours be more?'[1] Luciana chose the political and quasi-philosophical response that women must take their place in the chain of Degree below men. Pushed a step further back the justification is theological: God gave Adam authority over Eve as a penalty for the Fall. But the reformers could not help perceiving, as Mill perceived two centuries later, that the subjection of the wife saluted not abstract truth but the superior physical strength of the husband.[2] Adriana upbraids her husband, and he sends for a rope's end. Their extolling of the First Marriage with which God completed his Creation was not consistent with the concept of a subject and inferior wife. Such a being would have been a liability to Adam, not an asset. When the reformers declared for marriage rather than celibacy Eve was reinstated as the Good Wife God's gift, given to Adam 'to consummate and make up his happinesse.'[3] Physically she might be weaker, but spiritually she was man's equal. The road from Calvin and Bullinger to John Lilburne the Leveller is a long one, but its direction is the same. Lilburne's manifesto of equality: 'Every particular and individual man and woman that ever breathed in the world since [Adam and Eve] are and were by nature all equal and alike in power, dignity, authority and majesty, none of them having (by nature) any authority

---

[1] II.i.10.

[2] J. S. Mill, *The Subjection of Women*, p. 230.

[3] Thomas Gataker, *A Good Wife Gods Gift*, p. 9.

dominion or magisterial power one over . . . another,[4] grew from
the Protestant vision of the woman as partner. When the Puritans
set themselves to change the old idea of male authority over
women, they carried with them the dramatists, already nourished
on a Renaissance fascination with the whole question of authority
and the individual.

It is not surprising that Luciana answered her sister with a philo-
sophical rather than a theological argument. The theological basis
for women's subjection had been persistently queried and discredited throughout the sixteenth century. The Humanist Agrippa
protested against men 'which assume Authority to themselves over
Women by vertue of Religion, and doe prove their Tyranny out
of holy Writ.'[5] The *de iure* of right was too much like the *de facto* of
force. Vives admonished husbands in his pioneer tract written to
instruct not the woman but the man in the art of good marriage,
that 'some there be, that through evyll and rough handelynge and
in threatenynge of their wives, have them not as wives, but as
servauntes.'[6] In practice the Scriptures seemed to have authorised
unlimited domestic tyranny, and the Puritans, eager campaigners
against wife-beating, were anxious to divest Antipholus of his rope
even if it meant conceding an unBiblical liberty to his wife. Kate in
The Taming of the Shrew inhabits a world too sophisticated to
stomach the Du Bartas theology of subjection with which her for-
bear, the Kate of the anonymous *The Taming of a Shrew*, regales her
hearers. The earlier Kate begins with the Creation:

> Then to his image he did make a man,
> Olde *Adam* and from his side asleepe,
> A rib was taken, of which the Lord did make,
> The woe of man so termd by *Adam* then,
> Woman for that, by her came sinne to us,
> And for her sin was *Adam* doomd to die,
> As Sara to her husband, so should we,

[4] *The Free Man's Freedom Vindicated* (16 June 1646) pp. 11–12, quoted in H. N.
Brailsford, *The Levellers and the English Revolution*, p. 119.

[5] *The Glory of Women*, pp. 30–1.

[6] *The Office and Duetie of an Husband*, sigs. Kviii^v–Li.

Obey them, love them, keepe, and nourish them.[7]

Shakespeare's Kate is political:

Such duty as the subject owes the prince,
Even such a woman oweth to her husband;
And when she is froward, peevish, sullen, sour,
And not obedient to his honest will,
What is she but a foul contending rebel
And graceless traitor to her loving lord?
I am ashamed that women are so simple
To offer war where they should kneel for peace,
Or seek for rule, supremacy, and sway,
When they are bound to serve, love, and obey.[8]

The household was the microcosm of the State, and women's subjection a happy paradigm of civil order.

Luciana thus invokes the concept of women's position which it
would be the hardest for an Elizabethan or Jacobean feminist to
refute without becoming a revolutionary overnight. Shakespeare
would have heard many times from the pulpit the State-authorised
Homily 'Concerning Good Order and Obedience to Rulers and
Magistrates,' opening with an eloquent apostrophe to Degree
which makes Ulysses sound like a civil servant. Elizabeth, sponsor
of the Homilies, was as fine a propagandist as any of her Lancas-
trian ancestors. Wives are only one link in a comprehensive catalogue of relation: 'Some Kings and Princes, some Inferiors and
Subjects; Priests and Laymen, Masters and Servants, Fathers and
Children, Husbands and Wives, Rich and Poor: and every one
hath need of other: so that in all things is to be lauded and praised
the goodly order of God: without the which no house, no city, no
commonwealth, can continue and endure, or last.' Fearful prospects present themselves to the destroyers of order: 'No man shall
ride or go by the highway unrobbed; no man shall sleep in his own
house or bed unkilled; no man shall keep his wife, children, and
possessions in quietness.' Worst of all, that red dread: 'All things

[7] [xviii]. 31, in *Narrative and Dramatic Sources of Shakespeare*, I, 107.
[8] *The Taming of the Shrew*, v.ii.160.

shall be common: and there must needs follow all mischief and utter destruction both of souls, bodies, goods, and common-wealths.'⁹ Elizabeth was as determined as Henry V that the crown should sit securely on her head. Luciana describes to Adriana what the queen wished every subject to know, that subjection to authority is part of the divinely appointed order of Nature:

> Why, headstrong liberty is lashed with woe.
> There's nothing situate under heaven's eye
> But hath his bound, in earth, in sea, in sky.
> The beasts, the fishes, and the wingèd fowls,
> Are their males' subjects, and at their controls.
> Men, more divine, the masters of all these,
> Lords of the wide world, and wild wat'ry seas,
> Indued with intellectual sense and souls,
> Of more pre-eminence than fish and fowls,
> Are masters to their females, and their lords:
> Then let your will attend on their accords.¹⁰

Lilburne's claim for equality between the sexes was, for the Eliza-bethan establishment, a call to anarchy. Shakespeare gave Luciana a statement of decorous orthodoxy which, according to many critics, represents his own attitude to the hierarchy.

The cause of women's rights is the poor relation of democracy. Wherever and whenever men raise a voice for freedom from tyranny in the state, that inconspicuous figure becomes articulate too, shouting against the tyranny of men both in the home and outside it. The Elizabethan and Jacobean periods bred the con-ditions of a feminist movement; the breakdown of old ideas and forms in religion, in politics, in the structure of society: the begin-ning of a new economy; and the spirit of independence which the Puritans fostered in their followers not only in religion, but in their attitude to the ruling classes. The vociferousness of the Eliza-bethans about Order, and of James I about the divinity of kings – the first king to formulate the Divine Right – drowned the sound of domestic discontents and threatened uprisings, of the assassin-

⁹ *Book of Homilies*, pp. 95–6.
¹⁰ *The Comedy of Errors*, II.i.15.

ation of Henri IV in 1610 in uncomfortable proximity on the opposite side of the Channel. James I, significantly, proclaimed the authority of kings with the same breath in which he berated husbands for the insubordination of London women, and urged stricter domestic control. The spirit of unrest which moves men to recognise their rights as individual citizens, infects their women. The revolutionary fervour of the 1790's cast up Mary Wollstonecraft, declaring that 'the *divine right* of husbands, like the divine right of kings, may, it is to be hoped, in this enlightened age, be contested without danger.'[11]

The shrillness of the Elizabethans about the concept of Degree derived from a consciousness that they themselves had ruptured the chain at its highest point: the subordination of the temporal overlord to the spiritual, of the English king or queen to the Pope. Rebellion on this large scale might well set a precedent for sedition. Elizabeth's Homilist is explicit that 'we understand not these or such other like places – which so straitly command obedience to superiors, and so straitly punished rebellion and disobedience to the same – to be meant, in any condition, of the pretenced or coloured power of the Bishop of Rome. For truly the Scripture of God alloweth no such usurped power, full of enormities, abusions, and blasphemies: but the true meaning of these and such places be, to extol and set forth God's true ordinance, and the authority of God's anointed Kings, and of their Officers appointed under them.'[12] The Elizabethans soldered the breach in their own logic with a reassertion of Aristotelian order in the universe. It is no accident that Shakespeare gives the statement of Degree to his two most astute political figures: Ulysses in *Troilus and Cressida* and the Archbishop of Canterbury in *Henry V*. To see their doctrine as Shakespeare's own disregards both his dramatic technique and his sympathies. Alone among the dramatists of his time he never allowed any character to become the mouthpiece of a central philosophy which might be identified as his: hence Johnson's criticism

[11] *The Rights of Woman*, p. 46.
[12] 'An Exhortation concerning Good Order, and Obedience to Rulers and Magistrates', *Book of Homilies*, p. 104.

that he wrote without any moral purpose.[13] This is one reason why Shakespeare as a person remains elusive. The spirit of his plays, moreover, is profoundly democratic in that he sees men and women, from the milkmaid to the Empress, the Fool to the wise man, the Prince to the gravedigger, as equal, subject to the same passions and temptations, crawling from nativity to maturity, to the lean and slippered pantaloon and dusty death. The hierarchy is only one facet of his world. No wonder the movement to suppress and censor the theatres gathered impetus in the Elizabethan and Jacobean periods.

The chain of Degree was a political dogma bearing as much and as little relation to the lives of ordinary people as political dogmas generally do. But the dogma affected the debate on women because any questioning of their relation to male authority would throw the whole chain of subjection into disorder from the lowest to the highest, to the great alarm, in this period, of the highest. The Puritans were not concerned to accommodate the doctrine of Degree, but their opponents were.

Adriana retorts to her sister that she is not married – nor, with sisterly acid, likely to be: 'This servitude makes you to keep unwed.'[14] Adriana knew that her question about liberty was worth a better answer. If women were spiritually equal to men the questions about their subjection would have, at the least, to be rephrased, and this is exactly what the Puritans set themselves to do in their sermons and domestic conduct books. If they arrived at traditional conclusions it was by the way of new enquiries and new attitudes. Puritanism fostered a concern for the treatment of women which gave respectability to Adriana's discontent.

The Puritans did not repudiate the authority of the husband, but they qualified it. The picture of the uncompromising Puritan patriarch presiding over his family ignores the extent to which Puritans encouraged women to dispute his dominion. For the Puritans the only justification for a wife's submission was a diplomatic one that mutual comfort – to them the chief end of

[13] Preface to *The Plays of William Shakespeare* (1765), in *Samuel Johnson on Shakespeare*, p. 33.
[14] *The Comedy of Errors*, II.i.24.

marriage [15] – required it. For the late twentieth century this is a highly dubious and dangerous philosophy, but the change of direction which it recorded in male thinking about women made other changes possible because it released women from the strait-jacket of theology. If the criterion of good was domestic harmony, the conditions for achieving it might admit of infinite variety. Adam's rights over an erring wife allowed no such flexibility.

The Puritans reached the conclusion that marriage worked best if a wife offered her husband voluntary submission out of, and in return for, love; but on the way there they opened a Pandora's box of suggestion. A husband could not expect the gift of submission regardless of his own behaviour. Erasmus set the tone of their discussion in his retort to the discontented husband: 'A rare byrd in erthe (ye say) is an honest woman. And ymagine ye agayne youre selfe worthy to have a rare wyfe?'[16] The Puritans Dod and Cleaver cautioned in *A Godly Forme of Houshold Government* that 'as the wife ought with great care to endevour, and by all good means to labour to bee in favour and grace with her husband: So likewise the husband ought to feare to be in disgrace and disliking with his wife.'[17] The drama of Shakespeare's time espouses the idea of reciprocal obligation. Fallibility is no longer an exclusively female birthright. Cornelio's page in Chapman's *All Fools* needles his master about his shortcomings as a partner: 'Turn your eye into yourself. . . and weigh your own imperfection with hers. If she be wanton abroad, are you not wanting at home?'[18] The conviction that the husband is accountable for the wife's behaviour through his own, heralds a psychological approach to relations between men and women apparent as early as Vives and Erasmus. Erasmus pronounced:

> Beleve me, an evyll wyfe is nat wont to chaunce, but to evyll husbondes. . . . Of an evyll husbande (I wyll well) a good wyfe may be mard, but of a good the evyll is wont to be refourmed

[15] Haller and Haller, 'The Puritan Art of Love', *Huntington Library Quarterly*, v (1942) no. 2, 266, 270.

[16] *In Laude and Prayse of Matrymony*, sig. Diii[v].

[17] Sigs. L2[v]–L3.

[18] III.i.

and mended. We blame wyves falsly. No man (if ye gyve any credence to me) had ever a shrewe to his wyfe but thrughe hys owne defaute.[19]

Authority carries its own burdens, and as the heroine remarks in *The Miseries of Enforced Marriage*, having heard out the instructions of her betrothed about her subjection:

> We being thus subdued, pray you know then,
> As women owe a duty, so do men.[20]

Desdemona lightly upbraids her husband for his reluctance to gratify her wishes:

> I wonder in my soul
> What you could ask me, that I should deny?
> Or stand so mammering on?

In granting him the solitude he asks for, she pretends to reproach him for his wilfulness in contrast to her submission:

> Be it as your fancies teach you,
> Whate'er you be, I am obedient.[21]

The husband owns no monopoly of authority, nor the wife of submission.

The theatre was more susceptible than the pulpit to untying the Gordian knot of a domestic harmony fashioned not by theology but by diplomacy. The politics of the hearth interested the dramatists as vitally as the politics of the State, with less risk. In effect the Puritans preached for the wife what Lilburne proclaimed for the subject – the doctrine of mutual consent. Henry Smith might have said of husbands what Lilburne said of rulers: 'Neither have they or can they exercise any authority, but merely by institution or donation, that is to say . . . by mutual consent and agreement for the good . . . and comfort each of other and not for the . . . hurt or

---

[19] *In Laude and Prayse of Matrymony*, sig. Dii[v].
[20] George Wilkins, *The Miseries of Enforced Marriage*, I. p. 480.
[21] *Othello*, III.iii.69, 89.

damage of any.'[22] Portia accepts Bassanio in this spirit:

> Happiest of all, is that her gentle spirit
> Commits itself to yours to be directed,
> As from her lord, her governor, her king.
> Myself, and what is mine, to you and yours
> Is now converted. But now I was the lord
> Of this fair mansion, master of my servants,
> Queen o'er myself; and even now, but now,
> This house, these servants, and this same myself
> Are yours.[23]

But Portia's submission is part of the discrepancy in the play between outward precept and inward impulse.[24] Portia's obedience is
an act of courtesy, a ceremonial to the reality of love. In practice
she retains total independence. Submission is a garment she wears
as gracefully as her disguise. But her attitude to herself is entirely
different from that of the heroine who, owning 'the hereditary
strain of Puritan energy,' embraced 'the freedom of voluntary submission'[25] by marrying Casaubon. Dorothea's vision turns to dust
and ashes because she abdicates self, where Portia, truer to the spirit
of Puritanism, retains a separate identity from her husband. Tyse-
few in Marston's *The Dutch Courtezan* assures Crispinella that marriage will not compromise her independence: 'If you will be mine,
you shall be your own.'[26] Submission, in Puritan eyes, was the
handmaid of harmony in marriage, but the ideal it served was that
of freedom. The wife-tamer in Beaumont and Fletcher's *Rule a
Wife, and Have a Wife* grants his wife full liberty once she allows
him authority. It is her attitude that matters rather than her behaviour. Othello scoffs at the notion that he should restrict the liberty

[22] Lilburne, *The Free Man's Freedom Vindicated*, quoted in Brailsford, *The Levellers and the English Revolution*, p. 119. Cf. Stone, *The Crisis of the Aristocracy
1558–1641*, p. 669; James T. Johnson, 'The Covenant Idea and the Puritan View
of Marriage', *Journal of the History of Ideas*, XXXII (1971) no. 1, 107–18.

[23] *The Merchant of Venice*, III.ii.163.

[24] D. J. Palmer, '*The Merchant of Venice*, or the Importance of Being Earnest',
Shakespearian Comedy, Stratford-Upon-Avon Studies, *14*, 106.

[25] George Eliot, *Middlemarch*, chs. 1, 3.

[26] IV.i.85.

of a virtuous wife:

> 'Tis not to make me jealous,
> To say my wife is fair, feeds well, loves company,
> Is free of speech, sings, plays, and dances well;
> Where virtue is, these are more virtuous.[27]

Casaubon cast himself as Dorothea's conscience. In the world of
Middlemarch 'women were expected to have weak opinions; but
the safeguard of society and of domestic life was, that opinions
were not acted on. Sane people did what their neighbours did, so
that if any lunatics were at large, one might know and avoid
them.'[28] This is the attitude of Creon, of the Chorus, even of her
sister Ismene, to Sophocles' Antigone. Ismene protests at her proposal to bury her brother in defiance of Creon:

> O think, Antigone; we are women; it is not for us
> To fight against men; our rulers are stronger than we,
> And we must obey in this, or in worse than this.
> May the dead forgive me, I can do no other
> But as I am commanded; to do more is madness.[29]

Ismene's is the voice of submissive femininity. Society repudiates
Antigone's spirit: even she herself is forced to call it madness.
George Eliot, who later refers to Dorothea as 'a sort of Christian
Antigone,'[30] probably had Sophocles' play in mind when she
wrote of avoiding lunatics. The authority in matters of conscience
was the man.

In the sixteenth century the idea that women had consciences
which might operate independently from men's, might even judge
and oppose the male conscience, was revolutionary. Even in Elizabethan drama there are vestiges of the medieval schoolmen's debate about whether women had souls. Launce in *The Two
Gentlemen of Verona* makes his left shoe stand for his mother because

---

[27] *Othello*, III.iii.187.
[28] *Middlemarch*, ch. 1.
[29] *Antigone*, p. 128.
[30] *Middlemarch*, ch. 19.

'it hath the worser sole.'[31] Yet the reformers declared God to be no respecter of sexes, 'for in Christ,' said the Humanist Agrippa, 'Neither Male nor Female, but a new creature is accepted.' He argued, in a passage which recalls More's claim for women's spiritual equality in his letter to his daughters' tutor, Gunnell, that 'it is manifest that the difference of the Sexes consists only in the different Scituation of the parts of the Body, which the office of generation did necessarily require. But certain it is, he gave one and the same indifferent soule to Male and Female.'[32] When the Protestants supported the rights of the individual conscience against the authority of the Church, they created the conditions of support for the rights of individual women against the men in authority over them. If God created a partnership in Eden, He must have allowed freedom of conscience to both halves.

The Puritans had an interest in urging freedom of conscience for women in that the Puritan sects boasted a considerable female membership, perhaps for the general reason that women tend to be active in minority groups because they can exert more influence as individuals on a small new organisation than on a big one with traditional male dominance. More specifically the Puritan ideology backed women in a venture which was educative, politically orientated, and feminist in its implementation. Meetings of sects and Puritan lectures gave women a context outside the home. The sects admitted women on equal terms with men, allowed them to minister, and gave them an equal share in the government of the sect. They provided a sphere in which a woman might be independent of her husband. The more radical sects like the Anabaptists, the Brownists or the Family of Love – satirised in Middleton's play – held that a woman had no marital obligations to an unbelieving husband. In cases of difference the judge was her own conscience, and in cases of the antagonistic claims of husband and sect, her first loyalty should be to the sect.[33] John Knox in Geneva gathered round him a community which included emigré women like Anne

[31] II.iii.17.

[32] *The Glory of Women*, pp. 31, 1.

[33] Keith Thomas, 'Women and the Civil War Sects', *Past and Present*, XIII (1958) 44, 52, 49.

Locke who had fled the rule of an unregenerate husband.[34] Katherine Chidley, who was to be one of the most active leaders of the Levellers, and who wrote a pioneering pamphlet on the right of women to independence of conscience, left her husband, and, with her son, started a new Brownist community in Bury, Suffolk.[35] Women protested so militantly against the suppression of Puritan preachers that they went to prison for their activities.[36] Puritanism, which idealised the divine union of man and wife, operated, at least on the sectarian level, in a way which made women more conscious of their separateness from their husbands. Democracy develops out of a man's sense of an identity distinct from his relation to those who rule him, through which he can confront that rule. The Puritan sects offered women an identity apart from their husbands, which made it possible for them to challenge their husbands' authority.

That husbands felt challenged is indubitable. Freedom of conscience for wives spelled domestic insurrection. John Brinsley attacked the female sectarians on behalf of the male establishment:

> Let it be inquired with what warrant the Wife, who is under subjection, can upon a like pretext desert that Church, whereof her Husband is a Member . . . and ingage her self by Covenant unto another, and that without his consent, if not against it.

Such women are impossible to control: 'Their spirits will not stoop to any kinde of subjection, specially to their Husbands. . . . No, they are resolved they will have their wills.'[37] The woman preacher was a portentous figure. The New Englander Hugh Peters accosted Anne Hutchinson with: 'You have stepped out of your place; you have rather been a husband than a wife, and a preacher than a hearer; and a magistrate than a subject, and so you have thought to carry all things in Church and Commonwealth, as

[34] Patrick Collinson, 'The Role of Women in the English Reformation illustrated by the Life and Friendships of Anne Locke', *Studies in Church History*, II, 265.

[35] Brailsford, *The Levellers and the English Revolution*, p. 38.

[36] Collinson, *The Elizabethan Puritan Movement*, p. 93.

[37] *A Looking-Glasse for Good Women*, pp. 42, 39–40.

you would.'[38] Shades of Ulysses and Elizabeth's Homilist! Katherine Chidley's retort was not reassuring:

> I pray you tell me what authority [the] unbelieving husband
> hath over the conscience of his believing wife; it is true he hath
> authority over her in bodily and civil respects, but not to be a
> lord over her conscience.[39]

The dramatists reacted in three main ways to the controversy about freedom of conscience for women. In the first place, their satire on the sects took the form of demonstrating the licence of women sectarians as the most inflammatory area for arousing general opposition to sectarianism. They concentrated on the sects' annexing of property – both financial and sexual – through their women members, on their encouragement of mental insubordination, and on their motley class elements. The sects were predominantly lower-class in membership,[40] and when Quarlous in *Bartholomew Fair* scoffs at the 'good labourers and painful eaters'[41] class antagonism is as strong, if not stronger, than religious feeling. In *The Family of Love* Dryfat describes the sect as

> a crew of narrow-ruffed, strait-laced, yet loose-bodied dames,
> with a rout of omnium-gatherums, assembled by the title of the
> Family of Love: which, master doctor, if they be not punished
> and suppressed by our club-law, each man's copyhold will
> become freehold, specialities will turn to generalities. . . . Their
> wives, the only ornaments of their houses, and of all their wares,
> goods, and chattel[s], the chief moveables, will be made common.[42]

The idea of wives in common, the complaint of the husband in Chapman's *An Humorous Day's Mirth* of his sectarian wife, that

---

[38] Quoted in Thomas, 'Women and the Civil War Sects', p. 49.

[39] K. Chidley, *The Justification of the Independent Churches of Christ*, p. 26, quoted in 'Women and the Civil War Sects', p. 52.

[40] 'Women and the Civil War Sects', p. 45.

[41] Jonson, *Bartholomew Fair*, I.iii.89.

[42] Middleton, *The Family of Love*, V.iii.192.

'every man for her sake is a Puritan,'[43] was as distasteful to the middle-class family man as the picture of the wife embezzling his money to support the sect which Truewit evokes for Morose in *Epicoene*. The dramatists unerringly touched the tender areas of feeling about the sects, displaying witty and incorrigible women sectarians evading their husbands' control. Even Mrs Purge in *The Family of Love* eludes her husband's accusation that he has cuck-olded himself, swearing, with Falstaffian facility, that she knew him all along, and turning aside his plea that she attend the sect no more with the counter-argument of freedom of conscience:

> Truly, husband, my love must be free still to God's creatures: yea, nevertheless, preserving you still as the head of my body, I will do as the spirit shall enable me.[44]

Katherine Chidley might have said the same to her husband before she left.

Secondly, the dramatists focused on situations in which the wife's conscience took a different course from her husband's. The Puritans believed that a man must adhere to ethical standards with which his wife could identify; if he failed to do so, she had the right to disavow his authority. 'The husband saith, that his wife must obay him because he is her better, therefore if he let her be better than himselfe, he seemes to free her from obedience, and binde himselfe to obay her.'[45] Emilia in *Othello* is not alone in repudiating the rule of a husband inferior to her in virtue. Staring in horror at Iago disfigured by her new knowledge of him, she defies his command for her silence: ''Tis proper I obey him, but not now.'[46] A husband's villainy annuls his wife's duty to him. Middleton's Tho-masine in *Michaelmas Term*, watching her husband ruining another man, exclaims: 'Why am I wife to him that is no man?'[47] In *The Winter's Tale* Leontes responds to Paulina's curses on his cruelty to Hermione by turning to her husband: 'What! canst not rule her?' The retort comes not from a wife, but from an individual capable

---

[43] I.i.   [44] Middleton, *The Family of Love*, v.iii.425.

[45] Henry Smith, *A Preparative to Mariage*, p. 62.

[46] v.ii.197.   [47] II.iii.230.

of distinguishing good and evil without the intervention of a third party:

> From all dishonesty he can: in this —
> Unless he take the course that you have done,
> Commit me for committing honour — trust it,
> He shall not rule me.[48]

Women can be for God only, as well as men.

In some women obedience itself may have the impact of defiance, where rebellion would put the wife on the same level morally as her corrupted husband. When Othello strikes Desdemona as though she were his whore, her submission passes judgement on him more tellingly than a retaliation which would draw her into an ethical universe which settled moral issues with physical violence. Marriage on these terms is no better than a tavern brawl, the forays between Jonson's Cob and Tib in *Every Man In His Humour* where the wife adopts Henry Smith's reversal of roles, and agrees to take Cob back into favour only as 'my louing, and obedient husband.'[49] Desdemona's obedience bespeaks a clear conscience; her behaviour is independent of her husband's judgement of her. Lodovico marvels: 'Truly an obedient lady.' Othello's scorn fails to touch her, because her submission separates her from the confines of his moral vision:

> Sir, she can turn, and turn, and yet go on,
> And turn again, and she can weep, sir, weep;
> And she's obedient, as you say, obedient;
> Very obedient. Proceed you in your tears.

His unkindness cannot taint her goodness because its existence is not dependent on his favour. Othello's remorse scalds him the more for his wife's refusal to accuse him:

> When we shall meet at compt,
> This look of thine will hurl my soul from heaven,
> And fiends will snatch at it.[50]

[48] II.iii.46.   [49] Folio of 1616, v.v.65.
[50] *Othello*, IV.i.243, V.ii.274.

In *Cymbeline* Imogen's determination to obey Posthumus when she learns his desire for her death exposes his ignobility more devastatingly than defiance could: she prepares to kill herself:

> And thou, Posthumus, thou that didst set up
> My disobedience 'gainst the king my father,
> And make me put into contempt the suits
> Of princely fellows, shall hereafter find
> It is no act of common passage, but
> A strain of rareness.[51]

In both women submission is not the negative acquiescence of an indolent conscience but a mark of rareness which spots rebellion with commonness.

Thirdly, the Puritan debate about freedom of conscience made the dramatists interested in women on their own. Elizabethan drama has no Antigones. Surprisingly, in an age obsessed with the individual conscience, there are no plays about women vowed to great causes, unless one counts Dorothea, the Christian heroine of Massinger's particularly vile play about decadent Rome, *The Virgin Martyr*. The women of the political world – the Duchess of Malfi, Katherine in *Henry VIII*, even Margaret in the *Henry VI* plays and *Richard III* – are smaller, more domestic figures than Sophocles' heroine. The choices open to their consciences are more confused: they are more captive in the fact of womanhood and more impotent. The grand gesture of tragedy is less available to them than it is to a character like Racine's Bérénice. Shakespeare's theatre offers instead a consistent probing of the reactions of women to isolation in a society which has never allowed them independence from men either physically or spiritually. The struggle is not about issues – the gods and the State – it is about what Virginia Woolf called 'The Angel in the House,'[52] the male idea of womanhood. The dramatists took the concept of a man's dominion over his wife and daughters, and explored what it was like to be a woman under these conditions. The interplay between breaking free and submitting to the male world's view of

---

[51] III.iv.88.
[52] 'Professions for Women', *Collected Essays*, II, 285

women is inseparable from the characters of women as disparate as Goneril, Helena in *All's Well That Ends Well*, Portia in *The Merchant of Venice*, Lady Macbeth, or Vittoria in *The White Devil*. Tragedy is supposed to deal with the isolation of the human spirit, and one of the reasons for the Elizabethan and Jacobean preoccupation with heroines is that that isolation is more terrible in a being conditioned to dependence on men. Lady Macbeth, forever re-creating in her sleep-walking the inception of her separateness from her husband, still reaches for his hand. But Shakespeare's comedies evince the same fascination with women on their own, from the solitary sorrow of Julia in *The Two Gentlemen of Verona*, watching her lover court another woman, to Viola communing with her disguised self, 'How will this fadge?'[53] to Helena and Hermia, alternately exiled from the trio of competing lovers in *A Midsummer Night's Dream*.

Antigone's breeding has not quenched the fire of independence in her; her conscience is not a female one but a human one. In late Elizabethan drama the struggle for women is to be human in a world which declares them only female. The effect of Puritanism on the drama was to excite interest in what a woman's conscience would dictate to her if she were freed from subjection to the male conscience. Hamlet battles to make his mother independent of Claudius, taunting her with the possibility of breach of confidence:

> 'Twere good you let him know,
> For who that's but a queen, fair, sober, wise,
> Would from a paddock, from a bat, a gib,
> Such dear concernings hide?[54]

Freedom of conscience for women was still a new concept. Women had not been educated to form independent moral judgements. The dramatists asked themselves how the female conscience would work, given the authoritarian conditions of its nurture, or rather non-nurture. Mary Wollstonecraft urged that 'some degree

[53] *Twelfth Night*, II.ii.33.
[54] *Hamlet*, III.iv.188.

of liberty of mind is necessary even to form the person.[55] Polonius
dispatches his son to the university to sow his wild oats, to learn
through his errors how to be true to himself, and thus to other
men. But his daughter must not rely on her own judgement. Her
conviction of Hamlet's sincerity arouses contempt: 'Affection,
pooh! you speak like a green girl / Unsifted in such perilous cir-
cumstance.' He advises her to

> think yourself a baby
> That you have ta'en these tenders for true pay
> Which are not sterling.

Laertes expects Ophelia to heed his counsel that 'best safety lies in
fear.' Her whole education is geared to relying on other people's
judgements, and to placing chastity and the reputation for chastity
above even the virtue of truthfulness. Ophelia has no chance to develop an independent conscience of her own, so stifled is she by the
authority of the male world. The consequence is, that being false
to herself, allowing herself to acquiesce in the deception by which
her father and the king overhear her conversation with Hamlet,
she is inevitably false to Hamlet. His 'Get thee to a nunnery' mocks
a morality which thinks chastity compatible with hypocrisy.
Under this tutelage women are degraded into creatures with no
moral sense of their own, who have to be incarcerated in nunneries
to keep them virtuous. Polonius allows Ophelia no identity independent of his rule, a condition which makes her incapable of
coping with a world in which he has no part – the world of her relation to Hamlet. Her reason has not been educated to exercise
itself without his guidance: 'Lord, we know what we are, but
know not what we may be.' When Claudius laments 'poor Ophelia / Divided from herself and her fair judgment,'[56] the irony lies in
the fact that she was never allowed to have any judgement.

Mary Wollstonecraft's cynicism about the traditional attitude
that 'with respect to the female character, obedience is the grand

---

[55] *The Rights of Woman*, p. 84.

[56] *Hamlet*, I.iii.101, 43, III.i.121, IV.v.41, 83.

lesson which ought to be impressed with unrelenting vigour,'[57] was anticipated by sixteenth century Humanists when they argued that women need liberty to develop into people. Subjection, pointed out Agrippa, is self-perpetuating in women because:

> A woman by and by as soon as she is borne, and from the first beginning of her years is detained in sloth at home, and as uncapable of another Province, she is permitted to think of nothing besides her Needle or the like, when afterwards she reacheth to ripenesse of age, she is delivered up to the jealous rule of her husband, or else shut up in the perpetual Bridewell of Nuns.[58]

In Jonson's *Every Man In His Humour* Mrs Kitely suffers the jealous rule of a husband, where the treatment of Young Knowell recognises different principles. Knowell is unwilling to compel his son to virtue, preferring to give him his head to learn the meaning of virtue rather than its rules. Justice Clement reinforces his view: 'Your sonne is old inough, to gouerne himselfe: let him runne his course, it's the onely way to make him a stay'd man.'[59] The play ends, like *The Merry Wives of Windsor*, with the husband learning that what is sauce for the gander is sauce for the goose, and that a wife is more likely to be virtuous if trusted to be so than if compelled to be so, a compulsion which any woman of wit will evade. For both sexes, liberty is the soil in which conscience takes root. To preach freedom of conscience for women demanded recognition of their need for freedom from male authority.

Lack of liberty classes women not with men, but with boys. Even in a post-Pankhurst world men still hold Ganymede's view, pronounced with relish by Rosalind, that 'boys and women are for the most part cattle of this colour,'[60] owning the same caprices and irrational ways. Nora's children are her dolls, and Nora is Torwald's doll. The idea of woman as an undeveloped man dies hard. This feeling was much more intense at a time when women could not emerge, as the male child emerged, from the dependence

---

[57] *The Rights of Woman*, p. 30.
[58] *The Glory of Women*, p. 30.
[59] Folio of 1616, III.vii.86.
[60] *As You Like It*, III.ii.403.

of childhood. A woman obeyed her father until she obeyed her husband. But Puritanism sowed dissent and Beatrice speaks to the spirit of her time when she remarks caustically: 'It is my cousin's duty to make curtsy and say, "Father, as it please you." But yet for all that, cousin, let him be a handsome fellow, or else make another curtsy, and say, "Father, as it please me." ' Portia, Viola, Beatrice, are women set free from their fathers, and their voice is that of the adult world, where Hero is still a child.

Marriage could only be a partnership in Puritan terms if the woman was free to choose a husband, and was herself adult enough to be his partner. When the Puritans allowed the right of a daughter to query an arranged marriage they set a precedent for her independence from her father which influenced her attitude to her husband. Beatrice, free to make her own choice, is free also to dictate the conditions of that choice. She will not marry 'till God make men of some other mettle than earth. Would it not grieve a woman to be overmastered with a piece of valiant dust? to make an account of her life to a clod of wayward marl?'[61] John Stuart Mill held that the reason men feared emancipation for women was that they envisaged, not that women would refuse to marry, but that 'they should insist that marriage should be on equal conditions.' They were alarmed 'lest all women of spirit and capacity should prefer doing almost anything else, not in their own eyes degrading, rather than marry, when marrying is giving themselves a master, and a master too of all earthly possessions.'[62]

Women in the drama want to be married but not mastered, and this levels them with men who have always lamented loss of liberty in marrying. As Bacon pointed out, 'the most ordinary cause of a *Single Life*, is Liberty.'[63] The boast of liberty is a male prerogative where the spinster plucks with bony fingers at ever-receding sour grapes. But where Benedick and Beatrice both sound the hollowness of single liberty, they relinquish it only because they are confident of liberty within marriage. Women like Maria in Beaumont and Fletcher's *The Womans Prize, or The Tamer*

[61] *Much Ado about Nothing*, II.i.48, 54.
[62] *The Subjection of Women*, p. 245.
[63] 'Of Marriage and Single Life', p. 29.

Tam'd, or the city wives in Marston's *The Insatiate Countess*, marry on terms. The Epilogue to Beaumont and Fletcher's play — itself claiming to be an answer to *The Taming of the Shrew* — admonishes husbands that·

> They should not reign as Tyrants o'er their wives.
> Nor can the Women from this president
> Insult, or triumph; it being aptly meant,
> To teach both Sexes due equality;
> And as they stand bound, to love mutually.

Thomas Gataker said no less when he preached: 'Let both man and wife so esteeme either of other as joynd by Gods counsell, as given by Gods hand; and so receive either other as from God, bee thankfull either for other unto God, seeke the good either of other in God.'[64]

Puritan marriage abhorred an authoritarian climate whether in father or husband, and an anonymous handbook of common law printed in 1632, but written specifically for the instruction of women some thirty years earlier, stated categorically that in marriage 'the good-will of parents is required in regard of honestie, not of necessitie.'[65] As so often the spirit of Puritan reform belied the conservatism of their language. Preachers impressed on young people that clandestine marriage 'taketh much from the honour and dignity of marriage.'[66] But the impulse of Puritanism was to defend those helpless in the eyes of the law — children, Wards of Court, wives — against a system degrading to those in authority as well as to those under it. Desdemona's confronting of Brabantio with a 'divided duty' was perfectly orthodox in Puritan eyes. When they urged the desirability of equal marriage they owned the double purpose of exposing those parents condemned by Erasmus for regarding 'the greatness of Fortune,'[67] and of equipp-

---

[64] *A Good Wife Gods Gift*, p. 24.

[65] T. E., *The Lawes Resolutions of Womens Rights*, p. 53. I am grateful to Professor Alice Shalvi for pointing out that T. E. prepared for the press the book written at the turn of the century by one I. J.

[66] William Gouge, *Of Domesticall Duties*, p. 207.

[67] 'The Unequal Marriage', *All the Familiar Colloquies of Desiderius Erasmus*, p. 447.

ing a wife to match her husband so that marriage might be for women a partnership instead of a yoke.

The only woman in the drama who stands out for single life against marriage is Moll Cutpurse, the swaggering masculine heroine of Dekker and Middleton's *The Roaring Girl*. She forswears marrying in order to retain her freedom:

> A Wife, you know, ought to be obedient, but I fear I am too headstrong to obey, therefore I'll ne'er go about it. . . . I have the head now of myself, and am man enough for a woman: marriage is but chopping and changing, where a maiden loses one head, and has a worse i' th' place.[68]

Moll Cutpurse is the Germaine Greer of the Elizabethan stage. She goes further in her bid for independence from men than any other woman, but remains eccentric. Her way of life is not a viable one for other women, and in the end her claim to freedom is less powerful than that of women who make society recognise and harbour them within its framework. Dekker's shrew in *Patient Grissil*, warning her husband that her obedience may yet be forfeited through his ill-treatment, for ''tis not fid that poore womens should be kept alwaies vnder,'[69] marks a greater advance for the ordinary woman in undermining Adam's rights than Moll's retreat from the world in which those rights operate. The dramatists, like the Puritans, are no revolutionaries proposing a new order of society; their radicalism in their treatment of women consists in making change accessible to every woman whatever the state of life to which God has called her.

The Puritan vision of mystical union between man and wife was antagonistic to an authoritarian view of the husband's position. A divine conjunction demanded equal elements in its make-up. Donne declared in *The Good-Morrow* that 'What ever dyes, was not mixt equally.' The paradox of two in one fascinated preachers, poets and playwrights alike, prompting Gataker's image of 'two streames, that rising from severall heads, fall the one into the

[68] II.ii.39.
[69] v.ii.291.

other,'[70] Donne's 'stiffe twin compasses,' and *The Phoenix and Turtle* with its extraordinary abstract power:

> So they loved as love in twain
> Had the essence but in one;
> Two distincts, division none:
> Number there in love was slain.
>
> . . . .
>
> Property was thus appallèd,
> That the self was not the same;
> Single nature's double name
> Neither two nor one was callèd.

The Ghost in *Hamlet*, that curiously ambiguous figure escaped from the scourging of his sins to urge the Prince to the 'kinde of Wilde Justice'[71] which Bacon thought less noble than forgiveness, renders Hamlet's revenge virtually impossible by his injunction that Gertrude should be spared:

> Taint not thy mind, nor let thy soul contrive
> Against thy mother aught.

In Hamlet's ethics man and wife are one. While the union of Gertrude and Claudius makes a mockery of marriage because it grows from the division of Gertrude and Hamlet's father, it nevertheless denies Hamlet access to either Gertrude or Claudius as individuals. He is no longer her son, but Claudius' son also, 'too much in the "son."' When he takes leave of the king before going to England he salutes him with: 'Farewell, dear mother.' Claudius corrects him smoothly: 'Thy loving father, Hamlet,' and Hamlet bursts out: 'My mother — father and mother is man and wife, man and wife is one flesh, and so my mother.' His triumph after the play is that he has effected division: Gertrude is a stranger to Claudius' secret and Hamlet's upbraiding of her forges a link once again between her and her son. Claudius, like Macbeth, moves almost imperceptibly away from his wife. When he warns Laertes of the gradual decay of love he might be speaking of his love for

[70] *A Good Wife Gods Gift*, p. 5.
[71] 'Of Reuenge', p. 18.

Gertrude:

> But that I know love is begun by time,
> And that I see in passages of proof
> Time qualifies the spark and fire of it.

After the death of Polonius a separation of confidence sets in between him and the queen, symbolised by his curt request: 'Good
Gertrude, set some watch over your son.'[72] Hamlet's hand is stayed
against Claudius by a concept of marriage which strikes him with
irony and seems almost superstition, but which nonetheless constitutes the whole ground of his sense of sacrilege at his mother's
remarriage. To cast out a belief in the indivisibility of man and
wife is to justify Gertrude's faithlessness. Hamlet can only obey the
Ghost when Gertrude's death leaves Claudius unprotected, and
gives Hamlet a motive for revenge which seems to reunite his
parents against the intruder on their marriage.

The problem for the Puritans was that their enquiries about the
nature of the mystical union of marriage suggested the great extent
to which it was man-made, and man-made in the interests of man
rather than of woman. In common law the union of man and wife
meant loss of separate identity for the woman. The Puritan domestic conduct book's vision of beneficent sharing – 'a common par-
ticipation of body and goods'[73] – in law meant the husband's
annexing of those goods. Gataker's lyrical image of the two
streams acquires different associations under the pen of the author
of *The Lawes Resolutions of Women's Rights*: 'When a small brooke
or little river incorporateth with Rhodanus, Humber, or the
Thames, the poore Rivolet loseth her name, it is carried and recar-
ried with the new associate, it beareth no sway, it possesseth
nothyng.' In becoming one with her husband a woman 'hath lost
her streame.' But he offers women the consolation that in criminal
law they stand on their own. Humphrey of Gloucester in *Henry VI*
has no power to impede the legal disgrace of his wife Eleanor.
Unity is an allegory of harmony rather than a fact of existence. A
woman forfeits her separate identity in marriage only when it

[72] I.v.85, I.ii.67, IV.iii.48, IV.vii.110, v.i.290.

[73] Dod and Cleaver, *A Godly Forme of Houshold Government*, sig. F8ᵛ.

benefits her husband: she brings assets but not liabilities. He concludes:

> They are but one person, & by this a married Woman perhaps may either doubt whether shee bee either none or no more then halfe a person. But let her bee of good cheare, though for the neere conjunction which is betweene man and wife, and to tye them to a perfect love, agreement and adherence, they bee by intent and wise fiction of Law, one person, yet in nature & in some other cases by the Law of God and man, they remaine divers, for as Adams punishment was severall from Eves, so in criminall and other special causes our Law argues them severall persons.[74]

There was only one way in which a woman might seem to be immune from the penalties of her actions in law. If all her property belonged legally to her husband, it was impossible to fine her as an independent person and this was one reason why women were able to be active in the Catholic recusant movement. As long as the husband conformed it was difficult to convict the wife of subversive activity because she could not be fined separately, although some women did go to prison for their obduracy.[75] But the tone of T. E.'s remarkable little handbook is one of wry sympathy for women because of the way in which the myth of union masks her legal loss of identity.

The Puritans wanted to reconcile separate identity with union in marriage. They wanted the wife to be respected as an individual by her husband, and to share with him equal responsibility for the spiritual concord which made them one. In practice they perceived that mutual comfort was the consequence of compromise, and this perception made them write about marriage in a pragmatic way, however elevated their ideals might be. Their attitude has a political parallel. Richard II believed in a mystical union – articulated by James I – between king and crown. Bolingbroke saw it as a pragmatic relation, and, despite his uneasy conscience, bequeathed

---

[74] *The Lawes Resolutions of Womens Rights*, pp. 124–5, 4.

[75] R. Clifton, 'The Fear of Catholics in England 1637–45', unpublished D. Phil. thesis, University of Oxford, 1967.

to Henry V the politics rather than the religion of kingship:

> You won it, wore it, kept it, gave it me;
> Then plain and right must my possession be.[76]

The preacher Henry Smith speaks, in an age when the word 'policy' was redolent with Machiavellian association, of 'the best pollicie in Marriage.'[77] When Richard II parts from his queen he accuses Northumberland of effecting two divisions of parallel weight:

> Doubly divorc'd! Bad men, you violate
> A two-fold marriage – 'twixt my crown and me,
> And then betwixt me and my married wife.[78]

Richard relied on God to preserve his union with his crown – and probably also with his wife. But God could not keep him king without help, as the Bishop of Carlisle was swift to point out. The Puritans believed that God could not make marriage an ideal state of being without help from both partners, and the preachers continually asked themselves what kind of help it ought to be.

Unity, in Puritan eyes, conferred on man and wife an equal division of labour. Both are responsible as individuals for their joint identity as a couple. Adriana attacks her husband for a way of life he would not tolerate in her. He has divided the sacred union between them:

> How comes it now, my husband, O, how comes it,
> That thou art then estrangèd from thy self?
> Thyself I call it, being strange to me,
> That, undividable, incorporate,
> Am better than thy dear self's better part.
> . . . .
> How dearly would it touch thee to the quick,
> Shouldst thou but hear I were licentious,
> And that this body, consecrate to thee,

[76] *Henry IV* Part II, IV.v.221.
[77] *A Preparative to Mariage*, p. 58.
[78] *Richard II*, V.i.71.

By ruffian lust should be contaminate!
Wouldst thou not spit at me, and spurn at me,
And hurl the name of husband in my face,
And tear the stained skin off my harlot-brow,
And from my false hand cut the wedding-ring,
And break it with a deep-divorcing vow?

She urges him, with triumphant logic, to castigate her for a lust which infects her through their union:

I know thou canst, and therefore see thou do it.
I am possessed with an adulterate blot;
My blood is mingled with the crime of lust.
For if we two be one, and thou play false,
I do digest the poison of thy flesh,
Being strumpeted by thy contagion.
Keep then fair league and truce with thy true bed;
I live distained, thou undishonorèd.[79]

Her ideology is the one which determined the Puritan attack on the double standard.

Adriana is conscious, however, of chop-logic, a syllogism masked by the truthfulness of the spirit in which she argues. Unity can never be literal: it is only ever a 'wise fiction,' and the drama richly counterpoints the Puritan spirit of ideal union with the absurdity of taking it literally. The Provost in *Measure for Measure*, trying to recruit a hangman, asks Pompey if he can cut off a man's head. He asserts, with bawdy pun: 'If the man be a bachelor, sir, I can; but if he be a married man, he's his wife's head, and I can never cut off a woman's head.'[80] The man in Middleton's *The Old Law* who confides a secret to his wife on the grounds that telling her is no more than telling himself, bows to religion but offends common sense.

The doctrine of two in one describes a quality of feeling, the loyalty with which Mistress Arthur in *How a Man May Choose a Good Wife from a Bad* insists that to call her husband a villain is to

[79] *The Comedy of Errors*, II.ii.118.
[80] IV.ii.2.

implicate her:

> If he be call'd a villain, what is she,
> Whose heart and love, and soul, is one with him?

She accuses her father, in language weighty with the solemnity of Cranmer's marriage service, of trying, through his proposal to take her home, to separate her from her husband:

> Will you divorce whom God hath tied together?
> Or break that knot the sacred hand of heaven
> Made fast betwixt us? Have you never read,
> What a great curse was laid upon his head
> That breaks the holy band of marriage,
> Divorcing husbands from their chosen wives?[81]

Theology offers her a medium for articulating the passionate and exclusive involvement of marriage. Adriana opposes the Abbess in *The Comedy of Errors* on the same ground:

> I will not hence and leave my husband here;
> And ill it doth beseem your holiness
> To separate the husband and the wife.

Both women, Adriana unknowingly, address parents. Shakespeare wrote into the encounter between Adriana and the Abbess the instinctive, primitive hostility and competition for ownership between the mother of a man and his wife. Parents, who are one with their children through the tie of blood, are always the last to accept the metaphysical union which supersedes it, when the child forsakes his kin and cleaves to a stranger. The Puritans' gift to their world lay in the replacing of the legal union of the arranged marriage with a union born of the spirit.

The Comedy of Errors ends on a note of equilibrium. The natural equality of the twins becomes a symbol of a new concord between man and wife:

> We came into the world like brother and brother,
> And now let's go hand in hand, not one before another.[82]

---

[81] I.iii.   [82] v.i.109, 425.

Elizabethan obedience plays, with their motley multitude of shrews and patient husbands, gadders and gaolers, all resolve into a balance of power, disavowing exclusive authority in either husband or wife. The only outsider, disconcertingly, is *The Taming of the Shrew*, ending with a full-blown apostrophe to obedience, spoken by a woman who offers to place her hand under her husband's foot to 'do him ease.' A good Puritan would have been shocked by such excess, for the woman was not 'made of the fete (as though thou mightest spurne her a waye from the and nothing regarde her)'[83] reproves Bullinger in a passage dear to the writers of domestic conduct books. Audiences are dismayed by such obscurantism in a poet who always turns toward the light. Like Luciana's championing of domestic order in reproof of her sister's demand for equal liberty, Kate's rebuke of her fellow brides' perversity seems deceptively like an embodiment of the play's ultimate philosophy:

> Fie, fie, unknit that threat'ning unkind brow,
> And dart not scornful glances from those eyes,
> To wound thy lord, thy king, thy governor:
> . . . .
> Thy husband is thy lord, thy life, thy keeper,
> Thy head, thy sovereign; one that cares for thee
> And for thy maintenance; commits his body
> To painful labor, both by sea and land;
> To watch the night in storms, the day in cold,
> Whilst thou li'st warm at home, secure and safe,
> And craves no other tribute at thy hands,
> But love, fair looks, and true obedience.

As all the dramatists are liberal in their opposition to the idea of an authoritarian husband, it seems particularly disconcerting that Shakespeare, who in all other fields is more liberal than any of them, should make the most reactionary comment on women's obedience. But Kate's speech should not be taken at face value. When Beaumont and Fletcher wrote *The Woman's Prize, or The*

---

[83] *The Christen State of Matrimonye*, sig. Aiiij^v.

Tamer Tam'd about the wife who tamed a taming husband –
Maria, second wife to Shakespeare's Petruchio – they depicted
Kate, now deceased, as a lifelong shrew, resistant to a lifelong pro-
gramme of taming. What had happened to Petruchio's triumph at
the end of Shakespeare's play?

The extreme positions taken up by Kate and Petruchio – her
shrewishness, his undeterred and unqualified adherence to mercenary motives for marriage, her revolution into an obedience as absolute as St Paul could have wished – form part of a pattern of
transformation in the play. Just as Christopher Sly the beggar is
transformed into a lord for the duration of the play, with a player-
boy as the lady his wife – 'in all obedience' – so Kate and Petruchio
adopt the most hyperbolic postures open to man and wife in their
relation to each other, as the premise for real life.

Kate and Petruchio are players, fictions whom Shakespeare
allows to assume real proportions. Their reality is as much an illusion as Christopher Sly's lordliness. In the ephemeral real world
created for them in their play, reality is also tampered with. A
series of transformations – Lucentio into a tutor, Hortensio into a
musician, Tranio into Lucentio – undermine the characters' assumptions of what is real. Fact becomes irrelevant. Petruchio
wooes Kate as though she were the girl she is not:

> 'Twas told me you were rough and coy and sullen,
> And now I find report a very liar;
> For thou art pleasant, gamesome, passing courteous,
> But slow in speech; yet sweet as spring-time flowers.
> Thou canst not frown, thou canst not look askance,
> Nor bite the lip as angry wenches will,
> Nor hast thou pleasure to be cross in talk;
> But thou with mildness entertain'st thy wooers,
> With gentle conference, soft and affable.

Kate accepts her husband's version of old Vincentio's appearance:

> Young budding virgin, fair and fresh and sweet,
> Whither away, or where is thy abode?
> Happy the parents of so fair a child;

> Happier the man, whom favorable stars
> Allots thee for his lovely bedfellow!

Petruchio chooses to correct her:

> This is a man, old, wrinkled, faded, withered,
> And not a maiden, as thou say'st he is.

She accepts his judgement, not because this is the truth and the other is false, but because she has agreed to accept his judgement of what is true as the absolute truth. Whether the facts of the real world and his judgement of them concur is of no significance. She excuses herself disarmingly:

> Pardon, old father, my mistaking eyes,
> That have been so bedazzled with the sun,
> That every thing I look on seemeth green.

This cavalier sporting with reality culminates in the confrontation of the assumed Vincentio (the Pedant in disguise) with the genuine:

Pedant [to Petruchio]: Thou liest. His father is come from Mantua, and is here looking out at the window.

Vincentio: Art thou his father?

Pedant: Ay, sir, so his mother says, if I may believe her.

The authentic is routed by the make-believe. Vincentio almost doubts his own identity under reiterated accusations of impersonating the man he is. In the concrete world in which these people move, so many of the characters are impersonating someone else that those who are not impersonating anyone, have as tenuous a hold on reality as those who are. And this images the truth, which is that they are all impersonating human beings in their roles as players.

In this mirage Kate's new ideal obedience bears as fragile a relation to the actual world of human experience as her original curst shrewishness, or Christopher Sly's sudden splendour. Baptista's wondering observation: 'For she is changed as she had never been,' strikes the central note of ambiguity in the play – the magical change of a character whose identity was a fiction. The final lines of the play, as crucial to its understanding as the last couplet in *The Comedy of Errors*, cast doubt on the possibility of such a transformation in the world that Christopher Sly must now reinhabit. Hortensio, gazing after Petruchio, muses: 'Now go thy ways, thou hast tamed a curst shrow,' but Lucentio answers him with:

> 'Tis a wonder, by your leave, she will be taméd so.[84]

Shakespeare leaves the question open. To end the play with a return to the concreteness of Christopher Sly's beggary would mean insisting that it was only illusion which gave birth to the vision of domestic order. Slie in the earlier *The Taming of a Shrew* awakes, like Bottom, from 'a most rare vision,' and hurries home to face the music from his harridan wife. Shakespeare's story of Kate's taming allows the audience to feel that this is their own absolute factual world represented on the stage, while retaining their intellectual awareness that the humanity of the characters is momentary. Shakespeare lets the play-within-a-play usurp the real play: the audience has to take it seriously. But he casts a shadow of ambiguity across its conclusions without ever asserting categorically, by a crude reversion to the natural world, that they exist in a rarified and frangible context. Shakespeare postulates domestic harmony – the loving submission of the wife to her husband's cherishing authority – in an equivocal setting. Kate's transformation is a miracle in the world where miracles happen, the theatre, where beggars are lords.

Kate's submission gives her power over Petruchio. The Puritans interpreted a wife's submission as a mode of behaviour which could coexist with liberty. They retained the form of authority, but altered its spirit. The Clown in *All's Well That Ends Well* mocks his own subjection to the Countess, his mistress: 'That man should be at woman's command, and yet no hurt done! Though honesty be no puritan, yet it will do no hurt; it will wear the

[84] *The Taming of the Shrew*, v.ii.141, Ind.ii.107, II.i.245, IV.v.37, v.i.30, v.ii.120, 192.

surplice of humility over the black gown of a big heart.' Honesty is no Puritan because it obliges him, in his office as servant, to submit to a woman, and the Puritans declared for a man's authority in the household. But for each Puritan ousted from his pulpit for refusing to wear a surplice, there would be another who used the surplice to hide the Puritan black gown, maintaining his freedom within by submitting in externals. Helena submits to Bertram's command that she leave him unless she can prove herself his wife with his ring and his child, but her obedience defies his desire to be rid of her. She wears the vestment of humility over a big heart. The Puritans saw a woman's submission to her husband as a condition of freedom in the same way that a man submits to God 'whose service is perfect freedom.' This paradox, which pervades Christianity, not only posed to the reformers the question of freewill and predestination, but enhanced their consciousness that freedom of conscience imposed its own burdens, perhaps even more onerous to a man like Bunyan than the lack of freedom involved in recognising the authority of the Church. Puritan marriage is a hazardous ideal making demands on the individual man and woman by the side of which the arranged marriage almost looks easy. The thin ice, as regards the Puritans' attitudes to women, lay not in their actual reform of marriage practices, but in their assumption that goodwill on its own was strong enough to free a woman from a tyranny which grew, as Mill noticed, from male self-interest. They opened doors for good men, but provided no boots for kicking bad ones through them. Human nature, as the dramatists observed, is always the constant to the variable of human principle. As the Clown remarks in *All's Well That Ends Well*:

> If men could be contented to be what they are, there were no fear in marriage; for young Charbon the puritan and old Poysam the papist, howsome'er their hearts are sever'd in religion, their heads are both one; they may jowl horns together like any deer i' th' herd.[85]

Caroline drama mocked the Puritan idea of liberty in marriage, pointing aristocratic fingers at insubordinate city wives, and

[85] I.iii.89, 48.

applauding the woman who, like Mrs Wilding in the plot given to Shirley by Charles I for *The Gamester*, makes no retaliation to domestic tyranny. No doubt Charles heard the political undertones as clearly as the character in Suckling's *Brennoralt* who exclaims: ''Sfoot, let the king make an act that any man may be unmarried again: there's liberty for them! a race of half-witted fellows quarrel about freedom, and all that while allow the bonds of matrimony.'[86] The household was still the mirror of the State.

One critic argues that the Puritan doctrine of subordination in equality – some animals are more equal than others – arose from the problem of reconciling the belief in spiritual equality with adherence to the letter of the Scriptures,[87] containing as it did, St Paul's well-known advice about lesser vessels. But the Puritan answer to Adriana's question was a straightforward one: in marriage liberty was a process of checks and balances, of shifting authorities based on mutual consent. The democratic ideal, as conservatives were only too well aware, had its microcosm in the hearth. Petruchio could only play the part of lord if Kate agreed to the game.

2 *Women as Property*

When Moll Flanders declared her principle that 'a woman should never be kept for a mistress that had money to make herself a wife,'[1] Defoe, uncompromisingly Puritan himself, put his finger on the problem which perplexed the early Puritans. Wife or whore, 'a woman still is current ware,'[2] as a character remarks in Massinger's *The Fatal Dowry*.

It was easy for the Puritans to protest against the more grotesque aspects of treating women as property – forced marriages, prostitution, adultery for the sort of price that Volpone offers Corvino for Celia, and wife sale – the poor man's mode of divorce which features in Middleton's *The Phoenix*. But, like the Player Queen in

[86] I.iii.50.
[87] Christopher Hill, 'Clarissa Harlowe and her Times', *Essays in Criticism*, v (1955) no. 4, 333, 334.
[1] *Moll Flanders*, p. 69.
[2] v.ii.341.

Hamlet, prating her disapproval for 'base respects of thrift but none of love,'[3] the Puritans experienced a little difficulty when put to the test. Thrift was very dear to them, and they laboured for an attitude to the wife which would make love compatible with thrift without turning the woman into a good bargain. 'Pray, my dear aunt,' demands Elizabeth Bennet after the defection of Wickham in *Pride and Prejudice*, 'What is the difference in matrimonial affairs between the mercenary and the prudent motive? Where does discretion end, and avarice begin?'[4] The Puritans replied that avarice began when a man treated his wife like a whore.

A man's relation to his whore was that of owner. Her services had been bought and he might treat her in any way which gave him pleasure – as a goddess, as Brachiano treats Vittoria, darkly bartering his jewel for her jewel in *The White Devil*; as a bauble – Cassio's attitude to Bianca in *Othello*; as a servant to his interests, as Witgood considers the Courtesan in *A Trick to Catch the Old One*; even as a stimulus – Antipholus of Ephesus is happy to quit a shrewish hearth for a jaunty supper table:

> I know a wench of excellent discourse,
> Pretty and witty, wild and yet, too, gentle.
> There will we dine.

An Agony Aunt would advise Adriana to offer these attractions in her own dining-room, but she would have met a tart retort:

> His company must do his minions grace,
> Whilst I at home starve for a merry look.
> Hath homely age th'alluring beauty took
> From my poor cheek? Then he hath wasted it.
> Are my discourses dull? barren my wit?
> If voluble and sharp discourse be marred
> Unkindness blunts it more than marble hard.
> Do their gay vestments his affections bait?
> That's not my fault; he's master of my state.
> What ruins are in me that can be found

[3] III.ii.182.
[4] Jane Austen, *Pride and Prejudice*, ch. xxvii.

> By him not ruined? Then is he the ground
> Of my defeatures. My decayèd fair
> A sunny look of his would soon repair.
> But, too unruly deer, he breaks the pale
> And feeds from home; poor I am but his stale.

Luciana – Shakespeare's Agony Aunt – can only caution her sister against jealousy. Adriana is Antipholus' stale because without love their relation is one of property: 'He's master of my state.' His whore enjoys a partnership of the mind which should belong to his wife. Without it Adriana is no different from a whore except in being recognised socially. Antipholus' unwillingness to treat her as an equal mentally makes it impossible for her to be one. Voluble and sharp discourse requires exercise, which is why the wench's continues to be excellent when the wife's has grown dull. Luciana's real answer to her sister is reserved for Antipholus:

> If you did wed my sister for her wealth,
> Then for her wealth's sake use her with more kindness.[5]

Such logic is not gratifying to women, but it is likely to be intelligible to men.

The Humanists saw the pursuit of pleasure as the hallmark of lust. Men who courted women for their beauty made them whores by denying them equality of mind, which for men like Vives and More and Erasmus was the only thing which made marriage meaningful. 'Ther shalbe in wedlocke a certayne swete and pleasaunt conversation, without the whiche it is no maryage but a prysone,'[6] said Vives. Women must be educated because with an ignorant wife the sympathy which Erasmus described is impossible: 'It is an especyall swetnes to have one with whom ye may communycate the secrete affectyons of your mynde, with whom ye may speake even as it were with your owne self, whome ye may savely truste, whyche supposethe your chaunces to be his, what felycyte (thynke ye) have the conjunction of man and wyfe, than whych no thynge in the unyversall worlde may be founde outher

---

[5] *The Comedy of Errors*, iii.i.109, ii.i.87, iii.ii.5.
[6] *The Office and Duetie of an Husband*, sig. Nvii.

greater or fermer.'[7] A century later, poor Milton, mated with Mary who ran home to mother after a month of matrimony, came to the same conclusions: 'And what greater nakednes or unfitnes of mind then that which hinders ever the solace and peacefull society of the maried couple, and what hinders that more then the unfitnes and defectivenes of an unconjugal mind?' Milton believed that sexual inadequacies were less destructive of marriage than a mental incompatibility which would poison the sexual relation, and argued that if the spiritual union of man and wife brought them nearer to God, 'wherin can God delight, wherin be worshipt, wherin be glorify'd by the forcible continuing of an improper and ill-yoking couple?'[8] The Puritans cannot be blamed for falling short of Milton's radicalism about divorce: English law has taken more than three centuries to accept his arguments. William Perkins did at least insist that women have as much right as men to require divorce. 'The reason is, because they are equally bound each to other, and have also the same interest in one anothers bodie.'[9]

The Humanists denounced 'carnall lust and pleasure'[10] in the interests of the marriage of minds which Donne preached for man and wife: 'Not always like in complexion, nor like in years, nor like in fortune, nor like in birth, but like in minde, like in disposition, like in the love of God, and of one another.'[11] The whore could never rise out of the circle of pleasure into the sphere of partnership between equals. Plutarch's Portia is apologetic in her plea for Brutus' confidence; Shakespeare's demands it as her inalienable right – a demand which had both Humanist and Puritan backing:

> Within the bond of marriage, tell me, Brutus,
> Is it excepted I should know no secrets
> That appertain to you? Am I your self

[7] *In Laude and Prayse of Matrymony*, sigs. Cvi–Cvi[v].
[8] *The Doctrine and Discipline of Divorce*, pp. 244, 246, 277.
[9] *Christian Oeconomie*, p. 120.
[10] Thomas Paynell, Foreword to Vives, *The Office and Duetie of an Husband*, sig. Aij[v].
[11] *The Sermons of John Donne*, III, 247.

But, as it were, in sort or limitation?
To keep with you at meals, comfort your bed,
And talk to you sometimes? Dwell I but in the suburbs
Of your good pleasure? If it be no more,
Portia is Brutus' harlot, not his wife.[12]

That the suburbs housed harlots was no news to a Globe audience
on the South Bank. Portia repudiates the image of herself as a play-
thing in the interests of a more serious relation between husband
and wife, which, unlike Plutarch's heroine, she blames Brutus for
obstructing: she expects to find in marriage that identity of concern delineated by Erasmus.

To be permanently providing light relief to serious men, to be in
essence a symbol of that light relief in one's very being, allies
women with professional Fools, as Shakespeare perceived when he
depicted the peculiar sympathy between his Fools and his heroines.
– Celia and Touchstone, Viola and Feste, Cordelia and the Fool in
King Lear. Both stand on the periphery of the serious world of
men, assessing its wisdom from the perspective of not being of any
account. 'Thou art a fool,' scoffs Duke Frederick to Celia when she
defends Rosalind: 'She robs thee of thy name.'[13] The values of
women and Fools are an irritant to men: their function is to entertain, not to censure; but as critics they are not dangerous, because
they have no power. 'Take heed, sirrah; the whip,' might just as
well have been said by Antipholus to his wife as by Lear to his
Fool. With Cordelia in his arms, Lear murmurs: 'And my poor
fool is hang'd.'[14] His Fool and his daughter share the same area of
his consciousness.

Lydgate, in *Middlemarch*, destroyed by a wife who adorned and
entertained in the best tradition of feminine light relief, might
cherish the bitter knowledge that, like many husbands, he had got
what he wanted. Considering wives, he had previously reflected
that Miss Brooke 'did not look at things from the proper feminine
angle. The society of such women was about as relaxing as going

[12] *Julius Caesar*, II.i.280.
[13] *As You Like It*, I.iii.80.
[14] *King Lear*, I.iv.116, v.iii.305.

from your work to teach the second form, instead of reclining in a paradise with sweet laughs for bird-notes, and blue eyes for a heaven.'[15] Rosamund's angry indifference to his work contrasts with Dorothea's eagerness to lend him the money to free himself from Bulstrode. Lydgate saw wives as respectable and legalised whores, transferring to Rosamund the mindless adulation he had felt for the actress, Laure. But Mary Wollstonecraft had asked a question at the beginning of the century which focused what the Puritans, educated by Erasmus on marriage, felt to be the essential difference between wife and whore. She inquired: 'How then can the great art of pleasing be such a necessary study? It is only useful to a mistress. The chaste wife and serious mother should only consider her power to please as the polish of her virtues.'[16]

The pleasure which the Puritans felt a man should find in his wife did not arise from the gratification of the senses. Their interpretation of pleasure was more comprehensive. Barnaby Rich described the ideal wife: 'A man that wanteth a friend for pleasure, a servant for profit, a counsellour to advise him, a comforter to cherish him, a companion to solace him, a helper to assist him, or a spirituall instructor to informe him, a good and vertuous wife doth supply all these occasions.'[17] The role of counsellor and spiritual instructor makes its own comment on the view that women had no souls. Erasmus had urged the woman's right to be her husband's critic and adviser – that aspect of women's equality which even a man like Franklin Roosevelt, perhaps, like Lydgate, hankering for bird-notes and blue eyes after a difficult day – found hard to take.[18] When Erasmus warned the wife against abrasiveness he made no concessions to male sensitivity: elsewhere he makes it plain that husbands should be equally diplomatic: 'It is laufull that the wyfe tell the good man his faute, if that it be matter of substaunce . . . betwixt you two secretly he must be told his faute gently, or rather intreated, that in this thynge or that he play the better husbande, to loke better to his good name and fame and to his helth and this

[15] George Eliot, *Middlemarch*, p. 122.

[16] *The Rights of Woman*, p. 32.

[17] *The Excellency of Good Women*, p. 2.

[18] Joseph P. Lash, *Eleanor and Franklin*, p. 337.

tellyng must be myxt with mery conceites and pleasaunt wordes many times.'[19] Adriana had a perfect right to berate her husband for his treatment of her, but by Erasmus' standard her methods, like his in sending for the rope, were too violent.

When the Abbess effects a *volte face* from blaming Adriana for not criticising enough to criticising too much, Shakespeare dissects a traditional attitude to women nourished by the Church as well as by popular prejudice. If a marriage goes wrong, not only is the woman to blame, but it is her responsibility to put it right, whatever that may involve. The Puritans were not so facile; they sympathised with Adriana, wryly biting her lip at an ecclesiastical sleight of hand: 'She did betray me to my own reproof.'[20] Marriage, to a preacher like Henry Smith, was a two-way process, balancing weakness and strength equally in both partners. 'To begin this concord well, it is necessarie to learne one anothers nature, and one anothers affections, and one anothers infirmities, because ye must be helpers, and ye cannot help, unlesse ye know the disease.' The joy of marriage is not dependent, like the pleasure of whoredom, on youth and beauty, for 'mariage doth signifie merriage, because a playfellow is come to make our age merrie.'[21] This is the tone of Lorenzo's gay retort to Jessica's praise of Portia:

> Even such a husband
> Hast thou of me as she is for a wife.

She cries: 'Nay, but ask my opinion too of that!' He suggests they go to dinner first, and she answers: 'Nay, let me praise you while I have a stomach.'[22] Lorenzo laughs at his own male chauvinism, but he could not laugh at it were Jessica his whore, because then his power over her, the power of a man over his property, would make their inequalities too great and material, for jesting. Dorothy Osborne articulated the Puritan conviction that a wife possessed a relation to her husband different in kind from that of the whore to

---

[19] *A Mery Dialogue, declaringe the Propertyes of Shrowde Shrewes, and Honest Wyves*, sig. Avii[v].

[20] *The Comedy of Errors*, v.i.90.

[21] *A Preparative to Mariage*, pp. 59, 11–12.

[22] *The Merchant of Venice*, III.v.76.

her lover, when she wrote to Temple that 'there are a great many
ingredients must goe to the makeing mee happy in a husband, first,
. . . our humors must agree.'[23] For the Puritans the marriage of true
minds had to be marriage, not whoredom, because the conditions
of whoredom made such a relation impossible.

In late Elizabethan drama the view that the purpose of women is
to please is the prerogative of whores and whoremongers. Zanthia,
the whore in Marston's *Sophonisba*, speaks of

> We things cal'd women, only made for show
> And *pleasure*, created to beare children
> And play at shuttle-coke; we imperfect mixtures.[24]

Iago's insinuations to Cassio in praising Desdemona belittle her by
talking of her as a woman made to give pleasure – in other words a
whore: 'What an eye she has! Methinks it sounds a parley to
provocation.' Cassio, without knowing why, senses something
compromising to Desdemona, and replies: 'An inviting eye; and
yet methinks right modest.'[25] Cleopatra, despite her prevarica-
tions, is governed by the need to please, to refuel Antony's awareness that 'though I make this marriage for my peace, / I' the east my
pleasure lies.'[26] But in a woman like Hermione pleasure is a concept altogether inadequate to express the painful and yet durable
identity which binds her to Leontes and reunites them when youth
and beauty both are gone. The idea of love in the last scene of *The
Winter's Tale* – 'She embraces him!' / 'She hangs about his neck'[27]
– would be desecrated by the triviality of pleasure.

One of the difficulties for the Puritans was to decide how married sex differed from lustful sex – that is, sex outside marriage.
Erasmus enunciated two main principles; in marriage sexual union
completed and fulfilled the union of like minds: 'For what thynge
is sweter, then with her to lyve, with whome ye may be most
streyghtly copuled, nat onely in the benevolence of the mynd, but

[23] *The Letters of Dorothy Osborne to William Temple*, p. 105.

[24] I.ii.20.

[25] *Othello*, II.iii.22.

[26] *Antony and Cleopatra*, II.iii.38.

[27] v.iii.111.

also in the conjunction of the body.' Secondly, the joy of sexual love renewed the joy of marriage, and Erasmus is full of cogent advice about not quarrelling in the bedroom: 'Be wyse of this especyall that thou never gyve hym foule wordes in the chambre, or in bed, but be sure that all thynges there bee full of pastyme and pleasure. For yf that place which is ordeined to make amendes for all fautes and so to renew love, be polluted, eyther with strife or grugynges, then fayre wel al hope of love daies, or atonementes, yet there be some beastes so wayward and mischevous, that when theyr husbandes hath them in their armes a bed, they scholde and chyde.'[28] The Puritans repudiated the process by which sex completed a man's ownership of the wife he had bought. To them sexual union was meaningless unless it expressed spiritual union. But they were also anxious that married love should not be legalised lust – the quirk of law by which the Duke in *Women Beware Women* exonerates himself from guilt for his adultery with Bianca by planning to marry her.

The desire to distinguish the sexual impulse in marriage from its irregular counterpart prompted continual counsel about temperate sex in the sixteenth century, which sounds strange to a modern ear. Vives, always a peculiar mixture of liberal and conservative, said: 'Let everye man use his owne vessell in sanctification and holynes.'[29] Calvin preached moderation in marriage. Donne declared that without restraint 'marriage is but a continual fornication, sealed with an oath.'[30] If it seems on the surface like an attempt to harness the ascetic ideal to a non-ascetic state, in reality it demonstrated a concern to separate marriage from the impulses which dictate adultery and whoredom. Posthumus' account of Imogen's chastity proves not only his gullibility in believing her a whore, but the degree to which he himself had confused the married relation with the relation a man might expect with his whore:

> Me of my lawful pleasure she restrain'd,
> And pray'd me oft forbearance: did it with

[28] *In Laude and Prayse of Matrymony*, sig. Cvi; *A Mery Dialogue, declaringe the Propertyes of Shrowde Shrewes, and Honest Wyves*, sig. Bvi.
[29] *The Office and Duetie of an Husband*, sig. Rv.
[30] *The Sermons of John Donne*, II, 346.

> A pudency so rosy, the sweet view on't
> Might well have warm'd old Saturn; that I thought her
> As chaste as unsunn'd snow.[31]

Posthumus has not worked out for himself the difference between the wedded wife and the whore, and this makes him susceptible to Iachimo's innuendoes. When Othello requests that Desdemona accompany him to Cyprus he disclaims motives of lust: 'I therefore beg it not / To please the palate of my appetite,' dissociating himself from the sordid theft and seduction motif which dominates the conversation not only of Iago but of the father, Brabantio:

> Look to her, Moor, if thou hast eyes to see,
> She hath deceived her father, and may thee.[32]

Shakespeare is the only dramatist who understood what the Puritans meant by restraint: that it was a way of differentiating in kind between marriage and whoredom. For other playwrights it is a point of irony – Tamyra excusing herself in *Bussy D'Ambois* from lying with her husband after she has lain with her lover, on the grounds that coupling in the daytime – according to her Friar – spells luxury. Bianca in *Women Beware Women*, seduced by the Duke in the first fortnight of marriage to Leantio, pushes her returning husband away with an admonition to 'grow serious.'[33] In *Epicoene* Truewit mocks the reluctant Morose's escape from his own wedding-feast by construing it as haste to get to bed with his bride, reproving him: 'A man of your head and hair should owe more to that reverend ceremony, and not mount the marriage-bed like a town-bull or a mountain goat, but stay the due season and ascend it then with religion and fear.'[34] Petruchio leads Kate upstairs, and his servant reports that he is 'In her chamber, making a sermon of continency to her.'[35] When the Puritans preached temperate sex in marriage they wanted, by dissociating marriage from

---

[31] *Cymbeline*, II.iv.161.

[32] *Othello*, I.iii.261, 292.

[33] Middleton, *Women Beware Women*, III.i.166.

[34] Jonson, *Epicoene, or The Silent Woman*, III.v.42.

[35] *The Taming of the Shrew*, IV.i.170.

the heat of the brothel, to clarify their conviction that being a wife owed nothing to the commerce of being a whore.

Like Milton in *Paradise Lost* the playwrights of Shakespeare's theatre found it difficult to evoke a poetic image of sex in marriage which would be different from sex outside marriage. Vittoria's passion for Brachiano in *The White Devil* takes fire emotionally, where the chaste wife's (Isabella's) remains cold and querulous. Beatrice in Marston's *The Dutch Courtezan* is a pale and ineffectual figure beside the insouciant courtesan, and between her and Free-vill there is a complete lack of the dynamism which characterises his encounters with Franceschina. All of the dramatists except Shakespeare have trouble with married sex, growing either senti-mental or sententious. Outside Shakespeare's plays probably the exception is *The Duchess of Malfi*, in which Webster masters the art of suggesting the sensuous without making it simultaneously sinful. Marston, by contrast, makes married sex sinless – as in the union of Dulcimel and Tiberio in *The Fawn* – but he also makes it sexless. As poets the Elizabethans could not free themselves from the ancient poetic associations of chastity – Queen and huntress, chaste and fair, the austerity of Diana, the remoteness of Phoebe, an imaginative context of coldness and distance. Chastity in mar-riage is both creative and communicative, but in the drama the chaste wife – and the chaster she is, the more true this is – tends to be associated with loss. Octavia, who is 'of a holy, cold and still conversation,' never stands a chance against Cleopatra, 'That am with Phoebus' amorous pinches black, / And wrinkled deep in time'[36] – the competition of moon and sun. Virgilia in *Coriolanus* is downtrodden, wielding no influence over her husband despite her chastity. Katherine in *Henry VIII* is ousted by the whore who will bear the Virgin Queen. Desdemona is justified only in death:

> Cold, cold, my girl?
> Even like thy chastity.[37]

Shakespeare freed himself from the concept of sex in marriage as

---

[36] *Antony and Cleopatra*, II.vi.119, I.v.28.
[37] *Othello*, v.ii.276.

an act of power and possession, and in this he was true to one of the most difficult, and unfortunately least durable, aspects of Puritanism. Juliet's gift of love to Romeo defies the economics of property:

> My bounty is as boundless as the sea,
> My love as deep: the more I give to thee
> The more I have: for both are infinite.[38]

The generosity of sexual love in marriage permeates the last plays. Leontes laments to Paulina shortly before he sees the statue:

>   O, that ever I
> Had squar'd me to thy counsel! Then, even now,
> I might have look'd upon my queen's full eyes,
> Have taken treasure from her lips, –

Paulina completes his thought: 'And left them / More rich for what they yielded.'[39] If sex has nothing to do with property, then there is no loss involved in sexual love: Shakespeare realises Erasmus' logic in art. The image of sex as completion which grows from the Puritan interpretation of Eden dominates the reunion of Posthumus and Imogen in *Cymbeline*. Imogen embraces him: 'Think that you are upon a rock, and now / Throw me again.' He replies:

> Hang there like fruit, my soul,
> Till the tree die.[40]

When Shakespeare allowed Juliet to articulate passion in terms of property he pointed her innocence of a world in which love was subordinated to property:

> O, I have bought the mansion of a love,
> But not possessed it; and though I am sold,
> Not yet enjoyed.[41]

[38] *Romeo and Juliet*, II.ii.133.
[39] *The Winter's Tale*, v.i.51.
[40] v.v.262.
[41] *Romeo and Juliet*, III.ii.26.

The nature of sexual love in marriage was a quicksand on which several dramatists foundered. They were on much firmer ground when they demonstrated in the first place the similarities between whores and respectable women, and in the second, the conditions of life for which the ephemeral pleasures of lust were too high a price to pay.

The differences between the whore and the wife are obvious. The whore is a tradeswoman, 'A housewife that by selling her desires / Buys herself bread and clothes,'[42] as Iago describes Bianca. Whores and usurers are the twin parasites of Jacobean society, exploiting vice, and wealthy without labour or end product: an underworld aristocracy. The whore depends on the self-advertisement scorned by Coriolanus:

> Away, my disposition, and possess me
> Some harlot's spirit.[43]

The irony of her situation is that in one sense she 'is beholden to no trade, but lives of herself,'[44] while in another she conforms to a Puritan economic pattern by running her own business and supporting herself on it. She labours in her 'vocation.'[45] Like Moll Flanders, the whore in the drama copes with the restrictions society imposes on women without money. When Puritanism alerted the dramatists to the condition of ordinary women it aroused their curiosity about women who evaded that condition. The dramatists speak with a double voice about whores. On the one hand the whore – whether Mistress Mary in *How a Man May Choose a Good Wife from a Bad*, or the Courtesan in Middleton's *A Mad World, my Masters*, or Doll Tearsheet setting her cap at Prince Hal from the vantage point of Falstaff's knee – cocks a snook at a society which rewards virtue in women with subjection. On the other hand, she threatens the 'charities' of family life which Renaissance dramatists valued as highly as Milton did. They wanted to show that marriage offered a woman a better life, but

[42] *Othello*, IV.i.94.
[43] *Coriolanus*, III.ii.111.
[44] *How a Man May Choose a Good Wife from a Bad*, III.ii.
[45] Marston, *The Dutch Courtezan*, I.ii.144.

could not help observing that a whore like Mistress Mary seemed a less oppressed being than a wife like Mistress Arthur.

The position of the unmarried woman was only different from the position of the whore in being labelled respectable. In the arranged marriage the parent is the bawd of polite society. Becky Sharp in *Vanity Fair* is whorish in her pursuit of Josh Sedley not because it is a pursuit, but because she conducts it herself. Thackeray pleads indulgence for her, 'for though the task of husband-hunting is generally, and with becoming modesty, entrusted by young persons to their mammas, recollect that Miss Sharp had no kind parent to arrange these delicate matters for her, and that if she did not get a husband for herself, there was no one else in the wide world who would take the trouble off her hands.'[46] At the end of the sixteenth century fathers arranged the sale of their daughters over the port, as Clare's father arranges her marriage to Scarborow in *The Miseries of Enforced Marriage*. But where in the plays of Lope de Vega the relation of father and daughter is feudal, as in *Fuenteovejuna* where Laurencia accuses her father of not protecting her until her marriage, in Elizabethan drama it is capitalist. A daughter is a man's best investment, as others knew as well as Shylock – 'my ducats and my daughter' – and her assets are realised when she is bought by the consumer, her suitor. The bawd in *The Dutch Courtezan* boasts to the courtesan: 'And you had been mine own daughter, I could not ha' sold your maidenhead oft'ner than I ha' done.'[47]

For avaricious fathers love is for women and cash is for men. When the dramatists uphold the love match against the mercenary marriage, as they unfailingly do, they uphold women's values against men's, concluding with Fenton in *The Merry Wives of Windsor*, that if a woman escapes the degradation of being bought and sold: 'Th'offence is holy that she hath committed.'[48]

Kitty Scherbatsky, jilted by Vronsky in *Anna Karenina*, experiences disgust at 'the social relations of girls to men,' because they seem nothing more than 'shameful exhibitions of goods awaiting a buyer.'[49] Women in late Elizabethan drama feel the same indigna-

[46] ch. iii.
[48] v.v.216.
[47] Marston, *The Dutch Courtezan*, II.ii.13.
[49] Tolstoy, *Anna Karenina*, II.244.

tion. Kate demands of her father in *The Taming of the Shrew*: 'I pray you, sir, is it your will / To make a stale of me amongst these mates?'[50] In *Women Beware Women* Isabella parades before the foolish Ward who is her father's choice for her in order that he may inspect whether her legs are straight and her teeth white. Her only comfort lies in the prospect of deceiving him:

> But that I have th'advantage of the fool,
> As much as woman's heart can wish and joy at,
> What an infernal torment 'twere to be
> Thus bought and sold, and turn'd and pry'd into.[51]

In such a marriage, adultery is one way for a woman to preserve her self-respect, as to a certain extent Vittoria does in her relation with Brachiano, coupled as she is with the impotent and sottish Camillo. Webster – like the Puritans – sympathised with a woman whose marriage was intolerable, and exposed the institution rather than the individual. Under the system of arranged marriage a woman has to reject the world's assessment of her property worth, if she is to keep any human dignity. Perdita spurns the courtship of bribery:

> She prizes not such trifles as these are:
> The gifts she looks from me are pack'd and lock'd
> Up in my heart.[52]

In *Measure for Measure* Mariana's acceptance of Angelo, who had discarded her for want of a dowry and condemned Claudio for letting love anticipate finance, measures her worth against his. Her spirit is that of Chaucer's Griselda, refusing the Marquis' offer of her dowry as he turns her out of his house, with a charity which defines his quality as much as hers:

> My lord, ye woot that in my fadres place
> Ye dide me streepe out of my povre weede,

---

[50] I.i.57.
[51] Middleton, *Women Beware Women*, III.iii.33.
[52] *The Winter's Tale*, IV.iv.358.

> And richely me cladden, of your grace.
> To yow broghte I noght elles, out of drede,
> But feith, and nakednesse, and maydenhede;
> And heere agayn your clothyng I restoore,
> And eek your weddyng ryng, for everemore.[53]

When France takes Cordelia as his queen he recognises in her a quality of spirit not dependent either on Lear's estimate of her: 'When she was dear to us we did hold her so, / But now her price is fallen,' or on Burgundy's: 'Election makes not up in such conditions.' France sees in her a royalty beyond the majesty of wealth and land:

> Not all the dukes of wat'rish Burgundy
> Can buy this unpriz'd precious maid of me.

The contempt of buying echoes Cordelia's:

> Peace be with Burgundy!
> Since that respect and fortunes are his love,
> I shall not be his wife.

Lear, assessing Cordelia in terms of money – 'Nothing will come of nothing' – finds that he himself is nothing to Goneril and Regan without the property of a king. 'This is not Lear. . . . Who is it that can tell me who I am?' Lear, like Richard II, is one of the few men to enter the experience of women, and discover his own nullity in the eyes of the world once he is separated from his possessions. Cordelia's farewell to her sisters – 'the jewels of our father'[54] – points the irony of Lear's endowing of the daughters who bought his endowments with flattery, and loved him not for what he was, but for what he could give. Burgundy's suit to Cordelia acknowledged the same principles.

The Puritan answer to Elizabeth Bennet's question about motive would have been that Petruchio was mercenary: 'Thou know'st not gold's effect,'[55] Orsino imprudent: 'Tell her, my love,

[53] *The Clerk's Tale*, 862.
[54] *King Lear*, I.i.196, 90, I.iv.234, I.i.268.
[55] *The Taming of the Shrew*, I.ii.91.

more noble than the world, / Prizes not quantity of dirty lands,'[56] and Benedick wise:

> Rich she shall be, that's certain; wise, or I'll none; virtuous, or I'll never cheapen her; fair, or I'll never look on her; mild, or come not near me; noble, or not I for an angel; of good discourse, an excellent musician, and her hair shall be of what colour it please God.[57]

Property was only one of the ingredients Dorothy Osborne might have considered when matching with William Temple. Equality of estate – birth, age, wealth – seemed to the Humanists to further that equality of minds which made marriage more than a property arrangement. Sir Toby swears that his niece will have none of the Count: 'She'll not match above her degree, neither in estate, years, nor wit.'[58] In marriage the man owns the property but not the woman; in whoredom he owns the woman but no property.

Marriage only offered a woman a better life than whoredom, according to the Puritans, if her husband treated her as a partner instead of a possession. In the drama violence is something a man may use towards his whore because he has purchased her person; Othello's striking of Desdemona shocks Ludovico – 'What, strike his wife?'[59] – because it denies her a wife's dignity. Some productions make the point by having Cassio strike Bianca for plaguing him. Intimidation makes a mockery of marriage. Maria in *A Woman's Prize, or The Tamer Tam'd* proclaims:

> That childish woman
> That lives a prisoner to her Husbands pleasure
> Has lost her making, and becomes a beast,
> Created for his use, not fellowship.[60]

The Puritans would have approved of Adriana's restlessness under

---

[56] *Twelfth Night*, II.iv.81.

[57] *Much Ado About Nothing*, II.iii.27.

[58] *Twelfth Night*, I.iii.112.

[59] *Othello*, IV.i.265.

[60] Beaumont and Fletcher, *The Womans Prize, or The Tamer Tam'd*, I.ii.

her husband's rule: 'There's none but asses will be bridled so.'[61] A man may command his whore because their relation is one of property; but the power struggle, as Dekker pointed out when he transformed *Patient Grissil* into a domestic instead of a theological homily, stands in the way of that union of like minds without which marriage can only be a legalised fornication.

The principle of partnership between husband and wife is made more immediate in the drama between 1590 and 1625 by the fact that wives share their husbands' working lives. Wives, whether buying or selling, cajoling or cheating, are as vital to the commerce of Jacobean city life as their husbands, whether Mistress Mulligrub, tavern-keeper's wife in *The Dutch Courtezan*, or Viola, draper's wife in Dekker's *The Honest Whore*, or Mistress Quickly, presumably carrying on after the decease of a shadowy Mr Quickly. The dramatists invented no fiction when they drew wives who were working partners; Elizabethan wives enjoyed a working equality with their husbands which made foreigners declare them to be more liberated in practice than women in any other country.[62] The whore, relegated to the area of leisure, could have no place in a man's working world, and this confines her sphere of influence and makes her in Shakespeare's theatre both less free and less equal in her circumstances than a wife is able to be.

One difference between the position of wives in Caroline drama – a difference which was to dominate Restoration comedy – and of wives in the earlier plays, is that women cease to work. Written for people of leisure, Caroline plays project characters without a working context. There are no business relationships, only social ones. Women have already become part of the luxury of life, behaving in ways which enhance their desirability rather than their usefulness. In *The Way of the World* pleasure is the purpose of a woman's life: there is no longer any distinction between the function of a wife and the function of a whore. For the Restoration dramatist, all women are whores in being playthings; the socially

[61] *The Comedy of Errors*, II.i.14.
[62] William Brenchley Rye, *England as Seen by Foreigners: in the Days of Elizabeth and James the First*, pp. 7–8.

unacceptable woman is the one who gets caught. The friendship which the Puritans claimed for man and wife – an idea of friendship which the modern word no longer expresses – is in Caroline drama friendship between men, and this carries over into Restoration drama. Where the relation between Brutus and Portia had been more durable, and more equal than the relation between Brutus and Cassius, in Dryden's *Troilus and Cressida* Andromache disclaims her right to dissuade Hector from going to the battle in these terms:

> I would be worthy to be *Hectors* wife:
> And had I been a Man, as my Soul's one
> I had aspir'd a nobler name, his friend.[63]

The friends in Elizabethan drama are man and wife, and the playwrights owed this attitude to the Puritans; in the later drama the friends are man and man.

If the dramatists' first interest was to declare that the wife was a whore in all but name unless men's attitudes to her differed in essence from their attitudes to the whore, their second was to demonstrate the degradation which the whore endured from being merely a piece of property. In this degradation she inevitably engulfed her paramour.

'Pleasure will be paid, one time or another,'[64] observes Feste, the true Puritan to Malvolio's Puritan manner. To the Puritans the price of buying a woman for pleasure was fourfold: damnation, degeneration, bastards and beggary. The conventional ecclesiastical horror of adultery and whoredom gained impetus from Puritan articulation of the joys of marriage.

Renaissance drama surrounds adultery with an atmosphere of sacrilege. Elizabeth's Homilist condemned it as 'exceeding infamy of the name of Christ, the notable decay of true religion.'[65] Hamlet contemplates in his mother an act which

> makes marriage vows
> As false as dicers' oaths, O such a deed

---

[63] II.i.

[64] *Twelfth Night*, II.iv.70.

[65] 'Against Whoredom and Adultery', *Book of Homilies*, p. 108.

> As from the body of contraction plucks
> The very soul, and sweet religion makes
> A rhapsody of words.[66]

Plays like *The White Devil*, or *Women Beware Women*, or *The Changeling*, end with a Calvinist gnashing of teeth which tends to be a little disconcerting after a characterisation of individual adulteresses which is both humane and sophisticated. The playwrights record a dichotomy present in Puritanism itself, which, while pronouncing that 'adulterie and fornication are most grievous and open crimes, which do breake the very bond and covenant of mariage,'[67] tried to show that the individual adultery was not preordained through human corruption but induced through the evils of society. But although the Puritans' marriage reforms struck at the root causes of adultery, and in a sense demythologised its heinousness, men like the separatist John Greenwood still firmly maintained that it should be punished by death – in both parties – according to Mosaic law. Perhaps the separatists in particular were anxious to rebut accusations of sexual laxity readily cast in their direction, by an almost grotesque severity. But Luther himself had been less uncompromising, urging that if the sin were not made public, a husband might 'rebuke his wife privately and in a brotherly fashion, and keep her if she will mend her ways.'[68]

The dramatists span both points of view, repudiating the act, but seeing the individual as redeemable. Middleton and Webster and Marston, in analysing the pressures which society puts on women to commit adultery, achieve a remarkable insight into what it feels like to be a woman under such circumstances – the way in which Bianca in *Women Beware Women* is at the mercy first of her husband's whims and then of her lover's, the way in which the dice are loaded against Vittoria in the trial scene, or the refinements of the double standard which operate in the marriage of Zuccone and the Lady Zoya in Marston's *The Fawn*. But at the end of their plays adultery reasserts itself not as an individual dilemma, but as a way

[66] *Hamlet*, III.iv.44.
[67] Perkins, *Christian Oeconomie*, p. 118.
[68] *Luther's Works*, 45, 32.

of life inimical to marriage and the social order, and it is on these grounds that the individual is condemned and cast out from society. 'I am that of your blood was taken from you / For your better health,'[69] says Beatrice to her father at the end of *The Changeling*. *The White Devil* concludes with a homily which recalls Vittoria's image of her limb 'corrupted to an ulcer,' which she determines to cast away and 'go weeping to heaven on crutches.'

> Let guilty men remember their black deeds
> Do lean on crutches, made of slender reeds.[70]

Outside *Antony and Cleopatra* there is no play in the Jacobean period in which adulterous love creates its own moral universe. Even Ford, writing for the early years of Charles I's reign, denies in the resolution of *'Tis Pity She's a Whore* Giovanni's gesture of defiance towards the theological interpretation of adultery. Shakespeare alone creates passions without preconceptions. Where Hamlet expresses a Calvinist conviction that adultery is damnable, Cleopatra hastens death in case Iras should 'first meet the curled Antony,' and 'spend that kiss / Which is my heaven to have.'[71] Webster and Middleton have a powerful, but less flexible moral vision.

The Homily 'Against Whoredom and Adultery' prophesied the decay of valour, wit, beauty and youth through whoredom. But the Jacobeans were particularly fascinated by the subtle disintegration of moral fibre. Bianca's timorousness at the Duke's seduction turns into brazenness:

> I'm made bold now,
> I thank thy treachery; sin and I'm acquainted,
> No couple greater.[72]

In *The Changeling* Middleton traces in Beatrice the almost imperceptible stages by which her loathing of De Flores resolves into

[69] Middleton, *The Changeling*, v.iii.153.
[70] Webster, *The White Devil*, iv.ii.121, v.vi.300.
[71] *Antony and Cleopatra*, v.ii.300.
[72] Middleton, *Women Beware Women*, ii.ii.444.

love, and her love of Alsemero into the bravado of fear. Alsemero in his cry: 'O, thou art all deform'd,'[73] registers a degradation of which she herself is unconscious, so gradual has been its influence. The spirit of falsehood which overtook Anna Karenina in every encounter with her husband once Vronsky was her lover, in Jacobean tragedy infects all personal relations. Gertrude fears Ophelia because Ophelia is innocent:

> To my sick soul, as sin's true nature is,
> Each toy seems prologue to some great amiss,
> So full of artless jealousy is guilt,
> It spills itself, in fearing to be spilt.

Claudius' guilt stands between him and his love for Gertrude. She is 'my virtue or my plague;' his sin assumes the image of a whore:

> The harlot's cheek, beautied with plast'ring art,
> Is not more ugly to the thing that helps it,
> Than is my deed to my most painted word.[74]

In Elizabethan and Jacobean drama the relation between lovers is sterile, where in Restoration drama sterility is the handmaid of marriage. The Caroline dramatists fluctuated between the two, professing allegiance to marriage, but making it so boring that adultery seemed an attractive alternative. But the Jacobeans were unequivocal. Anne Frankford in *A Woman Killed with Kindness*, like Madame Bovary, finds in adultery the banality of marriage, and Beatrice in *The Changeling* forfeits the freedom which Isabella retains through faithfulness to her husband. Sin putrifies even a passion as intoxicating as that of Vittoria and Brachiano, induces further crime – Claudius moving from one poisoning to multiple poisonings – and prevents that parity of minds which lifts marriage out of the property market.

Adultery and whoredom spelled damnation and degeneration, but what was equally potent in Puritan eyes, they also spelled beggary. An adulterer wasted his substance in riotous living, pursuing

---

[73] v.iii.78.
[74] *Hamlet*, IV.v.17, III.i.51.

'his most filthy and beastly pleasure.'[75] Husbands in plays like *The
Miseries of Enforced Marriage*, or *A Yorkshire Tragedy* — those
heavily homiletic, popular domestic dramas — not only consume
their patrimony upon their whores, but run into gambling, theft
and perjury and become social pariahs. The implication is that
though men may court damnation without pallor because it is a future evil, they cannot remain impervious to present financial ruin.
Puritanism at the last post put godliness on a cash basis. The happy
ending of *The Miseries of Enforced Marriage* redeems Scarborow's
soul while simultaneously solving his financial problems. The
Caroline Brome satirises the marriage of God and Mammon in
Puritan morality when a character inquires in *The City Wit*:
'What should Citizens do with kind hearts; or trusting in any thing
but God, and ready money?'[76] But the Puritans were not conscious
of yoking incompatibles; the price of adultery was penury, and in
the drama the charnel house and the debtors' prison are on opposite sides of the same street.

Finally, the adulterer paid for his pleasure with his bastards.
Antony, accusing Cleopatra of courting Octavius' messenger,
exclaims:

> Have I my pillow left unpress'd in Rome,
> Forborne the getting of a lawful race,
> And by a gem of women, to be abus'd
> By one that looks on feeders.[77]

Renaissance emphasis on the joys of children heightened the sense
of what a man forfeited in fathering bastards. Social pressure
against a man's rearing illegitimate children, which operated from
the middle of the sixteenth century, and gained weight from Puritan ideas about the family, prompted regret for his bastards even in
a hardened whoremonger like Sir Walter Whorehound in
Middleton's *A Chaste Maid in Cheapside*. They detract from his eli-
gibility, and disturb the legitimate family.

Milton called marriage the 'true source / Of human offspring,'

[75] 'Against Whoredom and Adultery', p. 115.
[76] I.i.
[77] *Antony and Cleopatra*, III.xiii.106.

by which:

> Relations dear, and all the charities
> Of father, son, and brother, first were known.[78]

Edgar's speech to Edmund in *King Lear* sounds harsh:

> The Gods are just, and of our pleasant vices
> Make instruments to plague us;
> The dark and vicious place where thee he got
> Cost him his eyes.[79]

But the Elizabethans saw the bastard as an instrument of retribution for adultery not only in his birth, but in his nature, which mirrored the perfidy of his conception. Jonson records the popular prejudice in *Every Man In His Humour* where Kitely swears he would trust his life in the hands of his foundling, and Downright retorts:

> So, would not I in any bastards, brother,
> As, it is like, he is: although I knew
> Myselfe his father.[80]

The indifference of the parent to the sacred laws of wedlock is father to the lawlessness of the child. Hawthorne in *The Scarlet Letter* declares of Hester Prynne's child: 'In giving her existence a great law had been broken; and the result was a being whose elements were perhaps beautiful and brilliant, but all in disorder.'[81] Elizabethan drama demonstrates popular belief in the unreliability of bastards, from Laertes, declaiming his loyalty to his father: 'That drop of blood that's calm proclaims me bastard,'[82] to Joan of Arc repudiating hers in *Henry VI* or the bastard Spurio cuckolding his own father in *The Revenger's Tragedy*. Milton's sacred charities have no claim on a child born in defiance of those charities.

But in *King Lear* Shakespeare alters the perspective. Edmund

[78] *Paradise Lost*, IV.756.
[79] v.iii.170.
[80] Folio of 1616, II.i.24.
[81] Ch. VI.
[82] *Hamlet*, IV.v.117.

mocks the idea that his bastardy has made him what he is: 'Fut! I should have been that I am had the maidenliest star in the firmament twinkled on my bastardizing.' Edgar's simple analysis of cause and effect falters before Lear, destroyed by his legitimate daughters. Lear cries:

> Let copulation thrive; for Gloucester's bastard son
> Was kinder to his father than my daughters
> Got 'tween the lawful sheets.

In Lear's case Shakespeare complicates the moral issues by separating them from the fact of birth. Lear defies sacred charities not through physical adultery, but through disowning his legitimate daughter, an act as anarchic morally as Gloucester's actual disregard of his marriage vow:

> Here I disclaim all my paternal care,
> Propinquity and property of blood,
> And as a stranger to my heart and me
> Hold thee from this for ever.[83]

Lear himself casts away those duties which bind legitimate children to their parents. The retribution which falls on him is the bitter perception that his legitimate daughters hold their relation to him in as much contempt as he held his relation to Cordelia. Gloucester and he suffer for the same crime: a holding light of sacred obligations. But these obligations go much deeper than the fact of birth. Lear's own act licensed lawlessness in his daughters, as Gloucester's did in his son. That Gloucester's was registered by the fact of bastardy only proves Edmund's point that moral quality is independent of something so measurable as the physical fact of birth. Edmund's bastardy sinks into insignificance beside the legitimate Goneril and Regan. Shakespeare's interpretation of the price of adultery forms only part of a larger vision of what a man's acts cost him.

Mary Wollstonecraft asserted that 'a master and mistress of a family ought not to continue to love each other with passion. I mean to say that they ought not to indulge those emotions which

[83] I.ii.138, IV.vi.117, I.i.113.

disturb the order of society, and engross the thoughts that should be otherwise employed.'[84] If there was one weakness in the Puritan idea of marriage, it was that the Puritans underestimated the power of passion, and in particular the pleasure of illicit passion: this may be one reason for the witch-hunting of the Puritan period. Witchcraft explains those chaotic impulses which continue to sway a man's sexual nature in spite of all the Puritans' good advice. James I declared of witches that 'their power is speciall: as of weakening the nature of some men to make them unable for women: and making it to abound in others, more then the ordinary course of nature would permit.'[85] If women are no longer whores, the wicked ones must be witches, and in the drama of the time the two concepts go hand in hand, so that a witch like Hecate in Middleton's *The Witch* is little more than a bawd, and the wife in Heywood's *The Late Lancashire Witches* is plainly only a whore. When the Puritans rationalised the relation of man and wife to the very great advantage of the wife, who became an equal to an extent inconceivable under the arranged marriage, they also rationalised passion.

The Puritan commitment to certain kinds of equality for women had no lasting effect because its advocates failed to codify the ideal of partnership in the law. The handbook of common law which was printed for the instruction of women in 1632 names only two reasons for marriage: propagation and the avoidance of fornication. The concept of mutual comfort which had such a significant influence on changing attitudes to women changed only attitudes but not the facts of women's legal status. When Mrs Pankhurst limited her campaign to women's suffrage she left untouched many attitudes to women which declared their inequality more subtly than the lack of the vote, but no attitude will ever change permanently unless the conditions of change are recorded in the law. In the sphere of race relations this is a recognised fact; the conservative majority changes its behaviour not because its convictions have changed, but because the law compels change. For women, issues like equal pay only scratch the surface of the

84 *The Rights of Woman*, p. 35.

85 *Daemonologie*, Preface, xiii.

inequalities society inflicts on women, but it is only through the cut-and-dried process of legal change that the elusive pattern of attitudes to women can be forced into a different shape which will outlast the reformers who pioneer new attitudes.

Elizabethan and Jacobean feminism was a movement of minds but not of facts. Puritanism failed to give its ideas on women any permanent form, unless that form might be said to be the plays of Shakespeare.

CHAPTER III

Gods and Devils

1 Idolatry

Donne said of women: 'To make them Gods is ungodly, and to make them Devils is divillish; To make them Mistresses is unmanly, and to make them servants is unnoble; To make them as God made them, wives, is godly and manly too.'[1] Straddling like a Colossus a range of attitudes to women which stretch from Petrarch and the Ovidian religion of love to the medieval *querelle des femmes*, from the Humanists to the Puritans, Donne criticises from a social standpoint an idea of woman created by poetry.

Palamon in Chaucer's *The Knight's Tale*, spying Emelye in the garden, muses:

> I noot wher she be womman or goddesse,
> But Venus is it soothly, as I gesse.

Arcite justifies himself for falling in love with the same lady:

> Thou woost nat yet now
> Wheither she be a womman or goddesse!
> Thyn is affeccioun of hoolynesse,
> And myn is love, as to a creature.[2]

Chaucer's Knight, in ultimately rewarding Palamon's worship of Emelye beyond Arcite's, is true to the spirit of courtly love, which saw the lady as a deity before whom the lover abased himself. *The Knight's Tale* lacks only one element usually present in the courtly love romance: courtly love is adulterous in aim, if not in fact. Worship of the courtly lady releases impulses of idealism, self-

---

[1] *The Sermons of John Donne*, III, 242.

[2] 1101, 1156.

sacrifice and trial, an exalted and tender emotion not possible in the context of the business marriage, and therefore expressed in adultery.

Goddesses to the troubadours who sang to entertain the nobility in their great halls, women were devils to the satirists. Medieval satire on women, like courtly love, had its own elaborate forms and conventions, and played as significant a part in a reputable poet's repertoire as the courtly love romance. But satire had a more mongrel origin than adulation of women. It was a clerical hobby; the Wife of Bath's fifth husband, the clerk Jankyn, spends his evenings searching out proverbs which slander women till his wife puts an end to it: 'Al sodeynly thre leves have I plyght / Out of his book, right as he radde.'[3] It represented also a popular and bourgeois response – the *fabliaux* sources of some of Chaucer's Tales – to an exclusively aristocratic tradition.[4] Attitudes to women in satire and in courtly love complement each other, reflecting the Christian polarity between Eve and the Virgin Mary, and demonstrating a psychology of extremes, where the strains and excesses of worship find relief in the sibilants of satire. Both are part of an autonomous world of poetry, generating its own life independent of the social context which produced the poet.

The anti-Petrarchanism of the late sixteenth century protested against an outworn poetic manner:

> I grant I never saw a goddess go;
> My mistress, when she walks, treads on the ground.
> And yet, by heaven, I think my love as rare
> As any she belied with false compare.[5]

Metaphysical poetry broke away from the limited poetic world of the Petrarchan convention, both in content and in form. In prose, men like Bacon turned from *Euphues* to a terser delivery: 'more matter, with less art.'[6] But the attack on poetry as fiction which

[3] Chaucer, *The Wife of Bath's Prologue*, 790
[4] Cf. Francis Lee Utley, *The Crooked Rib: An Analytical Index to the Argument about Women in English and Scots Literature to the End of the Year 1568.*
[5] *Sonnet* 130.
[6] F. P. Wilson, *Elizabethan and Jacobean*, pp. 27–52.

Sidney countered in *An Apologie for Poetrie* grew from a wider Renaissance scepticism about fictions in general, whether in the field of religion or politics or the structure of the solar system. Shakespeare's lifetime marked the birth of scientific enquiry, the purpose of investigating nature for itself which Bacon passed on to the founders of the Royal Society. When Shakespeare claimed that his lady's fairness needed no fictions to enhance it, he pinpointed an attitude to women which was symptomatic of its time. Poets should portray women as they are, recognisable in nature, not as the gods and devils of literary mythology.

Meredith, in the proem to *Diana of the Crossways,* warns the novelist against turning his heroine into a deity: 'You have to teach your imagination of the feminine image you have set up to bend your civilized knees to, that it must temper its fastidiousness, shun the grossness of the overdainty.' Exaggeration of refinement, like Victorian prudery, is itself a mark of grossness. Meredith describes the process through which attitudes to women evolve, beginning in a desire to perfect nature:

> 'So well we know ourselves, that we one and all determine to know a purer,' says the heroine of my columns. Philosophy in fiction tells, among various other matters, of the perils of this in-timate acquaintance with a flattering familiar in the 'purer' — a person who more than ceases to be of use to us after his ideal shall have led up men from their flint and arrow-head caverns to intercommunicative daylight. For when the fictitious creature has performed that service of helping to civilize the world, it becomes the most dangerous of delusions, causing first the indi-vidual to despise the mass, and then to join the mass in crushing the individual.[7]

Courtly love made an art out of the crudities of nature. *The Knight's Tale, Troilus and Criseyde,* the debates between Gawain and the Lady in *Sir Gawain and the Green Knight* demonstrate the civilising influence of the concept of Courtesy on relations be-tween the sexes. Women may have enjoyed a more egalitarian position in society in the Anglo-Saxon period than in the post-

[7] Ch. I.

Norman world,[8] but Old English poetry celebrates primary masculine ideals. Courtly love stood for a refinement of spirit which led Theseus, out of his *gentillesse*, to take pity on the women of Thebes, and which created an attitude of reverence in the lover capable of the neo-Platonic progression from the love of woman to the love of God. It is a microcosm of the influence of Christianity itself. Whatever the truth behind C. S. Lewis' discussion in *The Allegory of Love* of the relation between homage to the Virgin Mary, and devotion to the courtly lady,[9] both bear witness to a development of sensibility which ennobled the spirit.

When Humanists like More and Erasmus attacked medieval romance for deifying women, they saw it, like Christianity, as forging its own fetters for the individual. Meredith's 'fictitious creature,' having civilised her world, had become for sixteenth century Humanists 'the most dangerous of delusions,' obliterating the individual woman, who was not a goddess but a rational being, capable of education on the same terms as men. The Humanist educators anticipated Protestantism in claiming the individual's right to a voice. They fought the idea of woman as symbol, either of good, as in romance, or evil, as in satire. The goddess had to be thrown out with the devil, because both denied women reason and individuality. Vives condemned the satirists' generalisations: 'Althoughe there be some evyll and lewde womenne, yet that doth no more prove the malice of their nature, then of men, and therefore the more ridiculous and foolish are they, that have invied agaynst the whole sect for a fewe evil: and have not with like fury vituperated al mankind because the part of them be theves, and part inchaunters.'[10]

To see a woman as a goddess is to silence her as a human being. George Eliot wrote that 'anything is more endurable than to change our established formulae about women, or to run the risk of looking up to our wives instead of looking down on them. *Sit divus, dummodo non sit vivus* (let him be a god, provided he be not living), said the Roman magnates of Romulus; and so men say of

[8] D. M. Stenton, *The English Woman in History*, pp. 1–28.

[9] p. 8.

[10] *The Office and Duetie of an Husband*, sigs. Pi^v–Pij.

women, let them be idols, useless absorbents of precious things, provided we are not obliged to admit them to be strictly fellow-beings, to be treated, one and all, with justice and sober reverence.'[11] The Victorian elevation of the wife to a household goddess dispensing feminine light with the angelic piety of Dickens' Agnes in *David Copperfield* had the same consequence as the deifying of the lady in courtly love, of excluding the woman from a rational world in which she might challenge male dominance. The myths of femininity in contemporary popular culture [12] are separated from the adulation of woman in medieval romance only by context and terminology: the sequence of attitudes is the same. To put a woman on a pedestal gives a man a Muse without allowing her any right of reply. Historically this attitude has been the most subtle influence in confining women's power to a sphere not governed by reason, difficult to combat because it is done in the name of respect and love.

The modern women's movement attacks gallantry, the outward manifestation of reverence, because it is the code of a society which pays homage to woman, while despising women. In *Anna Karenina* Vronsky's courtesy to his mother is the barometer of his contempt for her: 'In the depths of his heart he did not respect his mother and (though this he never acknowledged to himself) did not love her, but in accordance with the views of the set he lived in, and as a result of his education, he could not imagine himself treating her in any way but one altogether submissive and respectful, and the more submissive and respectful he was externally, the less he honoured and loved her in his heart.'[13] When the Humanists attacked reverence, they attacked scorn.

Virginia Woolf pointed at the gulf between women in literature and women in history. 'If woman had no existence save in the fiction written by men, one would imagine her a person of the utmost importance: very various; heroic and mean; splendid and sordid; infinitely beautiful and hideous in the extreme; as great as a man, some think even greater. But this is woman in fiction. In fact,

[11] 'Margaret Fuller and Mary Wollstonecraft', *Essays of George Eliot*, p. 205.

[12] Germaine Greer, *The Female Eunuch*.

[13] Tolstoy, *Anna Karenina*, I.68.

as Professor Trevelyan points out, she was locked up, beaten and
flung about the room.'[14] The barbarism of the arranged marriage
in the Middle Ages – the Pastons virtually sold their daughters –
itself stimulated the cult of courtly love. But Virginia Woolf
creates a contrast between women in Shakespeare's plays and in
Elizabethan society which did not exist, partly because the Humanists demanded from poetry not fictions, but discernible truth
about women. More's educational plans for women and his
ideas about marriage helped to develop an ideal for women, of
which Elizabeth herself was the best example, which the poet
could copy from nature – Sidney's defence of the poet against the
charge of invention. Elizabeth's court was not barren of Beatrices,
but to replace Dante with Benedick is to show how far the poet
had moved from the ideal to the real. Shakespeare's comedies acknowledge the double legacy of the myths of courtly love, and
Humanist scepticism about those myths.

If the art of courtly love tamed nature, the Humanists reasserted
the supremacy of nature in the relations between men and women.
The sexes are drawn together not through passion but through
reason and nature: 'They shuld first by nature and with reason
have judged, and then embraced that thinge with love, or with
hatred avoyded the same, the whiche yf man ought to do in
choosynge of frendes, howe much more diligently ought it to be
done in the choyce of a wife, the principal of al amitie and frend-
shippe.'[15] The Humanists saw the adultery of the courtly lover as
part of the corrupt aristocratic culture which More attacked in
Utopia. They rejected chivalry because it romanticised experiences
and attitudes which they felt to be degrading. More and Vives
would not have agreed with C. S. Lewis when he wrote: 'The
loves of Troilus and Cryseide are so nobly conceived that they are
divided only by the thinnest partition from the lawful loves of
Dorigen and her husband. It seems almost an accident that the third
book celebrates adultery instead of marriage. Chaucer has brought
the old romance of adultery to the very frontiers of the modern (or

[14] *A Room of One's Own*, pp. 43–5.
[15] Vives, *The Office and Duetie of an Husband*, sig. Di.

should I say the late?) romance of marriage.'[16] This interpretation sounds authentic to a modern ear, but Vives would have been horrified at the idea that Troilus' pursuit of, and abasement before, his lady, could possibly be translated into marriage. Vives repudiated the art of courtship: 'Yf the woman were a certayn kynd of merchaundise, peradventure it shuld not seme so unsembly by all maner of meanes and subteltie to obtayne her: . . . but consideryng that nowe she shalbe his felow for ever.' He would have found Troilus criminally extravagant in his emotions: 'Geve not thy self to those unmete and voluptuous love and lustes, by the whiche men are compelled to sai and do many thinges which are filthy and childish. . . . The poet doth speake of this erthly and blind love.'[17] Far from seeing the relation of Troilus and Criseyde as a harbinger of marriage contracted for love, Vives would have felt that it nourished attitudes hostile to the good fellowship of man and wife. The lover should not marry a mistress, but a wife. He would have considered Bacon's formulation that '*wiues* are young Mens Mistresses; Companions for middle Age; and old Mens Nurses,'[18] as the debauched frivolity of the confirmed bachelor. Vives advised: 'I wold not counsel ye to mary her, with whome thou hast bene in amors withal, whom thou flatterdest, whome thou didst serve, whom thou calledst thy hart, thy life, thy maistres, thy light, thy eyes, with other suche wordes as foolishe love doth perswade, usinge impietie agaynst God, which is the ende of al desire and goodnes.' A wife will not respect a husband she has enslaved as a lover. 'Thys submission is and shoulde be the cause, that she doth not regard thee, but disdayneth to serve thee, whose ladye she was as she estemed, and whom she found more obedient unto her, even with the peril and daunger of life, then any other slave that was bought for monie.'[19] The nurse of such folly is poetry, that anthology of idle romances about Tristan and Launcelot put together by Malory, or the miscellany of bawdry, full of 'lies' and 'wanton lust,' known as *The Decameron.* They kindle a 'beastly and filthy

[16] *The Allegory of Love,* p. 197.
[17] *The Office and Duetie of an Husband,* sigs. Cvii^v, Nv^v–Nvi.
[18] 'Of Marriage and Single Life', p. 30.
[19] *The Office and Duetie of an Husband,* sig. Kv.

desyre'[20] inimical to the reasonable relation which the Humanists placed at the centre of the Utopian family.

Roger Ascham, Elizabeth's tutor, clarified in *The Schoolmaster* another element in the Humanist position. The romances were Popish and ignorant, and behind those accusations lay a world of pioneered Biblical scholarship, anti-monasticism, and Erasmian contempt for superstitious ceremony. 'In our forefathers tyme,' observed Ascham, 'Whan Papistrie, as a standyng poole, covered and overflowed all England, fewe bookes were read on our tong, savyng certaine bookes Chevalrie, as they sayd, for pastime and pleasure, which, as some say, were made in Monasteries, by idle Monkes, or wanton Chanons: as one for example, *Morte Arthure*: the whole pleasure of which booke standeth in two speciall poyntes, in open mans slaughter, and bold bawdrye: In which booke those be counted the noblest Knightes, that do kill most men without any quarrell, and commit fowlest aduoulter[i]es by sutlest shiftes.' 'What toyes,' he concludes darkly, 'the dayly readyng of such a booke, may worke in the will of a yong ientleman, or a yong mayde, that liveth welthelie and idelie, wise men can iudge, and honest men do pitie.'[21] It might be Anne Elliot in *Persuasion* counselling a lovesick Captain Benwick to beware Byron. The Humanists saw the romances as the product of idle, ill-educated men who, vowed to a false shibboleth of celibacy, relieved their inward lusts by idealising adultery. Vives expostulates: 'As for learning, none is to be looked for in those men, which saw never so much as a shadow of learning themselves.'[22] In a sense the romances symbolised for More and Erasmus and Vives the dark ages into which medieval Christianity had fallen. Medieval poetry is the gargoyle on the face of the decaying building which the Humanists set themselves to clean and restore.

In *Utopia* More attacked an aristocratic culture without setting up a bourgeois one because there was no distinct social con-

---

[20] Vives, *The Instruction of a Christian Woman*, pp. 58–9; *The Office and Duetie of an Husband*, sig. Ovii[v].

[21] p. 80.

[22] *The Instruction of a Christian Woman*, pp. 58–9.

sciousness to absorb his attitudes.[23] When the Puritans purveyed Humanist ideas about marriage and the family and women to middle-class congregations, they made those ideas more definitively middle-class than they originally were, because Jacobean society included a substantial group of people who were identified by their antipathy to the court both in their values and in their style of life. In the plays of Shakespeare's contemporaries – even in Jonson – Humanist attitudes to women have narrowed to fit a specific social context. Playwrights like Dekker, Middleton and Heywood are confined within a Puritan bourgeois stance, because they lack Shakespeare's capacity for being at ease, like Bottom, in all worlds, whether court, country, city or temperate isle. Lyly's plays counterpoint opposing attitudes to romantic love, but always within the framework of the court, where Shakespeare is simultaneously in the court and outside it, defining it in relation to the work-a-day world which most of the Globe audience would return to after the holiday humour of play-going.

Late Elizabethan plays, produced by professional working dramatists to entertain a primarily citizen audience, present the art of poetry as a court pastime, cultivated by men with nothing to do except to create fictions about women and indulge in loose living, preferably at the expense of the middle classes. This pattern is evident, in its baldest terms, in Dekker's plays – in *Lust's Dominion*, or in the attempted seduction of the citizen wife in *Westward Ho* by an Earl, with full paraphernalia of poetic idolatry; discernable in the plays of Marston, Middleton, Webster, Chapman, some of Massinger and some of Beaumont and Fletcher; fragmented and flexible in Shakespeare.

The art of poetry is presented in the drama as peculiar to the court. Touchstone sighs for a breath of court nurture in Audrey: 'Truly, I would the gods had made thee poetical.' But his answer to her question: 'I do not know what "poetical" is: is it honest in deed and word? is it a true thing?' betrays his inclination for a touch of court falsehood: 'No, truly; for the truest poetry is the most feigning; and lovers are given to poetry; and what they swear

[23] J. H. Hexter, '*Utopia* and Its Historical Milieu', *The Complete Works of St. Thomas More*, IV, lvi.

in poetry it may be said as lovers they do feign.'[24] If Audrey were a poet, she might be less honest than she claimed, and then Touchstone could seduce her. The pattern – poetry, falsehood, seduction – is recurrent.

Poetry, in Jacobean tragedy, disguises lust, just as medieval romance disguised bold bawdry as chivalry:

> This madam takes physic, that t'other monsieur may minister to her: here is a pander jewelled; there is a fellow in a shift of satin this day, that could not shift a shirt t'other night: here a Paris supports that Helen; there's a Lady Guinever bears up that Sir Lancelot: dreams, dreams, visions, fantasies, chimeras, imaginations, tricks, conceits.[25]

There was nothing new in Shakespeare's version of the Trojan War in *Troilus and Cressida* – 'Lechery, lechery; still wars and lechery'[26] – presenting Helen as a drab deified. Marlowe made Faustus' worship of Helen his ultimate delusion of grandeur:

> Sweet Helen, make me immortal with a kiss.
> Her lips suck forth my soul. See where it flies!
> Come, Helen, come, give me my soul again.
> Here will I dwell, for heaven is in these lips,
> And all is dross that is not Helena.[27]

For Webster and Marston the courtly paramour is a potential Paris making love to another man's wife under the pretence of worshipping her. Flamineo sneers at Brachiano's courtship of Vittoria in *The White Devil*: 'What an ignorant ass or flattering knave might he be counted, that should write sonnets to her eyes, or call her brow the snow of Ida, or ivory of Corinth, or compare her hair to the blackbird's bill, when 'tis liker the blackbird's feather.'[28] In *The Malcontent* a character observes of the adulterer:

[24] *As You Like It*, III.iii.15.

[25] Marston, *The Malcontent*, I.i.92.

[26] v.ii.190.

[27] *Doctor Faustus*, v.i.101.

[28] Webster, *The White Devil*, I.ii.115.

> Now treads Ferneze in the dangerous path of lust,
> Swearing his sense is merely deified.

The art of courtship conceals the nature of seduction:

> Lust so confirm'd,
> That the black act of sin itself not sham'd
> To be term'd courtship.[29]

Court artifice and court vice are exposed either by the convention of the malcontent in Jacobean drama – Flamineo, Bosola, Marston's Malevole, and even Hamlet himself – or through confrontation with middle-class virtue. The subplot of Marston's *The Insatiate Countess* balances the court debauchery of the main plot with the bourgeois virtue of a pair of city wives, besieged in the court idiom by their own husbands, who hope to cuckold each other in pursuit of a private vendetta. One of the women reads out the love-letter sent by her husband to the other: 'Ay, marry, here's a stile so high as a man cannot help a dog o'er it. He was wont to write to me in the city phrase, *My good Abigail*. Here's *astonishment of nature, unparallel'd excellency, and most unequal rarity of creation!* – three such words will turn any honest woman in the world whore; for a woman is never won till she know not what to answer; and beshrew me if I understand any of these.'[30] Bertram's attempted seduction of Diana in *All's Well That Ends Well* brings into conflict two hostile cultures: the courtier wooing the middle-class girl with the religion of love, and the girl bred to the bourgeois ideal of the family. 'I would he lov'd his wife; if he were honester / He were much goodlier,' muses Diana of the young Count. Reflecting on his suit, she remembers:

> My mother told me just how he would woo
> As if she sat in's heart. She says all men
> Have the like oaths.

The goddess is an anachronism in this domestic setting. But Shakespeare goes beyond Marston's position as protagonist for middle-

[29] Marston, *The Malcontent*, II.i.2, v.iii.182.
[30] II.ii.21.

class virtue against court vice, because Bertram is himself condemned by the court – by the king, by his mother, by his own
peers. The first Lord remarks: 'He hath perverted a young gentlewoman here in Florence, of a most chaste renown, and this night
he fleshes his will in the spoil of her honour.'[31] The courtier who
profanes women in the name of chivalry is in this play as alien in
the court as in the city, and this mirrors More, who castigated the
aristocracy not from a middle-class standpoint, but from within its
own ranks.

Satire is the sister of the courtier's idolatry, conceived in indif-
ference to the individual woman, and obeying a law of extremes.
Claudio's disappointment is in proportion to his adulation of
Hero:

> You seem to me as Dian in her orb,
> As chaste as is the bud ere it be blown;
> But you are more intemperate in your blood
> Than Venus, or those pamp'red animals
> That rage in savage sensuality.

Beatrice's indignation: 'Is a' not approved in the height a villain,
that hath slandered, scorned, dishonoured my kinswoman?'[32] puts
a private and personal perspective on what in Claudio, whether
loving or hating, was impersonal and public. Both satire and idolatry submerge the individual in the image. Brachiano turns on
Vittoria:

> How long have I beheld the devil in crystal?
> Thou hast led me, like an heathen sacrifice,
> With music, and with fatal yokes of flowers
> To my eternal ruin. Woman to man
> Is either a god or a wolf.[33]

Troilus struggles to separate condemnation of Cressida from the
traducing of women in general:

[31] III.v.79, IV.ii.69, IV.iii.13.
[32] *Much Ado About Nothing*, IV.i.58, 300.
[33] Webster, *The White Devil*, IV.ii.88.

> Let it not be believed for womanhood!
> Think we had mothers; do not give advantage
> To stubborn critics, apt, without a theme,
> For depravation, to square the general sex
> By Cressid's rule.[34]

Shakespeare distinguishes, however, in a way that his contemporaries do not, between idolatry as the genuine effluence of passion metamorphosed into satire, and idolatry as the social veneer of contempt for women. In the plays of Marston and Middleton idolatry always assumes a Richard III cast: a mask donned to guarantee the success of seduction. Richard's seduction of Anne is a calculated experiment in courtly love conducted by one 'not shap'd for sportive tricks, / Nor made to court an amorous looking-glass.' He accosts Anne as 'divine perfection of a woman,' blaming her 'heavenly face' for his crimes. Her pity for him excites not the gratitude of the courtly lover, but scorn – 'Relenting fool, and shallow-changing woman.' He shrugs:

> Was ever woman in this humour woo'd?
> Was ever woman in this humour won?
> I'll have her, but I will not keep her long.[35]

Shakespeare gave the same mood to Suffolk in *Henry VI*, planning to woo Margaret for his king and to enjoy her himself:

> She's beautiful, and therefore to be woo'd,
> She is a woman, and therefore to be won.[36]

But in Shakespeare this is only one form of idolatry; in Marston and Middleton, even in Webster, it is the only form. Idolatry in their plays is always the excrescence of contempt. The paramour prostrates himself before the lady with whom he plans to commit adultery: 'Sweet women! most sweet ladies! nay, angels! by heaven, he is more accursed than a devil that hates you, or is hated by you; and happier than a god that loves you, or is beloved by

---

[34] *Troilus and Cressida*, v.ii.125.

[35] *Richard III*, i.i.14, i.ii.75, 182, iv.iv.434, i.ii.228.

[36] Part I, v.iii.78.

you.' Repulsed, he gives vent to his venom: 'Women! nay, Furies; nay, worse; for they torment only the bad, but women good and bad. Damnation of mankind! Breath, hast thou praised them for this? ... O, that I could rail against these monsters in nature, models of hell, curse of the earth, women!'[37] Marston is a ruthless satiriser of his own satirists of women. The pendulum of deity to devil through adultery is as predictable outside Shakespeare as More himself could have wished.

Marriage admits no deities, because the wife, declared Mary Wollstonecraft, 'cannot contentedly become merely an upper servant after having been treated like a goddess.'[38] Suffolk's pledge to Henry of his bride's submissiveness despite her godhead:

> And, which is more, she is not so divine,
> So full replete with choice of all delights,
> But with as humble lowliness of mind
> She is content to be at your command,[39]

would have exasperated Vives with its illogicality; Shakespeare uses it as a pointer both to Suffolk's disingenuousness, and Henry's gullibility. Jonson in particular allies himself to the Humanists in insisting that the courtly lover's attitudes to his mistress cannot be transposed into the setting of bourgeois marriage. Obsequiousness in the lover breeds despotism in the wife. 'Is this according to the instrument, when I married you?' demands Mistress Otter in *Epicoene*, 'That I would be princess, and reign in mine own house; and you would be my subject and obey me?'[40] Puritan marriage cannot be a perpetual 'wooing time;'[41] this insight lifts the Puritan domestic conduct book above the sphere of the modern woman's magazine where the continual charade of courtship is supposed to conceal the barrenness of the relation between husband and wife. But it cannot work, as romancers, husbands and wives all know. The deified wife of the rhapsodic Deliro in *Every Man Out of His*

[37] Marston, *The Malcontent*, I.i.20, I.ii.85.

[38] *The Rights of Woman*, p. 80.

[39] *Henry VI Part I*, v.v.16.

[40] III.i.28.

[41] Massinger, *The Fatal Dowry*, II.ii.

Humour seeks brisker satisfactions. He laments his inadequacy to serve a wife 'so passing-faire:'

> Shee weighs the things I doe, with what shee merits:
> And (seeing my worth out-weigh'd so in her graces)
> Shee is so solemne, so precise, so froward,
> That no obseruance I can doe to her,
> Can make her kind to me: if shee find fault,
> I mend that fault; and then shee saies, I faulted,
> That I did mend it.

Macilente gives him Vives' advice:

> You are too amorous, too obsequious,
> And make her too assur'd, shee may command you.

He tries to make Deliro confront the idol with the reality: 'Let me tell you, your wife is no proper woman, and by my life, I suspect her honestie, that's more, which you may likewise suspect (if you please:) doe you see?'[42] The voice is Hector's, arguing against the retention of Helen:

> 'Tis mad idolatry
> To make the service greater than the god;
> And the will dotes that is attributive
> To what infectiously itself affects,
> Without some image of th'affected merit.

The Humanist logic: 'To her own worth / She shall be prized,'[43] makes the gods and devils human, for better or worse.

The sub-plot of *Every Man Out of His Humour* parodies medieval romance by turning it into a pantomime between husband and wife performed every evening at his home-coming. Puntarvolo greets his wife:

> *What more than heauenly pulchritude is this,*
> *What magazine, or treasurie of blisse?*
> *Dazle, you organs to my optique sense,*

---

[42] Jonson, *Every Man Out of His Humour*, II.iv.52, IV.iv.60.
[43] *Troilus and Cressida*, II.ii.56, IV.iv.133.

> *To view a creature of such eminence:*
> *O, I am planet-strooke, and in yond sphere*
> *A brighter starre then VENUS doth appeare.*

'How! in verse!' exclaims one of the stage spectators. Puntarvolo
describes a quest worthy of Chaucer's Sir Thopas:

> I am a poore knight errant (lady) that hunting in the adjacent
> forrest, was, by aduenture in the pursuit of a hart, brought to this
> place; which hart (deare Madame) escaped by enchantment: the
> evening approching, (my selfe and seruant wearied) my suit is,
> to enter your faire castle and refresh me.

The lady acquiesces, with a middle-class demur which measures
her distance from her courtly counterpart: 'Sir Knight, albeit it be
not vsuall with me (chiefly in the absence of a husband) to admit
any entrance to strangers.' When Puntarvolo mouths gratitude:
'Most admir'd lady, you astonish me,' a wry comment interrupts
him: 'What, with speaking a speech of your owne penning?' In
showing Puntarvolo wooing his wife 'as shee were a stranger
neuer encounter'd before,' Jonson exposes one element in the incompatibility between courtly love and bourgeois marriage.
Worship of the lady demands distance and remoteness where marriage celebrates familiarity. A stranger may be the hero of
romance, as Mary Garth informs Fred Vincy, but he cannot feature
in marriage unless he is the lover, not the husband. Jonson's stage
audience dismiss Puntarvolo's interlude as 'a tedious chapter of
courtship, after sir LANCELOT, and queene GUENEVER,'
marvelling, in a way which brings Jonson closer to Shakespeare,
that the lady will put up with it. 'I mar'le in what dull cold nooke
he found this lady out? that (being a woman) shee was blest with
no more copie of wit but to serue his humour thus.'[44] That women
of wit and education preferred to be women rather than goddesses
was a perception which bound Jonson, as well as Shakespeare, to
the Humanist educators.

Idolatry by tradition emphasises the separate worlds of the two
sexes, because it is a homage paid *en bloc* by the male to the female,

---

[44] Jonson, *Every Man Out of His Humour*, II.iii.26, 47, II.i.138, II.iii.67.

thriving on the exaggeration and idealising of difference. Shakespeare's concern more than any of his fellow playwrights is to dissolve artificial distinctions between the sexes. His women, whether adored or despised, comment on men's idolatry from outside in the same way that his rustics and artisans comment on the frolics of the court. Even women whose shrines are worshipped preserve a sense of being outsiders because idolatry, set in motion, develops independently of the individual woman. The woman is an object. Julia gazes at the picture of Silvia which she is commissioned to carry to her own lover:

> If I had such a tire, this face of mine
> Were full as lovely as is this of hers:
>
> . . . .
>
> What should it be that he respects in her,
> But I can make respective in myself,
> If this fond Love were not a blinded god?[45]

The mood is Helena's, mourning over Demetrius' infatuation with Hermia:

> Through Athens I am thought as fair as she,
> But what of that? Demetrius thinks not so;
> But will not know what all but he do know.
> And as he errs, doting on Hermia's eyes,
> So I, admiring of his qualities.
> Things base and vile, holding no quantity,
> Love can transpose to form and dignity.
> Love looks not with the eyes, but with the mind:
> And therefore is winged Cupid painted blind.
> Nor hath Love's mind of any judgement taste:
> Wings and no eyes figure unheedy haste.

The awareness of the folly of idolatry – even when she accuses herself of idolising Demetrius – gives Helena the same perspective on the wood as Bottom, encircled by an idolatrous Titania. Scratching his ass's head, he remarks mildly: 'To say the truth, reason and love keep little company together now-a-days.'[46] Women, Fools,

[45] *The Two Gentlemen of Verona*, IV.iv.183.
[46] *A Midsummer Night's Dream*, I.i.227, III.i.136.

rustics, in Shakespeare's comedies are both actors and spectators of
their own play, involved, like Puck, in the drama, but also removed from it, in touch with the omniscience of Erasmus' Stultitia, which Shakespeare echoed in Puck:

> Yea, and it passeth, to see what sporte and passetyme the Goddes
> theim selues haue, at suche Folie of these selie mortall men. . . .
> Whiche syde of heauen bendeth most towardes the earth, there
> sitte they, and intentiuely beholde what mortall men dooe: and
> surely no spectacle can be more pleasaunt vnto theim. Good
> lorde, what a *Theatre* is this worlde? how many, and diuers are
> the pageantes that fooles plaie therin?[47]

Shakespeare remembered Erasmus in Puck's aside:

> Shall we their fond pageant see?
> Lord, what fools these mortals be!

The fairies share the wisdom which Shakespeare gave in *A Midsummer Night's Dream* to the Globe gods, those arbiters in the
heavens able to judge both the idolater and the man of reason. No
other of Shakespeare's plays gives the audience such omnipotence.
The lovers are exposed in all the bewilderment of their idolatry,
the action of love-in-idleness pointing a truth about its impersonal
nature, effusions of praise regardless of person:

> O Helen, goddess, nymph, perfect, divine!
> To what, my love, shall I compare thine eyne?
> Crystal is muddy. O how ripe in show
> Thy lips, those kissing cherries, tempting grow!
> That pure congealéd white, high Taurus' snow,
> Fanned with the eastern wind, turns to a crow,
> When thou hold'st up thy hand. O let me kiss
> This princess of pure white, this seal of bliss!

The audience sees the lovers' rapturous particularity about the
beauty irrespective of the lady mirrored in the misplaced trans-
ports of Pyramus and Thisbe:

[47] *The Praise of Folly*, p. 68.

These lily lips,
This cherry nose,
These yellow cowslip cheeks
Are gone, are gone:
Lovers, make moan:
His eyes were green as leeks.

But it can also assess not only the lovers' claims to reason –
Lysander's brag:

Who will not change a raven for a dove?
The will of man is by his reason swayed;
And reason says you are the worthier maid –

and the assurance with which the young courtiers scoff at the folly
of the bumpkin actors, but Theseus' scepticism. Theseus, born
among antique fables, brushes aside the lovers' story:

I never may believe
These antic fables, nor these fairy toys.

To such a man, imagination is delusion, and Shakespeare, the poet
of airy nothing, relishes his own exposure of the limits of Theseus'
vision:

Or in the night, imagining some fear,
How easy is a bush supposed a bear!

Only the audience knows that the bush and the bear were Puck.
But Shakespeare allows the women in *A Midsummer Night's Dream*
to partake of the audience's vision. Hippolyta lacks Theseus' cool
masculine conviction that he is right, and her doubt brings her
nearer the truth:

But all the story of the night told over,
And all their minds transfigured so together,
More witnesseth than fancy's images,
And grows to something of great constancy –
But howsoever strange and admirable.[48]

In Shakespeare's comedies women reach out to the world of the

[48] III.ii.114, 137, V.i.229, II.ii.122, V.i.2, 21.

audience, while men are contained within the play, whether
Viola, trapped within her own disguise and sharing her perplexity
with the audience, or Portia, displaying her talents as actress as
well as her acumen as lawyer. It is not a community of sympathy
confined to plays in which the heroine is disguised. Women are
forced to be watchers in a world ruled by men, and the power of
Shakespeare's heroines over the male world in the comedies comes
from their detachment from it, their standing aside from its assumptions. The women in *A Midsummer Night's Dream*, or *The Two
Gentlemen of Verona* or *Love's Labour's Lost*, are in some sense spectators of the idolatry directed towards them, and their independence
of the idolater's image of them bridges the gulf which idolatry
ordains between the world of men and the world of women.

Shakespeare metamorphosed the effect of the male cult of idolatry by making it reciprocal.[49] Romeo's worship of Rosaline, who
spurned him like any courtly lady, is new-minted in the encounter
with Juliet's return:

> Or, if thou wilt, swear by thy gracious self,
> Which is the god of my idolatry,
> And I'll believe thee.[50]

Mutual idolatry nourishes the intimacy which male idolatry dis-
courages. Ferdinand's first sight of Miranda recalls the reverence of
Chaucer's Palamon:

> Most sure the goddess
> On whom these airs attend! Vouchsafe my prayer
> May know if you remain upon this island.

But Miranda shares Ferdinand's wonder:

> What is't? a spirit?
> Lord, how it looks about! Believe me, sir,
> It carries a brave form. But 'tis a spirit.

The Tempest employs many of the conventions of the courtly love

---

[49] Cf. M. C. Bradbrook, *English Dramatic Form*, p. 97.
[50] *Romeo and Juliet*, II.ii.113.

romance – Ferdinand's trials, the chess-game, even the enchant-
ment, but Miranda is worlds apart from the courtly lady:

> I do not know
> One of my sex; no woman's face remember,
> Save, from my glass, mine own.[51]

Shakespeare uses reciprocal idolatry to reveal the nature of love
rather than to create, as male idolatry does, preconceptions about
the nature of women, the expectations which Keats describes:
'When I was a Schoolboy I though[t] a fair Woman a pure Goddess, my mind was a soft nest in which some of them slept, though
she knew it not – I have no right to expect more than their reality. I
thought them etherial above Men – I find them perhaps equal –
great by comparison is very small.'[52] Shared idolatry can grow into
equality, as with Romeo and Juliet, without the sense of decline
implicit in Keats' experience.

Shakespeare draws men and women together in idolatry by calling it the country of the young. He places it among people who
have moved beyond it – Theseus, after all one of the stormiest and
most mercurial of mythical lovers in his youth, Corin and Duke
Senior in *As You Like It*, the Friar in *Romeo and Juliet*. To the lover's
impatient eye these people inhabit a different universe, and are incapable of understanding the tumult of passion. Silvius breaks
away from Corin: 'No, Corin, being old, thou canst not guess,'[53]
and Romeo cries to the Friar: 'Thou canst not speak of that thou
dost not feel.'[54] Shakespeare intensifies but narrows idolatry by
realising the limits of the world which gives birth to it:

> Or, if there were a sympathy in choice,
> War, death, or sickness did lay siege to it –
> Making it momentany as a sound,
> Swift as a shadow, short as any dream,

---

[51] I.ii.424, III.i.48.
[52] Letter to Benjamin Bailey, July 1818.
[53] *As You Like It*, II.iv.24.
[54] *Romeo and Juliet*, III.iii.65.

Brief as the lightning in the collied night
That, in a spleen, unfolds both heaven and earth;
And ere a man hath power to say 'Behold!'
The jaws of darkness do devour it up:
So quick bright things come to confusion.[55]

He sees the alternative to the young lover's idolatry not as the
satire of the disillusioned idealist, but as the movement beyond infatuation into reason in love which distinguishes Beatrice and Benedick from Claudio and Hero in *Much Ado About Nothing*.
Benedick protests that he loves Beatrice 'no more than reason,' and
she retorts that her love for him is 'but in friendly recompense.'
The halting sonnets which belie their tranquillity are less important than the self-awareness and good humour, the sense of knowing the world in which their love has taken root, which lie behind
Benedick's 'By this light, I take thee for pity,' and Beatrice's 'By
this good day, I yield upon great persuasion, and partly to save
your life, for I was told you were in a consumption.'[56] Their love is
capable of surviving in the adult world, a world often inhospitable
to the idolatries of youth.

The more at home women are in the court in Shakespeare's
comedies, the more complicated their attitude to the courtly
lover's idolatry. Rosalind is chimeric where Phoebe is earth-
bound. Phoebe mocks the poetry of Silvius' passion because it tells
lies:

I would not be thy executioner.
I fly thee, for I would not injure thee . . .
Thou tell'st me there is murder in mine eye –
'Tis pretty, sure, and very probable,
That eyes, that are the frail'st and softest things,
Who shut their coward gates on atomies,
Should be called tyrants, butchers, murderers!
Now I do frown on thee with all my heart,
And if mine eyes can wound, now let them kill thee;

[55] *A Midsummer Night's Dream*, I.i.141.
[56] v.iv.77.

> Now counterfeit to swoon, why now fall down,
> Or if thou canst not, O for shame, for shame,
> Lie not, to say mine eyes are murderers!

Rosalind, bred in the court, sees beyond Orlando's versifying to the imaginative truth which Sidney claimed for poetry, where Phoebe, rubbing shoulders with Audrey, demands from it literal truth. Phoebe's scoffing at the theatricality of Silvius pretending to swoon, murdered by her eyes, anticipates Rosalind's real swoon, vainly disguised as theatrical. Rosalind's nurture gives her a finer perception of the distinction between the artificial and the genuine. Acting Ganymede, Rosalind also distances herself fom acting, where Phoebe cannot recognise her own histrionics. Rosalind has no time for Phoebe's cultivation of gentle manners; the courtly lover's abasement and his lady's pitilessness are as out of place in the country as Touchstone's hand-kissing:

> But, mistress, know yourself – down on your knees,
> And thank heaven, fasting, for a good man's love;
> For I must tell you friendly in your ear,
> Sell when you can – you are not for all markets.

Silvius is a rustic Troilus:

> You are a thousand times a properer man
> Than she a woman: 'tis such fools as you
> That makes the world full of ill-favoured children:
> 'Tis not her glass, but you, that flatters her,
> And out of you she sees herself more proper
> Than any of her lineaments can show her.[57]

Shakespeare places idolatry in the court, but he also confines to the court the capacity to see it in perspective.

The ladies in *Love's Labour's Lost* are in this respect the most courtly of any in Shakespearian comedy. Shakespeare challenges them with suitors in whom satire and idolatry of women are as inextricably entwined as in Pope's picture of Belinda in *The Rape of the Lock*. The young courtiers exclude woman from their

---

[57] *As You Like It*, III.v.8, 57.

academic refuge 'on pain of losing her tongue.' Their own inde-
fatigable chat: 'I'll prove her fair, or talk till doomsday here,'[58]
reverts to Erasmus' *The Praise of Folly*, enumerating 'these *Sophis-
trers* and *Logiciens*, beyng a race of men *more kackeling than a meny of
dawes*: eche of whom in bablyng maie compare with tenne
women.'[59] The sophists of the Inns of Court audience would have
taken Shakespeare's point. Moreover the young men consistently
under-rate the women's wit. Among themselves they recognise
two levels of talk – the rhetoric and intellectual juggling with
which they contrive to prove themselves right in the face of contrary evidence, and the common sense which surfaces when they
have to make a decision:

> Now to plain-dealing; lay these glozes by:
> Shall we resolve to woo these girls of France?

But they are incapable of plain-dealing with women, because they
do not credit them with enough sense to see through male
sophistry. Even after the King of Navarre's death their language
provokes the Princess's 'I understand you not.' The young men
court deities without recognising them as reasonable beings.

The ladies react to their suitors' idolatry as might be expected
from the high-bred, well-educated women of the Humanist ideal.
They display the impatience which Puntarvolo's wife should have
felt, or which Mistress Page and Mistress Ford convert into invention in routing a lovesick fat knight in *The Merry Wives of Windsor*,
transposed into a court setting. Women of wit do not want to be
idols. The ladies christen 'Some thousand verses of a faithful lover'
'A huge translation of hypocrisy,' sighing for shorter letters and
longer chains of pearl, and impervious to the language of compliment: 'If they do speak our language, 'tis our will / That some
plain man recount their purposes.' The language is foreign to them
in failing to communicate not only sense: 'How blow? how blow?
speak to be understood,' but good sense, which is violated by idolatry. Rosaline jests:

[58] I.i.122, IV.iii.271.

[59] p. 76.

Nay, I have verses too, I thank Berowne:
The numbers true; and, were the numbering too,
I were the fairest goddess on the ground.
I am compar'd to twenty thousand fairs.

They dash the courtiers' play 'like a Christmas comedy,' by taking
their courtship as a comic interlude:

We have receiv'd your letters full of love;
Your favours, the ambassadors of love;
And in our maiden council, rated them
At courtship, pleasant jest, and courtesy,
As bombast and as lining to the time.
But more devout than this in our respects
Have we not been; and therefore met your loves
In their own fashion, like a merriment.

The young men find themselves cast as Phoebes in a world of
Rosalinds.

The courtiers, used to dictating the terms of their own sport,
whether celibacy or courtship, confront in the ladies a sphere not
susceptible to manipulation through words and wit. The King
pleads:

Now, at the latest minute of the hour,
Grant us your loves.

The Princess retorts:

A time, methinks, too short
To make a world-without-end bargain in.

The ladies spoil the game of courtship by refusing to play:

Our wooing doth not end like an old play:
Jack hath not Jill: these ladies' courtesy
Might well have made our sport a comedy.

Shattering his play-world, Shakespeare asserts his characters' independence of its fictions. His women step back out of the play into
the world of the audience, forcing the fiction to accommodate
reality. The King attempts to console Berowne for the year's

interim: 'Come, sir, it wants a twelvemonth and a day, / And then
'twill end,' but Berowne, always more far-sighted than the others,
points out: 'That's too long for a play.' The play began with the
men in power, it ends with the women confining idolatry not only
to the court, but to the play.

The final scene of *Love's Labour's Lost* deals with plays spoilt by
the intrusion of life into art. The ladies wreck the Muscovite
masque when they change favours, by making it mirror the truth
that its protagonists are forsworn. Berowne remarks ruefully:

> The ladies did change favours, and then we,
> Following the signs, woo'd but the sign of she.
> Now, to our perjury to add more terror,
> We are again forsworn, in will and error.

Like the play in *Hamlet*, the Muscovite masque turns into an
instrument for exposing lies. The second play, the rustics' presentation of the Nine Worthies, founders beneath the jibes of the courtiers who restore their self-esteem, like Lysander and Demetrius
watching Pyramus and Thisbe, at the expense of Costard, Nathaniel and Holofernes. As the King points out: ''tis some policy / To
have one show worse than the king's and his company.'
Shakespeare's company was not called the King's Men until the
1600's, otherwise it would be tempting to see a joke at the actors
themselves. But the second play is also shattered by the intrusion of
a world of facts not susceptible to manipulation. Armado, as
Hector, declaims: 'This Hector far surmounted Hannibal, / The
party is gone – ' and Costard, no longer Pompey the Great, but
himself, interrupts: 'Fellow Hector, she is gone; she is two months
on her way.' Armado, like the courtiers, tries to play out the play,
but Costard stands for a level of reality not malleable in art: 'Faith,
unless you play the honest Troyan, the poor wench is cast away:
she's quick; the child brags in her belly already: 'tis yours.' The
end of Armado's courtship of Jaquenetta, with its precise aping of
the aristocrats both in its belittling of the beloved – 'the weaker
vessel,' 'a child of our grandmother Eve, a female; or, for thy more
sweet understanding, a woman' – and in its poetry: 'Assist me,
some extemporal god of rhyme, for I am sure I shall turn sonnet,' as

well as in its perjury, is pregnancy, the fact of life against the fiction of romance. The scene begins to cloud.

With the entrance of Marcade and the news of the King of France's death, Shakespeare spoils his own comedy. Death, like life, has intruded on the play-world, casting a shadow across its merriment, asserting a world which challenges the play's completeness by suggesting its limits. The final song opposes the fiction and the fact, the spring of courtship and the winter of marriage, the maiden and greasy Joan, with its reminder of Berowne's rueful reflection on the dark Rosaline: 'Some men must love my lady, and some Joan.' The singer's conclusion: 'The words of Mercury are harsh after the songs of Apollo'[60] returns to poetry and lies – Feste's benediction to Olivia: 'Now Mercury endue thee with leasing, for thou speakest well of fools!'[61] Mercury, god of lies, has the last word on Apollo, god of poetry. The rustic passes judgement on the courtly in the cuckoo who mocks married men. The court game of idolatry is a game only for the court.

Shakespeare drew court idolatry of women with a sympathy which brings him closer to the Elizabethan Lyly than to the Jacobean playwrights – Jonson or Marston or Middleton. But his evocation of the court has a perspective lacking in Lyly, which puts him again with the Jacobeans and the public theatre, the nurse of non-courtly attitudes. In Lyly the logical conclusion of idolatry in romance is the offering of the play to the queen, the goddess of the court poet. Images do not tarnish overnight, and idolatry of the Virgin Queen probably began to suffer in the 1590's – the decade of Shakespeare's comedies – the *fin de siècle* eclipse which darkened the Jacobean court and created the animus towards court manners which is a constant in Jacobean drama. Shakespeare's court is a prism, where Marston's is an opaque surface. Osric, Le Beau, Boyet, Jacques, Sebastian and Antonio in *The Tempest*, Cloten in *Cymbeline*, are creatures of Jacobean corruption paralleled in any of Marston's plays, where Hamlet, or Duke Senior in *As You Like It*, or Prospero, or Gonzalo stem from ideals which fashioned

[60] *Love's Labour's Lost*, IV.iii.367, V.ii.*passim*, I.i.259, I.ii.173, III.i.202, V.ii.920. Cf. Anne Righter, *Shakespeare and the Idea of the Play*, pp. 110–12.

[61] *Twelfth Night*, I.v.95.

Sidney, the courtier of Castiglione. The courts of Chapman or Jonson or Webster lack men of Elizabethan quality. But Shakespeare's court is more sharply defined than Lyly's because he brought to it a consciousness not only of the unideal courtier, but of worlds outside the court by which its virtues and vices, its refinements and its restrictions, might be measured. His criticism of idolatry of women as a courtly pursuit is a rapier to the cudgel in the hands of his fellow playwrights.

The line between the court and the workaday world is sharpest in *Love's Labour's Lost*, the least humane of Shakespeare's comedies. Only Costard breathes the life which animates Bottom and Dogberry – a man who thanks God that he is as he is, and other men are as they are. But Costard's fertility of spirit emphasises the aridity of the courtiers. Costard as a person cannot be dismissed with the aristocratic gesture of: 'Hence, Sirs; away!' He murmurs: 'Walk aside the true folk, and let the traitors stay.'[62] The values of non-courtly characters pass judgement on the courtiers. Costard's dignity, like Corin's in *As You Like It*, is internal to him, where the courtier's prestige is external. Corin tells Touchstone: 'Sir, I am a true labourer. I earn that I eat, get that I wear, owe no man hate, envy no man's happiness, glad of other men's good, content with my harm; and the greatest of my pride is to see my ewes graze and my lambs suck.'[63] Lear's envy of the beggar vibrates on Corin's creed for happiness: Shakespeare recapitulated in Lear's speech the rhythm of Corin's recital: 'Thou ow'st the worm no silk, the beast no hide, the sheep no wool, the cat no perfume.'[64] Corin holds his own against Touchstone by refusing to compete: 'You have too courtly a wit for me, I'll rest,'[65] a withdrawal inconceivable to the court jester, whose identity and livelihood depend on a perpetual renewal of sharpness at the expense of the world around him.

Court nurture and court leisure go together. Money and time breed imagination, as Virginia Woolf pointed out,[66] and imagination bodies forth idolatry of women. But Shakespeare always balances the world of leisure with the world of work. Theseus'

[62] IV.iii.209.   [63] III.ii.71.
[64] *King Lear*, III.iv.106.   [65] *As You Like It*, III.ii.67.
[66] *A Room of One's Own*.

nuptials summon the fairies, but also 'A crew of patches, rude mechanicals, / That work for bread upon Athenian stalls.' Playing is as alien to them as working is to the courtier:

> Hard-handed men that work in Athens here,
> Which never laboured in their minds till now;
> And now have toiled their unbreathed memories
> With this same play against your nuptial.

Bottom's fellows lament his translation because it deprives him of 'money, means and content,' Corin's priorities:

> O sweet bully Bottom! Thus hath he lost sixpence a day during his life: he could not have 'scaped sixpence a day. An the duke had not given him sixpence a day for playing Pyramus, I'll be hanged. He would have deserved it: sixpence a day in Pyramus, or nothing.[67]

Idolatry is the fume of an idle brain. Titania dotes on Bottom, while he is politely anxious to get out of the wood. Working men are tolerant of the whims and fancies of the lovesick courtier, but they would not contemplate annexing them to a working life. 'Away,' cries Holofernes the schoolmaster, after a happy disparaging of Berowne's love poetry: 'The gentles are at their game, and we will to our recreation.' Perhaps the final lines of *Love's Labour's Lost* – 'You that way, we this way' – are Shakespeare's own stage direction, defining, by dividing the actors, both the separation between the court and the world outside it which dominates the play, and the division between the play and the world of the audience which the final act of the play affirms. The actor speaks both to his fellow players, and to the departing crowd.

Shakespeare depicts courtiers who at their most ostentatiously courtly are less than courteous, and rustics, who at their rudest, know true gentleness. The audience is alienated from the smart young men who deflate a Worthy; its heart is with Holofernes in his reproach: 'This is not generous, not gentle, not humble.'[68] Adam's faithfulness in *As You Like It* judges both Oliver's

[67] *A Midsummer Night's Dream*, III.ii.9, v.i.72, IV.ii.16.
[68] IV.ii.164, V.ii.621.

treachery, and his nobility, in casting away as an 'old dog' the servant who has lost his teeth in his service. Snout's demur that the ladies will be 'afeard of the lion' and Bottom's careful remedy that 'half his face must be seen through the lion's neck' comment on the courtiers' inconsiderate behaviour at the play.

Love levels birth by making the courtier ignoble, and the poor man noble through feeling. Proteus is false to his friend and his mistress, violent towards Silvia. The wood pigeons in *A Midsummer Night's Dream* are at each other's throats, rending ancient amities and lashing each other into fresh frenzies of spite. Demetrius first threatens Helena with violence, then provokes her reproach for his extravagant praise:

> If you were civil and knew courtesy,
> You would not do me thus much injury.
>
> . . . .
>
> If you were men, as men you are in show,
> You would not use a gentle lady so.
>
> . . . .
>
> If you have any pity, grace, or manners,
> You would not make me such an argument.[69]

The young lords in *Love's Labour's Lost* are as self-absorbed in love as in study. But Silvius, the rustic, is ennobled by loving, becoming equal with the Duke's daughter. 'Jove, Jove!' cries Rosalind, stagily: 'This shepherd's passion / Is much upon my fashion.'[70] Silvius defines for the courtiers that distraction from self and capacity for living outside himself which Erasmus' Stultitia identified as the true lover's:[71]

> It is to be all made of fantasy,
> All made of passion, and all made of wishes,
> All adoration, duty and observance,
> All humbleness, all patience, and impatience,
> All purity, all trial, all obedience.[72]

---

[69] III.i.25, III.ii.147, 241.   [70] *As You Like It*, II.iv.58.
[71] *The Praise of Folly*, p. 126.   [72] *As You Like It*, v.ii.90.

These feelings put Armado's hand to the plough with the same willingness that dispatches a chastened Berowne to the sick-bed. Shakespeare placed idolatry at the centre of the court and characterised it from within with a sympathy absent in the plays of other dramatists, but at the same time he stepped outside the magic circle and showed how it looked to the world.

Women, and men not in love, see in idolatry the defiance of nature and reason offensive to the Humanists. Idolatry cannot accommodate the facts of the physical world – death, birth, age, sickness, sex. Romeo, cultivating his worship of Rosaline, is interrupted by a pang of hunger:

> Alas that Love, whose view is muffled still,
> Should without eyes see pathways to his will!
> Where shall we dine?[73]

The indifference of the lover to eating and sleeping – Celia is weary while Rosalind is rapturous – is a state which of nature must be impermanent. Speed nudges Valentine in *The Two Gentlemen of Verona*: 'Ay, but hearken, sir: though the chameleon Love can feed on the air, I am one that am nourished by my victuals; and would fain have meat.'[74] Music may be the food of love, but it will not sustain the body. Shakespeare's placing of Petrarchism in a physical world gives his comedies a dimension lacking in Lyly's. The symptoms of love are as likely to be Benedick's toothache or Beatrice's bad cold as Claudio's windy suspirations. The body is unromantically robust. Vives declared that 'love doth pain sometimes, but it never slayeth,'[75] and Rosalind, as Ganymede, assures Orlando that dying for love is a fiction of poetry:

> The poor world is almost six thousand years old, and in all this time there was not any man died in his own person, videlicet, in a love-cause: Troilus had his brains dashed out with a Grecian club, yet he did what he could to die before, and he is one of the patterns of love: Leander, he would have lived many a fair year,

---

[73] *Romeo and Juliet*, I.i.170.

[74] II.i.162.

[75] *The Instruction of a Christian Woman*, p. 106.

though Hero had turned nun, if it had not been for a hot midsummer night; for, good youth, he went forth to wash him in
the Hellespont and being taken with the cramp was drowned,
and the foolish chroniclers of that age found it was 'Hero of
Sestos.' . . . But these are all lies. Men have died from time to
time, and worms have eaten them, but not for love.[76]

Idolatry coexists with sex in Shakespeare's comedies not only in
the jesting of clowns like Launce and Speed, or in the mating of
non-courtly couples – Jaquenetta and Armado, Audrey and
Touchstone, Maria and Sir Toby – but in the consciousness of the
court lovers. Rosalind and Celia shock Le Beau with their salty
jests. Nerissa and Portia delight in catching each other in impro-
prieties. 'Why, shall we turn to men?' demands Nerissa, of their
projected disguise, and Portia retorts gleefully: 'Fie, what a question's that, / If thou wert near a lewd interpreter!'[77] Berowne
praises Rosaline's divinity but roots it in the earth; she owns
kindred with the Dark Lady:

> A whitely wanton with a velvet brow,
> With two pitch-balls stuck in her face for eyes;
> Ay and by heaven, one that will do the deed
> Though Argus were her eunuch and her guard.[78]

Shakespeare could never have resolved a play like *Twelfth Night* as
Lyly resolves *Gallathea*, allowing a woman to change sexes so that
another can marry her. Olivia's sexual nature demands a proper
man, and there is a sense of relief in the play when Sebastian strides
onto the stage dispelling shadows and false shapes, a bass voice
among the trebles: 'Are all the people mad?'[79] The fantasy is going
to end in fact, after all. In *A Midsummer Night's Dream*, the purest-
spoken of Shakespeare's comedies, Puck anchors the lovers' idolatries in the physical world. The poetry, the cruelty, the trials, the

[76] *As You Like It*, IV.i.90.
[77] *The Merchant of Venice*, III.iv.78.
[78] *Love's Labour's Lost*, III.i.193.
[79] IV.i.27.

potion, the divinities, the duellists, begin and end in four lovers lying on the ground, worn-out with the chase:

> And the country proverb known,
> That every man should take his own,
> In your waking shall be shown.
> Jack shall have Jill;
> Nought shall go ill;
> The man shall have his mare again, and all shall be well.[80]

The natural world reasserts itself, as Theseus enters with his bride and his hounds to enjoy the hunt. Shakespeare never allows the courtly lover's deifying of his lady to obscure the way of a man with a maid. The poetry only sets forth nature. The cult of idolatry has, in Shakespeare's plays, to step out of its male sanctuary.

Shakespeare saw women as closer to the physical process of birth and death than men, and consequently more conscious, like the women in *Love's Labour's Lost*, of the need for love to encompass change and growth: the perception which placed Donne in a new world from that of the Petrarchan poets. Leontes, gazing on the statue of his wife sixteen years later, speaks a truth which only love can render painless:

> Hermione was not so much wrinkled, nothing
> So aged as this seems.[81]

Women, whose beauty age must wither, turn a clear eye on the idolatry of youth. In *Love's Labour's Lost* the perception of the physical world shatters the play; in *As You Like It* it informs the whole philosophy and mood of the play. Shakespeare replaced the monotone youth of the early comedies with the pushing of one generation off the stage to make way for the next which Hazlitt noticed in *Romeo and Juliet*,[82] and instilled into Rosalind's spirit, as into Viola's, an awareness of mutability to intensify the experience of being fathom deep in love. 'Say "a day" without the "ever" . . .

---

[80] III.ii.458.
[81] *The Winter's Tale*, v.iii.28.
[82] *Characters of Shakespear's Plays*, p. 108.

No, no, Orlando, men are April when they woo, December when they wed; maids are May when they are maids, but the sky changes when they are wives.'[83] Time is the old justice who tries all, stealing on a love crowned with the prime with the swiftness with which he overtakes a thief to the gallows. The vividness of life in the comedies which centres on the women and radiates from them is brighter through their contact with the physical world of birth and death.

Victorian novelists tended to segregate their goddesses from the rawness of life, which they reserved for the working classes. Oliver Twist's mother giving birth in a workhouse, Nancy murdered by Bill Sikes, the pregnancy of Hetty Sorrel or the disgrace of Little Em'ly, contrast with the shadowy death in childbirth of the angelic Dora, the heavily sentimentalised birth of Amelia's baby after the death of George Osborne in *Vanity Fair*, the gentility of Rosamund's miscarriage in *Middlemarch*. Even Lady Dedlock is allowed a bastard shrouded in mystery and well-bred suffering. Men create peculiar problems and divisions for themselves when their image of ideal woman dictates, like the Virgin Mary, an evasion of nature. The extreme is Scott, in whose novels everything that is true to human experience retreats abashed from the polite circle of Lucy Bertrams and well-worshipped Julias into a sphere less inhibited by adulation of the feminine – the worlds of Meg Merrilies and Jeanie Deans. No English novelist wrote like Tolstoy in *War and Peace* of the experience of an upper-class woman in childbirth. In *Anna Karenina*, describing Kitty giving birth to Levin's child, Tolstoy completed the progression in Levin from worship of Kitty as unattainable, to love of her for herself and for her familiarity. Meredith, who called Diana Merion 'one of Shakespeare's women,' declaring through one of his characters that 'the bravest and best of us at bay in the world need an eye like his, to read deep and not be baffled by inconsistencies,' urged novelists to abjure the goddess and create woman as nature made her: 'As she grows in flesh when discreetly tended, nature is unimpeachable, flower-like, yet not too decoratively a flower; you must have her with the stem, the thorns, the roots, and the fat bed-

[83] IV.i.141. Cf. C. L. Barber, *Shakespeare's Festive Comedy*, pp. 230–38.

ding of roses.'[84] Shakespeare did not create upper-class women immune from nature. Jacquenetta the bumpkin bears a child, but so does Helena in *All's Well That Ends Well*, the most Humanist of Shakespeare's heroines, the least beholden to the Petrarchan religion of love. Pope's Clarissa tried to instil the ideal of good sense into the goddess, 'Angels called, and Angel-like adored:'

> Oh, if to dance all night, and dress all day,
> Charmed the smallpox, or chased old age away;
> Who would not scorn what housewife's cares produce,
> Or who would learn one earthly thing of use?
> . . . .
> But since, alas! frail beauty must decay,
> Curled or uncurled, since Locks will turn to grey;
> Since painted, or not painted, all shall fade,
> And she who scorns a man, must die a maid;
> What then remains but well our power to use,
> And keep good humour still whate'er we lose?[85]

In Shakespeare it is not women who need this counsel, but men. Shakespeare's aristocratic women, like Ascham, urge men to leave the monastery and sally forth into the world, to fashion the deity according to the flesh.

Longaville's sonnet in *Love's Labour's Lost* carries a logic reminiscent of the dispute between Palamon and Arcite about Emelye's godhead. He declaims:

> A woman I forswore; but I will prove,
>   Thou being a goddess, I forswore not thee:
> My vow was earthly, thou a heavenly love.

Berowne, passing judgements on fools' secrets like a Puckish demigod in his hiding-place, observes:

> This is the liver vein, which makes flesh a deity;
> A green goose a goddess; pure, pure idolatry.
> God amend us, God amend: we are much out o'th'way.

[84] *Diana of the Crossways*, chs. VIII, I.
[85] *The Rape of the Lock*, V.19.

The religion of love is suddenly an offence to religion. Dumain salutes his lady: 'O most divine Kate,' and Berowne retaliates: 'O most profane coxcomb.'[86] Idolatry of women took on a new aspect from its kinship with one of the hottest controversies of the time – the Protestant campaign against Catholic idolatry. The association would have been uppermost in Shakespeare's mind in *Love's Labour's Lost* because the historical Henri of Navarre was a Protestant who lost favour in England by turning Catholic. To make his followers idolaters had an appropriateness which the audience would have recognised. But the kinship between worship of women and worship of idols is not confined to this early play.

Vives had called the poet's idolatry of his lady 'impietie agaynst God,' but the Elizabethans had in the voluminous Homily 'Against Peril of Idolatry' a more immediate source for connecting the worship of women with the setting up of graven images. The popular image of Puritanism is still primarily concerned with a group of fanatics systematically destroying statues and stained glass in order to extirpate idolatry. Elizabeth's Homilist described the worship of idols – the statues in the Catholic Church, and the painted figures in the windows which had originally been put there to instruct the ignorant and then adored themselves even by the wise – as spiritual fornication. A man projected onto something worthless his own false idea of its value, exactly as a man decked his harlot with finery in defiance of her spiritual emptiness. The Homilist recalled Solomon, who, allowing his harlots to bring their false gods into his court, fell to worshipping them himself, his actual fornication creating a spiritual fornication.

Catholic shrines, Catholic pilgrimages, the Catholic homage to the Virgin differ, in the Homilist's view, only in name from pagan rites to Venus. He did not need Chaucer to tell him that in the merry ring-time, when birds do sing, 'Thanne longen folk to goon on pilgrimages.' 'It is too well known,' remarks the Homilist severely, 'That by such pilgrimage-going, Lady Venus and her son Cupid were rather worshipped wantonly in the flesh, than God the Father, and our Saviour Christ his Son, truly worshipped in the spirit.' *Amor vincit omnia* is as felicitously ambiguous as the Prioress

[86] IV.iii.62.

herself. The insistence on God the Father is significant. The Virgin, to Protestant eyes, attracted idolatry: 'When you hear of our Lady of Walsingham, our Lady of Ipswich, our Lady of Wilsdon, and such others, what is it but an imitation of the Gentiles Idolaters, Diana Agrotera, Diana Coriphea, Diana Ephesia &c. Venus Cypria, Venus Paphia, Venus Gnidia?' There can be no religion in a practice so allied to recognisable vice; the images 'be trimly decked in gold, silver, and stone, as well the images of men as of women, like wanton wenches, saith the Prophet Baruch, that love paramours; and therefore can they not teach us nor our wives and daughters, any soberness, modesty, and chastity.'[87]

Bertram wooes Diana in *All's Well That Ends Well* as a pagan goddess – ironically, of chastity: 'Titled goddess: / And worth it, with addition!' He invokes the religion of love: 'Be not so holy-cruel; love is holy.' But the Protestant spirit casts a blight on the shrines of false gods: 'Now God delay our rebellion! As we are ourselves, what things we are,'[88] as frosty as the touch of cold philosophy with which Appollonius withered Lycius' passion for the witch-goddess Lamia in Keats' poem. The Petrarchan goddess is in the drama of Shakespeare's time a profane idol in a pagan religion, not the being who can lead man, as Beatrice leads Dante, to God. Silvia promises her picture to Proteus despite the fact that she is 'loath to be your idol,' because the trappings of idolatry are congruous with his perfidy: 'Since your falsehood shall become you well / To worship shadows, and adore false shapes.'[89] The religion of love has itself become a heresy, a spiritual fornication.

Caroline drama lacked the Protestant incentive to cavil at idolatry of women, as well as the bourgeois impulse to reject attitudes fostered in a poetic art cultivated by courtiers and identified with the aristocracy. Dramatists like Suckling, Cartwright, Carlell and Denham are themselves the gallants – projecting courtly attitudes to women to a court audience – whom the Jacobeans mocked and exposed for the entertainment of the city. The transition is apparent in Beaumont and Fletcher, who were never happy consistently

[87] *Book of Homilies*, pp. 204, 237, 209, 206, 165.

[88] IV.ii.2, 32, IV.iii.18.

[89] *The Two Gentlemen of Verona*, IV.ii.125.

to ridicule and satirise the court in the way that Marston does. *The Maid's Tragedy* instances attitudes to royalty nearer Suckling than Shakespeare, a sentimental, pseudo-mystical allegiance to the king as symbol which James I, like Shakespeare's Richard II, would have liked to see in his subjects but found only in himself. Charles I found it in his dramatists. Francis Beaumont was the only Jacobean playwright who was one of the gentry, and had no need to work for a living. The Prologue to *The Woman-Hater* records a conciliatory gesture typical of all Beaumont and Fletcher plays, of never wanting to be at enmity with either city or court for too long, which creates in the plays a less sure relation both to the subject-matter and to the audience than in those of the other Jacobeans. The Prologue foretells of the play: '*You shall not find in it the ordinary and over-worn Trade of jesting at Lords and Courtiers, and Citizens, without taxation of any particular or new vice by them found out, but at the persons of them; such, he, that made this, thinks vile, and for his own part vows: That he did never think, but that a [Lord] born might be a wise man, and a Courtier an honest man.*' The honest courtier is as much a convention of Caroline drama, as the corrupt one is of late Elizabethan drama.

Platonic adulation of women in Caroline drama flatters Henrietta Maria. A character in Montague's *The Shepherd's Paradise* idolises Bellesa, played in the first performance by the queen: 'Shee's somwhat of her selfe; I know not what to call her, so unlike to all things sublunary, that we may better think the humility she beares chose rather to be a woman, then that heaven meant her one.'[90] There is plenty of ridicule of the Platonics in Caroline drama, but it never creates its own vocabulary in the way that mockery of idolatry did for the Elizabethans and Jacobeans. When Suckling tries to suggest a Miranda in *The Goblins* there is no sense of the new world into which Ferdinand's love baptises him. The hero sighs:

> Instruct me in what form I must approach thee,
> And how adore thee?[91]

[90] v. p. 120.
[91] III.vii.81.

but it is a stale salute in a setting of Gothic strangeness. Caroline drama is subservient to Henrietta Maria's ideas about women, where Elizabethan drama was independent. The absence of real opposition to the sentimental worship of women smothers the possibility of taking it seriously which gives subtlety to Shakespeare's criticism of it.

The rarity of sub-plots in Caroline drama restricts the means by which the dramatist can challenge his characters' attitudes.[92] But idolatry of women is a dull stereotype largely because the literary convention receives no challenge from life. Caring little about the implications of idolatry for actual men and women, dramatists like Suckling and Cartwright are simultaneously earnest and frivolous. Caroline dramatists were incapable of the sophisticated relation to courtly love which enabled Shakespeare to smile at Romeo's worship of Rosaline:

> When the devout religion of mine eye
> Maintains such falsehood, then turn tears to fires:
> And these who, often drowned, could never die,
> Transparent heretics, be burnt for liars,[93]

while couching the first encounter of Romeo and Juliet in a sonnet celebrating the worship of pilgrims at a shrine.

The Caroline theatre was the home of refined philosophy in a society of debaucheries.[94] Elizabethan drama made the theatre house both, and watched the action generated between them. From the clash of gods and devils emerges a new creature: the Humanists' rational woman.

2 Satire

The rational woman is as likely to emerge from a dust-bath of contumely as from a Cytherean sea of adoration. Satire on women is perhaps man's oldest pastime (if one exclude gardening), born with the weeds which transformed the leisure of Paradise into a

[92] Harbage, *Cavalier Drama*, p. 40.
[93] *Romeo and Juliet*, I.ii.91.
[94] *Cavalier Drama*, p. 77.

lifetime of labour. When invention flags, the bluntest pen can wring a grin out of an audience of nodding Slys with a jibe at women.

At first sight satire on women seems to enjoy its heyday in late Elizabethan and Jacobean drama. If by satire one means the proverbial compilation of female failings which spurred a contributor to 'jab his pen on the paper as if he were killing some noxious insect as he wrote,'[1] it was as popular in Shakespeare's theatre as murder, adultery, ghosts and jokes about foreigners. Jacobean dialogue carries a cynicism about women difficult to reconcile with either Puritanism or feminism.

Shakespeare and his fellow playwrights contrived nevertheless to have it both ways − to reap the audience's laughter at the satirist's sallies against women without compromising their own position as defenders of women. They wrote for people not likely to take satire at face value, and they could as a result fashion it into a fine-edged dramatic tool. The dramatists use scurrility about women for a variety of purposes, but never as a flat statement of their own point of view.

Any of Shakespeare's audience could buy a broadside ballad reeking with satire on women, the remnant of a long and loftier tradition. Medieval satire on women was an elaborate art-form, testing a poet's invention as a stylist in refurbishing a tatty Galatea, that gallimaufry of lust, inconstancy, greed, caprice, extravagance and hypocrisy which God had foisted onto Adam. But doubt about the troubadour's goddess went hand in hand with scepticism about the satirist's harpy. The Humanists, insisting on women's right to be individuals, shared Bullinger's contempt for the spleeny rhymer who put men off marriage: 'The wife is not in the scriptures called an impediment or necessary evil, as certain poets and beastly men who hated women have foolishly jangled; but she is the help or arm of the man.'[2] When Luther accused misogynist pens of blaspheming God's work he pointed out that 'if women were to write books they would say exactly the same about men.'[3]

[1] Virginia Woolf, *A Room of One's Own*, pp. 32–3.
[2] *The Decades of Henry Bullinger*, pp. 397–8.
[3] *Luther's Works*, 45, 36.

The satirist of women, like the poet of courtly love, was continually called to account throughout the sixteenth century by reformers who saw his venom as a celibate's perversion, by Humanist supporters of women's education, by defenders who pointed to the example of living women, and ultimately by women themselves. The English *querelle des femmes* of the midsixteenth century lacked the éclat of a feminist leader like Christine de Pisan, who half a century earlier had astounded French intellectuals by seizing a pen to answer the satirist. But England shared with France an intellectual climate hospitable to feminism. Italian Humanism, with its egalitarian approach to noblewomen, was as vital an influence in the courts of Catherine of Aragon, of Catherine Parr, and of Elizabeth herself, as in the circle surrounding Marguerite of Navarre. The presence of learned women gave an edge to Edward Gosynhill's waspish sneer in *The School House of Women*, first printed in 1541, that:

> In the woman
> Is lyttell thynge, of prayse worthye
> Lettred or unlerned.[4]

This piece, itself conventional enough, could hardly have sparked off the English quarrel about women without an already created concern.

Men ready to argue women's rights, whether in education or in the home, felt the challenge of a satire on women which up to the sixteenth century had enjoyed the impunity of poetry. Edward More's retort to Gosynhill reflects the reformers' enthusiasm for marriage:

> And more mete in dede I thought it also for a marryed man, who in defendyng of women myght partly gratyfye hys owne wyfe, whose honest behavyor sobernes wytt and true love theryn semyng to be apparent, myght redoune, and sounde not a lyttle to hys owne honestie; and also wolde be a greate encrease of love betwene them although they skant loved before.[5]

He addresses himself 'especially' to English women. Throughout Shakespeare's lifetime defenders of women exposed the satirist's

[4] Sig. Diii^v. [5] *The Defence of Women*, Preface, sig. Aii.

lies by pointing to the virtue of actual women. 'They use continually to visite Hospitalles, Prisons, and other places of wants, to give assistance to the miseries of men,'⁶ declared Anthony Gibson in *A Woman's Worth*, dedicated to the Countess of Southampton. The poet perpetrated fictions about women, which, whether slanderous or flattering, were equally false.

Satire on women is a siren, summoning the dramatist to an attractive but treacherous haven. Less ephemeral than political satire, its impact is as immediate. Its subject-matter is appealing and accessible; the experiences it records are the property of Everyman. Where other kinds of satire form and speak to their own élites, satire on women creates a comprehensive élite: the male world. But as a consequence it tends to exchange the exclusiveness of political satire for a lowest common factor of jest. Dullness is always in the wings ready to envelop the actor mouthing satire on women. His jibes lack the salt of provoking retaliation which gives savour to Dryden's scorn of the Earl of Shaftesbury in *Absalom and Achitophel*. Chapman, Jonson and possibly Marston were imprisoned for satire on James I in *Eastward Ho*. No playwright risked imprisonment for satire on women even when a queen was on the throne. Women offered the dramatist a too amorphous and silent target; satirising them was like berating a dumb waiter for a cold meal. Tudor dramatists demolished both women and foreigners with tedious ease. Neither knew how to answer back.

Tudor drama did not in any case create women capable of countering satire through their own characters as women might outside the theatre. The hybrid morality play is abstract: action clings perilously to ideas; characters embody types – the shrew, the improvised standard human being (disobedient child or what you will). Satire on women provides one element in a string of homilies; cynical instead of serious, its natural home is the Vice. As early as John Heywood's *The Play of Love* the Vice emerges as the enemy of romantic values.⁷ Conditions, Haphazard, Ill Reporte, Ambidexter, Politicke Perswasion,⁸ and many others of dubious prom-

⁶ p. 30.   ⁷ Bernard Spivack, *Shakespeare and the Allegory of Evil*, pp. 440, 226, 294.
⁸ In, respectively, *Common Conditions, Appius and Virginia, The Most Virtuous & Godly Susanna, Cambyses, The Play of Patient Grissell*.

ise, delight in naming love lust, and advising both the protagonists on the stage and the audience, on how to manage 'the craftiest cattell in Christendome.'[9] Congruous with the Vice's inherited and professed nature as a residual devil, who is more likely to blast his victims with fireworks than with eternal bonfire, the Vice's satire on women has its own music-hall propriety in plays which would make good pantomime. But it is never put to the test by any single woman. Women remain, like Hester, relentlessly godly, or, like Tom Tyler's wife, resoundingly shrewish. The satire on women which little William might have heard delivered by a strolling player could have been funny, or instructive, or scurrilous, or dull, but it would not have been dramatic.

When Shakespeare began writing he could have culled from the controversy about women suggestions for using satire in the theatre. Vives' attack – taken up by Jane Anger, the first woman defender, in 1589 – on men who condemned the all for the few, surfaced again in the miniature *querelle des femmes* ignited by Joseph Swetnam's *The Araignment of Lewde, Idle, Froward, and Unconstant Women*, printed in 1615. Its torch-bearers were three women who wrote – two of them under pseudonyms – with a vigorous articulateness which reminds one of the militant women sectarians, and of the women petitioners to Parliament in the 1640's. The slandered worm had at last turned. 'What if you had cause to be offended with some (as I cannot excuse all) must you needs shoot your paper-pellets out of your potgun-pate at all women?' The satirist indulges his own scurrilous fantasies: 'Why should you imploy your invention to lay open new fashions of lewdnesse, which the worst of women scarce ever were acquainted with?'[10] demanded Constantia Munda. Women are defamed by posturing poets:

[9] John Phillip, *The Play of Patient Grissell*, 1.433.

[10] *The Worming of a Mad Dogge: or A Soppe for Cerberus the Jaylor of Hell*, pp. 7, 9. All three defences appeared in 1617; Constantia Munda's real name is unknown, but Ester Sowernam's was Joane Sharp (according to the envoy of her pamphlet) and Rachel Speght wrote under her own name. Cf. Louis B. Wright, *Middle-Class Culture in Elizabethan England*, pp. 465–507, for a full account of the English *querelle des femmes*.

It hath ever beene a common custome amongst Idle, and hume-
rous Poets, Pamphleters, and Rimers, out of passionate discontents, or having little otherwise to imploy themselves about, to
write some bitter Satire-Pamphlet, or Rime, against women: in
which argument he who could devise any thing more bitterly,
or spitefully, against our sexe hath never wanted the liking, al-
lowance, and applause of giddy headed people.[11]

Rachel Speght saw in Swetnam an embittered bachelor envying
Puritan wedded bliss:

So the single man is by marriage changed from a Batchelour to a
Husband, a farre more excellent title; from a solitarie life unto a
joyfull union and conjunction, with such a creature as God hath
made for man, for whom none was meete till she was made.[12]

The satirist blames women for his own bile: 'Forbeare to charge
women with faults which come from the contagion of Masculine
serpents.'[13] The drama registers all these attitudes to the satirist of
women: nothing new emerged in the attack on Swetnam except a
play, *Swetnam the Woman-Hater Arraigned by Women*, in which
Swetnam is tried, found guilty and tortured by angry Amazons.
The stage was still a woman's best friend.

Articulate polemics identify the final direction taken by the
amoeba of discontent. A wish to vindicate women against the
satirist's accusations had long been in the air. Swetnam's dreary
diatribe offered an opportunity to express it. But Puritanism, and
the petty warfare in the popular press, had already created an alertness in Shakespeare's audience which the playwrights could
exploit. The dramatists mock the popular satire-monger. The
virtuous wife in Marston's *The Insatiate Countess* imagines her husband turning satirist in revenge for his own disappointed lust:

---

[11] Ester Sowernam (pseud.), *Ester hath Hang'd Haman*, pp. 31–2.
[12] *A Mouzell for Melastomus: The Cynical Bayter of, and Foule Mouthed Barker against Evahs Sex*, p. 14.
[13] Ester Sowernam (pseud.), *Ester hath Hang'd Haman*, p. 48.

    Abigail: They say mine has compiled an ungodly volume of
             satires against women, and calls his book *The Snarl*.
    Thais: But he's in hope his book will save him.
    Abigail: God defend that it should, or any that snarl in that
             fashion.[14]

Jonson's Corvino curses Celia for her reluctance to gratify Volpone:

                I hop'd that she were onward
    To damnation, if there be a hell
    Greater then whore, and woman; a good catholique
    May make the doubt.[15]

The dramatists could be confident of their audience's alienation from the satirist.

If satire is sharpened by opposition and danger, there was enough opposition to the satirist of women in the Jacobean theatre to give his satire a new vitality. Furthermore, with a misogynist king on the throne, sensitive to scorn from a stage eager to scorn him, there was a political frame of reference in satirising women which approximated to danger. The dramatists used satire on women as a stick to beat the court, aware of the popularity of such a practice with an audience of disapproving burghers. Satire thrives on risk, and exposing satirists of women acquired its own audacity.

Defenders of women hazard earnestness, the bad taste of resenting what was meant in jest. When Robert Copland in the early sixteenth century satirised the feigned grief of widows, he concluded with a conciliatory Envoy urging widows 'to take it as in play.'[16] One might argue that no one was imprisoned for satirising women because no one took it seriously. But the satirist's best joke is that society in its judgement of women has always taken him seriously,

[14] III.iii.36.
[15] IV.v.128.
[16] *The Seven Sorowes that Women Have When theyr Husbandes Be Deade*, Lenvoy, sig. Ciiii^v.

as a celibate clergy has only to demonstrate. His assertions carry at
the least a no-smoke-without-fire conviction. In a world swarm-
ing with male hypocrites, gluttons and lechers, hypocrisy, greed
and lechery were still the inheritance of Eve, and to keep a woman
in check was the short way of keeping in check what she brought
with her: vices to overwhelm her innocent spouse. When the Humanists argued for women's education, they noticed the extent to
which the treatment of women was determined by the satirist's fictions about woman. It was all very well to declare that this was
poetry, airy nothing, folly and fantasy, but Bacon's notion of
examining nature for its own sake was new and strange in the sixteenth century, and the poet's view of woman's nature offered a
simple, all-embracing definition hallowed by time and by ac-
cumulated male ecclesiastical wisdom. Shakespeare's audience
needed no convincing that what Leontes said about women would
have serious consequences for his wife.

The occupation of satirist acquired status in the Renaissance. The
pen was not mightier than the sword in the 1590's, but writing was
just as much a form of action as fighting, a positive response to experience, constituting action in a world where the active and contemplative were not divided but integrated. Posthumus' decision
to write against women in revenge for Imogen's faithlessness
becomes, in a more passionate man, the strangling of a wife:

> I'll write against them,
> Detest them, curse them: yet 'tis greater skill
> In a true hate, to pray they have their will
> The very devils cannot plague them better.

In a play where satire on women initiates the whole action –
Iachimo's jibe that 'if you buy ladies' flesh at a million a dram, you
cannot preserve it from tainting,' – there is an ironic fitness in
making the hero, at the height of his tragedy, sound like Swetnam.
Shakespeare deliberately draws in Posthumus a character of untra-
gic stature, satirising in him the leap from life into the fictions of
poetry:

> Could I find out
> The woman's part in me – for there's no motion

> That tends to vice in man, but I affirm
> It is the woman's part: be it lying, note it,
> The woman's: flattering, hers; deceiving, hers:
> Lust, and rank thoughts, hers, hers: revenges, hers:
> Ambitions, covetings, change of prides, disdain,
> Nice longing, slanders, mutability;
> All faults that name, nay, that hell knows, why, hers
> In part, or all: but rather all. For even to vice
> They are not constant, but are changing still;
> One vice, but of a minute old, for one
> Not half so old as that.[17]

The determination to write is a form of action comparable to the malcontent's assumption of a disguise, and carries the same prestige. The Renaissance satirist enjoyed a social cachet mirrored in the drama in the distinction attached to Don John's churlishness in *Much Ado About Nothing*, or in the confidence accorded to the penniless Flamineo by the Duke Brachiano in *The White Devil*. Jacques in *As You Like It* exchanges the inconsequence of the libertine for the status of the critic. The satirist of women offered the dramatists an antagonist worth confronting.

The feminism of the dramatists consists in containing the satirist within his own curiously contorted world. Their preoccupation is not with what he says, but with why he says it, its influence both on himself, and on others. In the drama satire tells more about the nature of the masculine serpent than about the nature of women.

The theatre is the natural arena for satire on women because the satire itself embraces elements of the theatrical. The satirist plays with his own illusions, like the jealous man. Hermione confronts Leontes:

> Sir,
> You speak a language that I understand not:
> My life stands in the level of your dreams,
> Which I'll lay down.

Leontes' obsession with the satirist's premises about women is not a

[17] *Cymbeline*, II.iv.183, I.v.39, II.iv.171.

vitriolic reaction to a woman's betrayal of him, but the breeding-ground for his conviction of betrayal:

> Should all despair
> That have revolted wives, the tenth of mankind
> Would hang themselves. Physic for't there's none;
> It is a bawdy planet, that will strike
> Where 'tis predominant; and 'tis powerful, think it,
> From east, west, north, and south; be it concluded,
> No barricado for a belly. Know't,
> It will let in and out the enemy,
> With bag and baggage.[18]

The satirist constructs his own fantasy world peopled with monstrous women. Othello's joy in Desdemona as a unique being is transformed by Iago into a vision of bestial generality:

> O devil, devil!
> If that the earth could teem with women's tears,
> Each drop she falls would prove a crocadile.[19]

In *The Duchess of Malfi* Ferdinand's hallucinations in his madness are not more weird than the dark web of lust which he weaves round his sister, seeing in her the epitome of medieval frailty, where the Duchess feels only her own bewildered chastity:

> Why might I not marry?
> I have not gone about, in this, to create
> Any new world, or custom.

Webster found the story in Painter's *Palace of Pleasure*, where the Duchess' suffering falls on her as retribution for lust in marrying again. Webster gave this interpretation of her situation to Ferdinand – 'They are most luxurious / Will wed twice,'[20] – while himself pointing the futility of the Duchess' virtue in a society convinced of women's innate corruption. The satirist is his own

[18] *The Winter's Tale*, III.ii.79, I.ii.198.

[19] IV.i.239.

[20] *The Duchess of Malfi*, III.ii.109, I.i.297.

dramatist, creating women to fit his book, his lurid stage-lighting blinding him to the real characters of the women around him.

The satirist's perception describes not a life outside himself but his own nature, so that Iago sees in Emilia and in Desdemona only his own negation of love and goodness:

> Come on, come on, you are pictures out o' doors;
> Bells in your parlours; wild-cats in your kitchens;
> Saints in your injuries; devils being offended;
> Players in your housewifery; and housewives in your beds.

Iago easily convinces himself, or claims to convince himself, that Desdemona is lustful and inconstant because a woman, for he himself conceives love as 'merely a lust of the blood, and a permission of the will.'[21] Iachimo in *Cymbeline*, weaker and less destructive than Iago, shares with him the habit of seeing in other men only himself. Conjuring up an image of Posthumus cavorting in Rome, freed from the shackles of a wife, Iachimo sketches a self-portrait:

> The jolly Briton
> (Your lord, I mean) laughs from's free lungs: cries 'O,
> Can my sides hold, to think that man, who knows
> By history, report, or his own proof,
> What woman is, yea what she cannot choose
> But must be, will's free hours languish for
> Assured bondage?'[22]

Elizabethan drama, despite its secular and naturalistic setting and its evocation of individual character, retains traces of the morality Vice. Iago, Edmund of Gloucester, Richard III, the Bastard in *King John*, revel in the stratagems, disguises, self-dramatisation, and manipulation of other characters which are the Vice's dramatic legacy. If satire on women was the property of the Vice in the morality play, his descendants in Shakespeare's theatre annex it. Where the satire of a man like Leontes is theatrical because akin to the delusions of madness, men such as Bosola in *The Duchess of Malfi*, or Flamineo in *The White Devil*, or Iago himself, recall the

[21] *Othello*, II.i.109, I.iii.335.
[22] I.vii.67.

Vice's self-conscious assumption of a role, and his trick, in being two-faced, of taking the audience into his confidence. Flamineo is not far removed from Conditions or Subtle Shift:

> It may appear to some ridiculous
> Thus to talk knave and madman; and sometimes
> Come in with a dried sentence, stuff'd with sage.
> But this allows my varying of shapes, –
> Knaves do grow great by being great men's apes.[23]

Satire on women is an indispensable element in the performance of such men.

The dramatic role of the Vice is often fused in the drama with the social separation of the Italian malcontent. Detached from the play-world and commenting bitterly on its iniquities, the malcontent is a less uneasy figure than the Vice because his satire is part of a philosophy, not simply a frivolous extension of a stage licence. Webster married the Vice and the malcontent in both Bosola and Flamineo, but Bosola, nearer the malcontent than the Vice, is the more flesh-and-blood character. Like the Duchess, Bosola rejects the world around him. But her repudiation of corruption postulates belief in man's capacity for virtue. Bosola's is a nihilistic retreat into isolation, his denial of goodness in human nature making him turn even from the woman whose virtue contradicts his negation, merely because she is a woman:

> Foolish men,
> That e'er will trust their honour in a bark
> Made of so slight, weak bulrush as is woman,
> Apt every minute to sink it![24]

Flamineo, like the Vice, deflates romance with gadfly satire. No poetic passions can survive his nudging, Pandarus-like commentary. Shakespeare separates Enobarbus' satire from the encounters between Antony and Cleopatra, allowing the passion truth as well as the criticism of it; but the love scenes between Brachiano and Vittoria are perpetually orchestrated by Flamineo's cynicism

---

[23] Webster, *The White Devil*, IV.ii.243.

[24] *The Duchess of Malfi*, II.v.33.

about women. He encourages Brachiano to woo Vittoria by assuring him of women's lust:

> What is't you doubt? her coyness? that's but the superficies of lust most women have; yet why should ladies blush to hear that nam'd, which they do not fear to handle? O they are politic, they know our desire is increas'd by the difficulty of enjoying; whereas satiety is a blunt, weary and drowsy passion, – if the buttery-hatch at court stood continually open there would be nothing so passionate crowding, nor hot suit after the beverage.

He urges Vittoria: 'Come, sister, darkness hides your blush, – women are like curst dogs, civility keeps them tied all daytime, but they are let loose at midnight, then they do most good or most mischief.' At the height of a passionate dispute occasioned by Brachiano's jealousy, Flamineo advises:

> Fie, fie, my lord,
> Women are caught as you take tortoises,
> She must be turn'd on her back.[25]

The comparable dramatic crisis in *Antony and Cleopatra*, when Antony suspects Cleopatra of fawning on Caesar's messenger, culminates in a change of tone possible because private:

> *Antony*: Cold-hearted toward me?
> *Cleopatra*:   Ah, dear, if I be so,
> From my cold heart let heaven engender hail,
> And poison it in the source, and the first stone
> Drop in my neck: as it determines, so
> Dissolve my life.[26]

Flamineo sullies even the authenticity of grief, when Vittoria weeps for Brachiano's death:

> Had women navigable rivers in their eyes
> They would dispend them all; surely I wonder
> Why we should wish more rivers to the city,

---

[25] Webster, *The White Devil*, I.ii.17, 298, IV.ii.150.
[26] III.xiii.158.

When they sell water so good cheap. I'll tell thee,
These are but moonish shades of griefs or fears,
There's nothing sooner dry than women's tears.

Flamineo's satire on women, unlike that of the Vice, is central to
the morality of the play: like Enobarbus's, it exposes the issues
involved in adultery. But it is misleading to see his belittling of
love as the psychological policy of a fully motivated character.
Flamineo's satire is not, like that of Leontes, or Hamlet, indicative
of a state of mind. He is a literary creation with a hereditary predi-
lection for degrading love and women. Webster places a semi-
allegorical figure in a situation where his theatrical villainy and
cynicism can masquerade as human motive. In a society where
women merit his censures his satire passes for spontaneous commentary on the world around him. Webster disguises Flamineo's
ancestry by stressing the deleterious influence on him of the court:

I visited the court, whence I return'd,
More courteous, more lecherous by far.

Flamineo claims that his disillusion with women represents a
mature judgement on the idolatry of his youth:

I myself have loved a lady and pursued her with a great deal of
under-age protestation, whom some three or four gallants that
have enjoyed would with all their hearts have been glad to have
been rid of: 'tis just like a summer bird-cage in a garden, – the
birds that are without, despair to get in, and the birds that are
within despair and are in a consumption for fear they shall never
get out.[27]

But this is Webster's way of dressing the Vice in motive and
human verisimilitude. In Flamineo Webster gave the Vice a local
habitation and a name. In Bosola he created a character capable of
suggesting life outside the theatre.
    Iago's satire on women in *Othello* is congruous with his Vice-like
nature and dramatic role, but it is more evil than Flamineo's.
Where Webster merely finds an appropriate secular setting and

[27]   *The White Devil*, v.iii.181, i.ii.325, 40.

outlet for the Vice's satire about women, Shakespeare draws a character who applies the judgements of a literary mode to real people in a real world. For Iago, cynicism about women is both motive and commentary and vindication, not the excrescence of 'motiveless malignity.' Iago is morally involved in the tragedy and his satire exists in a moral universe, whereas the Vice's exists in the theatre and in literature.

The malcontent is to tragedy as the Fool is to comedy, an outsider with a licence to criticise. Like the Fool, he adopts a role towards the other players. Satire on women forms part of the dramatic equipment of both characters. Launce in *The Two Gentlemen of Verona* punctuates Speed's reading of his (Launce's) letter to his lady with attacks on women which he disguises as defence, refusing to blame his love for slowness in speech:

> O villain, that set this down among her vices!
> To be slow in words is a woman's only virtue.

Hearing her accused of pride he cries: 'Out with that too; it was Eve's legacy, and cannot be ta'en from her.'[28] Aping the love-letter between Valentine and Silvia, Launce's satirical improvisation is a theatrical act which nevertheless exposes the theatrical elements in romantic love. Malevole in Marston's *The Malcontent* wearies of his role as cynic and satirist of women:

> No cuckold but has his horns, and no fool but has his feather; even so, no woman but has her weakness and feather too, no sex but has his – I can hunt the letter no farther. – [*Aside*] O God, how loathsome this toying is to me![29]

Truth about the nature of women emerges, in both the Fool and the malcontent, from a palpable staginess.

Malevole discards satire on women when he sees the hypocrisy of the men who denigrate them, and the virtue of individual women. By contrast, Hamlet's satire on women in general is a reaction to corruption in one. 'Frailty thy name is woman!' For him satire is no longer a poet's paradox, but a revelation of truth:

[28] III.i.330.

[29] v.ii.136.

The power of beauty will sooner transform honesty from what
it is to a bawd, than the force of honesty can translate beauty into
his likeness. This was sometime a paradox, but now the time
gives it proof.

Hamlet's father's goodness had no power to translate Gertrude's
beauty into its own likeness. Hamlet sees Ophelia as the representative of a sex who deserve the poet's venom. The chaste woman is
one who has never been asked:

If thou dost marry, I'll give thee this plague for thy dowry – be
thou as chaste as ice, as pure as snow, thou shalt not escape
calumny; get thee to a nunnery, go, farewell. Or if thou wilt
needs marry, marry a fool, for wise men know well enough
what monsters you make of them: to a nunnery, go, and quickly
too, farewell.

Hamlet, moving among the falsehoods of the court and discerning
truth only in the Player, in his relation to Ophelia himself becomes
a player, obscuring the real woman with the satirist's fictions:

Hamlet: Is this a prologue, or the posy of a ring?
Ophelia: 'Tis brief, my lord.
Hamlet: As woman's love.[30]

Obliterating the individual woman, satire initiates tragedy.
   The misogynist is as theatrical in his satire on women as the malcontent. Benedick, asked by Claudio to approve Hero, demands:
'Do you question me as an honest man should do, for my simple
true judgement? or would you have me speak after my custom, as
being a professed tyrant to their sex?' He vows never to marry:

That a woman conceived me, I thank her: that she brought me
up, I likewise give her most humble thanks: but that I will have a
recheat winded in my forehead, or hang my bugle in an invisible
baldric, all women shall pardon me. Because I will not do them
the wrong to mistrust any, I will do myself the right to trust
none: and the fine is – for the which I may go the finer – I will
live and die a bachelor.

[30] I.ii.146, III.i.111, 137, III.ii.150.

Having slyly insinuated women's extravagance as well as their inconstancy, Benedick steps with debonair security into Shakespeare's trap:

> I do much wonder, that one man seeing how much another man is a fool when he dedicates his behaviours to love, will after he hath laughed at such shallow follies in others, become the argument of his own scorn by falling in love. And such a man is Claudio.

But Benedick's self-awareness distinguishes him even from Berowne in *Love's Labour's Lost*. In the midst of his mockery of Claudio doubt of his own immunity grazes him: 'May I be so converted, and see with these eyes? I cannot tell – I think not.' He recognises the pose in his imperviousness to women. Casting it aside as no longer appropriate, he turns all his spirit to defending his new position. 'I did never think to marry. I must not seem proud. Happy are they that hear their detractions, and can put them to mending.' The audience nurses no antagonism to such a man: it delights in his escape from shame where in *Love's Labour's Lost* it enjoys seeing the young lords set down. Benedick always stands a little outside himself, amused at his own performance:

> I may chance have some odd quirks and remnants of wit broken on me, because I have railed so long against marriage: but doth not the appetite alter? a man loves the meat in his youth that he cannot endure in his age. Shall quips and sentences and these paper bullets of the brain awe a man from the career of his humour? No – the world must be peopled. When I said I would die a bachelor, I did not think I should live till I were married.[31]

Claudio's histrionic reviling of Hero cures both Beatrice and Benedick of their taste for acting.

Jonson's Morose is a less rounded character than Benedick, one of those men of humours who in Jonson's comedies are funny without ever being sad, and thus never quite so funny as Shakespeare's characters. The audience laughs at Morose, never with him. As an extravaganza on the misogynist the play bodies

---

[31] *Much Ado About Nothing*, i.i.159, 225, ii.iii.7, 21, 223.

forth the perception that satire on women is good comedy not for
what it says about women, but for what it says about men. Morose
is the stage manager of his own show, which consists of a completely silent household about to be blessed with a completely
silent bride. Jonson saddles him with a producer's blunder. His
principal woman turns out to be not only everything the satirist
predicted – domineering, garrulous, extravagant – but an
impostor, a puny boy actor in petticoats.

Elizabethan dramatists invented a variety of situations to demonstrate the satirist's relation to what he says about women. That
the satirist nurses sexual frustration is the Protestant's easiest, and
probably least interesting weapon against Catholic celibacy. Webster shows the Cardinal in *The Duchess of Malfi* making merry with
his whore while persecuting his sister for her marriage. Chapman's
Friar in *Bussy D'Ambois* satirises women's frailty while arranging
Tamyra's seduction. To see satire as an occupational disease,
whether of priest or pander – and in Renaissance drama they are
much the same thing – is to turn the satirist's paper pellets against
himself.

Satire on women flatters and soothes the vanity of the disappointed man. It is less painful to reflect that the whole sex are
duds, than that one has oneself shown the folly to choose a dud. In
Dekker's *Westward Ho* a husband solaces his unfounded jealousy of
his wife with the reflection:

> All wiues loue clipping, there's no fault in mine.
> But if the world lay speechles, euen the dead
> Would rise and thus cry out from yawning graues
> Women make men, or Fooles, or Beasts, or Slaues.[32]

Amintor in *The Maid's Tragedy* would prefer to explain Evadne's
treachery not as retribution for his own desertion of his betrothed,
Aspatia, but as cosmic female wickedness: 'For the rareness /
Afflicts me now.'[33] Conviction of the commonness of vice in
women provides a refuge for male pride.

By the same token it is consoling to 'fallen' persons of either sex

[32] II.i.233.
[33] Beaumont and Fletcher, *The Maid's Tragedy*, III.ii.52.

to reflect that their condition is pre-ordained by the nature of women. Satire on women is consequently the trademark of bawds, courtesans, rakes and panders. The Courtesan in Middleton's *A Mad World, my Masters* declares:

> Pooh, all the world knows women are soon down: we can be sick when we have a mind to't, catch an ague with the wind of our fans, surfeit upon the rump of a lark, and bestow ten pound in physic upon't: we're likest ourselves when we're down; 'tis the easiest art and cunning for our sect to counterfeit sick, that are always full of fits when we are well; for since we were made for a weak, imperfect creature, we can fit that best that we are made for.[34]

If frailty is endemic to the sex, the individual woman feels less responsibility for her own weakness. Evadne in *The Maid's Tragedy*, in lines which George Eliot misinterpreted when she put them at the head of the first chapter of *Middlemarch* to imply the impotence of women to act, laments women's natural inclination to evil:

> Since I can do no good, because a woman,
> Reach constantly at something that is near it.[35]

Cressida, surrendering to Diomed, sighs:

> Ah, poor our sex! this fault in us I find,
> The error of our eye directs our mind.[36]

These women bow to the satirist's judgement of women partly from policy, because it alleviates their guilt, partly from a blunted moral perception which blinds them to goodness in other women.

Satire on women is a sop to the virtuous woman's sense of superiority. I thank God that I am not as other men are acquires a new dimension if one is a woman. Isabella in *Measure for Measure* assents enthusiastically to Angelo's suggestion: 'Nay, women are frail, too:'

---

[34] II.vi.30.
[35] Beaumont and Fletcher, *The Maid's Tragedy*, IV.ii.258.
[36] *Troilus and Cressida*, V.ii.109.

Ay, as the glasses where they view themselves,
Which are as easy broke as they make forms.
Women? – Help, heaven! Men their creation mar
In profiting by them. Nay, call us ten times frail:
For we are soft as our complexions are,
And credulous to false prints.

Angelo takes his cue: 'Be that you are, / That is, a woman; if you
be more, you're none.' Women have always struggled against the
judgements of men who, estimating women low, proclaim those
who rise above their estimate not to be women. But Isabella, a
stronger character than any of the men in the play, accepts the
view of woman promulgated by the Church which she is about to
enter as a nun. Women's frailty is part of her theology; but it also
feeds the same moral superiority which allows Angelo to muse:

Ever till now
When men were fond, I smil'd, and wonder'd how.[37]

Women disarm their detractors by admitting the justice of their
accusations. The knowledge that men expect the worst of them be-
stows freedom: Nature has given them a licence for waywardness
and irrationality. Julia in *The Two Gentlemen of Verona*, weighing
the merits of her suitors, asks Lucetta what she thinks of Proteus.
Hearing him preferred, she demands the reason. Lucetta retorts:

I have no other but a woman's reason;
I think him so because I think him so![38]

In Middleton's *More Dissemblers Besides Women*, Aurelia, knowing
herself faithless, protests loyalty to her lover:

More than thyself what woman could desire,
If reason had a part of her creation?[39]

Women's irrationality justifies her infidelity. Rosalind's impor-
tunity about Orlando provokes Celia's protest: 'I would sing my

[37] II.iv.123, II.ii.186.
[38] I.ii.22.
[39] II.iii.41.

song without a burden – thou bring'st me out of tune.' Rosalind
excuses herself: 'Do you not know I am a woman? when I think, I
must speak.'[40] The satirist offers women, as well as men, a part to
play. Women enjoy assuming a stage personality in real life.

Satire on women in Shakespeare's theatre is, perhaps more than
anything else, a class symbol. The dramatists, expecting Puritan attitudes to women from their audience, make satire the badge of the
courtier who menaces both city morals and city money. City disapproval of satire coalesces with class antagonism. Two stock characters dominate late Elizabethan comedy: the gallant who seduces
a citizen's wife while tapping her for her husband's money, and the
gallant who, failing to seduce, revenges himself by broadcasting
success. The seducer persuades himself of the ease of his assignment
by reflecting that women are 'apple-eaters all, deceivers still.' A
gallant in Middleton's *The Roaring Girl* observes of his bene-
factress:

> By this light, I hate her, but for means to keep me in fashion with
> gallants; for what I take from her, I spend upon other wenches;
> bear her in hand still: she has wit enough to rob her husband, and
> I ways enough to consume the money.[41]

Out of this cardboard convention of the court intruder on bourgeois respectability grows Falstaff, making love simultaneously to
Mistress Ford and Mistress Page while planning inroads on their
husbands' wealth: 'I will be cheaters to them both, and they shall
be exchequers to me,'[42] and reproached by a defrauded yet devoted
Mistress Quickly:

> Thou didst swear to me then, as I was washing thy wound, to
> marry me, and make me my lady thy wife. Canst thou deny it?
> Did not goodwife Keech the butcher's wife come in then and
> call me gossip Quickly? – coming in to borrow a mess of vin-
> egar, telling us she had a good dish of prawns, whereby thou
> didst desire to eat some, whereby I told thee they were ill for a

[40] *As You Like It*, III.ii.245.
[41] III.iii.262, II.i.89.
[42] *The Merry Wives of Windsor*, I.iii.68.

green wound? And didst thou not, when she was gone down-
stairs, desire me to be no more so familiarity with such poor
people, saying that ere long they should call me madam? And
didst thou not kiss me, and bid me fetch thee thirty shillings? I
put thee now to thy book oath, deny it if thou canst.[43]

Finding the city woman more virtuous than satire suggests, the
gallant boasts imaginary conquests. Jonson's Epicoene warns the
collegiates against courtiers: 'They, what they tell one of us, have
told a thousand and are the only thieves of our fame.' Sir John Daw
and Sir Amorous Lá Foole brag of the times they have slept with
Epicoene – at first from bravado, and then to give Morose grounds
for divorce – banishing hesitation with the recollection that 'she is
but a woman, and in disgrace.' At the end of the play Truewit confronts them with the 'woman' they have deflowered:

> Nay, Sir Daw and Sir La Foole, you see the gentlewoman that
> has done you the favors! We are all thankful to you, and so
> should the womankind here, specially for lying on her, though
> not with her! You meant so, I am sure? . . . This Amazon, the
> champion of the sex, should beat you now thriftily for the com-
> mon slanders which ladies receive from such cuckoos as you are.
> You are they that, when no merit or fortune can make you hope
> to enjoy their bodies, will yet lie with their reputations and
> make their fame suffer. Away, you common moths of these and
> all ladies' honors.[44]

Moll Cutpurse berates the gallant who tried to seduce her in language worthy of Constantia Munda:

> Thou'rt one of those
> That thinks each woman thy fond flexible whore;
> If she but cast a liberal eye upon thee,
> Turn back her head, she's thine; . . .
> . . . .
> How many of our sex by such as thou,
> Have their good thoughts paid with a blasted name

[43] *Henry IV* Part II, ii.i.88.
[44] iv.vi.28, v.iv.91, 207.

> That never deserv'd loosely, or did trip
> In path of whoredom beyond cup and lip!
> But for the stain of conscience and of soul,
> Better had women fall into the hands
> Of an act silent than a bragging nothing.[45]

A character in Middleton's *No Wit, no Help Like a Woman's* plans to manifest his breeding by aping the gallant's satire on women, though acknowledging its origin in thwarted lechery:

> I'll give it out abroad that I have lain with the widow myself, as 'tis the fashion of many a gallant to disgrace his new mistress when he cannot have his will of her, and lie with her name in every tavern, though he ne'er come within a yard of her person; so I, being a gentleman, may say as much in that kind as a gallant; I am as free by my father's copy.[46]

Satire on women identifies the courtier to an audience of citizens.

In the drama the satirist creates his own fiction about women and judges individuals according to its terms. But the dramatists are perfectly clear that its terms belong to literature, not to life. The page who upbraids the jealous husband in Chapman's *All Fools* harks back to Bullinger's contempt of the poet:

> Now, sir, for these cuckooish songs of yours, of cuckolds, horns, grafting, and such-like; what are they but mere imaginary toys, bred out of your own heads, as your own, and so by tradition delivered from man to man, like scarecrows, to terrify fools from this earthly paradise of wedlock, coined at first by some spent poets, superannuated bachelors, or some that were scarce men of their hands; who, like the fox, having lost his tail, would persuade others to lose theirs for company?

The Puritans and the playwrights band together against the celibate and the idle rhymer. 'To conclude,' observes Chapman's Page, 'Let poets coin, or fools credit, what they list.'[47]

[45] Middleton and Dekker, *The Roaring Girl*, III.i.72.
[46] III.i.59.
[47] III.i.

Satire on women in Elizabethan and Jacobean drama is nearly always taken by critics at face value, as an expression of anti-feminism. Noticing its absence in Caroline drama Harbage concludes that those plays were more feminist.[48] But clean-mouthedness has nothing to do with women's rights; it is a sign of the separation of men from women when talk is censored for the sex of the hearer, like the censoring of oaths for children. Periods of emancipation for women often reflect greater freedom of speech, with that surface degeneration of standards of purity which is easily confused with a contempt in reality little allied to it. Caroline drama salutes propriety. Shakespeare and his fellows, by bringing the satirist's venom into the open, gave women a chance to answer it both in what they said and in what they did. Nothing is so daunting to fictions about woman as the facts about women. Shakespeare's women are not the only ones to belie the satirist's image as well as the idolater's.

Meredith lamented that in the creation of women in literature 'your recurring rose-pink is rebuked by hideous revelations of the filthy foul; for nature will force her way, and if you try to stifle her by drowning, she comes up, not the fairest part of her uppermost.'[49] Rejecting the simplifications of literature, whether rose-pink or filthy foul – or in Donne's words, whether god or devil – Shakespeare and his contemporaries used the theatre to explore the real nature of women.

[48] *Cavalier Drama*, p. 40.
[49] *Diana of the Crossways*, ch. I.

CHAPTER IV

Femininity and Masculinity

1 Women and Education

To talk about concepts of femininity and masculinity is to change them, because in no other field are the constants, the perceptible natures of men and women, so variable. When the sixteenth century Humanists discussed women's education, they found themselves redefining femininity.

Vives argued that the nature of women was unchanging: 'As man can not be chaunged, nor utterly delivered of his affections, so let no man hope to chaunge a woman from her proper and native nature.' He may improve her, but the raw material will remain the same, 'for as it is not in him to make of a woman no woman, so it is not in him to make of a man no man.' But when Vives started defining women's native nature, he noticed that he knew men like that too. It was not easy to divide feminine nature from human nature. 'All these foresayde thinges are of nature, and not of women them selves, and therfore they are not onelye found in women, but also in such men, as . . . are woman like.'[1] Nature seemed sometimes to parcel out the feminine to the wrong sex, and the tart-tongued Virgin Queen stood evidence to the Elizabethans that the goddess also distributed masculinity a little carelessly. The Humanists, addressing themselves to women's education, had to decide whether femininity was natural or social, eternal or ephemeral, absolute or relative. Shakespeare's public, including, at one time or another, the woman-ruler scorned by John Knox, a homosexual king surrounded by long-haired men, and the doubleted Amazon who swaggered the London streets to the horror of Philip Stubbes, brought to the theatre the alertness to preconceived

[1] *The Office and Duetie of an Husband*, sigs. Eiiij^v, Eij^v–Eiij.

notions of femininity which More carried into his daughters' schoolroom.

More, and the Humanists who followed his lead, saw that women's upbringing, based on the assumption that women were by nature weak in the head, led to situations where their ignorance and frivolity confirmed the belief. Education defined a woman's sphere, placing the needle in her hand, and the pen or the sword in her brother's. If learning was for men, a learned woman must be masculine. The Abbot in Erasmus' Colloquy assures the educated woman that 'women have nothing to do with Wisdom; Pleasure is Ladies Business.'[2] It is unfeminine to find pleasure in books. The proper areas of work and leisure left no room for Lady Jane Grey declaring that games in the Park were 'but a shadoe to that pleasure, that I find in Plato,'[3] or for the Puritan Lucy Hutchinson, describing how, like Maggie Tulliver, 'my father would have me learn Latin, and I was so apt that I outstripped my brothers who were at school. . . . My mother would have been contented I had not so wholly addicted myself to that as to neglect my other qualities. As for music and dancing I profited very little in them, and would never practise my lute or harpsichord but when my masters were with me; and for my needle I absolutely hated it.'[4] More and Erasmus not only attacked the idea that only men could enjoy books, they attacked the system of segregating girls from boys so that they learnt their ideas about life from women whose education had been totally restricted, who required the kind of conformity which Lucy Hutchinson's father was less anxious to inflict than her mother. Erasmus scoffed at the notion that needlework could improve the mind, or that the daily round of 'rouging and hair-dressing,' going to church for the sake of being seen, gossiping, reading romances and associating mainly with servants[5] could create any idea of the feminine nature which was not synonymous

---

[2] 'The Abbot and the Learned Woman', p. 254.

[3] Ascham, *The Schoolmaster*, p. 47.

[4] *The Life of Mrs. Lucy Hutchinson*, in *Memoirs of the Life of Colonel Hutchinson*, by his widow Lucy, p. 14.

[5] William Harrison Woodward, *Desiderius Erasmus: concerning the Aim and Method of Education*, pp. 149, 150, 152.

with folly.

When More instructed his daughters' tutor to educate their minds irrespective of their sex he claimed for women not only the capacity for education denied by those who held that women's moral fibre was too weak to withstand the dynamite of that knowledge so fatally purchased by Eve; not only their right, as human beings rather than women, to the spiritual heritage monopolised by men; he claimed that femininity could coexist with that expansion of the spirit usually described as masculine. His strongest argument was to point to Catherine of Aragon, the woman responsible for bringing the Spanish Vives to England to educate her own daughter, who commanded for her own learning a devoted admiration from the greatest Humanist scholars, which was perhaps not even quite equalled by the loyalty which later scholars such as Ascham and Cheke felt for the last of Henry's queens, Catherine Parr. Significantly More's tribute to Catherine of Aragon stresses her womanly qualities. He knew her to be a scholar. What he wanted to demonstrate was that her scholarship was not incompatible with an idea of women's nature which had always declared learning to be masculine:

> She it is who could vanquish the ancient Sabine women in devotion, and in dignity the holy, half-divine heroines of Greece. She could equal the unselfish love of Alcestis or, in her unfailing judgment, outdo Tanaquil. In her expression, in her countenance, there is a remarkable beauty uniquely appropriate for one so great and good. Cornelia, that famous mother, would yield to her in eloquence; Penelope, in loyalty to a husband.[6]

Such a woman is as far from the bluestocking feminism of Marie de Gournay, illegitimate daughter of Montaigne, who claimed equality for men and women, as Hermione is from Marston's Crispinella. More was a politician as well as an educational philosopher and he judged that the most persuasive claim for women's education was that it made them better women.

More cannot, however, be accused of pressing education into the service of sexual attraction as the nineteenth century did when

[6] *The Latin Epigrams of Thomas More*, p. 142.

it dressed a woman in 'feminine' accomplishments to make her a more formidable competitor in the marriage market. Mr Brooke, George Eliot's ideas-man, is nervous about his niece's reading Greek to her betrothed, fearing that it will be 'too taxing for a woman,' and is comforted to hear that she will read without comprehension:

> Ah, well, without understanding, you know – that may not be so bad. But there is a lightness about the feminine mind – a touch and go – music, the fine arts, that kind of thing – they should study those up to a certain point, women should; but in a light way, you know. A woman should be able to sit down and play you or sing you a good old English tune. That is what I like; though I have heard most things – been at the opera in Vienna: Gluck, Mozart, everything of that sort. But I'm a conservative in music – it's not like ideas, you know.[7]

If More was merely proposing education as a feminine grace, his siege of the male fort of education stopped this side of the drawbridge. The battle for women is to move beyond the realm of elegant amateurism which made the arts an after-dinner entertainment for the nineteenth century gentleman, Mary Bennet whacking through her concerto to the boredom of the Netherfield dance party, and Darcy insisting that women be well-read as well as expert coffee-table designers. One of the reasons why women gravitated towards novel-writing was not only that, as Virginia Woolf pointed out, paper was cheap, and if a woman sat in a dining-room with two doors, like Mrs Gaskell, she could run the house at the same time, but that the writing of fiction has always retained an amateur image, for love not for money, easily pushed under the blotting-paper if an important – or indeed any – visitor called. The Romantic idea of the artist dashing down his fine frenzy helped to ward off the truth of ninety percent sweat, 'the little bit (two Inches wide) of Ivory on which I work with so fine a Brush as produces little effect after much labour,'[8] which turns a feminine accomplishment into a profession; and professions are for

[7] *Middlemarch*, ch. 7.

[8] Jane Austen, *Letters 1796–1817*, p. 189.

men. Even now many parents, and the higher their class status the more likely this is to be, regard university education for girls, especially if it be Oxford or Cambridge, as a superior finishing school which will end, in every sense, in marriage. Education for women on these terms is not going to make them masculine, and offers no menace to the world's view of feminine nature.

To remain an enhancement instead of becoming a drawback in the marriage stakes, education for women must, in the male view of More's time, of the nineteenth century, and to a considerable extent, of the twentieth century, stop short of an excellence which a husband may construe as competition. Monsieur Paul in *Villette* instructs Lucy Snowe in Latin and Greek with perfect good humour until she starts to get the hang of it and really work hard, when his smiles turn to severity:

> 'Women of intellect' was the next theme: here he was at home. A 'woman of intellect,' it appeared, was a sort of 'lusus naturae,' a luckless accident, a thing for which there was neither place nor use in creation, wanted neither as wife nor worker. Beauty anticipated her in the first office. He believed in his soul that lovely, placid and passive feminine mediocrity was the only pillow on which manly thought and sense could find rest for its aching temples; and as to work, male mind alone could work to any good practical result.[9]

G. H. Lewes, the year before he met George Eliot, wrote that the ideal woman was one who could write, but did not;[10] Virgil's Spare Sisters must have spun his thread with a sardonic smile. More knew as well as any nineteenth century feminist that men feared that education would spoil women for the domestic round, making them discontented, combative, rebellious and uncomfortable to live with. His praise of Catherine of Aragon takes care to deny the incompatibility of learning with the duties of wife and mother. More pointed elsewhere to the practical advantages of a wife who would teach the children to read, and who would offer

9 Charlotte Brontë, *Villette*, ch. xxx.
10 Inga-Stina Ewbank, *Their Proper Sphere: A Study of the Brontë Sisters as Early-Victorian Female Novelists*, p. 9.

her husband the joy of intellectual companionship: 'It will be your
pleasure to spend days and nights in pleasant and intelligent conversation. . . . When she speaks, it will be difficult to judge between her extraordinary ability to say what she thinks and her
thoughtful understanding of all kinds of affairs.'[11] Milton would
have agreed fervently with Vives that whereas a stupid wife may
be a tolerable, though hardly a delightful, mate for a stupid man,
for a clever man she is insufferable.[12] More claimed that Orpheus
would not have bothered to fetch Eurydice from the underworld
if she had been ill-educated.[13] Educated wives would be more
tractable than ignorant ones, for 'there is nothing so hard to control as ignorance, in dealing with which reason and argument are
of no avail,'[14] argued Erasmus. A learned wife would be an asset,
not a liability.

If this vision of the educated woman enhancing a man's happiness and prestige were More's only contribution to the history of
women's education he could make no just claim to have freed
women from the male idea of the feminine nature. His arguments
undermine the narrowest conception of femininity, encouraging
Lady Jane Grey to prefer Plato to croquet without feeling freakish.
But women are still seen through male eyes, as dependants of the
male world, rather than as independent beings.

More, however, was not basically concerned to make a little
Latin a little lovesome. He urged that learning would not detract
from a woman's feminine attractions only because he was so
strongly convinced of women's inalienable right to education that
he was prepared to use almost any argument which would further
the cause. His real contention was twofold; he believed that mentally and spiritually women were not feminine but human, that
they had an equal claim with men to education as the means
through which the human spirit grows:

[11] *The Latin Epigrams of Thomas More*, p. 182.
[12] Vives, *The Office and Duetie of an Husband*, sig. Gvii.
[13] *The Latin Epigrams of Thomas More*, pp. 182–3.
[14] Woodward, *Desiderius Erasmus: concerning the Aim and Method of Education*, pp.
150–1.

The difference between the sexes has nothing to do with the matter, for in the time of harvest it is all one whether the hand which sowed the seed belongs to a man or a woman. Both possess the same reason which distinguishes men from animals. Both are therefore capable of those studies by which reason is perfected and fertilised, like a field over which the seed of good instruction has been sown.[15]

Secondly, he held that when educated on the same terms as men, women would prove as well-fitted as they for many professions previously debarred them on the grounds of their natural incapacity. In *Utopia* all men and women flock to lectures ('ac foeminae multitudo maxime audiendo lectiones'), all women have a craft; they may practise agriculture, and the more venerable – which also applies to men – may become priests.[16]

More was not simply stating the fact which even now is not accepted as obvious, that, given the appropriate education and training, women can do the same jobs as men, with the exception of those requiring unusual physical strength; though even this proviso, as primitive cultures show, is dictated by custom rather than by nature.[17] He wanted to reshape the patterns of society, breaking down its artificial divisions into the world of women, which stood for leisure, and the world of men, which stood for work. Men in *Utopia* have time to go to lectures because they have very short working hours. More explains: 'This phenomenon you too will understand if you consider how large a part of the population in other countries exists without working. First, there are almost all the women, who constitute half the whole.'[18] More's radicalism consisted in envisaging social conditions which would make many of the distinctions of his own time between the masculine and the feminine seem both arbitrary and irrelevant. His ideas about women's education formed one element in a larger vision which

[15] More to Gunnell, quoted in Karl Kautsky, *Thomas More and his Utopia*, pp. 99–100.

[16] pp. 129, 127, 125, 229.

[17] Margaret Mead, *Male and Female*.

[18] p. 129.

sought to free men as well as women. *Utopia* rises out of the same intellectual ferment which twenty years later produced Rabelais' Abbey of Thelema, where men and women live together in a free, equal and harmonious community.[19] Rabelais satirised, in creating the Abbey, both the anti-feminism and the authoritarianism of monastic life. Its motto, 'Do What Thou Wilt,' expresses More's ideal of concord instead of division between the masculine and the feminine.

More did not think of education as training women for work. Instead, like Agrippa, who protested that 'publicke Offices are forbidden them by Lawes, it is not permitted that any one plead in judgement, be she never so wise,'[20] he contested the confinement to the home which perpetuated an exaggerated view of the differences between men and women. He campaigned not for jobs for the girls, but for a community of ability irrespective of sex.

The Renaissance was hospitable to new ideas about women's education. Humanist concern for the education and upbringing of children highlighted the responsibilities of the mother as educator, a role she could only fulfil if educated herself. Montaigne, addressing the Countess of Gurson on the education of her children, assures himself of her diligence: 'So, (noble Ladie) forsomuch as I cannot perswade my selfe, that you will either forget or neglect this point, concerning the institution of yours, especially having tasted the sweetnesse thereof, and being descended of so noble and learned a race.'[21] In England girls from noble families received their education in the household of some other great lady, and were either educated by her alone, or with the help of a tutor from Oxford or Cambridge. Lady Brilliana Harley sent her daughter to the Lady Vere, and writes anxiously to her son: 'Deare Ned, send me word how my ladey Veere vsess her, and how shee carriers herself.'[22] The range of that education depended on the interests of the lady herself, and the Puritan Lady Margaret Hoby, whose diary

[19] *Gargantua and Pantragruel*, I, 119–33. Cf. M. A. Screech, *The Rabelaisian Marriage*, pp. 34–5.

[20] *The Glory of Women*, p. 30.

[21] *The Essayes of Montaigne*, I, 154.

[22] *Letters of Lady Brilliana Harley*, p. 158.

records an astringent diet of sermons – Babington, Gifford, Greenham – no doubt offered a practical rather than intellectual training, in household management, in the midwifery which well-born women practised, and in estate management. '[I] . . . walked with Mr. Hoby about the toune to spye out the best places where Cotiges might be builded.'[23] Dorothea Brooke would have envied her.

Lady Anne Clifford, of whom Donne declared that 'she knew well how to discourse of all things, from Predestination to Sleasilk,'[24] was a bigger intellectual fish for mothers to seek out for their daughters. Her diary records the reading of *The Faerie Queene*, Ovid, Turkish history, Chaucer, Sidney's *Arcadia*, Montaigne and Josephus. But her charges may have had a more tempestuous time than Lady Hoby's, for she notes: 'I fell out with Kate Burton and swore I would not keep her and caused her to send to her Father. The 18th Sir Edward Burton came hither and I told him I would not keep his daughter.'[25]

The education of children provided both noble and middle-class women with a function. For the many unable, as Erasmus feared, to teach anything but needlework and scandal, there must have been some like Mrs Garth, modelled on George Eliot's own mother, who instructed her children in Roman history while rolling out her pastry in the kitchen. The translation of the Bible in the sixteenth century provided ordinary women with a rich source of history, politics, philosophy and poetry; its fruits were nonconformity, the right to a free interpretation of the text. Compulsory state education robs women of a purpose which dignified their position, and leaves them, just as the removal of domestic industry to the factory left them, in increasing redundancy in the home. The Renaissance bred a less sentimental attitude to the educated mother than that of a society which puts the business of educating children in the hands of professionals. Educate a women, educate a family is the seductive slogan of a world in which the mother has little to do with formal education, and is

---

[23] *Diary of Lady Margaret Hoby 1599–1605*, p. 65.

[24] *The Sermons of John Donne*, I, 130, n. 36.

[25] *The Diary of Lady Anne Clifford*, pp. 52, 104, 66, 76, 41, 111, 106.

encouraged to have less. The woman who, like More's ideal wife, teaches her little ones to read, probably uses the wrong method. In More's time, if the middle-class woman failed to teach her children to read, no one else was going to do it.

The men of the Renaissance had thus in one sense a utilitarian attitude to women's education: it was essential to the virtuous upbringing of children. In another sense they were non-utilitarian, and this was also to women's advantage. To More, Erasmus, Vives, Ascham, Montaigne, Bacon, education meant more than book-learning, that shrunken pursuit of letters for its own sake which proves so inadequate to the needs of the young men in *Love's Labour's Lost*. Navarre's study would people the world not with men like Sidney, but with reproductions of Holofernes, preambulating arts-man. Montaigne declared that 'a meere bookish sufficiencie is unpleasant,' and that 'the good that comes of studie (or at least should come) is to prove better, wiser, honester.' A man demonstrated his education 'not by the testimonie of his memorie, but by the witnesse of his life.'[26] Nurtured on Castiglione's *The Courtier* with its evocation of the 'compleat' gentleman, Renaissance educators saw education as a means to virtue. They did not divorce, as the monasteries had done, the active from the contemplative life; Sidney was a soldier and a statesman as well as a scholar and a poet, and Erasmus' Prince, like Hamlet, acquired education to make him a virtuous ruler. Education opened a man's eyes to the fullness of life, colouring his mind; through the recognising and ordering of his passions it fitted him, as Prospero's art eventually fits him, not for the seclusion of the library (which proved fatal to Prospero's political position) but for responsibility in the world. The Humanist paradise admitted no noble unknowing savage. Man was given reason in order that he might learn the good life. In Erasmus' view the pivot of Christ's teaching was the Sermon on the Mount. Education, the nurse of virtue, led to God.

If God were no respecter of souls, the Humanists argued that it was illogical and pernicious to deny women that nurturing of the

[26] 'Of the Institution and Education of Children: to the Lady Diana of Foix, Countesse of Gurson', pp. 158, 157, 155.

spirit conducive to good in men. If the woman was indeed 'endued with the same rational power, and Speech with the man, and indeavoreth to the same end of blessednesse,'[27] her education should be the same as his. 'That they are no better, it is our falt, inasmuch as we do not our duetyes to teache them,'[28] remarked Vives. If the classics help a man to bear the slings and arrows of outrageous fortune, then, according to More: 'Happy is the woman whose education permits her to derive from the best of ancient works the principles which confer a blessing on life. Armed with this learning, she would not yield to pride in prosperity, nor to grief in distress – even though misfortune strike her down.'[29] Lady Anne Clifford recorded after one of her frays with her husband, Lord Dorset: 'My soul was much troubled and afflicted to see how things go, but my trust is still in God, and compare things past with things present and read over the Chronicles.'[30] The perspective of philosophy, the solace of the kingdom of the mind, was not just for men. The learned woman in Erasmus' Colloquy observes that 'this is Wisdom, to know that a Man is only happy by the Goods of the Mind. That Wealth, Honour and Descent, neither make a man happier nor better.'[31]

Christianity, which in its Pauline interpretation must bear responsibility for suppressing women's claim to education, contains within it the logic of emancipation, granted the equality of souls. The parable of the talents applies to women, as Lucy Snowe stoutly decided in the face of Monsieur Paul's pique: 'Whatever my powers – feminine or the contrary – God had given them, and I felt resolute to be ashamed of no faculty of his bestowal.'[32] The decline of Christianity as the focus of society has, ironically, weakened one of the strongest ideological justifications for educating women. The ideal of self-fulfilment, however worthy, is narrower and more inward-looking than the concept of custodianship of the

[27] Agrippa, *The Glory of Women*, p. 1.
[28] *The Office and Duetie of an Husband*, sig. Pv[v].
[29] *The Latin Epigrams of Thomas More*, p. 182.
[30] *The Diary of Lady Anne Clifford*, p. 56.
[31] 'The Abbot and the Learned Woman', p. 254.
[32] Charlotte Brontë, *Villette*, ch. xxx.

gifts of God which impelled all the Brontë sisters to pursue their calling,[33] and which influenced the feminist argument perhaps into the 1930's, but not beyond.

More and Vives did not ask themselves the modern question about what they were educating women for, because they did not ask it about men. Education for the practical purpose of service in the commonwealth was the corollary of the Humanist ideal, but not its starting-point. Modern bourgeois society, having abandoned Colet's concept of classical education, embraces an increasingly specific view of education as a training for a particular function. More wrote for men and women who owned their own libraries. To the modern state, financing education itself, women are a worse investment than men unless they can demonstrate that they are being educated for jobs on the same terms as men, hence the drive for nurseries. Women's right to the same education as men was a simpler and more watertight claim in the Renaissance because it bore no relation to economics. The differences of life-style between men and women, in the bearing and raising of children, were irrelevant to the argument.

More, like Bruni in Italy, conceived of an education for noble women. Vives asserted that a middle-class woman only needed to understand her religion and the management of her home. The Frenchman Jean Bouchet, writing in 1538, pointed out that only aristocratic women would have time for education, as they would have servants to run their homes.[34] Montaigne later averred that learning would be sullied by base-bred minds.[35] The tributes to learned women in the sixteenth century are all addressed to noblewomen. Ascham wrote of the Princess Elizabeth that 'beside her perfit readines, in Latin, Italian, French, and Spanish, she readeth here now at Windsore more Greeke every day, than some Prebendarie of this Chirch doth read Latin in a whole weeke.'[36] Nicholas

---

[33] Ewbank, *Their Proper Sphere*, p. 49.

[34] Lula McDowell Richardson, *The Forerunners of Feminism in French Literature of the Renaissance*, p. 72.

[35] 'Of the Institution and Education of Children: to the Lady Diana of Foix, Countesse of Gurson', p. 153.

[36] *The Schoolmaster*, p. 67.

Udall, dedicating a translation of Erasmus by the Princess Mary to her stepmother, Catherine Parr, marvelled at the number of noble women 'geven to the studie of humaine sciences and of straunge tongues,' at their 'pennynge of godlye and fruitfull treatises,' and their translations from Greek and Latin for the benefit of the ignorant.[37] For all this More, as the pioneer of classical learning for English women, must take credit. But emancipation for the few is emancipation only in a limited sense, assuming means, leisure and domestics, that trilogy which even Mrs Pankhurst took for granted.

More's influence was not confined to the circle for which he wrote. When the Puritans proclaimed Humanist ideas about marriage, they could hardly escape Humanist attitudes to women's education. Lucy Hutchinson's education compares with that of More's daughters. Slightly higher on the social scale, Lady Brilliana Harley probably read Greek, and certainly knew Latin so well that she chose it for light reading on her sick-bed:

> Haueing bine offtin not well, and confined to so sollatary a place as my beed, I made choys of an entertainment for meself, which might be eassy and of some benifit to meself; in which I made choys to reade the life of Luther, rwite by Mr. Calluen. I did the more willingly reade it, becaus he is generally branded with ambistion, which caused him to doo what he did, and that the papis doo so generally obrade us that we cannot tell wheare our religion was before Luther. . . . Theas resons made me desire to reade his life, to see vpon what growned theas opinions weare biult; and finding such satisfaction to meself, how fallsly theas weare raised, I put it into Inglisch, and heare in closed haue sent it you.[38]

But women diarists and letter writers – Grace Sherrington, Lady Margaret Hoby, Dorothy Osborne, Lady Brilliana Harley herself – are few on the ground, and perhaps too exceptional to suggest what education Shakespeare's sister might have received (had one

[37] James Kelsey McConica, *English Humanists and Reformation Politics Under Henry VIII and Edward VII*, pp. 231–2.
[38] *Letters of Lady Brilliana Harley*, p. 52.

indeed been certain of what he received himself).

More himself would have been the first to repudiate a classi-
fication which equated education with proficiency in languages.
Jonson was a classical scholar and Shakespeare was not, but only
the twentieth century, judging education by what a man knows
rather than by what he is, would call Jonson more educated. The
quality of education of any group, whether women, or children,
or a social class, can only be judged by the individuals it produces,
the kind of society they want, and the kind that they make. That
society's values, prejudices, capacity for change, tell more about
the education of its members than the sum of their learning, as
More perceived when he contrasted the pagan Utopians with the
corrupt Christian Europeans.

More's campaign for women's education had two consequences
which affected the condition of middle-class women. In the first
place it resulted in a circle of noblewomen, centred round Elizabeth, who had all been educated on equal terms with men, and
who could therefore assess the validity of society's attitudes to
women from a standpoint denied to most women. Individual
women themselves have always presented the strongest challenge
to the male idea of the feminine. John Knox inveighed against
Mary Tudor, the New Englanders imprisoned Anne Hutchinson
for preaching, reviewers complained of the feminine indelicacy of
Wuthering Heights, and sycophants sighed with relief when they
heard that George Eliot, despite her masculine cranium, spoke in a
very feminine voice. The prominence of educated women in Elizabethan and Jacobean society made the Elizabethans sensitive to
the whole area of masculinity and femininity, to the way in which,
as More argued, women's nature was dependent on women's upbringing.

Secondly, in Shakespeare's lifetime middle-class women began
to have a voice. Education breeds articulateness. Just as the bourgeois Marie de Gournay inherited the pen of Marguerite of
Navarre, so the women who repudiated the satirists of their sex,
who spoke in separatist meetings, who, like Elizabeth Grymeston
and Emilia Lanyer, wrote poetry, who justified the 'mankind'
woman in breeches, were the heirs of Catherine of Aragon and

Margaret Roper and Elizabeth herself. The discovery of Æmilia Lanyer, poet, pearl in the oyster of Brown Ladies, adds another voice to those heard from the silent multitude. The title-page of her poems advertises 'Eves Apologie in defence of Women' – an extended argument for Adam's superior responsibility for the Fall. Her character of Pilate's Wife claims that Pilate's sin is greater than Eve's:

> Then let us have our Libertie againe,
> And challendge to yourselves no Sov'raigntie;
> You came not in the world without our paine,
> Make that a barre against your crueltie;
> Your fault beeing greater, why should you disdaine
> Our beeing your equals, free from tyranny?
> If one weake woman simply did offend
> This sinne of yours hath no excuse, nor end.[39]

Theology is still the pointer to politics; More would have rejoiced at the education which prompted the women petitioners of Parliament in 1648 to claim that 'since we are assured of our creation in the image of God, and of an interest in Christ equal unto men, as also of a proportionable share in the freedoms of this commonwealth . . . Have we not an equal interest with the men of this nation in those liberties and securities contained in the *Petition of Right*, and other the good laws of the land?'[40] Middle-class women in Shakespeare's time may have had no more Latin than he had himself, and less Greek, but they were less silent than they had been fifty years earlier, and more to be reckoned with. Shakespeare wrote both about, and for, women aware of what it was like to be feminine in a culture which labelled not only physical, but mental strength, masculine. This consciousness both he and they owed to More.

St Paul's demand for silence in women debarred them from the whole spectrum of Scholastic education in the Middle Ages, which

[39] Æmilia Lanyer, *Salve Deus Rex Iudaeorum* (1611), sig. D 2. Professor Kenneth Muir very kindly drew my attention to these poems.
[40] From a *Petition of Women, Affecters and Approvers of the Petition of Sept. 11, 1648* (5 May 1649), in A. S. P. Woodhouse, *Puritanism and Liberty*, p. 367.

in its emphasis on rhetoric, logic, grammar, oratory, gave the spoken word primary importance. Where disputation was the medium of instruction a silent woman was bound to be an ignorant one. Yet the insistence on silence in women, like the call to chastity, goes hand in hand with complaints of its opposite, the garrulity of the sex. Silence appears not as the natural state, but as a condition imposed by men to keep the talking animal in check. When More commended Catherine of Aragon's eloquence, and Agrippa argued that women have speech and reason on the same terms as men, they scaled a tower which men had labelled Babel for many centuries.

Shakespeare and his fellow playwrights suggest neither that silence is natural to women and speech to men, nor that femininity requires silence. But their women characters relate in one form or another to the assumption that eloquence and argument are masculine. Their feminism consists in suggesting the Protean nature of silence in women.

Virgilia in *Coriolanus* is the only one of Shakespeare's women who conforms to the masculine ideal of feminine silence. Coriolanus, triumphant from battle, greets his wife:

> My gracious silence, hail!
> Wouldst thou have laughed had I come coffined home,
> That weep'st to see me triumph?

But her silence is impotent to sway him, and Volumnia, urging him to pity Rome, turns irascibly on her daughter-in-law:

> Daughter, speak you,
> He cares not for your weeping.

When Virgilia, in a flash of forthrightness, accosts Sicinius: 'You shall stay too. I would I had the power / To say so to my husband,' he retorts: 'Are you mankind?' (meaning masculine). But the reward of feminine silence is insignificance. In a play which circles round the power of the voice to vote, to plead, to scorn, to sway and to betray, the dramatic climax salutes not the power of silence in women, but Volumnia's masculine eloquence which turns Coriolanus to Aufidius, demanding: 'Were you in my stead, would you have heard / A mother less?'[41]

The silence which separates Virgilia from the centre of action makes Cordelia the focus of it in *King Lear* where eloquence bespeaks the hypocrisy of Goneril and Regan, or the well-oiled deference of Oswald. Cordelia's intransigent silence allies her with Kent, refusing to speak smooth to the Earl of Cornwall. Kent's honesty recognises the mainspring of Cordelia's reluctance to flatter:

> Nor are those empty-hearted whose low sounds
> Reverb no hollowness.

Offering himself in disguise as a servant to the king who banished him, Kent describes himself as one 'to converse with him that is wise, and says little.' Lear's rage with his daughter: 'Let pride, which she calls plainness, marry her,' anticipates Cornwall's sarcasm about Kent: 'An honest mind and plain, he must speak truth.'[42] Yet to Hazlitt, plainness is 'manly plainness,'[43] despite the fact that Shakespeare portrays it equally in Kent and Cordelia. To the confusion of convention, Cordelia's refusal to speak salutes a rule of femininity in a context which gives her bluntness masculine strength. Later in the play, moreover, the restraint and inarticulateness of her grief recalls not Constance, but Brutus or Macduff:

> Faith, once or twice she heav'd the name of 'father'
> Pantingly forth, as if it press'd her heart;
> Cried 'Sisters! sisters! Shame of ladies! sisters!
> Kent! father! sisters! What? i' th' storm! i'th'night?
> Let pity not be believ'd!' There she shook
> The holy water from her heavenly eyes,
> And clamour moisten'd, then away she started
> To deal with grief alone.

The Renaissance image of the temperate man mastering his passions becomes feminine:

---

[41] II.i.165, V.iii.155, IV.ii.15, V.iii.192.

[42] I.i.153, I.iv.16, I.i.129, II.ii.100.

[43] *Characters of Shakespear's Plays*, p. 119.

> It seem'd she was a queen
> Over her passion; who, most rebel-like,
> Sought to be king o'er her.

In Cordelia the strength which men look for in other men coexists
with the compassion and gentleness which they seek in women:

> Her voice was ever soft,
> Gentle and low, an excellent thing in woman.[44]

The intractability of Cordelia's silence in a world where silence in
women spells submission is part of the inversion which clothes the
ferocity and self-interest of her sisters in superficial docility and sex
appeal. The strictures on women which erupt from the inner chaos
of Lear's mind show him grappling with the consciousness that his
idea of the feminine failed to interpret the natures of his own
daughters.

Shakespeare's women, however independent they are, always
retain a sense of how they look to men, even if, like Goneril, they
reject its suggestions. They speak against a backcloth of feminine
silence. Imogen repulses Cloten:

> I am much sorry, sir,
> You put me to forget a lady's manners,
> By being so verbal.[45]

The Victorians' favourite heroine was Imogen, partly because in
her Shakespeare softens the initiative of the comic heroine with a
susceptibility to decorum. Drawing attention to the manners she
ignores, she escapes their restrictions while declaring allegiance to
them. She discards feminine behaviour harmoniously, where Kate,
galled by Petruchio, casts it boisterously aside; the difference in
manner disguises the similarity of the gesture:

> Why, sir, I trust I may have leave to speak,
> And speak I will. I am no child, no babe.
> Your betters have endured me say my mind,

---

[44] *King Lear*, IV.iii.26, V.iii.272.
[45] *Cymbeline*, II.iii.105.

And if you cannot, best you stop your ears.
My tongue will tell the anger of my heart
Or else my heart, concealing it, will break,
And rather than it shall, I will be free
Even to the uttermost, as I please, in words.[46]

Women free themselves through a conscious dissociation from their image in men's eyes, as Beatrice does, or Helena, or Desdemona, escaping the nature her father wants to find in her:

A maiden never bold;
Of spirit so still and quiet that her motion
Blushed at itself.[47]

Portia disclaims Brutus' view of her as a woman:

I grant I am a woman; but withal
A woman that Lord Brutus took to wife.
I grant I am a woman; but withal
A woman well-reputed, Cato's daughter.
Think you I am no stronger than my sex,
Being so fathered and so husbanded?
Tell me your counsels; I will not disclose 'em.
I have made strong proof of my constancy,
Giving myself a voluntary wound
Here, in the thigh. Can I bear that with patience,
And not my husband's secrets?

Shakespeare would not weary his audience with a repetition from Brutus to Portia of the plot they already know. But when the day dawns on Portia alone in the house which Brutus has left for the Capitol, her agitation demonstrates her knowledge:

O constancy, be strong upon my side,
Set a huge mountain 'tween my heart and tongue!
I have a man's mind, but a woman's might.
How hard it is for women to keep counsel.[48]

[46] *The Taming of the Shrew*, IV.iii.73.   [47] *Othello*, I.iii.94.
[48] *Julius Caesar*, II.i.292, II.iv.6.

Brutus bowed to a strength he perceived only when his wife explicitly denied its femininity. Women's freedom in late Elizabethan drama is always wrested from the chains of the masculine idea of woman, whether silent, passive or silly, where men's freedom is their birthright.

Women are swift to see other women in men's terms, because other women reflect themselves, thus declaring their own impact on the male world. Gertrude's first comment on the play which the players stage at Elsinore criticises the Player Queen: 'The lady doth protest too much methinks.'[49] Gertrude is not guileful, deflecting comparisons between herself and the hypocritical queen by anticipating and bringing them into the open. She is a stupid, straightforward woman of blunted sensibility. The Player Queen is interesting to her because a woman, and as such a competitor for attention in the world of men; with a flatulant Elsinore sigh, Gertrude decides that she talks too much, and will therefore not convince men of her sincerity. For a woman like Gertrude, as, on a different scale, for Goneril and Regan, what matters is not whether the Player Queen is sincere, but whether she will be successful in making men think she is sincere. When women look at other women they momentarily become men. Meredith wrote that 'what a woman thinks of women, is the test of her nature.'[50] Cleopatra frets for a description of Octavia that she may judge how attractive her rival will be to Antony. She demands: 'Didst hear her speak? is she shrill-tongu'd or low?' Hearing that she is low-voiced, she muses: 'That's not so good: he cannot like her long,' and translates the phrase into her own 'dull of tongue,' prompting her informant to a vivid evocation of lifelessness:

> She shows a body, rather than a life,
> A statue, than a breather.[51]

Cleopatra is momentarily taken aback by Octavia's soft voice; Lear was not the only one to like low voices in women. But recollecting her own shrill outbursts she brushes aside the man's

[49] *Hamlet*, III.ii.229.
[50] *Diana of the Crossways*, ch. 1.
[51] *Antony and Cleopatra*, III.iii.12, 20.

vision of the attractive woman, and recasts Octavia in her own terms, measured by a standard she knows to be Antony's, however it may contradict, as Rosaline contradicted for Berowne, the male idea of female beauty. But her confidence is won through a glimpse of Octavia from the man's point of view, it is not an instantaneous self-confidence.

The injunction to silence affects women's position in domestic life, but also in public life. If eloquence is inappropriate in a woman she is automatically excluded from office in the Church, in the State, or in the Courts of Law. More knew how revolutionary was his depiction of women priests in *Utopia*. The State had to give way to women before any other male stronghold in the sixteenth century, but when John Knox attacked the woman-ruler he expatiated on the whole field of public activity for women, relating his arguments back to St Paul's embargo. He declared:

> Hereof it is plaine, that the administration of the grace of God is denied to all woman. By the administration of Goddes grace, is understood not only the preaching of the Worde and administration of the Sacramentes, by the whiche the grace of God is presented and ordinarilie distributed unto man, but also the administration of Civile Justice, by the whiche vertue oght to be mainteined, and vices punished. The execution wherof is no less denied to woman, then is the preaching of the Evangile.[52]

The Humanist Agrippa had regretted that a woman could not plead in judgement, however wise she might be. Women made no inroads on the closed shop of the law in the sixteenth century despite their prominence in politics and the emergence of some women preachers. A woman judge is still newsworthy. But a woman could speak at her own trial. The drama shows women defending themselves in court while conscious that men condemn them for masculine presumption in so doing.

The heroines of Shakespeare's last plays stand halfway between the comic heroines and women in the tragedies. Women dominate the last plays emotionally, dwarfing the men, just as the comic

---

[52] *The First Blast of the Trumpet against the Monstrous Regiment of Women, The Works of John Knox*, IV, 386.

heroines control the male world. But the women in the last plays
encounter a hostility in men which in tragedy emerges in the raw,
unalleviated by comic sportiveness. Katherine's trial in *Henry VIII*
allies her not to women in the histories, but to Hermione in *The
Winter's Tale.*

Hermione and Katherine plead their own cause in courts which
have prejudged the issue. The public hearing which Leontes
arranged to prove his own impartiality turns into a public shaming, almost comparable to Hero's in *Much Ado About Nothing.*
Leontes scoffs at his wife's defence:

> I ne'er heard yet
> That any of these bolder vices wanted
> Less impudence to gainsay what they did
> Than to perform it first.

He interprets her eloquence as effrontery, urging condemnation of
her not for what she says, but for saying it at all. Fearless speech
spells shamelessness, a masculine disregard for feminine propriety.
Leontes essays the same technique for silencing Paulina, calling her
'dame Partlet:'

> A callat
> Of boundless tongue, who late hath beat her husband,
> And now baits me!

But Shakespeare demonstrates in this play almost more than in any
other, that conventions of femininity have no relevance in the tribunal of right and wrong. Paulina's conscience, like Hermione's
innocence, compels speech:

> I'll use that tongue I have: if wit flow from 't
> As boldness from my bosom, let 't not be doubted
> I shall do good.

Paulina bows to femininity with an orator's subtlety, talking inces-
santly of subjects on which she protests womanly silence:

> Alas! I have show'd too much
> The rashness of a woman: he is touch'd

> To th' noble heart. What's gone and what's past help
> Should be past grief. Do not receive affliction
> At my petition; I beseech you, rather
> Let me be punish'd, that have minded you
> Of what you should forget. Now, good my liege,
> Sir, royal sir, forgive a foolish woman:
> The love I bore your queen – lo, fool again!
> I'll speak of her no more, nor of your children:
> I'll not remember you of my own lord
> (Who is lost too): take your patience to you,
> And I'll say nothing.

The morals of silence are as unstable in *The Winter's Tale* as time itself. The eloquence of Hermione and Paulina contrasts with the cowardly silence of Leontes' courtiers. But words, which give shape to Leontes' imaginings, seem in the end suspect and inexpressive:

> The silence often of pure innocence
> Persuades, when speaking fails.[53]

After sixteen years, Leontes and Hermione embrace silently. The trial scene desecrated words between them.

Vittoria in Webster's *The White Devil* suffers, like Hermione, from being a woman speaking for herself in a court. The Lawyer begins by addressing her in Latin, which she refuses to answer not because she fails to understand it herself, but because half the audience in court will, through ignorance of the language, be unable to judge the justice of her sentence:

> I will not have my accusation clouded
> In a strange tongue: all this assembly
> Shall hear what you can charge me with.

The prejudice of the court against her immediately erupts in Monticelso's expostulation that a foreign tongue will guard her credit better than her own. But when Vittoria scoffs at the Lawyer's jargon – 'Why this is Welsh to Latin,' – the Lawyer

[53] *The Winter's Tale*, III.ii.54, II.iii.90, II.ii.52, III.ii.220, II.ii.41.

takes refuge in the masculine freemasonry of the law into which
women can never be initiated:

> My lords, the woman
> Knows not her tropes nor figures, nor is perfect
> In the academic derivation
> Of grammatical elocution.

Flamineo later adopts the same tack against his sister's pleas for life:

> Leave your prating,
> For these are but grammatical laments,
> Feminine arguments, and they move me
> As some in pulpits move their auditory
> More with their exclamation than sense
> Of reason, or sound doctrine.

As soon as Vittoria begins her defence against the charges of
whoredom and murder Monticelso interrupts to label her 'A
woman of a most prodigious spirit,' pointing to her defiance of the
court's conviction of her guilt as evidence of her unfeminine immodesty:

> She comes not like a widow: she comes arm'd
> With scorn and impudence: is this a mourning habit?

Her retort that had she planned her husband's death she would
have ordered her mourning habit is construed as contempt of
court. But Vittoria makes explicit what the whole trial illustrates,
that her defence convicts her as a woman as completely as any of
her deeds, because every word she utters proclaims her a rebel to
the nature which St Paul declared to be womanly:

> My modesty
> And womanhood I tender; but withal
> So entangled in a cursed accusation
> That my defence of force like Perseus
> Must personate masculine virtue.[54]

---

[54] III.ii.18, v.vi.67, III.ii.58, 120, 132.

If eloquence is a masculine virtue, then feminine virtue consists in silent acquiescence to charges of guilt. The logic is that of witch-ducking: if she swims she is guilty and burned at the stake; if she drowns she is innocent, but dead anyway. Webster is never so fully behind Vittoria as in the court scene where he depicts a justice which is only for men.

Wolsey in Shakespeare's *Henry VIII*, who knew from the case of the Surveyor's trumped-up charges against Buckingham, how nearly his own contrivances had been thwarted by the rationality and integrity of the queen, urges Henry to provide his wife with advocates instead of letting her plead her own defence in the marriage dispute. The trial goes as badly as he had feared. Katherine addresses her case directly to her husband with an eloquence which spurs Wolsey to try and hustle her away, leaving the decision to the assembled 'reverend fathers;' like Monticelso, he seeks to establish an impenetrable cabal of the learned to which the accused woman will have no access. But having attempted to silence her, Wolsey is taken aback by her next move. Campeius declares:

> The queen is obstinate,
> Stubborn to justice, apt to accuse it, and
> Disdainful to be tried by't. 'Tis not well.
> She's going away.

The queen is deaf to calls to return, resolving amongst her attendants:

> They vex me past my patience. Pray you pass on.
> I will not tarry; no, nor ever more
> Upon this business my appearance make
> In any of their courts.

Her silence outwits her accusers because her presence is necessary to the exercise of the law against her. Katherine defies the male world by refusing to listen if she is not allowed to speak.

The two cardinals, Wolsey and Campeius, try then to settle the case out of court. Katherine, addressed in Latin by Wolsey, makes Vittoria's protest, not because she is unlearned, but because she needs the support of her attendants:

O, good my lord, no Latin!
I am not such a truant since my coming
As not to know the language I have lived in.
A strange tongue makes my cause more strange, suspicious.
Pray speak in English. Here are some will thank you,
If you speak truth, for their poor mistress' sake.

Katherine's politics are to conciliate her adversaries with disarming plaints of womanly weakness:

If I have used myself unmannerly,
You know I am a woman, lacking wit
To make a seemly answer to such persons.[55]

Her assumed diffidence, so different from her behaviour at the beginning of the play, is the only weapon she has against a world in which eloquence in women, like Cadmus' dragon's teeth, breeds enemies. Katherine, like Hermione, has no power to halt the court's decree; her capacity to plead exasperates because it obstructs decisions already taken for her by men.

Renaissance drama places in a hostile environment women whose education renders them as eloquent and as rational as men. Claudio's confidence in his sister's powers are not misplaced:

She hath prosperous art
When she will play with reason and discourse,
And well she can persuade.[56]

Isabella's rhetoric constitutes an element in the strong self around which Isabella constructs her own convent wall of carefully cultivated feminine weakness. She entices Angelo, cold to other women, because she addresses him as a human being rather than as a man. Her oblivion of his sex is aphrodisiac. A man's eloquence – as Isabella anticipates of her own – liberates itself from masculine identity, but a woman's, as she painfully discovers, is always coloured by her sex. Portia is a second Daniel only while she wears

[55] II.iv.119, III.i.42, 176.
[56] *Measure for Measure*, I.ii.174.

breeches: as a wife Bassanio portrays her as an illogical being to whom rings and things are more important than gratitude. Portia, playing the part of the affronted wife, confirms a vision which is Bassanio's, not her own. As the young lawyer predicted, a rational wife 'would not hold out enemy for ever / For giving it to me,'[57] and nor does Portia, despite her return to the skirt. Mary Wollstonecraft argued that 'the desire of being always women, is the very consciousness that degrades the sex.'[58] More attacked an education which insisted that women were always women by educating his daughters as though they were men, and thus equipping them to challenge the male idea of femininity. Shakespeare and his contemporaries create women ready to forget the fact of womanhood in a society determined to remember it. The dramatists saw that society makes women in its own image and informs the rebels that they are not women, but men. But Luther himself pointed out that the acquired associations of the word 'woman' were different from those of the Hebrew word used to describe Eve in *Genesis*, which suggested rather 'a She-man, . . . a heroic woman who performs manly acts.'[59] The feminism of the drama consists, like More's, in constant pressure against the boundaries which, in defining the feminine, determine also the masculine, making the sword as restrictive as the skirt. If the finest man in Shakespeare's theatre is Volumnia, the finest woman is Hamlet.

Virginia Woolf observed that 'the history of men's opposition to women's emancipation is more interesting perhaps than the story of that emancipation itself.'[60] More tilled a soil to bring forth Helena and Isabella, Beatrice and Portia and Hermione, but among the wheat waved the thriving tares of Jonson's intellectual ladies.

Jonson reacts to learned women much as the gentlemen of the *Athenaeum* might react to mixed membership. He resists the intrusion of women on a territory he considers exclusively and justifia-

---

[57] *The Merchant of Venice*, IV.i.443.
[58] *The Rights of Woman*, p. 109.
[59] *Luther's Works*, *1*, 137.
[60] *A Room of One's Own*, p. 57.

bly male. Truewit in *Epicoene* declares of the collegiates: 'Why, all
their actions are governed by crude opinion, without reason or
cause; they know not why they do anything; but as they are
inform'd, believe, judge, praise, condemn, love, hate, and in emulation one of another, do all these things alike.'[61] Erasmus and
More would have agreed, but blamed men for failing to educate
women's judgement. But Jonson contends that education will only
produce the stale wit of the lady intellectual in *Every Man Out of
His Humour*, or the effusions of a Lady Politick Would-be:

> Which o' your poets? PETRARCH? or TASSO? or DANTE?
> GVERRINI? ARIOSTO? ARETINE?
> CIECO di Hadria? I haue read them all.[62]

Women can only drag standards of scholarship down to their own
level of indistinction. Like Molière, who allows his learned
ladies to be duped by imposters in *Les Précieuses Ridicules*, Jonson
believes women's brains to be bright but halcyon, turning with
every breath of fashion, and balking at mental discipline. Truewit
warns Morose of the literary pretensions of a wife: 'She may censure poets and authors and styles, and compare 'em, Daniel with
Spenser, Jonson with the t'other youth, and so forth.'[63] Hebrew
causes the lady scholar impersonated by Doll in *The Alchemist* to
fall into her fit, and discourse 'learnedly of genealogies.'[64] The ability to digest inwardly, in Jonson's view, is masculine.

Jonson's hermaphrodites in *Epicoene*, 'a new foundation, sir, here
i' the town, of ladies that call themselves the collegiates, an order
between courtiers and country madams, that live from their husbands, and give entertainment to all the Wits and Braveries o' the
time, as they call 'em – cry down or up what they like or dislike in
a brain or a fashion with most masculine or rather hermaphroditi-
cal authority,' derive from no organised social clique of intel-

[61] IV.vi.56.
[62] *Volpone*, III.iv.79.
[63] *Epicoene, or The Silent Woman*, II.ii.110.
[64] II.iii.240.

lectual women such as Molière satirised in *Les Femmes Savantes*, drawing on the *précieuses' salons* of his day. Jonson exploits instead the obsession of his own time with the idea of femininity and masculinity, depicting women who are masculine because they live away from their husbands, because of their intellectual pretensions, or because, like Mrs Otter and the bride Epicoene, they command where women should obey. Men are effeminate because foppish like Sir John Daw and Sir Amorous, or unmanned, as Morose claims when trying to divorce Epicoene on the grounds of his own incapacity, or because enslaved by women, as Otter is. But where so many are unnatural, the stability of nature itself is undermined, just as the stability of the real is undermined in *The Taming of the Shrew*, and like Shakespeare's play, Jonson's comes to rest not in social certainty, but in the truth of the theatre. Epicoene, ultra-feminine, silent and submissive, and then ultra-masculine – 'her masculine and loud commanding, and urging the whole family, makes him think he has married a fury,'[65] – is not a woman at all. The boy actor provides the final comment on the baseless fabric of jarring opposites. Beneath the superficial certainties of Jonson's moral world, in which learned women are masculine while displaying all the inadequacies of femininity, seethes an anarchy which sucks even those certainties into its own vortex, making Jonson the precursor of Swift.

Whether or not middle-class women in Shakespeare's time shared Queen Elizabeth's scholarship, they partook of the wit which is the side product of education, that child of prose and logic which is to the highly cultivated and self-aware society as poetry is to the primitive culture. Elizabeth's apocryphal sharpness made its own comment on the conviction that wit, the fruit of learning, was a masculine attribute. Wit contradicts the male ideal of the silent submissive woman because its nature is combative and verbal. Leonato fears that Beatrice will not get a husband if she is so sharp-tongued. Defying one set of standards for women, wit inevitably suggests defiance of another – the witty woman is often accused of loose living. Meredith describes a witty woman as 'a character swimming for life:'

[65] I.i.70, IV.i.8.

Cleverness is an attribute of the selector missionary lieutenants of Satan. We pray to be defended from her cleverness: she flashes bits of speech that catch men in their unguarded corner. The wary stuff their ears, the stolid bid her best sayings rebound on her reputation.[66]

When Edward IV spies the Lady Elizabeth in *Henry VI* he reflects:

> Her looks doth argue her replete with modesty;
> Her words doth show her wit incomparable.[67]

The assumption is that in women modesty and wit are incompatible.

The influence of Elizabeth's example in combining the untouchability (at least in the myth) of the Virgin Queen with a sharpness which survives in Shakespeare's noble ladies, together with the actual situation of middle-class women in Jacobean society, gave the witty woman noticeable status in the drama. Without being learned in More's sense, city women display something of the native quickness of the Cockney cab-driver: a race of everyday Beatrices. Although sometimes, as with Middleton's Mrs Allwit in *A Chaste Maid in Cheapside* or Mrs Purge in *The Family of Love*, wit is the let-out for lightness, in many plays, such as Dekker's *Westward Ho*, or Marston's *The Insatiate Countess*, wit in city women preserves chastity and reputation with the ingenuity and determination with which Mistress Page and Mistress Ford deflect the advances of Falstaff in *The Merry Wives of Windsor*.

Mirroring a society on the move, the dramatists relish, despite their surface mockery, the wit which enables men and women to rise in the world. In a bourgeois society education becomes not More's vision of the good life, but the means of moving up socially. Those at the top value it least, because they have nowhere to move to. Higgins has to explain away Eliza Doolittle's sharpness as the new small talk to upper-class women reared on the idea that the more boring and conventional the speech the more well-bred the speaker. The dramatists are ambivalent. Women like Gertrude

[66] *Diana of the Crossways*, ch. 1.
[67] *Henry VI* Part III, III.ii.84.

in Chapman's *Eastward Ho* who scorn their own class, and court worthless gallants, meet their own come-uppance in the collapse of their ambition. But wit is also the traffic of a new world in which Anne Boleyn, the daughter of a knight, captivated a king, and Anne Page outwitted her father and married Fenton. Education used to be a way of changing regional accents; in Elizabethan theatre it is the city woman's road to elegant speech and social success. Dauphine remarks satirically of Mrs Otter in *Epicoene*: 'What an excellent choice phrase this lady expresses in,' and Truewit replies: 'O sir, she is the only authentical courtier, that is not naturally bred one, in the city.'[68] The court ladies in Jonson's *Poetaster* warn Chloë against betraying her background: 'Your cittie mannerly word (forsooth) vse it not too often in any case.'[69] Hotspur boisterously berates his wife for refusing, in terms reminiscent of the affected gentility of the city woman, to sing:

Not yours, in good sooth! Heart! you swear like a comfit-maker's wife – 'not you, in good sooth', and 'as true as I live', and 'as God shall mend me', and 'as sure as day' –

> And givest such sarcenet surety for thy oaths,
> As if thou never walk'st further than Finsbury.
> Swear me, Kate, like a lady as thou art,
> A good mouth-filling oath, and leave 'in sooth',
> And such protest of pepper-gingerbread,
> To velvet-guards and Sunday citizens.[70]

If wit irons out the distinctions between the masculine and feminine spirit, making Beatrice more akin to Mercutio than to Ophelia, it also levels social difference, making the Bastard King John's right-hand man, and Maria not Olivia's servant but her kinswoman, the Lady Toby Belch. Sir Toby, crowing over the gulled Malvolio, exclaims: 'I could marry this wench for this device,' and swears to follow her 'to the gates of Tartar, thou most excellent devil of wit!'[71]

[68] Jonson, *Epicoene, or The Silent Woman*, III.ii.23.   [69] IV.i.33.
[70] *Henry IV* Part I, III.i.247.   [71] *Twelfth Night*, II.v.185, 208.

In Caroline drama wit in women is *déclassé*. The hero in Glapthorne's *Wit in a Constable*, a play imitative of *Much Ado About Nothing*, reproves the heroines – and Glapthorne makes the common Caroline mistake of juxtaposing two witty women, where Shakespeare complements Beatrice with Hero, and Rosalind with Celia – for a wit which shows city breeding. My Lady Tongue needs the reminder that 'we are / Gentlemen Ladies, and no city foremen.'[72] Jacobean drama looks at city wit from within and takes pride in it; Caroline drama gazes at it from without and expresses contempt. Both men and women accept the equation of wit and immodesty, even though a character like Fowler in Shirley's *The Witty Fair One*, dizzy from defeat in the war of words, recognises that the charge of unchastity marks only a man's revenge for being routed by a woman.

Henrietta Maria's Platonics, the forbears of Molière's *précieuses*, do not challenge the male world in the way that More's educated women, or the Jacobean city women do. The cult cherishes the separation of the sexes, claiming for women not the equality of intellect in which More believed, but the superiority of the feminine Ariel in a world of masculine Calibans. As a character observes to her daughter of her gross fleshly husband in Molière's *Les Précieuses Ridicules*: 'Mon Dieu! ma chère, que ton père a la forme enfoncée dans la matière! que son intelligence est épaisse, et qu'il fait sombre dans son âme!'[73] (Material, gross, unenlightened.) The Platonics assign separate spheres to men and women, rebuilding the barriers between the masculine and feminine which More sought to rescind.

Nathaniel Hawthorne described the way in which the outcast Hester Prynne in *The Scarlet Letter* earned her living: 'It was the art, – then, as now, almost the only one within a woman's grasp – of needlework. . . . Women derive a pleasure, incomprehensible to the other sex, from the delicate toil of the needle.'[74] Hawthorne perceived no relation between an extraordinary feminine delight

[72] ii.i.

[73] v.p. 16.

[74] Ch. v.

in sewing and the social fact that there was nothing else to do. When More and Erasmus attacked the needle as the sceptre of the feminine empire, they suggested for women other pleasures as well as other work. The Humanists believed that women might escape from the traditional male circumference of the feminine without becoming masculine. More set the stage on which Shakespeare and his fellows asked questions about the nature of women which could not be answered by society's definition of femininity.

2 *Disguise and the Boy Actor*

The boy actor had a special affinity with those women who offended Elizabethan and Jacobean society by wearing men's clothes. Condemned by opponents of the stage for dressing as a woman, he was often also guilty of disguising that woman as a man. Viola's melancholy reflection when she sees Olivia's ring fell on well-tuned ears:

> My master loves her dearly
> And I (poor monster!) fond as much on him.[1]

Viola was a monster on two counts: a man acting a woman and a woman in breeches. The woman in theatrical disguise aroused the same fear in moralists as the masculine woman in breeches. When Greene's Dorothea in *James IV* asks her dwarf whether she looks like a man in her disguise as squire, he retorts: 'If not a man, yet like a manly shrew.'[2] Trousers on a woman, whether on the stage or off it, spelled insubordination.

The dramatists recognised the kinship between the 'mankind' woman, attacked by Elizabethan and Jacobean moralists for wearing men's clothes, and the disguised heroine. Stubbes, fanatical Puritan Jeremiah, attacked the doublet-and-hose woman in *The Anatomy of Abuses*, printed in 1583: '*Proteus*, that Monster, could neuer chaunge him self into so many fourmes & shapes as these

[1] *Twelfth Night*, II.ii.33.

[2] IV.iv.9.

women doo!'[3] Less than ten years later, Julia in *The Two Gentlemen of Verona* reproaches Proteus for the inconstancy which has forced her into the allegedly monstrous shape of the man-woman sporting breeches:

> O Proteus, let this habit make thee blush.
> Be thou asham'd that I have took upon me
> Such an immodest raiment; if shame live
> In a disguise of love!
> It is the lesser blot modesty finds,
> Women to change their shapes, than men their minds.[4]

Shakespeare mocked Stubbes again in *The Merchant of Venice*. Stubbes had declared the masculine woman to be the victim of Medea's sorcery:

> I neuer read nor heard of any people, except drunken with *Cyrces* cups, or poysoned with *exorcisms* of *Medea*, that famous and renoumed Sorceresse, that euer woulde weare suche kinde of attire as is not onely stinking before the face of God, offensiue to man, but also painteth out to the whole world the venereous inclination of their corrupt conversation.[5]

Jessica gazes into the night for the returning Portia (associated elsewhere in the play with Medea [6]) who assumed the man's robe of lawyer to renew Antonio's life:

> In such a night
> Medea gathered the enchanted herbs
> That did renew old Æson.[7]

Defending their own theatrical practice the dramatists reinforced the feminism of the masculine woman. They claimed that

[3] p. 73.
[4] v.iv.103.
[5] *Philip Stubbes's Anatomy of the Abuses in England in Shakspere's Youth A.D. 1583*, pp. 73–4.
[6] Cf. D. J. Palmer, '*The Merchant of Venice*, or the Importance of Being Earnest', *Shakespearian Comedy*, Stratford-Upon-Avon Studies, *14*, 101–4.
[7] *The Merchant of Venice*, v.i.12.

all clothes are a form of disguise and that theatrical disguise could be a revelation of truth about men and women. Secondly, they suggested that society's modes of identifying sexual behaviour required from its members not moral stability but good acting. If femininity and masculinity have any permanent validity, it exists independent of the clothes society ordains for men and women to wear. Thirdly, a woman in disguise – or the masculine woman in breeches – is changed by her male dress only because it allows her to express desires and delights which society suppresses in the interests of that narrow femininity which More had attacked. Disguise makes a woman not a man but a more developed woman.

Acting a woman disguised as a boy, the boy actor looked all too like himself. The consciousness that they were not dealing with women actors spurred the dramatists to discover a femininity more durable than that which might be put on or taken off with a suit of clothes. The boy actor encouraged the dramatist to observe the similarities between the sexes, the way in which boyishness itself formed an element in femininity. But he also made it necessary for them to understand what made the sexes different if they were to evade the accusation that the heroine was a kind of monster, a palpable boy parading a skirt.

Stubbes' 'Hermaphroditi, that is, Monsters of bothe kindes, half women, half men,'[8] represented more than the London under-world of Middleton and Dekker's Moll Cutpurse. William Harrison noted in his *Description of England* in 1587 a general fashion: 'Some of these trulls in London so disguised that it hath passed my skill to discern whether they were men or women. . . . Thus it is now come to pass that women are become men and men transformed into monsters.'[9] James I saw the woman in breeches as a threat to respectable society and, according to one of John Chamberlain's letters, instructed the clergy in 1620 to 'inveigh vehemently against the insolencie of our women, and theyre wearing of brode brimed hats, pointed dublets, theyre hayre cut short or shorne, and some of them stilettos or poniards, and such other trinckets of like moment.'[10]

[8] *Anatomy of Abuses*, p. 73.   [9] p. 147.
[10] Quoted in Louis B. Wright, *Middle-Class Culture in Elizabethan England*, p. 493.

The masculine woman is a symptom of Jacobean feminism; it has been said that 'the ideal of any "emancipated" age is necessarily a creature half man and half woman.'[11] Protests against dress articulate complex aversions. Difference of taste is impregnable where difference of judgement is assailable: the deploring of finery may mask complex antagonisms. The Elizabethans had a consuming interest in clothes, and the court boasted fantastic 'bravery'. Questions about clothes and cost, clothes and class, the cloth and the hypocrite, the wife and the wardrobe hustled each other through the press and out of the pulpit. Foreign visitors saw in women's lavishness their unprecedented liberty.[12] Women's finery became the emblem of that confusion of classes which led Barnaby Rich to lament that 'wee canne hardly knowe . . . a Lady from a Landresse.'[13]

Clothes, which Nature had given to man to identify his sex and station, at the turn of the sixteenth century ceased to do either with any reliability. Women, crowding into London in their new coaches,[14] decked in a tradesman's feathers and ready to pollute the best blue blood by bribing it into city marriage, seemed to conservatives the heralds of social anarchy. Women's assumption of men's dress mirrored the effeminacy of the Jacobean court. 'And from whence commeth this wearing and this imbrodering of long lockes, this curiositie that is used amongst men in freziling and curling of their hayre? this gentlewoman-like starcht bands, so be edged, and be laced, fitter for Mayd Marion in a Moris dance, then for him that hath either spirit or courage that should be in a gentleman?'[15] cried Barnaby Rich. The masculine woman jeopardised the balance of society between male and female just as the velvet

---

[11] James Laver, *Dress: How and Why Fashions in Men's and Women's Clothes Have Changed during the Past Two Hundred Years*, pp. 30–1.

[12] Rye, *England as Seen by Foreigners: in the Days of Elizabeth and James the First*, pp. 7–8.

[13] *The Honestie of this Age*, p. 65.

[14] Stone, *The Crisis of the Aristocracy 1558–1641*, p. 391.

[15] *The Honestie of this Age*, p. 50.

laundress destroyed its distinction between high and low. Fear of changing fashion is a universal rallying-point. Wearing breeches and learning Latin might be different ways of saying the same thing but the breeches were the more outspoken intrusion on the male world. More wanted his daughters to think like men; he might not have wanted them to dress like men.

Clothes, ceasing to advertise the real nature of the wearer, became a disguise. Nashe denounced 'England, the players' stage of gorgeous attire,' and blamed the land for 'wanton disguising thyself against kind.'[16] The fine woman, according to Stubbes, is herself a player: 'So that when they haue all these goodly robes vppon them, women seeme to be the smallest part of themselves, not naturall women, but artificiall Women; not Women of flesh & blod, but rather puppits or mawmets of rags & clowtes compact together.' Stubbes reviles the common player in the same terms:

> Do these Mockers and Flowters of his Maiesty, these dissembling *Hipocrites*, and flattering *Gnatoes*, think to escape vnpunished? beware, therfore, you masking Players, you painted sepulchres, you doble dealing ambodexters.[17]

The player in his shreds and patches, the monk in his cowl, the citizen's wife tricked up to look like a lady, the woman in a man's dress, practise the art of illusion. To find one monstrous was to find all monstrous. The theme of moralists like Stubbes is that of Molière's Cléonte against the social climber in *Le Bourgeois Gentilhomme*: 'Toute imposture est indigne d'un honnête homme, et qu'il y a de la lâcheté à déguiser ce que le Ciel nous a fait naître.'[18] The dissembler had a hateful fascination for the Elizabethans. His clothes were the stage properties of his hypocrisy.

Nashe's is the traditional view, that, as one critic observes, 'apparel proclaims the man and does not disguise him.'[19] But the Elizabethans were not simply traditionalist; their ideas grew out of

[16] *Christs Teares over Ierusalem*, quoted in Dover Wilson, *Life in Shakespeare's England*, p. 125.

[17] *Anatomy of Abuses*, pp. 75, 141.

[18] III.xii.

[19] M. C. Bradbrook, *Shakespeare and Elizabethan Poetry*, p. 42.

a constant tension between old and new, and the new in this case
asserted that all clothes were a disguise. More in *Utopia* denies the
distinctions contained in clothes, and disparages men

> who think themselves the better men, the better the coat they
> wear. In this one thing they make a twofold mistake: they are no
> less deceived in thinking their coat better than in thinking them-
> selves better. If you consider the use of the garment, why is wool
> of finer thread superior to that of thicker? Yet, as if it were by
> nature and not by their own mistake that they had the advant-
> age, they hold their heads high and believe some extra worth
> attaches to themselves thereby. Thus, the honour which, if ill-
> clad, they would not have ventured to hope for, they require as
> if of right for a smarter coat.[20]

Clothes create artificial diversity among men. Custom ordains difference where there is none, according to Montaigne: 'If we consider a Cottager and a King, a noble and a handy-crafts man, a
magistrate and a private man, a rich man and a poore, an extreme
disparitie doth immediately present it self unto our eies, which, as a
man may say, differ in nothing, but in their clothes.'[21] All
Shakespeare's kings carry this consciousness. Lear, seeing in the
naked beggar an image of himself, strips off his clothes as the lend-
ings of a flattering society:

> Through tatter'd clothes small vices do appear;
> Robes and furr'd gowns hide all.[22]

The despised Jacobean creation of new peers, the mushroom
knights who had sprung up overnight, gave an edge to the Shepherd's Son's final flouting of Autolycus: 'See you these clothes? say
you see them not and think me still no gentleman born: you were
best say these robes are not gentleman born: give me the lie: do;
and try whether I am not now a gentleman born.'[23]

The player became the emblem of man's equality beneath the

[20] p. 167.

[21] 'Of the Inequalitie that is Betweene us', p. 296.

[22] *King Lear*, IV.vi.166.

[23] *The Winter's Tale*, V.ii.130.

distinction of his dress. Montaigne makes the parallel:

> For, as enterlude-plaiers, you shal now see them on the stage,
> play a King, an Emperor, or a Duke, but they are no sooner off
> the stage, but they are base rascals, vagabond abjects, and port-
> erly hirelings, which is their naturall and originall condition:
> Even so the Emperor whose glorious pomp doth so dazzle you
> in publicke:. . . View him behinde the curtaine, and you see but
> an ordinarie man, and peradventure more vile, and more seely,
> than the least of his subjects.[24]

Vincentio in *The Taming of the Shrew*, one of the actors hired to entertain the deceived Sly, rebukes his son's servant Tranio for wearing the young nobleman's clothes in defiance of social difference:

> What am I, sir? Nay, what are you, sir? O immortal gods! O
> fine villain! A silken doublet, a velvet hose, a scarlet cloak and a
> copatain hat! O I am undone, I am undone! While I play the
> good husband at home, my son and my servants spend all at the
> university.

Tranio's finery lends him effrontery: 'Sir, you seem a sober ancient
gentleman by your habit, but your words show you a madman.
Why sir, what 'cerns it you if I wear pearl and gold? I thank my
good father, I am able to maintain it.' Vincentio, the player, complains of the social climber, and Tranio gives the actor's answer,
that they are equals and Vincentio's claim of difference only a
madman's illusion.

The player justified the unreliability of his outward show by
declaring that clothes could not change his nature. Petruchio
defends his wedding gear:

> To me she's married, not unto my clothes.
> Could I repair what she will wear in me
> As I can change these poor accoutrements,
> 'Twere well for Kate and better for myself.[25]

Theatrical disguise borrows only the garment. 'Edgar I nothing

[24] 'Of the Inequalitie that is Betweene us', p. 296.
[25] v.i.56, III.ii.113.

am' is true for Lear and Gloucester seeing the pitiful rags of Poor
Tom, but not for Edgar himself, who can assure his unconscious
father:

> You're much deceiv'd; in nothing am I chang'd
> But in my garments.[26]

A man's nature will out whatever he wears. Neither his princely
costume nor Posthumus' clothes can disguise Cloten's baseness in
Cymbeline. When he accosts Guiderius: 'Know'st me not by my
clothes?' the authentic prince in peasant's tunic scoffs:

> No, nor thy tailor, rascal,
> Who is thy grandfather: he made those clothes,
> Which (as it seems) make thee.

Belarius marvels of his two stolen boys:

> How hard it is to hide the sparks of Nature!
> These boys know little they are sons to th' king,
> Nor Cymbeline dreams that they are alive.
> They think they are mine, and though train'd up thus
> meanly,
> I' th' cave wherein they bow, their thoughts do hit
> The roofs of palaces, and Nature prompts them
> In simple and low things to prince it, much
> Beyond the trick of others.[27]

The costume of queen of the sheep-shearing discovers in Perdita a
natural royalty:

> Methinks I play as I have seen them do
> In Whitsun pastorals: sure this robe of mine
> Doth change my disposition.[28]

Bacon gave the dramatist's justification of theatrical disguise when
he observed: 'A Mans Nature is but perceiued in Priuatenesse, for
there is no Affectation; In Passion, for that putteth a Man out of his
Precepts; And in a new Case or Experiment, for there Custome

[26] *King Lear*, II.iii.21, IV.vi.7.

[27] IV.ii.81, III.iii.79.

[28] *The Winter's Tale*, IV.iv.133.

leaueth him.'[29] Disguise, instead of concealing, reveals the truth about a man's nature because it places him in a new case or experiment. Florizel might answer Stubbes on the player's behalf:

> Apprehend
> Nothing but jollity. The gods themselves,
> Humbling their deities to love, have taken
> The shapes of beasts upon them: Jupiter
> Became a bull, and bellow'd; the green Neptune
> A ram, and bleated; and the fire-rob'd god,
> Golden Apollo, a poor humble swain,
> As I seem now.[30]

The masculine woman was as potentially subversive as the player. Born subject because female, by taking a man's clothes she threatened not only to usurp his authority but to annex his nature. Men dislike their own characteristics when they observe them in women, and an angry pamphleteer in 1620 attacked the masculine woman for being

> man-like . . . in every condition: man in body by attyre, man in behaviour by rude complement, man in nature by aptnesse to anger, man in action by pursuing revenge, man in wearing weapons man in using weapons: And in briefe, so much man in all things, that they are neither men, nor women but just good for nothing.[31]

A woman in man's clothes seemed to the Jacobeans not simply eccentric in dress, but really in part a man, and thus monstrous and unnatural – half-man and half-woman, a horrible counterpart to the homosexual courtier.

But this freak remained irritatingly unrepentant. She pointed gaily to the changing seasons, and protested against the rigidity of a custom which would have 'poore woman such a fixed Starre,

[29] 'Of Nature in Men', p. 161.
[30] *The Winter's Tale*, IV.iv.24.
[31] *Hic Mulier: or The Man-Woman: being a Medicine to Cure the Coltish Disease of the Staggers in the Masculine-Feminines of our Times*, sig. B 2.

that shee shall not so much as move or twinkle in her owne Spheare.'[32] What was particularly annoying was that she could claim good authority for distrusting custom. Montaigne had argued that if Nature had meant men and women to wear breeches and petticoats she would have taken care to protect those parts of the body which clothes left exposed – eyes, face, mouth, nose, ears.[33] More, claiming the same propensity for good in women as in men, attacked custom for distorting their nature. Custom may ordain breeches for men, but custom is itself the casualty of growth and decay, Time's subject:

> Since it is in my power
> To o'erthrow law, and in one self-born hour
> To plant and o'erwhelm custom.[34]

Time in *The Winter's Tale* becomes the dramatist himself, creating and destroying custom within the two hours' traffic of the stage.

Reviled as a player, the masculine woman had a natural ally in the playwright when she claimed for women that 'we are as free-borne as Men, have as free election, and as free spirits, we are compounded of like parts, and may with like liberty make benefit of our creations.'[35] The dramatists asked themselves what breeches might reveal about the nature of women when it was freed from the custom of femininity.

In the world of simplified emotions and stratified personal relations which Lyly constructed for the little eyases, those chorister competitors to Hamlet's common player, male dress on a woman affronts femininity. When Phyllida in *Gallathea* hears that she must dress as a boy to avoid Neptune's demand for virgin sacrifice, she exclaims: 'It will neither become my body nor my mind.' She predicts a continual blushing at her 'long hose and short coat.'

[32] *Haec-Vir: or The Womanish-Man: being an Answere to a Late Booke intituled Hic-Mulier*, sig. B 1. This pamphlet and its companion piece, *Mulde Sacke: or The Apologie of Hic Mulier: to the Late Declamation against Her*, printed three years after the attacks of Rachel Speght, Ester Sowernam and Constantia Munda on Swetnam, may possibly also have been written by women.

[33] 'Of the Use of Apparell', p. 240.

[34] *The Winter's Tale*, IV.i.4.

[35] *Haec-Vir: or The Womanish-Man*, sig. B 2ᵛ.

Gallathea, also disguised, cries: 'How now, Gallathea, miserable Gallathea, that having put on the apparel of a boy thou canst not also put on the mind.'[36] If breeches had exerted as little influence on the minds of Long Meg of Westminster and Moll Cutpurse as on those of Lyly's heroines, Stubbes would have had nothing to worry about. Lyly, coping with little actors only too at home in hose and short coats, had to rely – like the Fairy in *A Midsummer Night's Dream* insisting on the minuteness of Titania's train – on language to create the illusion of feminine distaste. Lyly's drama is deliberately small-scale: the Children's theatre allowed him no room to ask whether femininity in the mind meant any more than a preference for petticoats. But Lyly was the first playwright to realise that disguise invites the dramatist to explore masculinity and femininity, where in a Tudor romance like *Clyomon and Clamydes* the heroine's disguise as a man promotes only intrigue.

Many plays seize the opportunity to make the woman in disguise comment on the masculine woman controversy. In Beaumont and Fletcher's *Love's Cure, or The Martial Maid* Clara is an upper-class Moll Cutpurse, reared from childhood as a boy, with a brother who has been reared as a girl. Their parents try unsuccessfully to make them revert to nature. The custom of masculinity has usurped Clara's femininity. The question hovers in the air as to whether the vapid femininity she has been spared is not an equal, though different, usurpation of a woman's nature. Clara casts Erasmian contempt on the women's pastimes for which she is required to forfeit the freedom of a man:

> I had rather meet ten enemies in the field
> All sworn to fetch my head, than be brought on
> To change an hours discourse with one of these
> Smooth City-fools, or Tissue-Cavaliers,
> The only Gallants, as they wisely think,
> To get a Jewel, or a wanton Kiss
> From a Court-lip, though painted.

The dramatists do not condemn her robustness any more than they rule out of court the gentleness which makes Lucio, revived to

[36] II.iii.16, II.iv.1.

valour, a more restrained and merciful opponent than the traditional masculine aggressor. But, tantalisingly laying the scent for a new marriage of the feminine and the masculine within the individual nature, predictably they get cold feet, and endorse the old marriage after all.

The transformations in *Love's Cure*, unlike those in Shakespeare's comedies, owe nothing to human ingenuity. Clara, having defended her lover with her own sword, feels its temper soften in her hand under the influence of Cupid's dart:

> I begin to find
> I am a woman, and must learn to fight
> A softer sweeter battel, than with swords.

Putting off the breeches of the mind, Clara assures an apprehensive lover of total feminine submission:

> I here abjure all actions of a man,
> And will esteem it happiness from you
> To suffer like a woman: love, true love
> Hath made a search within me, and expell'd
> All but my natural softness, and made perfect
> That which my parents care could not begin.

The sword becomes a symbolic Freudian weapon. One of the characters reproves Clara in the days of her aggression: 'Remember Mistriss; nature hath given you a sheath only, to signifie women are to put up mens weapons, not to draw them.'[37] When Clara takes it off, Lucio puts it on. When his father is in danger, manly courage suddenly surges into his flat but effeminate breast. Discovering his masculine skill with weapons Lucio moves from the market-place to the drawing-room and woos his lady, hampered by his ignorance of the facts of life, but feeling the genuine Erasmian pricks and itchings. Beaumont and Fletcher did not need Freud to tell them that sex is power, and that women may wear swords and short coats and hose if they want to, but it is all a futile attempt to contradict Nature's gift of the weapon to the man.

If Beaumont and Fletcher gave the sword to the man, Shake-

[37] I.iii, II.ii, IV.ii, II.ii.

speare called that man Sir Andrew Aguecheek. Breeches of themselves bestow no bravery on either the natural inmate or the
usurper. Viola discovers when she puts on a sword a diffidence no
greater than that of her male adversary to whom Nature had not
given a sheath: but rather the way in which the world finds difference in similarity. Pacifism in women is cowardice in men. While
Viola, pressed into a duel at the point of Sir Toby's sword, gasps:
'Pray God defend me! A little thing would make me tell them how
much I lack of a man,' Sir Andrew hears in trembling that 'a terrible oath, with a swaggering accent sharply twanged off, gives
manhood more approbation than ever proof itself would have
earned him.' Both 'men' need instruction in manhood – the man
terrified as a girl, and the girl terrified because taken for a man. If
there is to be any killing between these two it will be 'by the look,
like cockatrices.'[38] Custom gives a man a sword and teaches him
how to use it, so that when Sebastian strides across the stage strew-
ing it with broken pates Shakespeare establishes that this is the male
twin and Cesario's masculinity a pastiche. But Nature endows
the will to fight indiscriminately: Sir Andrew hangs back while
Beatrice curses a convention which keeps her hand from killing
Claudio:

> O that I were a man for his sake! or that I had any friend would
> be a man for my sake! But manhood is melted into curtsies,
> valour into compliment, and men are only turned into tongue,
> and trim ones too: he is now as valiant as Hercules, that only tells
> a lie and swears it. I cannot be a man with wishing; therefore I
> will die a woman with grieving.[39]

Masculinity and femininity require of men and women that they
learn their parts and give a satisfactory performance. The farth-
ingale can be no vehicle for valour, however true Virginia
Woolf's observation that 'in every human being a vacillation from
one sex to the other takes place, and often it is only the clothes that
keep the male or female likeness.'[40] When Chapman's Charlotte in

[38] *Twelfth Night*, III.iv.300, 183, 199.
[39] *Much Ado About Nothing*, IV.i.316.
[40] *Orlando*, p. 133.

The Revenge of Bussy D'Ambois urges the revenge of Bussy, Clermont and her husband advise her to convert bloodthirsty thoughts
into care for her appearance:

> And with these
> Womanly practices employ your spirit;
> This other suits you not, nor fits the fashion.[41]

Taking literally her own metaphor of casting off the shame of
delay with her woman's attire, Charlotte disguises herself as a man
and challenges Bussy's murderer. Disguise makes actual aspects of
her nature – courage, moral stamina, physical strength – which are
out of her part as long as she wears a woman's clothes. Stubbes
feared the 'mankind' woman because her male clothes showed
society someone less easily subjugated than a she in a skirt. The gallant in *The Roaring Girl* takes no liberties with a Moll Cutpurse
armed like a man. Bess Bridges in Heywood's *The Fair Maid of the
West* finds in her breeches the power to quell the masculine bully:

> Me thinkes I could be valiant on the sudden:
> And meet a man i' th' field.
> I could doe all that I have heard discourst
> Of *Mary Ambree* or *Westminsters Long-Meg*.[42]

The masculine woman and the woman in disguise are both disruptive socially because they go behind the scenes and find that manhood describes not the man inside the clothes, but the world's
reactions to his breeches. Masculinity is as much a mask as femininity, and the face it hides may be Sir Andrew Aguecheek's, or
Petruchio's, or Volumnia's, or Moll Cutpurse's, or Portia's, or that
of Coriolanus himself, bewildered by emotions the mask cannot
express:

> Like a dull actor now,
> I have forgot my part, and I am out,
> Even to a full disgrace.[43]

[41] I.i.

[42] Part I, II.i.

[43] *Coriolanus*, V.iii.40.

A woman in disguise smokes out the male world, perceiving masculinity as a form of acting, the manner rather than the man. But the charade only works if the sexes stick to their parts. When the lover fails to importune the lady in *Love's Cure*, she must relinquish reluctance if she is to bring him to the sticking-point. Beatrice, called on to admire Benedick's valour, mischievously delivers the wrong speech:

> *Beatrice*: He is a very valiant trencherman; he hath an excellent stomach.
> *Messenger*: And a good soldier too, lady.
> *Beatrice*: And a good soldier to a lady; but what is he to a lord?[44]

Rosalind can play the man as convincingly as a coward:

> Were it not better
> Because that I am more than common tall,
> That I did suit me all points like a man?
> A gallant curtle-axe upon my thigh,
> A boar-spear in my hand, and in my heart
> Lie there what hidden woman's fear there will,
> We'll have a swashing and a martial outside,
> As many other mannish cowards have
> That do outface it with their semblances.[45]

Portia revels in the prospect of her own boyish braggardism; the world will see her and Nerissa

> in such a habit,
> That they shall think we are accomplished
> With that we lack; I'll hold thee any wager
> When we are both accoutered like young men,
> I'll prove the prettier fellow of the two,
> And wear my dagger with the braver grace,
> And speak between the change of man and boy,
> With a reed voice, and turn two mincing steps
> Into a manly stride; and speak of frays

[44] *Much Ado About Nothing*, I.i.48.
[45] *As You Like It*, I.iii.114.

> Like a fine bragging youth: and tell quaint lies
> How honourable ladies sought my love,
> Which I denying, they fell sick and died:
> I could not do withal: – then I'll repent,
> And wish for all that, that I had not kill'd them;
> And twenty of these puny lies I'll tell,
> That men shall swear I have discontinued school
> About a twelvemonth: I have within my mind
> A thousand raw tricks of these bragging Jacks,
> Which I will practise.[46]

Society values the rules of masculine and feminine behaviour because they are easy to follow. The dramatist of Shakespeare's theatre values them because they help him to turn his boy actors into women. Shakespeare affirms Portia's femininity by assigning her the woman's view that masculinity is a charade. The boy actor imagines a boy's pranks; declaring what he is, he gives the illusion of being what he is not: a woman acting a boy. Shakespeare draws attention to the boy actor only to confirm his woman's nature. Bianca in *The Taming of the Shrew* petulantly brushes aside her importunate tutor:

> I am no breeching scholar in the schools.
> I'll not be tied to hours nor 'pointed times,
> But learn my lessons as I please myself.[47]

The woman is born from the boy's petulant denial of his own identity. She mocks the boy who creates her. Imogen interrupts Pisanio's recital of the waggish tricks which must take the place of feminine foibles once she is disguised as a man:

> Nay, be brief:
> I see into thy end, and am almost
> A man already.

None of the men in the play resemble Pisanio's sketch of a man, any more than Imogen herself resembles his idea of a woman,

[46] *The Merchant of Venice*, III.iv.60.

[47] III.i.18.

except in the one respect in which she is different from most women. 'Change/Command into obedience,'[48] instructs the attendant of a princess, forgetting that women obey and men command. But when the playwright makes his boy actors act women, who are to act men, he gives them a sexual identity too positive to be confused with the change in their clothes. The woman character acquires independence from the boy who acts her.

One element in her independence lies in her detachment from the role of femininity. The woman is aware of herself as actress not in the theatre, but in a social setting. The Wise-woman of Hogsdon in Heywood's play advises one of the heroines, whom she believes to be a boy, how to act a girl: 'Thou shalt be tyred like a woman; can you make a curtesie, take small strides, simper, and seeme modest? me thinkes thou has a womans voyce already.' Luce assures her: 'Doubt not of me, Ile act them naturally.'[49] The Lord in the Induction to *The Taming of the Shrew* summons his page to play Sly's lady:

> Sirrah, go you to Barthol'mew my page
> And see him dressed in all suits like a lady.
> That done, conduct him to the drunkard's chamber
> And call him madam; do him obeisance.
> Tell him from me — as he will win my love —
> He bear himself with honorable action
> Such as he hath observed in noble ladies
> Unto their lords, by them accomplishèd:
> Such duty to the drunkard let him do
> With soft low tongue and lowly courtesy,
> And say, 'What is't your honor will command
> Wherein your lady and your humble wife
> May show her duty and make known her love?'
> And then with kind embracements, tempting kisses,
> And with declining head into his bosom,
> Bid him shed tears, as being overjoyed
> To see her noble lord restored to health

[48] *Cymbeline*, III.iv.155.
[49] *The Wise-woman of Hogsdon*, II.i.

> Who for this seven years hath esteemèd him
> No better than a poor and loathsome beggar.
> And if the boy have not a woman's gift
> To rain a shower of commanded tears,
> An onion will do well for such a shift,
> Which in a napkin being close conveyed
> Shall in despite enforce a watery eye.
> I know the boy will well usurp the grace,
> Voice, gait, and action of a gentlewoman.

When the players begin their entertainment for Sly, *The Taming of the Shrew* itself, two young ladies enter: Kate the curst, and Bianca, full of 'mild behavior and sobriety,' like the lady played by Bartholomew. Her father rages at the elder:

> Why, how now, dame, whence grows this insolence?
> Bianca, stand aside. Poor girl, she weeps.[50]

Shakespeare seasons the sorrow of Bianca with the suspicion of an onion close conveyed in a napkin. The boy feigns the woman's sorrow, and the woman's sorrow is feigned.

Disguise makes explicit in women what one writer describes as 'an ambiguity which corresponded to an ambiguity in the self, divided between surveyor and surveyed.'[51] The woman observes her disguised self. But when the woman is played by a boy, she watches two people, herself disguised, and the boy who plays her. Julia in *The Two Gentlemen of Verona*, disguised as the page Sebastian, describes to Silvia the lady Julia, who is

> About my stature: for at Pentecost,
> When all our pageants of delight were play'd,
> Our youth got me to play the woman's part,
> And I was trimm'd in Madam Julia's gown,
> Which served me as fit, by all men's judgments,
> As if the garment had been made for me;
> Therefore I know she is about my height.
> And at that time I made her weep agood,

[50] i.104, I.i.71, II.i.23.

[51] John Berger, *G*, p. 167.

> For I did play a lamentable part.
> Madam, 'twas Ariadne, passioning
> For Theseus' perjury, and unjust flight;
> Which I so lively acted with my tears,
> That my poor mistress, moved therewithal,
> Wept bitterly; and would I might be dead,
> If I in thought felt not her very sorrow.[52]

Julia watches a boy put on Julia's gown and play a woman deserted by her lover. When he weeps she weeps in pity for him and he feels her sorrow, for the boy actor is Julia herself. Cleopatra shares with Antony, in a passion at once both real and theatrical, a highly developed aesthetic sense of self which allows the artist both to be and to observe himself being – the Callas temperament. Cleopatra dreads not death, but the image of her own femininity amateurishly acted:

> The quick comedians
> Extemporally will stage us, and present
> Our Alexandrian revels: Antony
> Shall be brought drunken forth, and I shall see
> Some squeaking Cleopatra boy my greatness
> I' the posture of whore.[53]

Cleopatra, professional player of her own part as woman, spurns the boy who is also herself. The woman is audience to the boy.

In *As You Like It* Rosalind disguised as Ganymede watches her own performance as a boy. She consents shamefacedly to Oliver's friendly jibe: 'You a man! / You lack a man's heart,' protesting that she was only acting. 'Well then,' cries Oliver, 'Take a good heart, and counterfeit to be a man.' Rosalind, no longer acting, sighs: 'So I do: but i'faith, I should have been a woman by right.' Disguise makes Rosalind a man-woman. Trudging into Arden with Celia wilting on her arm as a shepherdess, she muses: 'I could find in my heart to disgrace my man's apparel, and to cry like a woman: but I must comfort the weaker vessel, as doublet and hose

---

[52] IV.iv.156.

[53] *Antony and Cleopatra*, v.ii.215.

ought to show itself courageous to petticoat.' Breeches compel her bravery, but the bravery is her own, perceived in the woman by the boy. As Ganymede she draws her own portrait for Orlando:

> I will be more jealous of thee than a Barbary cock-pigeon over his hen, more clamorous than a parrot against rain, more new-fangled than an ape, more giddy in my desires than a monkey: I will weep for nothing, like Diana in the fountain, and I will do that when you are disposed to be merry; I will laugh like a hyen, and that when thou art inclined to sleep.[54]

Rosalind revels in Orlando's discomforture at a boy's vision of the contrary wife of whom Erasmus had urged that 'she be not mery when he murneth nor dysposed to play when he is sad.'[55] Projecting a woman's incorrigibility, the boy is incorrigible. 'But will my Rosalind do so?' asks Orlando, bemused. 'By my life,' she rejoins, 'She will do as I do.' Being a woman, she thrives on not being a woman: 'I thank God I am not a woman, to be touched with so many giddy offences as he hath generally taxed their whole sex withal.'[56]

Acting a man in the forest, acting a woman for Orlando, Rosalind acquires a Puckish insight into the theatrical nature of masculinity and femininity. Recognising the two roles, she travels from one to the other with the versatility of the Elizabethan player obliged to double parts. As a boy she is Orlando's equal; as a woman she is Celia's equal. Meredith might have had Rosalind in mind when he wrote:

> The heroines of Comedy are like women of the world, not necessarily heartless from being clear-sighted: they seem so to the sentimentally-reared only for the reason that they use their wits, and are not wandering vessels crying for a captain or a pilot. Comedy is an exhibition of their battle with men, and that of men with them: and as the two, however divergent, both look on one object, namely, Life, the gradual similarity of their

[54] IV.iii.164, II.iv.4, IV.i.144.
[55] *A Mery Dialogue, declaringe the Propertyes of Shrowde Shrewes, and Honest Wyves*, sig. A vii.
[56] *As You Like It*, IV.i.152, III.ii.342.

impressions must bring them to some resemblance. The Comic poet dares to show us men and women coming to this mutual likeness; he is for saying that when they draw together in social life their minds grow liker; just as the philosopher discerns the similarity of boy and girl, until the girl is marched away to the nursery.[57]

The boy actor was a spur to the creation of heroines of allegedly masculine spirit. The high spirits and sharp repartee which characterised the Children's companies are reborn in the quick wits, audacity and independence of Shakespeare's heroines. But where Phyllida and Gallathea in Lyly's play are accessible to boy actors because they embody a boy's view of women, Shakespeare's women are both women and boys.

Encountering only each other, Phyllida and Gallathea learn nothing new about men from their disguise. But Rosalind sees Orlando through a man's eyes because he treats her as he might treat another man. Orsino in *Twelfth Night*, who can only address the high fantastical to the Lady Olivia, talks to his page as to a rational being. Had Rosalind worn a skirt, Orlando might have courted her with the masculine panache which she delights to display in the boy Ganymede. Theatrical disguise robs courtship of the artificial exaggeration of masculine and feminine difference sustained in the skirmishes between Phoebe and Silvius.

Yet Shakespeare, faced with actors who were literally the same, focused his imagination on creating out of more and more likeness, a sense of difference. Benedick and Beatrice speak more alike, act more alike than Orlando and Rosalind because Beatrice never looks like a man, so Shakespeare can afford to have her, as More would have wished, talk and think like one. Rosalind, who looks like one, is all vivacity, spirit, speed, susceptibility and fancy to an Orlando silent, melancholic, never drawn wholly into her sphere, wanting a world of substance as well as shadows: 'O, how bitter a thing it is to look into happiness through another man's eyes! . . . I can live no longer by thinking.' As Corin is to Touchstone, so Orlando is to Rosalind; he cannot compete, but nor does he want

[57] *An Essay on Comedy*, p. 248.

to, any more than he wants to be cured of his love, and in this play his tranquil ease beside her greater brilliance marks masculinity beside a femininity not obscured by breeches.

Celia keeps before the audience a Rosalind who is always a woman. Affirming the fiction of boyhood, Celia continually destroys it. Rosalind laments Orlando's tardiness: 'Never talk to me, I will weep.' Celia retorts: 'Do, I prithee – but yet have the grace to consider that tears do not become a man.' Insisting that Rosalind is a man, Celia draws attention to the illusion of manhood. Rosalind assures Orlando: 'And I am your Rosalind,' and an anxious sisterly voice nudges the forgetful Ganymede: 'It pleases him to call you so; but he hath a Rosalind of a better leer than you.' In the play of shepherd and shepherdess the actors dry up and require a prompter, so that Celia, startled at Rosalind's swoon, cries: 'There is more in it . . . Cousin, Ganymede.' Celia stands witness that Rosalind is not changed from the girl of the first scenes. To that girl, the presence of Orlando in the forest is a delight at first marred by her own masculine appearance: 'Alas the day, what shall I do with my doublet and hose?' A woman in love demands the licence of womanhood: 'Good my complexion! dost thou think, though I am caparisoned like a man, I have a doublet-and-hose in my disposition?' Celia stands evidence to a fixed point in Rosalind's nature to which the moving foot of her acting of the masculine and the feminine always hearkens back. 'You have simply misused our sex in your love-prate: we must have your doublet and hose plucked over your head, and show the world what the bird hath done to her own nest.'[58] Shakespeare separates his women from the boy actors who play them: at their most boyish they are still women watching their own performance as boys.

Shakespeare's actors gave him none of the actress' short-cuts to femininity – pre-packaged sex appeal, bosoms, hair, the tricks of the feminine trade which the female child may learn as soon as she sees she is admired. Shakespeare wrote into his text, just as he wrote blood and darkness into *Macbeth*, a femininity which would survive the most gangling of Ganymedes. Actresses tend to play Shakespeare's heroines too feminine; like elaborate scenery, too

[58] *As You Like It*, v.ii.42, iii.iv.1, iv.i.62, iv.iii.159, iii.ii.217, 194, iv.i.196.

much archness has the effect of tautology. Shakespeare used poetry to evoke a scene he could not reproduce in the theatre; to suggest the physical passion which his actors could not demonstrate realistically; to create women when he had only men. To annex to his plays too much of what he had not is only to waste what he gives. Some of the finest Shakespearian women are still schoolboys.

Boys make bewitching girls, where women make lumbering youths. Slighter than the adult actor, a boy could still make a convincing girl even when disguised as a boy. The age at which a boy actor ceased to act women is a moot point. Malvolio describes Cesario as 'not yet old enough for a man, nor young enough for a boy; as a squash is before 'tis a peascod, or a codling when 'tis almost an apple: 'tis with him in standing water between boy and man.'[59] Portia proposes to 'speak between the change of man and boy, / With a reed voice,'[60] implying one harsher than her normal speaking voice. The natural transition from playing women to playing men is at the breaking of the voice, but boys' voices broke later in Shakespeare's time than now, and a trained voice not only tends to break later than an untrained one, but its alto tone may be prolonged even into the late teens.[61] Nathan Field, boy actor and dramatist, may have played women's parts into his late teens or even till he was twenty, but it is unlikely that he continued to play them once his voice was really broken.[62] The dramatists draw attention to women's high voices. Hamlet accosts the Player who will play the Queen: 'Pray God your voice, like a piece of uncurrent gold, be not cracked within the ring.'[63] Quince instructs Flute to 'speak as small as you will.'[64] The comedy of Flute's name and profession as bellows-mender consists in the gruffness artificially repaired with which he renders Thisbe's dulcet tones. The vocal

[59] *Twelfth Night*, I.v.156.

[60] *The Merchant of Venice*, III.iv.66.

[61] W. Robertson Davies, *Shakespeare's Boy Actors*, p. 37.

[62] *The Plays of Nathan Field*, pp. 8–9, 8, n. 53. The belief that Field continued to play women's parts after his voice had broken is based on the dubious authority of Malone.

[63] *Hamlet*, II.ii.432.

[64] *A Midsummer Night's Dream*, I.ii.46.

contortion is part of his amateurishness, not comic at all if Hippolyta declares it to be the silliest stuff she has ever seen in a tenor voice. The disguised heroine's lightness of voice gives her the skittishness of Lyly's boy pages which makes Cesario seem at once saucy to Maria and the Fool, and wistful to Orsino:

> For they shall yet belie thy happy years,
> That say thou art a man: Diana's lip
> Is not more smooth and rubious; thy small pipe
> Is as the maiden's organ, shrill and sound —
> And all is semblative a woman's part.[65]

Shakespeare may have used poetry to enhance a difference not easily discernible without its suggestion. But it seems more likely that when Arviragus and Guiderius sing the dirge for the youth Fidele (Imogen in disguise) Arviragus mentions their broken voices because he noticed that Fidele's was unbroken, intuitively associating the unknown sister with his mother:

> And let us, Polydore, though now our voices
> Have got the mannish crack, sing him to th' ground,
> As once to our mother: use like note and words,
> Save that Euriphele must be Fidele.[66]

The point about the encounter between Sir Andrew and Viola is not that they both look like men but that they both look like girls. Young men wore their hair long, as Barnaby Rich had bitterly complained. When Julia disguises herself as a boy Lucetta reminds her to cut her hair, but she replies:

> No, girl, I'll knit it up in silken strings,
> With twenty odd-conceited true-love knots.[67]

In an age of effeminate fashions, it was easy for the boy actor to look like a woman.

The respectability of the theatre depended on the dramatist's

[65] *Twelfth Night*, I.iv.30.
[66] *Cymbeline*, IV.ii.235.
[67] *The Two Gentlemen of Verona*, II.vii.43. Victor Oscar Freeburg, *Disguise Plots in Elizabethan Drama*, p. 26.

ability to suggest that the boy actor was not *Haec-Vir*, the feminine man, any more than the woman he acted was *Hic Mulier*, the masculine woman. One way was to juxtapose the woman in disguise with the effeminate male adult actor. Middleton's Lactantio in *More Dissemblers Besides Women* is a typical Jacobean courtier, 'This perfum'd parcel of curl'd powder'd hair.' He is debauched: attended by one pregnant mistress disguised as a page, he contrives for a second also to disguise herself, pretending to be shocked by her masculine immodesty in her new attire:

> I arrest thee
> In Cupid's name; deliver up your weapon,
>   [*Takes her sword.*
> It is not for your wearing, Venus knows it:
> Here's a fit thing indeed.

The author of *Haec-Vir* might have retorted that Lactantio had surrendered all manhood except the power of begetting, and had thus obliged his women to assume masculine bearing in his stead. The girlishness of the page measures the hero's girlishness, just as Viola's manhood queries Sir Andrew's. Dondolo describes

> a young gallant lying a-bed with his wench, if the constable should chance to come up and search, being both in smocks, they'd be taken for sisters, and I hope a constable dare go no further; and as for knowing of their heads, that's well enough too, for I know many young gentlemen wear longer hair than their mistresses.

Femininity and masculinity become a Lewis Carroll joke in a looking-glass world; when the dancing master hears his boy pupil cry for a midwife, he expostulates:

> A midwife? by this light, the boy's with child!
> A miracle! some woman is the father.
> The world's turn'd upside down: sure if men breed,
> Women must get; one never could do both yet.

The effeminate man's reward for his inversion of nature is a wife in breeches:

> He durst not own her for his wife till now;
> Only contracted with her in man's apparel,
> For the more modesty, because he was bashful,
> And never could endure the sight of women.[68]

The masculine woman in *Haec-Vir* justified herself by pointing to the womanish man: 'What could we poore weake women, doe lesse (being farre too weake by force to fetch backe those spoiles you have unjustly taken from us) then to gather up those garments you have proudly cast away, and therewith to cloath both our bodies and our mindes; since no other meanes was left us to continue our names, and to support a difference?'[69]

Virginia Woolf claimed that 'it was a change in Orlando herself that dictated her choice of a woman's dress and of a woman's sex.'[70] The dramatists declared that whereas an instability in Lactantio's nature made him wear feminine clothes, the boy actor's clothes were only a theatrical device. In *The Roaring Girl* Middleton conceived a scene between a woman in disguise, her lover, and Moll Cutpurse in the masculine woman's breeches. Despite the fact that they not only all three look like men, but are men, there is no mistaking the two who are women. Moll comments when Sebastian kisses his disguised mistress: 'How strange this shows, one man to kiss another.' Sebastian retorts:

> I'd kiss such men to choose, Moll;
> Methinks a woman's lip tastes well in a doublet.[71]

Clothes, in the theatre and out of it, manifest only that nothing that is so, is so.

The man-womanishness of disguise may have helped to rebut accusations that boy actors excited homosexuality. Orlando and Orsino develop love for a playfellow and confidant rather than for a sexual opposite – Erasmus' idea of love born from the harmony of like minds. When the woman in disguise is wooed by a woman

[68] IV.ii.122, I.ii.172, I.iv.71, V.ii.224, 219.
[69] Sig. C 2 .
[70] *Orlando*, p. 133.
[71] IV.i.46.

she reverts to boyhood while protecting her womanhood. Rosalind is masculine to Phoebe's femininity – scornful, down-to-earth, impatient at the follies of women. Viola is robust in her relation to Olivia – proud, uncompromising, scrupulous: the lady, being of her element, is not in her welkin. In Lyly's *Gallathea* two girls woo each other without lasciviousness: passion reaches the audience filtered through comic distance. The image of love is fantastic, grotesque, lyrical, asexual, a pastime for gods and nymphs. Cupid haunts the grove disguised as a nymph, and nymphs haunt the grove disguised as boys in order to evade Neptune. Lyly's love-struck girls inhabit the same uncomplicated emotional climate as the boys in the Elizabethan friendship plays. There is little overt homosexuality in Elizabethan drama outside Marlowe's *Edward II*. Nor would it arguably have been politic for the dramatists, despite their capacity for evasion, to nurture on stage propensities for which moralists condemned the theatre.

Caroline drama compromises with the homosexual situation in a way that Elizabethan drama never does. Women disguised as men woo other women with more sense of physical involvement, less moral keenness and less honesty when the subterfuge is discovered. In Ford's *The Lover's Melancholy*, or Brome's *A Mad Couple Well Match'd*, or Suckling's *Brennoralt* or Shirley's *The Sisters*, ladies disappointed by suitors turned feminine are left high and dry with no questions asked and unreal protestations of eternal friendship covering unequivocal amorous betrayal. So many feelings are cavalierly swept under the carpet that the only conclusion possible is that these are not feeling beings. The earlier playwrights took care to develop in the disguised woman an unmistakable allegiance to the fact of her womanhood, while freeing her from its restrictions. Caroline drama, less interested in the restrictions, is also less interested in the woman, or in the man she might become. Blasé about both nature and custom, the Caroline dramatist peopled the theatre with monsters without noticing it.

Obliged to convince the audience of the boy actor's femininity even when he looked, because of his disguise, exactly like the boy he was, Shakespeare and his fellow playwrights created a femininity to outlast the boy actor's changes of costume. Not having a natural woman on the stage, the dramatists concentrated on making audiences believe in the fiction of real women. The fact that the boy actor gave them no help freed them to look beyond the acquired manners of femininity, as the masculine woman herself had done when she cast aside a woman's dress.

Women share with other women experiences which men can never have. The Duchess of York in *Richard II* despairs of finding in the Duke that love for a child which is born with the struggle for life:

> Had'st thou groan'd for him
> As I have done, thou wouldst be more pitiful.[72]

Imogen compares her longing to see Posthumus with a mother's longing for delivery:

> Ne'er long'd my mother so
> To see me first, as I have now.[73]

Giovanni in *The White Devil* cites his mother Isabella's feeding of him as a proof of her love:

> I have often heard her say she gave me suck,
> And it should seem by that she dearly lov'd me,
> Since princes seldom do it.[74]

Lady Macbeth's image of dashing the babe from her breast evokes her femininity even more potently for Shakespeare's time because a noblewoman, like Juliet's mother, would not have been expected to suckle her child. On this primal level a woman's nature diverges from a man's, forging the tie which Hermione allows to be stronger than the tie of childhood amity:

> To tell, he longs to see his son, were strong:
> But let him say so then, and let him go;
> But let him swear so, and he shall not stay.
> We'll thwack him hence with distaffs.[75]

[72] v.ii.102.

[73] *Cymbeline*, iii.iv.2.

[74] Webster, *The White Devil*, iii.ii.336.

[75] *The Winter's Tale*, i.ii.34.

The Duchess of Malfi's last thought is for her children:

> I pray thee, look thou giv'st my little boy
> Some syrup for his cold, and let the girl
> Say her prayers, ere she sleep.[76]

Women are one with other women in the experience of mother-
hood in a way that men are with other men on the battlefield, both
united against the isolation of violence and fear of death. The
dramatists place the boy actor in a spiritual community of women.
  Women are intimate not just as individuals, but as women.
Brought up together in separation from the male world, women
develop a loyalty to their sex, while the male child in their midst
prepares himself to move into the company of men. Challenged to
choose between her father and her childhood playmate, Celia embraces the feminine tie:

> I was too young that time to value her,
> But now I know her: if she be a traitor,
> Why, so am I: we still have slept together,
> Rose at an instant, learned, played, eat together,
> And wheresoe'er we went, like Juno's swans,
> Still we went coupled and inseparable.[77]

Helena reproaches Hermia not only with betraying a friend, but
with betraying her sex to men:

> Is all the counsel that we two have shared,
> The sisters' vows, the hours that we have spent,
> When we have chid the hasty-footed time
> For parting us – O! is all forgot?
> All school-days' friendship, childhood innocence?
> We, Hermia, like two artificial gods,
> Have with our needles created both one flower,
> Both on one sampler, sitting on one cushion,
> Both warbling of one song, both in one key;
> As if our hands, our sides, voices, and minds,

[76] Webster, *The Duchess of Malfi*, IV.ii.203.
[77] *As You Like It*, I.iii.71.

Had been incorporate. So we grew together,
Like to a double cherry, seeming parted,
But yet an union in partition,
Two lovely berries moulded on one stem:
So, with two seeming bodies, but one heart,
Two of the first, like coats in heraldry,
Due but to one, and crownéd with one crest.
And will you rend our ancient love asunder,
To join with men in scorning your poor friend?
It is not friendly, 'tis not maidenly –
Our sex, as well as I, may chide you for it;
Though I alone do feel the injury.

Women are reared in closeness to become competitors for male favour; the intrusion of a man converts intimacy into enmity. They have few weapons with which to war on each other; Hermia threatens scratching where Lysander draws a sword on Demetrius. Women try instead to influence a man against another woman, talking not to each other but to their defenders: 'She was a vixen when she went to school.' Helena turns to the two men who have deserted her friend:

I pray you, though you mock me, gentlemen,
Let her not hurt me. I was never curst:
I have no gift at all in shrewishness:
I am a right maid for my cowardice:
Let her not strike me. You perhaps may think,
Because she is something lower than myself,
That I can match her.[78]

When the sewing stops, the needle which worked the sampler pricks the helping hand. Women grow up knowing that men have power: father, brother, husband. To fight other women they enlist a man. If the four lovers in the wood all wore breeches there would still be no mistaking the women.

Born unequal in the eyes of the world, but with infant opportunity to observe each other's equality, brothers and sisters cherish

[78] *A Midsummer Night's Dream*, III.ii.198, 324, 299.

a closeness streaked with hostility. Isabella fears Claudio's weakness because she knows it as well as she knows her own strength. Her rage at his wavering is a nursery laceration, unmoderated by acquired respect:

> O, you beast!
> O faithless coward! O dishonest wretch!
> Wilt thou be made a man out of my vice?
> Is't not a kind of incest, to take life
> From thine own sister's shame? What should I think?
> Heaven shield my mother play'd my father fair:
> For such a warped slip of wilderness
> Ne'er issued from his blood.[79]

Society hands all the cards to Claudio, and he asks Isabella for her only one – her chastity. The brother inherits his father's authority towards his sister: Ferdinand and the Cardinal have absolute power over the Duchess. But the sister who bows to the parent's yoke is restive under the brother's. The Duchess of Malfi secretly goes her own way. Ophelia, subject to her father's preaching, rebels at her brother's – the faintest hint of insurrection to presage the revolt of insanity:

> I shall the effect of this good lesson keep
> As watchman to my heart. But good my brother
> Do not, as some ungracious pastors do,
> Show me the steep and thorny way to heaven,
> Whiles like a puffed and reckless libertine
> Himself the primrose path of dalliance treads,
> And recks not his own rede.[80]

The sister sees the libertine before society takes the boy out of smocks like her own and gives him breeches and the right to rule her, and she refuses to obliterate the memory of a being like herself. The boy actor, literally the same beneath a woman's clothes, entered naturally into the sister's role.

[79] *Measure for Measure*, III.i.135.

[80] *Hamlet*, I.iii.45.

Women have a delightful sense of confederacy with their own sex when they are in love, where men find other men tiresome. Benedick mocks Claudio and betrays his passion to Don Pedro; Proteus is a gadfly to the moony Valentine. Enobarbus talks to Antony about war and the need to leave Cleopatra. Cleopatra talks to her women about Antony, and imagines him talking of her:

> O Charmian!
> Where think'st thou he is now? Stands he, or sits he?
> Or does he walk? or is he on his horse?
> O happy horse to bear the weight of Antony!
> Do bravely, horse, for wot'st thou whom thou mov'st,
> The demi-Atlas of this earth, the arm
> And burgonet of men. He's speaking now,
> Or murmuring, 'Where's my serpent of old Nile?'
> For so he calls me.[81]

In *As You Like It* Celia's discovery to Rosalind of Orlando's love is an enchanting game whose rules both women know. Celia enhances Rosalind's joy by prolonging the disclosure: 'O Lord, Lord! It is a hard matter for friends to meet; but mountains may be removed with earthquakes and so encounter.' Rosalind is eager, inconsequential: 'Is it a man?' insatiable and irrational: 'But doth he know that I am in this forest and in man's apparel? Looks he as freshly as he did the day he wrestled?' A woman's love is not complete without a listener.

In the same scene, immediately following, Orlando and Jacques converse about Rosalind. Jacques informs the lover: 'I do not like her name.' Orlando retorts: 'There was no thought of pleasing you when she was christened.' Jacques calls Orlando's love his worst fault, and the lover rejoins: ' 'Tis a fault I will not change for your best virtue. . . . I am weary of you.' The man wants to protect his passion from idle stares where the woman wants to feed hers by communicating it. As Jacques dawdles laconically from the stage, a saucy lackey accosts Orlando. Shakespeare frames the lovers' first meeting with an interchange between two women, and an inter-

[81] *Antony and Cleopatra*, I.v.18.

change between two men. The boy actor steps out of the feminine world as unmistakably as Orlando emerges from the masculine.

Shakespeare often places in among the boy actors a man on whom they may prove their femininity. Women treat a man alone in their company with a tantalising mixture of flirtation and exclusion. The presence of Alexas spices the vivacity of Cleopatra and Charmian and Iras. The ladies in *Love's Labour's Lost* rehearse their mockery of the lords on Boyet. Both Le Beau and Touchstone are whetstones to the wit of Rosalind and Celia, where a woman would not do. Touchstone is not taken in. After a complicated witticism from the heroine he glances at the gallery to which both the Fool and the lady play: 'You have said: but whether wisely or no, let the forest judge.'[82] Women together make a single man among them feel an alien being, a Bottom among the fairies. A man either pays attention to a woman or he does not; a woman acknowledges his presence with delicate indirection. Beatrice assures Benedick at the end of his speech of her own inattention to it: 'I wonder that you will still be talking, Signior Benedick. Nobody marks you.'[83] A real man on the stage throws into relief the boy actor's femininity.

The more traditionally feminine the woman the more ill at ease she is in breeches. Rosalind and Portia thrive on the masculine life where Imogen wilts beneath it. The young princes sense her otherness: were she a woman they would woo her. Imogen's presence emanates refinement and delicacy, even fastidiousness; life becomes an art:

> But his neat cookery! he cut our roots in characters,
> And sauced our broths, as Juno had been sick
> And he her dieter.

Femininity is all things to all men. Guiderius admires Imogen for her housewifery, Arviragus for her singing: 'How angel-like he sings.' What a man finds feminine defines not the nature of women, but his own nature. Nevertheless, Imogen's disguise discomforts her. When she urges the youths to hunt as usual, she

[82] *As You Like It*, III.ii. *passim*.
[83] *Much Ado About Nothing*, I.i.103.

might be speaking of herself:

> Stick to your journal course: the breach of custom
> Is breach of all.[84]

Breaking custom in her apparel, Imogen obstructs the current of her own life. Femininity is so deeply ingrained in her that to annihilate it is a kind of death, like Ophelia's madness, or Lady Macbeth's hallucinatory sleep-walking. Rosalind, Portia, even Viola, whose minds travel easily between the world of men and the world of women, extend rather than endanger their sense of self when they assume a man's dress. Imogen, less versatile, more vulnerable, herself more fully realised in the traditional feminine world, never acquires the double image of the comic heroines, the man-woman spirit, which is perhaps why the Victorian actress, Helena Faucit, preferred her above all Shakespeare's heroines. She spoke of 'Imogen, in whom all that makes a woman most winning to unspoiled manly natures is unconsciously felt through the boyish disguise.'[85] Mrs Jameson wrote in 1832 that 'the preservation of her feminine character under her masculine attire, her delicacy, her modesty, and her timidity, are managed with the same perfect consistency and unconscious grace as in Viola.'[86] But Viola disguised is in part Sebastian, her own natural division of herself, watching Viola the woman:

> She never told her love,
> But let concealment like a worm i' th' bud
> Feed on her damask cheek: she pined in thought,
> And with a green and yellow melancholy
> She sat like Patience on a monument,
> Smiling at grief. Was not this love, indeed?
> We men may say more, swear more – but indeed
> Our shows are more than will; for still we prove
> Much in our vows, but little in our love.[87]

[84] *Cymbeline*, IV.ii.49, 10.
[85] *Shakespeare's Female Characters*, p. 199.
[86] *Shakespeare's Heroines*, p. 200.
[87] *Twelfth Night*, II.iv.110.

Imogen never sees herself as a man; the moment of her unmasking
is as a consequence the least ambivalent dramatically and psychologically of any in Shakespeare's plays. Forgetting her disguise –
which Viola or Rosalind would never have done – she presses forward to alleviate the anguish of Posthumus' remorse. He turns on
her, enraged that a page should steal his scene:

> Shall's have a play of this? Thou scornful page,
> There lie thy part.

Posthumus, histrionic, always playing to his own private amphi-
theatre of over-heated, under-rehearsed passions, encounters his
wife as another player on his own stage. Art and life marry. All
disguises vanish before the question Imogen had to disguise herself
in order to ask: 'Why did you throw your wedded lady from
you?'[88]

When disguise gives a woman a double image of herself the
dramatist has more difficulty getting her out of her breeches. Virginia Woolf described 'Shakespeare's mind as the type of the
androgynus, of the man-womanly mind. . . . It is one of the tokens
of the fully developed mind that it does not think specially or
separately of sex. . . . It is fatal for anyone who writes to think of
their sex. It is fatal to be a man or woman pure and simple; one
must be woman-manly or man-womanly.'[89] The experience of
Rosalind, or Viola, or Portia as men colours their character as
women. A man's attire, like a man's education, allows them to be
more complete and fully developed women. Disguise draws men
and women together in the comedies through their discovery of
the artifice of difference which social custom sustains. Lyly solved
the awkwardness of resolving disguise by allowing one of his girls
to change sex, but his mechanical plot device was innocent of any
symbolism of harmony between the masculine and the feminine.
Shakespeare's heroines integrate their experience as men with their
feelings as women, which makes it harder for the dramatist to
return them to their skirts. Orlando tires of the disguise before
Rosalind. Rosalind is a perfect woman when a man; as a woman

[88] *Cymbeline*, v.v.28, 261.

[89] *A Room of One's Own*, pp. 97, 102.

she needs more of a man than Orlando. Rejoicing with her in the saturnalian revelry of her masculinity in Arden, the audience regrets relinquishing her to her father to be formally given to a husband. Its playfellow must again become the possession of the male world. Shakespeare himself wanted his heroine to escape and brought her back as insouciant and elusive as ever to tell the audience that she was still Jove's own page: 'If I were a woman, I would kiss as many of you as had beards that pleased me, complexions that liked me, and breaths that I defied not: and, I am sure, as many as have good beards, or good faces, or sweet breaths, will for my kind offer, when I make curtsy, bid me farewell.'[90]

Viola, as isolated in her sorrow as Julia in *The Two Gentlemen of Verona*, cherishes a special unacknowledged intimacy with the audience. When Viola tells Orsino that she knows:

> Too well what love women to men may owe:
> In faith they are as true of heart as we,

the audience shares her doubleness. It identifies with the two selves with whom the actor himself has intercourse, where its relation with the Fool is only one of straightforward dialogue. Viola's love is nourished in the secrecy, suppression and melancholy of her disguise. The audience is committed not to her success but to her sadness. To be queen of a fancy so opal as Orsino's seems an unenviable bliss and Orsino, having squandered his treasury of love, is himself loth to lose his page: 'Cesario, come! / For so you shall be, while you are a man.' Outfaced by his own eloquence, he can find – like Cordelia – no genuine currency in which to court Viola except

> Give me thy hand,
> And let me see thee in thy woman's weeds.

This is exactly what the audience does not want to do; Viola is Viola in her breeches. Constant where Orsino is changeable, possessing a moral sensitivity which places Olivia in the same hemisphere as Cressida, Viola's other self is not the man she loves, but her brother:

---

[90] *As You Like It*, Epilogue, 16.

> One face, one voice, one habit, and two persons,
> A natural perspective, that is and is not.

Viola sees herself in his mirror:

> If spirits can assume both form and suit
> You come to fright us.

Sebastian's presence exorcises the wickedness of disguise; Nature has clothed his spirit in a shape to question Viola's 'masculine usurp'd attire:'

> A spirit I am indeed,
> But am in that dimension grossly clad,
> Which from the womb I did participate.[91]

In the magical reunion of the twins, man and woman, Shakespeare soothes the mind with an illusion of concord between the masculine and feminine only to dispel the illusion by separating Viola from the second self with whom she has learnt to live. She is diminished by a return to a world where she must be Orsino's lady after the momentary freedom of a Twelfth Night masculinity which restored Nature's wholeness.

Shakespeare evaded in *The Merchant of Venice* the problems that he created for himself in *Twelfth Night* and *As You Like It*. Portia's disguise scenes are a dramatic performance produced and presented with faultless fluency, like that other well-staged charade, the casket lottery at Belmont. The audience is never private with the young Daniel; it hears no catch in the voice, sees no panic, no laughter and alarm, no inner life. Shakespeare arouses no special affection for Portia in her breeches and therefore has none to disengage when he returns her to her gown. Disguise is contained within the stage scene. Shakespeare exploits the mockery of discovery without risking its embarrassment. Disguise expresses Portia's poise and control of the male world, but it is a poise present in Belmont itself and there is no sense of loss when the heroine returns home. Portia's clothes effect no metamorphosis on her spirit: the lawyer was never the lady, although the lady is always

---

[91] *Twelfth Night*, II.iv.105, v.i.384, 215, 234.

something of a lawyer. But the comedy is less perfect for lacking that imperfection in romantic resolution which fascinated Shakespeare as early as *Love's Labour's Lost*. The audience admires Portia, but it loves Viola.

The woman in disguise is a reveller in her own masque; her masculinity intrudes on the order of society making her, like the servant who plays the master in the Twelfth Night festivities, a mistress of misrule. Like the court masquer's, her unmasking reveals not the chameleon player, who might be anyone, but a new reality affirmed against the illusion of the play. The court masquer unmasks into the real world of the court,[92] and the woman in disguise discovers herself as part of the movement of the play out of the theatre into life – out of Arden, out of Twelfth Night into the rain that raineth every day.

In 1632 Henrietta Maria caused a sensation by acting in Montague's masque *The Shepherd's Paradise*. The event was not so revolutionary as its Puritan critic William Prynne made out in an attack which, if it was meant for the French troupe who performed with actresses in London in 1629, was taken by the court for abuse on the queen and chastised accordingly. The masque traditionally dissolves as the masque draws into its orbit the real monarch. Playing the queen of the shepherd's paradise in Montague's masque, Henrietta merged a dramatic role and a real one in a perfectly conventional way, as queen of a court which parallels the shepherds' retreat in the nobility of its inmates. She had acted in masques in France without impropriety. Charles I's first sight of her had been in a masque at the French court which he attended in disguise on his way to woo the Infanta of Spain. Prynne's attack probably took fire because of the queen's unpopularity in other spheres – her French attendants, the aversion created by her mother Marie de Medici's long sojourn in London, her religion, her interference in politics.[93] But it turned the event of noblewomen acting in private performances into a royalist cause, and playwrights like Cartwright felt an obligation to create plays for

[92] Orgel, *The Jonsonian Masque*, p. 118.

[93] Harbage, *Cavalier Drama*, p. 13. Oman, *Henrietta Maria*, pp. 16–17, 35, 45–8, 103.

the queen and her ladies to take part in. Professional actresses were not seen on the English stage till after the Restoration, when Charles II introduced the fashion allegedly to reform morals, on the grounds that male actors provoked homosexuality. As Nell Gwyn epitomised the Restoration actress's way of life the reform of morals seems to have been a straw in the wind. It was a long time before professional actresses ceased to have courtesan status. The amateur productions of the thirties staged by court ladies were altogether different in tone from the Restoration professional theatre, and judging from Montague's masque, deadeningly blameless. But some of the changes which the presence of women made on the later stage began in the private performances of the 1630's.

The first was a wholesale clean-up of dialogue between women, which impoverished the presentation of female character. Feminine propriety is a boy actor's joke in Shakespeare's theatre. Celia in Middleton's *More Dissemblers Besides Women* casts a sideways glance at the little page – in reality a pregnant woman in disguise – smirking: 'I must not talk / Too long of women's matters before boys.'[94] Middleton exploits a double ambiguity: in the illusion of the play they are all women together, though she thinks the page a boy; in the reality of the theatre they are all boys. Epicoene's interchanges with the collegiates share the same club-room feminine exclusiveness. Once there is really a woman on the stage the playwright feels the need to bow to the male idea of female modesty. Nice women do not crack dirty jokes, at least in public; it is not amusing to see them do so. Raciness becomes a male prerogative. Shakespeare and his contemporaries knew as well as anyone else that women are quite as racy as men when they are on their own together, but they had no social inhibitions to overcome because their women's racy jokes – the fun which Portia and Nerissa have, the audacious jesting of Celia and Rosalind which amazes the courtier Le Beau, with his conventional idea of woman – are spoken by boy actors. The personality and image of the actor does not interpose itself between the playwright and his conception of his character. The boy actor is an instrument, and Shake-

[94] v.i.141.

speare uses him with the sense of his possibilities and limits which Beethoven brought to writing concertos for a piano smaller than the modern concert grand, or Mozart to composing a horn concerto for a different kind of technical mechanism. The woman actress was not the dramatist's tool in the same way; Victorian actresses fussed about having to dress as boys. Shakespeare put a woman's qualms about breeches into the play. He did not want to have to bother with them in his actors. The boy actor gave the dramatist more freedom to imagine what women were like without having to accommodate their imagined likeness to the whims and preconceptions not only of a woman actress, but of the audience, about what it was proper for a woman to say whoever she might be acting. It has been said that the Children's companies initiated the tragedy of sex and violence in the Jacobean period.[95] The more impersonal the actor, the more dissociated he is in the audience's mind from what he projects as a professional, the greater the freedom of the dramatist to explore and take risks. The Children of their nature provided the maximum contrast between the bawdy or vicious talk of, for example, Marston's courtiers, and the actual presence of the boy actor.[96] Shakespeare exploited this dissociation in his women characters, making women as lively and uninhibited as boys because boys had to speak their parts. Montague's Platonic love dialogues are written by a man to be spoken by well-bred women: a good recipe for politeness, but a poor one for a play.

Caroline drama initiated the custom of having women play serious men's parts. In Shirley's *The Bird in a Cage* a masque is staged with a woman playing the hero, and her stage passion gets out of hand to an uneasy degree which the playwright seems to have ignored, or found titillating: 'Beshrew the bell-man,' exclaims the man-woman, 'an you had not wak'd as you did, madam, I should have forgot myself, and play'd Jupiter indeed with you; my imaginations were strong upon me, and you lay so

---

[95] R. A. Foakes, 'Tragedy of the Children's Theatres after 1600: A Challenge to the Adult Stage', *The Elizabethan Theatre II*, p. 59.

[96] Michael Shapiro, 'Children's Troupes: Dramatic Illusion and Acting Style', *Comparative Drama*, III (1967) 43–6.

sweetly.'[97] Under these terms drama moves into theatrical convention in a way that Shakespeare's plays, conceived for an equally arbitrary condition – an all male cast as opposed to an all female – never did. Men performed by ladies tend to be operatic, requiring the degree of suspension of disbelief necessary in Gluck's *Orfeo*, as the contralto expresses her longing for Eurydice, or in *Der Rosenkavalier*, where an inevitably buxom operatic youth woos the ageing countess. This is only tolerable if real questions are not asked – about sexual contact, emotions, psychology. Drama deals primarily with those questions an opera like Strauss's urges one to ignore. But where the woman actor obstructs questions about men the boy actor provokes questions about women. The apparently artificial stage convention of boys playing women leads to a portrait of the individual woman which courts naturalism.

Restoration drama boasts neither female heroes nor male heroines. But the woman actor offers no challenge to the dramatist to understand femininity beyond its surface appearance. If the audience knows that when a woman enters, that is what she is, the dramatist need not ask himself how to make her womanhood convincing beyond charming speeches for Millamant and what Meredith called 'boudoir Billingsgate'[98] for Lady Wishfort. All the questions behind the Elizabethan and Jacobean creation of female character become a stage anachronism. The world knows a woman when it sees one.

Shakespeare's feminism is not optional, to be taken or left according to the critic's taste. The masculine woman's claim that feminine clothes did not necessarily express a feminine nature was vital to the theatre's justification of the boy actor and the woman in disguise. The boy actor prompted the creation of boyish heroines. Disguise freed the dramatist to explore, in Bacon's new case or experiment, the natures of women untrammelled by the customs of femininity. More would have approved of Shakespeare's suggestion that the masculine spirit can liberate women from the constraints of traditional femininity.

[97] IV.ii.
[98] *An Essay on Comedy*, p. 252.

3 *Politics and Violence*

For the Elizabethans successful politics meant successful wars. The fact that women's physical weakness debarred them from the battlefield seemed perhaps an even stronger argument against their involvement in politics than the ideological ones which Knox mustered against women-rulers. A modern Prime Minister may decide to embark on war, but he is not required to head a cavalry charge. Shakespeare's Henry V answered at Agincourt the Elizabethan acid test of the strong monarch as surely as Richard II failed it on the coast of Wales. Yet it is no accident that in a play full of compliment to the queen Shakespeare married Theseus to the queen of the Amazons. When Spenser traced the queen's lineage back to the martial maid Britomart in *The Faerie Queene*, he accused men of prejudice in not recording the warlike exploits of women:

> Here have I cause in men just blame to find,
> That in their proper praise too partiall bee,
> And not indifferent to woman kind,
> To whom no share in armes and chevalree
> They doe impart, ne maken memoree
> Of their brave gestes and prowesse martiall.

Spenser claims that despite the niggardly tribute of poets

> By record of antique times I finde
> That wemen wont in warres to beare most sway,
> And to all great exploites them selves inclind,
> Of which they still the girlond bore away;
> Till envious Men, fearing their rules decay,
> Gan coyne streight lawes to curb their liberty:
> Yet sith they warlike armes have laide away,
> They have exceld in artes and pollicy,
> That now we foolish men that prayse gin eke t'envy.

Britomart excelled in battle before men deprived women of arms; Elizabeth, the champion of a later age, translates her ancestor's glory into arts and policy:

> Of warlike puissance in ages spent,
> Be thou, faire Britomart, whose prayse I wryte;
> But of all wisdom bee thou precedent,
> O soveraine Queene![1]

That the queen rules by wisdom rather than by the sword measures the advance of civilisation, not the inadequacy of the woman-ruler. The disgruntled Jacobeans, comparing their inglorious male monarch with Gloriana, might well have felt that the female sovereign had given her people the best of both worlds, proving herself to be the lodestar of valour in men, while nurturing all the excellent arts of peace. Shakespeare and his fellow playwrights register, as Spenser did, the devaluing of women consequent on denying them physical strength, but the dramatists also establish values which declare physical strength untempered by wisdom to be the emblem of barbarity.

The dramatists wrote for a period fascinated by the question of women's political capacity. Sixteenth century Europe boasted a plethora of notorious female sovereigns: Bloody Mary Tudor, who persecuted the Protestants and provoked Knox's original outburst against female Catholic monarchs; Catherine de Medici, who aroused the same anguished protests in France after the massacre of the Huguenots on St Bartholomew's Day; Mary Queen of Scots; the Scottish Queen Regent, Marie of Lorraine; Henri IV's widow, the Regent Marie de Medici, hated mother of Henrietta Maria; and Elizabeth herself, possibly the most respectable apple in a fairly rotten crop. None of these women could be accused of shirking the violent action which defines manhood. As politicians they might severally have set the murderous Machiavel to school.

Elizabeth's success as a political ruler perhaps strengthened the convictions of some Humanists about women's capacity for public life. If women might enter the law or even the priesthood there was no logic in excluding them from government. Women's political consciousness developed fast in the century between

---

[1] Book III, Canto II, i–iii. The first three books of *The Faerie Queene* were published in 1589, shortly before Shakespeare wrote the *Henry VI* plays.

Elizabeth's accession and the end of the Civil War. Women demonstrated in the streets against the suppression of Puritan preachers;
they canvassed for the Levellers; they wrote tracts and petitioned
Parliament.[2] The victims of political decisions, they demanded the
right to make them:

> Are any of our lives, limbs, liberties, or goods to be taken from
> us, no more than from men, but by due process of law and con-
> viction of twelve sworn men of the neighbourhood? And can
> you imagine us to be so sottish or stupid as not to perceive, or not
> to be sensible when daily those strong defences of our peace and
> welfare are broken down and trod underfoot by force and arbi-
> trary power?[3]

The handbook of common law – written specifically for women –
which T.E. published in 1632 argued that women ought to know
the principles on which men made decisions affecting them:
'There bee some things in these Bookes which are not Latin, yet
even these may enable you the better to understand the reasons and
arguments of Law, and to conferre and enquire what the Law is.'[4]

Elizabeth's pre-eminence underlined the ambiguity of women's
position in politics. The fate of Henry VIII's wives – her own
mother was beheaded – and even of Mary Queen of Scots, admonished the queen of the special precariousness of a woman's political
triumph. Towards the end of her reign she became more and more
obsessive in her precautions against poisoning and sudden attacks
on her person. The insecurity of her state, and the contrast between
her power and the myth of feminine weakness, obtruded on
playwrights who already possessed a literary model for exploring
the plight of women in politics.

When Thomas Newton collected together the Elizabethan
translations of Seneca's *Tenne Tragedies* he provided Shakespeare
and his fellow playwrights with a gallery of women enmeshed in

---

[2] Collinson, *The Elizabethan Puritan Movement*, p. 93; Brailsford, *The Levellers
and the English Revolution*, pp. 316–17.

[3] From a *Petition of Women, Affecters and Approvers of the Petition of Sept. 11, 1648*
(5 May 1649), in Woodhouse, *Puritanism and Liberty*, p. 367.

[4] *The Lawes Resolutions of Womens Rights*, p. 403.

the male world of politics, whether as its pawns, like Hecuba and her women in *Troas* — Seneca's version of Euripides' *The Trojan Women* — or as its instruments of vengeance and destruction. Seneca's Clytemnestra looks back to Aeschylus' more powerful heroine, forward to Margaret in Shakespeare's history plays and ultimately to Goneril. Seneca's women suffer atrocious violence, but they also commit it, whether governed by the private passions of a Phaedra or the entangled personal and political motives of Clytemnestra and, to a degree, Medea. The compelling figure of Medea thrust itself on Shakespeare's imagination again in Golding's translation of Ovid. Seneca, tawdry and tedious as he is, and as his translators have faithfully rendered him, nevertheless made accessible to Shakespeare and his contemporaries that astounding array of heroines in Greek classical drama who consistently contradict male images of female weakness, mental and physical.

The woman-ruler accepted an office fashioned by masculine tradition. John Knox, intransigent Scots Presbyterian, held that she could only perform it by becoming a man, and thus a monster. Circe, the *alter ego* of Medea in Greek mythology, is for him, as for Stubbes, the patron sorceress of the masculine woman. Knox imagines Aristotle and the Greek philosophers gazing on a European queen:

> I am assuredlie persuaded, I say, that suche a sight shulde so astonishe them, that they shulde judge the hole worlde to be transformed into Amazones, and that suche a metamorphosis and change was made of all the men of that countrie, as poetes do feyn was made of the companyons of Ulisses, or at least, that albeit the outwarde form of men remained, yet shuld they judge that their hartes were changed frome the wisdome, understanding, and courage of men, to the foolishe fondnese and cowardise of women.

For Knox the political and the domestic cannot be separated. God made woman subject to man and to grant her sovereignty over him is sacrilegious:

> Nature, I say, doth paynt them furthe to be weake, fraile,

impacient, feble and foolishe; and experience hath declared
them to be unconstant, variable, cruell, and lacking the spirit of
counsel and regiment.[5]

Knox's notorious *First Blast of the Trumpet against the Monstrous
Regiment of Women*, printed in 1558, was written particularly
against the two Catholic monarchs, Mary Tudor and the Scottish
Queen Regent, Marie of Lorraine. Braving the storm of protest
which his outburst occasioned Knox tried to conciliate Elizabeth
by claiming that her extirpation of idolatry both in herself and in
her kingdom reconciled him to her reign, at least. But his letter to
her demonstrates in a manner not likely to deceive that sharp-eyed
sovereign that being a woman is not redeemed by being a Protestant. Knox counsels the queen to attribute her triumphs to God's
mercy, 'which onlie maketh that truthfull to your Grace, which
nature and law denieth to all weomen.'[6] The queen must practise
self-abasement even in her exalted station. Knox has it both ways:
a strong woman-ruler is manly and monstrous; but a woman-ruler
attending to his advice would be bound to be weak, in which case
his point would be proven – women are unfitted for sovereignty.

Knox – whose polemics were far from popular in a world more
sympathetic to Spenser's view of Britomart's descendant – equated
physical and moral strength. Finding women deficient in the one,
he assumed their deficiency in the other. He quoted Tertullian to
prove that 'he that judgeth it a monstre in nature that a woman
shall exercise weapons, must judge it to be a monstre of monstres
that a woman shalbe exalted above a hole realme and nation.'[7] The
playwrights assign to many characters Knox's view that to be
feminine is to be effeminate: that all the qualities which degrade a
man lodge in women. Melantius, vowing revenge in *The Maid's
Tragedy*, cries:

> Forsake me, then, all weaknesses of nature,
> That make men women![8]

[5] *First Blast of the Trumpet against the Monstrous Regiment of Women*, pp. 375, 374.

[6] Knox to Queen Elizabeth, *The Works of John Knox*, VI, 49.

[7] *The First Blast of the Trumpet against the Monstrous Regiment of Women*, p. 383.

[8] Beaumont and Fletcher, *The Maid's Tragedy*, IV.i.99.

If physical force is the ultimate arbiter of supremacy women must be inferior in a world which denies them weapons. But the inferiority comes to embrace a much wider sphere than that of the physical weakness which first decided it. A man who refuses to strike is irresolute, cowardly, ill-judging. Romeo castigates himself for his reluctance to fight Tybalt: 'O sweet Juliet, / Thy beauty hath made me effeminate.'9 Patrochlus languidly presents Achilles with a portrait of the inactive man:

> To this effect, Achilles, have I moved you.
> A woman impudent and mannish grown
> Is not more loathed than an effeminate man
> In time of action.¹⁰

A society which values action above everything else offers women no middle position between monstrosity and womanishness.

In such a world moral strength consists in banishing the feminine. Cassius measures Caesar's worth by the susceptibility of his body:

> That tongue of his that bade the Romans
> Mark him and write his speeches in their books,
> 'Alas,' it cried, 'give me some drink, Titinius,'
> As a sick girl! Ye gods, it doth amaze me
> A man of such a feeble temper should
> So get the start of the majestic world
> And bear the palm alone.¹¹

A man strikes where a woman weeps, swoons and curses. Macduff medicines grief by remembering that tears are not his only weapon:

> O, I could play the woman with mine eyes
> And braggart with my tongue. – But, gentle heavens,
> Cut short all intermission; front to front,
> Bring thou this fiend of Scotland, and myself;
> Within my sword's length set him.

⁹ *Romeo and Juliet*, III.i.112.
¹⁰ *Troilus and Cressida*, III.iii.216.
˙ *Julius Caesar*, I.ii.125.

Malcolm approves: 'This tune goes manly.'[12] Hamlet sees in
Laertes and Fortinbras the rebuke of his effeminate inaction, that
he

> Must like a whore unpack my heart with words,
> And fall a-cursing like a very drab.[13]

If a man lacks physical power he becomes a woman, not respected
because not feared, a contemptible onlooker on the world of
action. When Lear gives his daughters his kingdom and his army
he gives them his manhood:

> You see me here, you Gods, a poor old man,
> As full of grief as age; wretched in both!
> If it be you that stirs these daughters' hearts
> Against their father, fool me not so much
> To bear it tamely; touch me with noble anger,
> And let not women's weapons, water-drops,
> Stain my man's cheeks! No, you unnatural hags,
> I will have such revenges on you both
> That all the world shall – I will do such things,
> What they are, yet I know not, but they shall be
> The terrors of the earth. You think I'll weep;
> No, I'll not weep:
> I have full cause of weeping, but this heart
> Shall break into a hundred thousand flaws
> Or ere I'll weep.[14]

A woman suffers continually from the impotence which is
exceptional in a man. The playwrights suggest how the condition
of powerlessness affects individual women. At moments of crisis
women in the drama are painfully aware that their only weapon is
words. Vittoria in *The White Devil* exclaims at her trial:

> O woman's poor revenge
> Which dwells but in the tongue, – I will not weep,

[12] *Macbeth*, IV.iii.230.
[13] *Hamlet*, II.ii.589.
[14] *King Lear*, II.iv.274.

> Nor I do scorn to call up one poor tear
> To fawn on your injustice.[15]

The Duchess of York demands in *Richard III*: 'Why should calamity be full of words?' and Queen Elizabeth replies:

> Windy attornies to their client woes,
> Airy succeeders of intestate joys,
> Poor breathing orators of miseries!
> Let them have scope: though what they will impart
> Help nothing else, yet do they ease the heart.[16]

Women use words to create the illusion of action. Andromacha in Seneca's *Troas* – that evocation of the hopeless grief of the Trojan women about to be led into slavery – places before Ulysses a portrait of herself as Amazon avenger:

> As fierce as dyd the Amasones
>   beat downe the Greekes in fight,
> And Menas once enspyrde with God,
>   in sacryfice dothe smyght:
> With speare in hande, and while with fu-
>   rious pace she treades the grounde,
> And woode as one in rage: she strikes
>   and feelythe not the wounde:
> So wyll I ronne on midst of them
>   and on theyr weapons dye,
> And in defence of Hectors tombe,
>   among hys asshes lye.[17]

Ulysses bids her desist from womanish fury and open Hector's tomb as he commands, which she of course does. Women construct their own theatre where they watch themselves making 'an act of tragic violence.'[18] The theatricality of Constance's grief in

[15] Webster, *The White Devil*, III.ii.283.
[16] IV.iv.126.
[17] III.i.1705.
[18] *Richard III*, II.ii.39.

King John comforts her; like Richard II lacking an army, she
peoples her imagination with subjects:

> To me and to the state of my great grief
> Let kings assemble; for my grief's so great
> That no supporter but the huge firm earth
> Can hold it up: here I and sorrows sit;
> Here is my throne, bid kings come bow to it.

Her appeal to the Heavens to fight on her behalf looks forward to
Lear:

> Arm, arm, you heavens, against these perjur'd kings!
> A widow cries; be husband to me, heavens!
> Let not the hours of this ungodly day
> Wear out the day's in peace; but, ere sunset,
> Set armed discord 'twixt these perjur'd kings!
> Hear me, O, hear me![19]

Shakespeare as a poet cherishes a special sympathy with the men
and women whose sphere of action is words rather than deeds.

The effect of impotence is to turn women against each other
rather than against the men who injure them. The famous
slanging-match between Eleanor and Constance in *King John* –
sometimes cut as unseemly – is psychologically apt. Constance
knows that her most vulnerable enemy is not a man, but the
woman who has succeeded – where she herself has failed – in setting up a man on her behalf. Both women are aware that Eleanor's
position is as precarious as her rival's. The forsaken queens in
Richard III lacerate with their tongues not the men who have
wronged them, but the women attached to those men. A woman
can only commit vicarious physical violence – like Hecuba in
Troas urging Menelaus to kill Helen; her violent passions are more
likely to impress women than men, because women cannot escape
to a world of action.

The frustrations of women trapped in the political world are
many-sided. They are Cassandras, foreseeing doom but unheeded.

[19] II.ii.70, III.i.33.

In Tacitus' *Germania* women are revered for possessing a gift of 'holiness and prophecy,'[20] and men attend to their advice. Shakespeare's women dream and see visions in vain, surviving to suffer the devastation they predict. Decius interprets Calphurnia's dream to flatter Caesar, and sketches the scorn which would attend his hearkening to his wife's fears:

> Besides, it were a mock
> Apt to be rendered, for some one to say
> 'Break up the Senate till another time,
> When Caesar's wife shall meet with better dreams.'[21]

Hector's parting words to Andromache express his impatience of his wife's foreboding; Troilus shrugs off 'This foolish, dreaming, superstitious girl.'[22] When in Aeschylus' *Agamemnon* Clytemnestra announces that she has seen the beacons aflame which declare the end of the Trojan War, the Chorus suggests that she has dreamt it. She turns on them with the pent-up scorn of a strong woman never listened to because a woman: 'Dream! Am I one to air drowsy imaginings?'[23]

The first to divine events, women are the last to know them. Richard II's queen feels only an undefined grief; she learns of the deposition by overhearing a gardener's gossip. Her fury with him is the offshoot of a helplessness so palpable that men do not trouble to inform her of events which radically affect her life:

> Nimble mischance, that art so light of foot,
> Doth not thy embassage belong to me.
> And am I last that knows it?[24]

Constance hears of the alliance between France and England, which will destroy Arthur's claim, second-hand through Salisbury. She is incredulous:

[20] *On Britain and Germany*, p. 107.
[21] *Julius Caesar*, II.ii.96.
[22] *Troilus and Cressida*, V.iii.79.
[23] p. 52.
[24] *Richard II*, III.iv.92.

It cannot be; thou dost but say 'tis so.
I trust I may not trust thee, for thy word
Is but the vain breath of a common man.
Believe me, I do not believe thee, man;
I have a king's oath to the contrary.[25]

Lady Macduff learns of her husband's flight – disastrous to herself
and her children – from another man. She can only offer the
woman's bitter, but also slightly querulous reproach to an inatten-
tive male world: 'He loves us not.' She feels the feebleness of her
self-justification to the murderers:

I have done no harm. But I remember now
I am in this earthly world, where, to do harm
Is often laudable; to do good, sometime
Accounted dangerous folly: why then, alas!
Do I put up that womanly defence,
To say, I have done no harm?[26]

Women's harmlessness in the political world, as Clytemnestra
knew only too well, was their worst enemy. Shakespeare understood that in politics power hangs on the power to inflict injury.
Women are not told events because they cannot alter them.

Women parry powerlessness by becoming adept plotters, chan-
nelling into premeditation the energy which men expend in performance. Feminine cunning is proverbial. Golding, translator of
Ovid's *Metamorphoses*, finds in the story of Medea the moral 'That
women both in helping and in hurting have no match / When they
too eyther bend their wits.'[27] The evil, scheming stepmother in
Seneca's *Octavia* anticipates the Queen in *Cymbeline*. Clytemnestra
and Medea prefigure many Renaissance heroines – Vittoria using
her dream to instruct her lover how to do away with her husband,
or Beatrice in *The Changeling* plotting to evade responsibility for
violence enacted on her behalf. Seneca's Creon finds in Medea a
devilish mixture of 'shamelesse womans wilie braine / and manly

[25] *King John*, II.ii.6.
[26] *Macbeth*, IV.ii.8, 73.
[27] Epistle, 147.

stomack stoute.'²⁸ The 'craftye guyles / of wicked women kynd'²⁹ acquired topical interest for the Jacobeans from the case of the Countess of Essex who contrived the slow poisoning of Thomas Overbury in revenge for his exposing her character as a wife.

A skilful woman acquires a man to act on her behalf. But women who contrive without the power to accomplish tend, like Middleton's Beatrice committing murder through De Flores' agency, to live in a fantasy world immune from the realities of action. A woman's distance from the arm that strikes heats her imagination, where for a man the necessity of acting chills ambition. Eleanor is more intransigent than John, Volumnia fiercer than Coriolanus; Eleanor in *Henry VI* urges where Duke Humphrey demurs, and her successor, Lady Macbeth, is deaf to promptings which give Macbeth pause. Impotence makes women dangerous.

Lady Macbeth is dangerous because she miscalculates the consequences of her strategy. The witches work on Macbeth's image of himself as king; Lady Macbeth works on his image of himself as man. To spur him to action she embraces manhood herself:

> Come, you Spirits
> That tend on mortal thoughts, unsex me here,
> And fill me from the crown to the toe top-full
> Of direst cruelty! make thick my blood;
> Stop up th'access and passage to remorse;
> That no compunctious visitings of Nature
> Shake my fell purpose nor keep peace between
> Th'effect and it!

She tries to shame him with her own resolution:

> I have given suck, and know
> How tender 'tis to love the babe that milks me:
> I would, while it was smiling in my face,
> Have pluck'd my nipple from his boneless gums,
> And dash'd the brains out, had I so sworn
> As you have done to this.

²⁸ *Medea*, II, 942.

²⁹ Seneca, *Agamemnon*, II, 826.

Macbeth marvels, like Flamineo paying tribute to Vittoria's courage at the end of *The White Devil*, at her ability to shake off the trammels of feminine weakness:

> Bring forth men-children only!
> For thy undaunted mettle should compose
> Nothing but males.

But Lady Macbeth's fiction of masculinity is never more than a valour of the tongue. She cannot repress her nature: 'Had he not resembled / My father as he slept, I had done't.' Violence destroys her as Macduff imagined that it would:

> O gentle lady,
> 'Tis not for you to hear what I can speak:
> The repetition in a woman's ear
> Would murder as it fell.

Unlike Goneril's, Lady Macbeth's sense of self is rooted in a traditional pattern of femininity – mother, wife, helpmeet. Repudiating her womanhood to make Macbeth a man, Lady Macbeth forfeits her closeness to him. Seeking to be more than a woman she becomes less than one – the shadow of the sleep-walking scene, as unsexed as the witches themselves.

Lady Macbeth's idea of masculinity is devastatingly conventional: a man is one who acts:

> Art thou afeard
> To be the same in thine own act and valour
> As thou art in desire?

Macbeth has more feeling for the limits of action:

> I dare do all that may become a man;
> Who dares do more, is none.

His wife ignores his insinuation:

> What beast was't then,
> That made you break this enterprise to me?
> When you durst do it, then you were a man;

And, to be more than what you were, you would
Be so much more the man.

Her only means of rallying him when he sees Banquo's ghost is to
taunt him with effeminacy: 'Are you a man?'

O! these flaws and starts
(Imposters to true fear), would well become
A woman's story at a winter's fire,
Authoris'd by her grandam.

But Macbeth is too unmanned by his own excess of manly action
to heed her jibes. Gazing at Banquo's stool, he murmurs: 'Why,
so; — being gone, / I am a man again.' Lacking virtue, Macbeth's
action in killing Duncan reduces him to the level of the hired murderer whose claim to be a man excites his scorn:

Ay, in the catalogue ye go for men;
As hounds, and greyhounds, mongrels, spaniels, curs,
Shoughs, water-rugs, and demi-wolves, are clept
All by the name of dogs.

The deed which Lady Macbeth prophesied would make Macbeth
more of a man reduces the warrior of the opening battle —
'Valour's minion' — to the shrinking, superstitious, bragging, hys-
terical wretch at Dunsinane who cannot look his enemy in the
face, for he has 'cow'd my better part of man.'

Shakespeare denies that masculinity ordains action, and in doing
so undermines the logic which declares women to be weak and
ignoble because incapable of fighting. Physical strength, as in
Ajax, is the attribute of a beast unless tempered by judgement.
Macbeth envies Banquo his discretion:

'Tis much he dares;
And, to that dauntless temper of his mind,
He hath a wisdom that doth guide his valour
To act in safety.[30]

---

[30] *Macbeth*, I.v.40, I.vii.54, 73, II.ii.12, II.iii.83, I.vii.39, III.iv.57, III.i.91, I.ii.19,
v.ix.18, III.i.50.

Valour without wisdom defeats Hotspur at Shrewsbury. Albany in *King Lear* becomes a man at the moment when he defends himself for not acting: 'Where I could not be honest, / I never yet was valiant.'[31] Laertes in *Hamlet* comes the nearest in Shakespeare's plays to Seneca's Pyrrhus, content to avenge Achilles in a manner which desecrates Athene's shrine – the origin of all the Greek troubles on the return voyage from Troy. Hamlet, trying to urge his reluctant spirit to revenge, requests from the Player the description of Pyrrhus slaughtering Priam. But Hamlet is more of a man for his inability to proclaim with Laertes: 'Conscience and grace to the profoundest pit,' or to agree with Claudius, an expert on murder, that

> No place indeed should murder sanctuarize,
> Revenge should have no bounds.[32]

Hamlet is less noble contriving the death of Rosencrantz and Guildenstern – his first positive action – than in his unwillingness to act. If manhood really means killing rather than being killed, it is only another name for barbarity. The wisdom which makes physical strength valuable is as accessible – as Spenser pointed out – to women as to men, perhaps more so because they are not tempted to exercise the brute force which unmans Macbeth.

Shakespeare's successful military men all evince elements of barbarity. A good soldier cultivates ruthlessness and even unscrupulousness at the expense of compassion, generosity, tenderness of conscience. Edmund informs the Captain whom he hires to execute Lear and Cordelia:

> Know thou this, that men
> Are as the time is; to be tender-minded
> Does not become a sword.[33]

Warriors have no time for second thoughts; they live in the present. Henry V's verdict on the fiery-nosed Bardolph brushes aside the ambassador of memory: 'We would have all such offenders so

[31] v.i.23.
[32] *Hamlet*, IV.v.132, IV.vii.126.
[33] *King Lear*, V.iii.31.

cut off.' Action quells reflection:

> We'll cut the throats of those we have,
> And not a man of them that we shall take
> Shall taste our mercy.[34]

The imperviousness to other people which guarantees success in ruling them diminishes a man. Bolingbroke repels the audience's sympathy as long as he disclaims vulnerability:

> Little are we beholding to your love,
> And little look'd for at your helping hands.[35]

The weary, tormented king of *Henry IV* compels more concern. Octavius Caesar is an austere, ascetic, cold man who seems a boy in spirit compared with Antony, primitive where Antony is civilised – raw, unschooled and relentlessly Roman. Just as Shakespeare endowed Falstaff with all the creative warmth which he denied Henry V – what Bradley called 'the inexplicable touch of infinity'[36] – so he gave to Antony and Cleopatra a colour, poetry and richness which dwarfs Octavius, leaving him as lean and hungry as Cassius, the man who had no music in his soul. Shakespeare recaptured in many plays the rhetoric of war, but he felt the poetry of peace. A new life is infused into *Henry V* when Burgundy heralds peace:

> Let it not disgrace me
> If I demand before this royal view,
> What rub or what impediment there is,
> Why that the naked, poor, and mangled Peace,
> Dear nurse of arts, plenties, and joyful births,
> Should not in this best garden of the world,
> Our fertile France, put up her lovely visage?
> . . . .
> The even mead, that erst brought sweetly forth
> The freckled cowslip, burnet, and green clover,
> Wanting the scythe, all uncorrected, rank,

---

[34] *Henry V*, III.vi.111, IV.vii.65.
[35] *Richard II*, IV.i.160.
[36] 'The Rejection of Falstaff', *Oxford Lectures on Poetry*, p. 273.

Conceives by idleness, and nothing teems
But hateful docks, rough thistles, kecksies, burrs,
Losing both beauty and utility.
And as our vineyards, fallows, meads, and hedges,
Defective in their natures, grow to wildness,
Even so our houses and ourselves and children
Have lost, or do not learn for want of time,
The sciences that should become our country,
But grow like savages, as soldiers will
That nothing do but meditate on blood,
To swearing and stern looks, diffus'd attire,
And every thing that seems unnatural.[37]

Shakespeare shared the Humanists' scepticism about war even in his most military play. He drew men who, when only soldiers, grow something like savages. Antony, whom Plutarch sternly rebukes for squandering in Egypt 'the most precious thing a man can spend, as Antiphon saith: and that is, time,'[38] develops in *Antony and Cleopatra* from the slick politician and reputed reveller of *Julius Caesar* into a man who does not need war to show his quality. Cleopatra, for whom Plutarch has not a good word to say, in Shakespeare bodies forth all that Rome lacks – the beauty, art, leisure and non-utilitarianism which war denies. Britomart's descendant excelled not in war, but in the arts and policy of peace.

The soldier, living in a world of men, develops a particular attitude to women. Cleopatra recognises the contempt behind Octavius' conciliation of her: 'He words me, girls, he words me, that I should not / Be noble to myself.' Classing all women together, Octavius plays into Cleopatra's hands; he instructs:

From Antony win Cleopatra, promise,
And in our name, what she requires; add more,
From thine invention, offers: women are not
In their best fortunes strong; but want will perjure
The ne'er-touch'd vestal.

Cleopatra flatters his masculine superiority:

[37] v.ii.34.   [38] *Shakespeare's Plutarch*, II, 41.

> Sole sir o'the world,
> I cannot project mine own cause so well
> To make it clear, but do confess I have
> Been laden with like frailties, which before
> Have often sham'd our sex.[39]

Her pretence that she retains her treasure to propitiate two women she hates — Livia and Octavia — convinces Octavius because it accords with his idea of feminine corruptibility. The soldier sees women as the luxury of peace and the impediment of war. Enobarbus' impatience of Antony's entanglement with Cleopatra is of the same order as Hotspur's brushing aside of his wife:

> Away,
> Away, you trifler! Love! I love thee not.
> I care not for thee, Kate; this is no world
> To play with mammets, and to tilt with lips;
> We must have bloody noses, and crack'd crowns,
> And pass them current too.

Hotspur offers a man of action's love, strong, instinctive — 'Whither I go, thither shall you go too,' — but recognising in his wife no equality: 'Thou wilt not utter what thou dost not know.'[40] Shakespeare named Lady Percy Kate in defiance of history, perhaps because he associated Hotspur with that other rough wooer, Petruchio in *The Taming of the Shrew*. Shakespeare's Kates — Henry V's queen as well — all get the same kind of man. The soldier's woman must accommodate herself to the limits in his perception of her. Hotspur is a fine match for Kate, but he would bore Cleopatra.

Enobarbus projects a soldier's image of himself — unemotional, cynical about women, hard-headed about his profession. But just as Cleopatra's magic draws from him the most exotic tribute of the whole play, so in his broken-heartedness at his treachery to Antony his emotional nature rebels against the man of action's mask of toughness:

---

[39] *Antony and Cleopatra*, v.ii.190, III.xii.27, v.ii.119.
[40] *Henry IV* Part I, II.iii.90, 116.

> Throw my heart
> Against the flint and hardness of my fault,
> Which being dried with grief, will break to powder,
> And finish all foul thoughts. O Antony,
> Nobler than my revolt is infamous,
> Forgive me in thine own particular,
> But let the world rank me in register
> A master-leaver, and a fugitive:
> O Antony! O Antony![41]

When Dr Johnson grumbled at the extravagance of Enobarbus' conceit he missed the point about Enobarbus which specially interested Shakespeare in a character he almost entirely invented, and to whom he chose to give North's beautiful rendering of Plutarch's description of Cleopatra's barge. Shakespeare created in *Antony and Cleopatra* a contrast between the three soldiers: Octavius without feeling, Enobarbus in whom feeling is disastrously suppressed in the interests of masculine hardness, and Antony whose excess of feeling draws on him accusations of effeminacy. There is no doubt whom Shakespeare considered to be the fullest man of the three.

Shakespeare admired the temperate man as Hamlet admired Horatio, but he was more engaged by the character who did not stop short at Horatio's view that ' 'Twere to consider too curiously, to consider so.'[42] In *Julius Caesar* Brutus' self-government seems the epitome of manhood beside the chiding spirit which Cassius blames on his mother. He swallows Portia's death as stoically as the wine which quenches the quarrel with Cassius. Where Richard III is a trembling wreck after the visitations of ghosts before Bosworth, Caesar's ghost finds Brutus almost laconic: 'Why, I will see thee at Philippi then.'[43] Nevertheless, commanding his own emotions, Brutus underestimates the way in which other men are swayed by theirs. Brutus may have more integrity than Antony but he is obtuse about passions which Antony understands. In the same way the extravagant sensibility of Malcolm is as inaccessible

---

[41] *Antony and Cleopatra*, IV.ix.15.

[42] *Hamlet*, v.i.200.

[43] IV.iii.286.

to Macduff as Richard II's is to Bolingbroke. Macduff confirms the facts of his family's slaughter but conceals his grief; Malcolm rallies him:

> Merciful heaven! –
> What, man! ne'er pull your hat upon your brows:
> Give sorrow words; the grief that does not speak,
> Whispers the o'erfraught heart, and bids it break.

Macduff's self-control is surer than Enobarbus's because it is founded on the recognition of emotion. When Malcolm urges him to 'Dispute it like a man,' he replies:

> I shall do so;
> But I must also feel it as a man.[44]

Denying that action proves the man, Shakespeare also denies that passion proves him a woman.

Shakespeare believed that for a man to be more than a boy, as for a woman to be more than a child, the masculine and the feminine must marry in his spirit. Claudius speaks to the enraged Laertes as to a tantrummy schoolchild: he is more afraid of Hamlet. Coriolanus is reared to a masculinity unmoderated by femininity because his mother is more manly than himself: 'Thy valiantness was mine, thou suck'st it from me.'[45] As a consequence he never fully attains manhood; he remains trapped in a world where only action is valued. His relation to his mother is more like that of a son to his father; but by spurring him to greater masculinity Volumnia deprives him of the opportunity to develop a manhood to complement her womanhood.[46] Shakespeare greatly expanded the relationship between Coriolanus and his mother which he found in Plutarch. Like Macbeth, Coriolanus is less of a man for being more than a man; like Octavius, he needed a Cleopatra.

Aufidius accuses Coriolanus of womanishness in his tears of relenting, knowing that it will gall him. But in Shakespeare's plays

[44] *Macbeth*, IV.iii.207, 220.
[45] *Coriolanus*, III.ii.129.
[46] Cf. I. R. Browning, 'Coriolanus: Boy of Tears', *Essays in Criticism*, V (1955) no. 1, 18–31.

tears are not the emblem of feminine impotence. When Cranmer weeps for gratitude at Henry VIII's trust in him, his tears attest his truth: 'Look, the good man weeps: / He's honest on mine honor!'[47] Even Lewis in *King John*, hard-boiled politician, is moved by Salisbury's grief at betraying his country, a grief redemptive of that treachery:

> Let me wipe off this honorable dew,
> That silverly doth progress on thy cheeks:
> My heart hath melted at a lady's tears,
> Being an ordinary inundation;
> But this effusion of such manly drops,
> This shower, blown up by tempest of the soul,
> Startles mine eyes.[48]

When Macbeth imagines tears drowning the wind in pity for Duncan's murder he sees in his mind's eye the king's tears of joy for his subjects' loyalty. Shakespeare disavows the womanishness of weeping. Some of his noblest women do not weep. Katherine at her trial turns to Wolsey:

>   Sir,
> I am about to weep; but, thinking that
> We are a queen (or long have dreamed so), certain
> The daughter of a king, my drops of tears
> I'll turn to sparks of fire.[49]

Hermione begs the lords not to stint their compassion for her because of her lack of tears:

>   Good my lords,
> I am not prone to weeping, as our sex
> Commonly are; the want of which vain dew
> Perchance shall dry your pities: but I have
> That honourable grief lodg'd here which burns
> Worse than tears drown.[50]

---

[47] *Henry VIII*, v.i.152.   [48] v.ii.45.

[49] *Henry VIII*, ii.iv.67.   [50] *The Winter's Tale*, ii.i.107.

Shakespeare refuses to divide men and women into the active and the passive, the stoic and the sentient.

Spenser declared that men had defeated their own ends by robbing women of weapons, because as a consequence women surpassed them in art and policy. Shakespeare uses the women who seem the most at the mercy of the male world to assert values which measure its worth and find it wanting. In *Henry VIII* marriage provides Katherine with no political protection. Henry assures his wife magniloquently at the beginning of the play of her share in his sovereignty:

> Arise, and take place by us. Half your suit
> Never name to us; you have half our power.
> The other moiety ere you ask is given.
> Repeat your will and take it.

But the virtue as a wife which gives Katherine power while queen is only of value in the political world as long as she is queen. Ungilded by princely favour, a women's virtues declare only her weakness. Anne Bullen's subtlety stands her in better stead than Katherine's straightforwardness:

> There's nothing I have done yet, o' my conscience,
> Deserves a corner. Would all other women
> Could speak this with as free a soul as I do!

Henry, even as Katherine leaves the court, can only praise her goodness:

> Go thy ways, Kate.
> That man i' th' world who shall report he has
> A better wife, let him in naught be trusted
> For speaking false in that. Thou art alone
> (If thy rare qualities, sweet gentleness,
> Thy meekness saint-like, wife-like government,
> Obeying in commanding, and thy parts
> Sovereign and pious else, could speak thee out)

> The queen of earthly queens. She's noble born,
> And like her true nobility she has
> Carried herself towards me.

Katherine might have retorted for all women: 'As flies to wanton boys, are we to th' Gods.' Politics sanctions a moral inversion where the virtues of a good woman enable men to consider her of no account. Cressida, daughter of a traitor, rootless in an enemy setting, has the measure of the male political world better than any of Shakespeare's virtuous queens and daughters; where Katherine's womanhood evinces her weakness Cressida's is a political bargaining point, gaining her favour despite her precarious circumstances. But Cressida's accommodation to the values of politics extends the turpitude of the Trojan War. Shakespeare was more interested in the criticism of political values offered by Katherine than in Cressida's acclimatisation to those values. The Epilogue to *Henry VIII* declares what the author considered to be the heart of the play:

> All the expected good w'are like to hear
> For this play at this time, is only in
> The merciful construction of good women,
> For such a one we showed 'em.[51]

Women, who live to be the grievous survivors of wars men make and die in, stand in Shakespeare's history plays for permanence and fidelity against shifting political sands. The cruelty of political marriage lies in its harnessing of vows of stability to the fickleness of political allegiance. In the cases of both Octavia in *Antony and Cleopatra* and Blanche in *King John* Shakespeare accelerated the crises which rupture the marriages, thus emphasising the anomalies of the woman's situation. The sixteenth century had plenty of occasion to doubt the diplomacy of political marriage. Erasmus declared that its consequence 'is not the absence of wars, but rather the cause of making wars more frequent and more atrocious; for while one kingdom is allied to another through marriage, whenever anyone is offended he uses his right of relationship

[51] III.ii.366, I.ii.10, III.i.30, II.iv.131, Epilogue, 8.

to stir up the others.'[52] Where Plutarch showed Octavia to be a successful ambassador between her brother and her husband, Shakespeare makes her the pretext for Octavius' renewed aggression against Antony. Octavius complains of the indignity of her arrival in Rome as 'a market-maid'. His followers are ostentatious in defence of her honour, self-righteously condemning the abominations of the adulterous Antony. Plutarch's Octavia is a more fully developed character than Shakespeare's – a noble Roman lady universally beloved, who bore Antony two children and held his love until he was obliged to return to Asia, and there succumbed again to Cleopatra. Shakespeare's Octavia is more ruthlessly the victim of politics, holding no power over the heart she tries to sway:

> O my good lord,
> Believe not all, or, if you must believe,
> Stomach not all. A more unhappy lady,
> If this division chance, ne'er stood between,
> Praying for both parts.

She pleads in vain for the trust which Agrippa had optimistically promised between brother and brother-in-law:

> By this marriage,
> All little jealousies which now seem great,
> And all great fears, which now import their dangers,
> Would then be nothing: truths would be tales,
> Where now half tales be truths: her love to both
> Would each to other and all loves to both
> Draw after.[53]

Octavia is instead, as Erasmus predicted, the rankling point between rivals.

The humiliation of Octavia's situation lies in its lip-service to love. Shakespeare's Antony makes the marriage for his peace. He has no use for his holy cold wife and her attempts to influence him

---

[52] *The Education of a Christian Prince*, p. 242.

[53] *Antony and Cleopatra*, III.vi.51, III.iv.10, II.ii.131.

demonstrate only the self-deception which the political bride is
obliged to practise to conceal from herself the crude buying and
selling in which she is only a coin passed between hands. Blanche's
situation in *King John* is more extreme; the marriage vows between
her and Lewis consolidating the alliance between England and
France have hardly died on the air – a sensational speeding up and
telescoping of Holinshed's version – before Pandulph, the Roman
legate, arrives to divorce the unholy alliance of the faithful and the
apostate country. Blanche is the casualty of diplomacy. Her new
husband urges his father to arms against his new wife's land.
Blanche cries:

> Upon thy wedding-day?
> Against the blood that thou hast married?
> What, shall our feast be kept with slaughter'd men?
> Shall braying trumpets and loud churlish drums,
> Clamours of hell, be measures to our pomp?
> O husband, hear me! ay, alack, how new
> Is 'husband' in my mouth! even for that name,
> Which till this time my tongue did ne'er pronounce,
> Upon my knee I beg, go not to arms
> Against mine uncle.

No one except Blanche believes the fiction of love which civilises
political marriage. Lewis does not even answer her when she
upbraids him:

> Now shall I see thy love: what motive may
> Be stronger with thee than the name of wife?[54]

Blanche transgresses the gentleman's agreement by which her
marriage is only serious politics, not serious passion. Erasmus had
described the heartlessness of political marriage for the women
involved;[55] Shakespeare condensed his source material in these two
plays to make the human tragedy of Octavia and of Blanche
comment on the political transaction.

[54] III.i.226, 239.
[55] *The Education of a Christian Prince*, p. 243.

Shakespeare never allows the political world independence from the personal. Blanche's plea for faith acts as a foil to the fabric of infidelity which begins with Lady Faulconbridge and the argument about the Bastard's birth – Shakespeare's own invention – which casts its shadow across John's political legitimacy and his claims in France. The women in the histories, like Falstaff in Eastcheap and Shallow in Gloucester, offer a perspective on political life which subdues its sound and fury. Most of them can be sure, like Blanche, only of 'Assured loss.'[56] But their losses undercut the gains of the male world.

The women in *Richard II* – the Duchess of Gloucester, the Duchess of York, Richard's queen, whose characters are Shakespeare's creation – assess the values of the political world. Opening with the political quarrel between Mowbray and Bolingbroke the play moves immediately onto the domestic plane of the Duchess of Gloucester vainly urging Gaunt to revenge her husband:

> Finds brotherhood in thee no sharper spur?
> Hath love in thy old blood no living fire?

Finding family loyalty cold, she proceeds to the more cunning persuasion of self-interest:

> Call it not patience, Gaunt, it is despair;
> In suff'ring thus thy brother to be slaught'red,
> Thou showest the naked pathway to thy life,
> Teaching stern murder how to butcher thee.
> That which in mean men we intitle patience
> Is pale cold cowardice in noble breasts.
> What shall I say? to safeguard thine own life,
> The best way is to venge my Gloucester's death.

Gaunt commends her to a guardian as impotent in Shakespeare's histories as women themselves, 'God, the widow's champion and defence,' and the Duchess acknowledges the value of such succour with a sigh: 'Why then, I will.' The scene is virtually Shakespeare's invention, prominently placed in the play to make

[56] *King John*, III.i.262.

the point often reiterated in his histories that politics, born among
men, is never confined to the male world. The tournament at
Coventry acquires a new dimension from the solitary figure who
intrudes between the decision and the event, murmuring:

> Alack, and what shall good old York there see
> But empty lodgings and unfurnish'd walls,
> Unpeopled offices, untrodden stones,
> And what hear there for welcome but my groans?

York hopes to cement his loyalty to the new king by exposing
the treachery of his son, Aumerle. His zeal is the fruit of his own
perfidy, punishing himself in his offspring. The Duchess is indifferent to her husband's political prestige; she leaps to the defence of
her young:

> Why, York, what wilt thou do?
> Wilt thou not hide the trespass of thine own?
> Have we more sons? Or are we like to have?
> Is not my teeming date drunk up with time?
> And wilt thou pluck my fair son from mine age
> And rob me of a happy mother's name?
> Is he not like thee? Is he not thine own?

As early as *Henry VI*, where son unwittingly slays father and father
son in Civil War, Shakespeare recorded in domestic division the
division of a kingdom. He intensifies the Duchess' plea for family
unity against political difference by making her Aumerle's real
mother instead of his stepmother. But in the scene where child and
parents plead in chorus to Bolingbroke for pardon or punishment
the Duchess' values triumph. The scene opens with the successful
usurper reflecting on his unsuccessful heir, the madcap Prince of
Henry IV: 'Can no man tell me of my unthrifty son?' The Duchess
argues that York's harshness to Aumerle will mirror his love to the
king: 'Love loving not itself none other can.' York begs the new
king not to acquit the traitor on his father's account:

> So shall my virtue be his vice's bawd,
> And he shall spend mine honour with his shame,
> As thriftless sons their scraping fathers' gold.

Bolingbroke's mind flits back to the unthrifty son spending and whoring in the taverns, of whom he has such hopes. Loving none other, the politician loves his son. He pardons Aumerle. The Duchess' fidelity to the primal tie comments on York's faith to the political one, but it also recalls the larger treachery of the play. She falls before Bolingbroke as a 'god on earth,' and gathers the sinner to her: 'Come, my old son, I pray God make thee new.'[57] The image of original sin redeemed is full of irony. Aumerle's sin was the virtue of not turning against the deputy appointed by the Lord. The Duchess' truth to her son exposes the instability of political loyalty. Women undermine the subtleties of politics by clinging to values not susceptible to manipulation.

If women go to war themselves they cease to offer an alternative to the male world of politics and violence. When the Bastard in *King John* wants to express the subversive effects of Salisbury's treachery he describes women fighting:

> Blush for shame:
> For your own ladies ánd pale-visag'd maids
> Like Amazons come tripping after drums,
> Their thimbles into armed gauntlets change,
> Their needl's to lances, and their gentle hearts
> To fierce and bloody inclination.[58]

Ferocity is bestial in Shakespeare's plays in both men and women, but ferocity in women challenges the stability of the civilised world. Margaret's violence in *Henry VI* reflects the pattern of moral inversion – unscrupulousness, infidelity, meaningless vengeance – set in motion by Civil War. Her scorn of Henry's weakness, her adultery with Suffolk, her own military prowess, look forward to Goneril. Oswald, in *King Lear*, describing to Regan Albany's indecision at arms, declares: 'Your sister is the better soldier.' Goneril scoffs that she 'must change arms at home, and give the distaff / Into my husband's hands.' She demands of Albany:

> Where's thy drum;
> France spreads his banners in our noiseless land,
> With plumed helm thy state begins to threat,
> Whil'st thou, a moral fool, sits still, and cries
> 'Alack! why does he so?'

Where Margaret's cruelty is the imposthume of war, Goneril's is more terrible because it predates war, finding in the battlefield a means of expression. But Margaret's bestiality – York calls her she-wolf, tiger, Amazonian trull – is part of the ordered pattern of Shakespeare's histories. She is an avenger, able in the earlier plays to translate vengeance into violence, where, by the time of *Richard III*, she can only haunt her enemies with curses and her friends with ghoulish injunctions, like the ghost of Andrea in *The Spanish Tragedy*. Margaret acquires the legitimacy of the Greek Furies, insisting on retribution in future generations.

Aeschylus – and Seneca after him – gave the same sanction to Clytemnestra, making her the tool of the gods' vengeance on Agamemnon for the crimes of the house of Atreus, and for the slaughter of Iphigenia. Shakespeare, however, saw in Goneril – whose character mirrors the strength, indomitable will, imperturbable ability to deceive, of the Greek heroine – a more anarchic being: 'The laws are mine, not thine: / Who shall arraign me for't?' Her adultery with Edmund is part of that ruthless gratification of the will which makes her scorn Albany's refusal to strike her: 'Howe'er thou art a fiend, / A woman's shape doth shield thee.' She shrugs: 'Marry, your manhood – mew!' Clytemnestra, having ruled on her own until her husband's return, has more reason for bitterness at her subjection to her overbearing and faithless husband than Goneril. Goneril and Regan manifest human nature reduced to the predatory with none of the grandeur of Clytemnestra's rebellion against the lot of womanhood. Albany turns on his wife:

> See thyself, devil!
> Proper deformity shows not in the fiend
> So horrid as in woman.

Cornwall's violence is as vile as Regan's, more vile than Goneril's, which, despite the brutality of her treatment of Lear, only takes the form of poisoning her sister and stabbing herself. But the outrage which provokes even a servant to retaliation is the sight of a woman revelling in the violence which she ought to restrain in men:

> If she live long,
> And in the end meet the old course of death,
> Women will all turn monsters.

Lady Macbeth's rejection of femininity is paltry beside the sisters' reduction of human dignity. The loyalties which Goneril condemns as effeminate and womanish Shakespeare upholds as the dividing line between men and women, and beasts.

Regan's violence is more repulsive, though perhaps less dangerous, than Goneril's, because she is more conventionally feminine. The first interchange between the sisters declares their difference:

Regan: We shall further think of it.
Goneril: We must do something, and i' th' heat.[59]

Regan meditates while Goneril acts. Regan is not a woman to stand on her own; Goneril leads her, Cornwall takes action on her behalf. Her husband dead, she invests Edmund with her power. She needs to exercise power through a man, where Goneril holds it in her own hands. Like Margaret, accustomed to the impotence of politics, Regan regards the enactment of physical violence with almost Bacchic satisfaction, as one of the luxuries of power. She plucks Gloucester's beard with gratuitous savagery, bids the servants bind him hard, urges Cornwall to put out the other eye. Margaret's mockery of York with the paper crown and the mole-hill throne and a napkin dyed in his son's blood, is performed with the same fine-scale, torture-chamber thoroughness. The weak woman, like the weak man, given the chance makes the most vicious tyrant.

The violent woman in Shakespeare's theatre is nearly always an

---

[59] *King Lear*, IV.v.3, IV.ii.17, 55, V.iii.158, IV.ii.66, 59, III.vii.99, I.i.307.

adulteress – Tamora in *Titus Andronicus*, Evadne in *The Maid's Tragedy*, Bianca in *Women Beware Women*, Goneril herself, and any number of others. Pericles mouths a moral slogan – more reminiscent of Fletcher than Shakespeare – which dogs Renaissance tragedy:

> One sin, I know, another doth provoke;
> Murder's as near to lust as flame to smoke.
> Poison and treason are the hands of sin,
> Ay, and the targets, to put off the shame.[60]

Murder and adultery were twins, leaping together from the rind of the same apple tasted. The adulteress, taking the initiative in illicit sexual activity, forces on her husband the passivity of the cuckold. The adulterous woman adopts a male role; her femininity no longer stands in the way of physical violence. Similarly, the cuckold can only recover respect through the violent re-establishment of his manhood. Imagining himself wronged, Othello feels his identity as a man of action dissolve:

>   O now for ever
> Farewell the tranquil mind, farewell content;
> Farewell the plumèd troop, and the big wars,
> That make ambition virtue: O farewell,
> Farewell the neighing steed, and the shrill trump,
> The spirit-stirring drum, the ear-piercing fife;
> The royal banner, and all quality,
> Pride, pomp, and circumstance of glorious war!
> And, O ye mortal engines, whose wide throats
> The immortal Jove's great clamour counterfeit;
> Farewell, Othello's occupation's gone.[61]

When the adulteress breaks the taboo which debars her from violence, she also breaks the taboo which protects her from it. In the drama the ultimate horror of adultery is not the woman with the dagger drawn against a man, but the body of a woman – like

[60] *Pericles*, I.i.138.
[61] *Othello*, III.iii.353.

Tamyra's in Chapman's *Bussy D'Ambois* – tortured by a husband's vengeance. Albany's nobility emerges in his recognition that to stop his wife's mouth with her own letter to her lover is a more apt comment on her worth than killing her would have been. In some ways the Elizabethan tragedy of adultery is the woman's version of the revenge tragedy. Adultery is a woman's only weapon of vengeance, not only for the particular wrongs of a husband, but for the helplessness of women in a world where action is strength. Seneca's Medea sets a precedent for the frequent association in the drama of sorcery and adultery. But just as Seneca is divided between repulsion and compassion for his tormented heroine, so the Elizabethans and Jacobeans see in the enforced passivity of women a justification for the unnatural activities of the adulteress.

It would be tempting to assume that the presence of a female monarch on the throne fosters feminism. Certainly women in the plays of Shakespeare and his contemporaries demonstrate, as Elizabeth herself demonstrated, that power is not confined to the power to strike. Eleanor in *King John* chides the king for the political ineptitude which allowed Constance to bring her grievances as far as the battlefield instead of keeping them round the negotiating table. Marston's Sophonisba, ideal woman-ruler, uses her femininity as a political weapon, disarming opposition by talking about women's weakness while she instructs her followers what to do. Cleopatra is useless as a queen only when she tries to be a man, leading her fleet to battle. She is at her most queenly when claiming to be

> No more but e'en a woman, and commanded
> By such poor passion as the maid that milks,
> And does the meanest chares.[62]

Where Knox used conventional ideas about femininity to attack the woman-ruler, Shakespeare, like Spenser, attacked the ideas instead. The woman-ruler is a spur to feminism because her position forces men to ask questions about the relation between femininity and power. Shakespeare saw the nature of women as the

---

[62] *Antony and Cleopatra*, IV.xv.73.

inevitable product of their powerlessness in a masculine world, but he also saw it as the guardian of a civilisation which had moved beyond the primitive struggle of brute strength. Elizabeth's ascendancy is nobler than Britomart's. When the Humanists devalued war they upgraded women.

Shakespeare

Shakespeare's feminism consists of more than a handful of high-born emancipated heroines: it lies rather in his scepticism about the nature of women.

Shakespeare inherited ideas about women as well-defined and apparently impregnable as the principles of the Ptolemaic universe. Theology authorised a view of woman as a separate and inferior species, a view which pervaded the popular culture of proverbs, ballads and folk wisdom, but which also determined women's political and social position. Poetry offered an exotic choice between beauty and the beast, the goddess and the devil. The new dramatist might have imagined that the nature of women, so thoroughly and wearisomely familiar to everyone, was a good deal less interesting than the nature of men.

Had Shakespeare chosen to accept ideas about women formulated by Adam – gazing back at the apple-tree over the wall as he stumped out of Eden hand-in-hand with a pregnant wife – most writers, most readers, and most audiences, both before and since, would not have blamed him. Kitto declared acidly when writing on Greek drama, that 'most men are interested in women, and most women in themselves,'[1] but it would be easier to prove that most men are interested in themselves, and most women in men. Shakespeare need not have challenged preconceptions about women. Nevertheless, born into a world of Olympian uncertainties, the choice of the old gods would have placed Shakespeare outside the bounds of the new world at a time when intellectual vitality meant a seeking-out of new heaven and new earth. The men who dominated the spiritual life of the sixteenth century in England – Luther, Erasmus, Calvin, More and many of the Hu-

[1] The Greeks, p. 219.

manists – were all concerned to change the position of women. They all knew that that position could not be altered without a changed view of the nature which had determined it.

Calvin had to obliterate the image of Eve as temptress if he were to extricate marriage from the obloquy of spiritual second-rateness. More and Erasmus, with that total absence of mental insularity which characterised the Renaissance scholar, had gone further than Calvin. They saw in the aristocratic emancipated women of fifteenth century Italy – women educated as men's equals – a challenge to the whole philosophy and practice of education as applied to English women. More's observation of his own family, as well as of Catherine of Aragon and other famous women scholars in the Renaissance, bred in him the conviction voiced three centuries later by John Stuart Mill, that 'what is now called the nature of women is an eminently artificial thing – the result of forced repression in some directions, unnatural stimulation in others.'[2] Shakespeare demonstrated his susceptibility to the most powerful intellectual influences of his time when he drew Ophelia, chained into femininity by Polonius, and Helena in *All's Well That Ends Well*, determined to escape those chains. He recognised that the nature of women, as More pointed out, is only the product of society's expectations – expectations which in governing the treatment of women are bound to be self-fulfilling.

The reformation theologians – Bullinger, Latimer, Thomas Becon – had done their work in destroying the image of the seductive serpent who slithered across a man's hearth to dissuade him from celibacy. The Puritans accepted the more testing task of resetting, in everyday terms, men's attitudes to their wives, daughters, sisters, mothers. The medieval Eve was as incongruous a figure in Puritan marriage as a puppet in a full-scale play. Shakespeare's theatre – commercially run, and boasting adult actors like Burbage – was less hospitable to puppets, male or female, than the Tudor great hall, or the schoolroom or university hall, or the court itself had been in the heyday of the morality play, or in the years when Lyly's Children carried all before them. The Puritan sermon on home life provided Shakespeare and his fellow dramatists with

[2] *The Subjection of Women*, p. 238.

raw material for plays no longer devoted to life as it ought to be in defiance of life as it is. Social and psychological drama – like the novel, its natural heir – places women in the centre of the stage, which is perhaps one reason why Euripides was pre-eminently the favourite dramatist of Renaissance Humanist scholars.

The feminism which inevitably surrounded Elizabeth – herself reared on Humanist principles under the eye of Catherine Parr – had by James I's reign moved down into the middle classes. Puritanism gained its strongest foothold in the citizenry who constituted the bulk of the Globe audience – men and women who shared with the dramatists values defined by antipathy to the court. When the playwrights defended women against defamation they identified themselves with the social ideals of an audience hostile to aristocratic debauchery.

Literary critics tend to allow themselves a majestic unconcern about the precise relation between a man of genius and his own society. As one of the marks of genius is a liberation from time it is easy to talk about a great artist as though he were born into the world full-grown, like Minerva leaping from Jupiter's skull. Yet Milton would have been a totally different poet without the Puritan movement. Shakespeare had none of Milton's specific political involvement in Puritanism, but it is absurd to imagine that the Puritan spirit, which has had such a vast influence on English life, rubbed off on Spenser but left no traces on a man earning his living by entertaining a city buzzing with Puritan activity. Puritanism was the last manifestation in England of that astounding concentration of intellectual energy which created the Renaissance. Operating in a narrower sphere than the Humanists, the Puritans nevertheless embodied values upheld by Erasmus. The greatest works of art nearly always grow out of the mainstream of a tradition – like Mozart's operas – achieving greatness in their power to transcend that tradition. Shakespeare took the best of the Puritan spirit – its freshness, its rethinking of old authorities, its passionate moral intensity – and discarded its partisanship, so evident in the plays of men like Dekker and Heywood. Had he turned aside from the wellspring of talent which Puritanism tapped in the early seventeenth century he would have isolated himself from what was most vital in his own culture. Drama, which asks many questions which are not literary, and which in Shakespeare's time spoke to an audience of whom only a part possessed a literary culture, cannot afford to bypass the social and spiritual concerns of its time, however it may transmute them. What a critic says about a writer depends on the questions he asks himself; but what that writer himself says depends on the questions in his own mind. His own world, in one form or another, suggests his questions. Genius is a process of selecting what to ask as much as, if not more than of deciding what and how to answer. Drama has been called 'the poetry of the city.'[3] Shakespeare's theatre came magnificently of age in a London where women's influence was sharply felt and attitudes to them keenly debated. The feminism of the city provided one of those curious catalysts through which genius is crystallised.

Feminism nevertheless sounds a strange bedfellow for poetry, more like a joke in Aristophanes than a serious statement in Shakespeare. Shakespeare was not concerned to register in his plays his own presence as defender of women. He wrote no theses on the position of women – as did most of his contemporaries in one form or another, Marston, Dekker, Heywood, and even Middleton and Jonson. But Virginia Woolf was deceived by the poet's own unobtrusiveness when she declared that 'it would be impossible to say what Shakespeare thought of women.'[4] Shakespeare saw men and women as equal in a world which declared them unequal. He did not divide human nature into the masculine and the feminine, but observed in the individual woman or man an infinite variety of union between opposing impulses. To talk about Shakespeare's women is to talk about his men, because he refused to separate their worlds physically, intellectually, or spiritually. Where in every other field understanding of Shakespeare's art grows, reactions to his women continually recycle, because critics are still immersed in preconceptions which Shakespeare discarded about the nature of women.

[3] M. C. Bradbrook, *English Dramatic Form*, p. 41.
[4] *A Room of One's Own*, p. 97.

Works Cited

PLAYS

Aeschylus. *The Oresteian Trilogy*, trans. Philip Vellacott. 1959.
Beaumont and Fletcher. *The Works of Francis Beaumont and John Fletcher*, ed. A. R. Waller. Cambridge, 1905.
———. *The Maid's Tragedy. Five Stuart Tragedies*, ed. A. K. McIlwraith. 1953.
Brome, Richard. *The Dramatic Works of Richard Brome*. 1873.
Chapman, George. *The Works of George Chapman: Plays*, ed. Richard Herne Shepherd. 1889.
Dekker, Thomas. *The Dramatic Works of Thomas Dekker*, ed. Fredson Bowers. Cambridge, 1953–61.
Dryden, John. *Troilus and Cressida*. 1679.
Field, Nathan. *The Plays of Nathan Field*, ed. William Peery. Austin, 1950.
Ford, John. *The Dramatic Works of John Ford*, ed. William Gifford and Alexander Dyce. New York, 1965.
Heywood, Thomas. *The Dramatic Works of Thomas Heywood*. 1874.
———. *A Woman Killed with Kindness*, ed. R. W. Van Fossen. 1961.
How a Man May Choose a Good Wife from a Bad. Dodsley's Old English Plays, ed. W. Carew Hazlitt, IX. 1874.
Glapthorne, Henry. *The Plays and Poems of Henry Glapthorne*. 1874.
Jonson, Ben. *Ben Jonson*, ed. C. H. Herford and Percy Simpson. Oxford, 1954.
———. *Epicoene, or The Silent Woman*, ed. I. A. Beaurline. 1966.
Killigrew, Thomas. *Comedies and Tragedies*. 1664.
Lyly, John. *Gallathea and Midas*, ed. Anne Begor Lancashire. 1970.
Marlowe, Christopher. *The Complete Plays of Christopher Marlowe*, ed. Irving Ribner. New York, 1963.

Marston, John. *The Works of John Marston*, ed. A. H. Bullen. 1887.
Massinger, Philip. *The Plays of Philip Massinger*, ed. W. Gifford. Baltimore, 1856.
Middleton, Thomas. *The Works of Thomas Middleton*, ed. A. H. Bullen. 1885.
Molière. *The Plays of Molière*, in French, trans. A. R. Waller. Edinburgh, 1907.
Montague, Walter. *The Shepheard's Paradise*. 1659.
Seneca. *His Tenne Tragedies*, ed. Thomas Newton. 1927.
———. *Jasper Heywood and his Translations of Seneca's Troas, Thyestes and Hercules Furens*. *Materialen zur Kunde des älteren Englischen Dramas*, ed. W. Bang, 41. Vaduz, 1963.
———. *Studley's Translations of Seneca's Agamemnon and Medea*. Bang's *Materialen*, 38.
Shakespeare, William. *The Complete Pelican Shakespeare*. 1969. Used for *Errors, Shrew, H. VIII, Tit., Caesar, Troi., Oth., Cor., Per., Sonn., Phoenix*.
———. *Arden*. Used for *T.G.V., L.L.L., Merch., All's W., Meas., H. VI, H. IV, H. V, R. II, R. III, John, Lear, Macb., Antony, Cym., Temp., The Winter's Tale*.
———. *New Cambridge*. Used for *Dream, Twel., A.Y.L., Wives, Ham., Much*.
Shirley, James. *The Dramatic Works and Poems of James Shirley*, ed. William Gifford and Alexander Dyce. 1833.
Sophocles. *The Theban Plays*, trans. E. F. Watling. 1947.
Suckling, Sir John. *The Works of Sir John Suckling in Prose and Verse*, ed. A. Hamilton Thompson. 1910.
Lope de Vega. *Five Plays*, trans. Jill Booty, ed. R. D. F. Pring-Mill. New York, 1961.
Webster, John. *The Duchess of Malfi*, ed. John Russell Brown. 1964.
———. *The White Devil*, ed. John Russell Brown. 1960.
Wilkins, George. *The Miseries of Enforced Marriage*. Dodsley's *Old English Plays*, ed. W. Carew Hazlitt, IX. 1874.

OTHER WORKS

Adams, Robert P. *The Better Part of Valor: More, Erasmus Colet, and*

Vives, on Humanism, War, and Peace, 1496–1535. Seattle, 1962.

Agrippa, Henricus Cornelius. *The Glory of Women,* trans. Edward Fleetwood. 1651.

Anger, Jane. *Jane Anger her Protection for Women.* 1589.

Arnold, Matthew. *Culture and Anarchy,* ed. J. Dover Wilson. Cambridge, 1966.

Ascham, Roger. *The Scholemaster,* ed. Edward Arber. 1923.

Bacon, Francis. *Essays.* 1937.

Barber, C. L. *Shakespeare's Festive Comedy.* Princeton, 1959.

Bradbrook, M. C. *English Dramatic Form.* 1965.

——. *The Rise of the Common Player.* 1962.

——. *Shakespeare and Elizabethan Poetry.* 1964.

——. *Themes and Conventions of Elizabethan Tragedy.* Cambridge, 1935.

Bradley, A. C. *Oxford Lectures on Poetry.* 1965.

Brailsford, H. N. *The Levellers and the English Revolution,* ed. Christopher Hill. 1961.

Brinsley, John. *A Looking-Glasse for Good Women.* 1645.

Browning, I. R. 'Coriolanus: Boy of Tears'. *Essays in Criticism,* v (1955) no. 1, 18–31.

Bullinger, Heinrich. *The Christen State of Matrimonye,* trans. Myles Coverdale. 1541.

——. *The Decades of Henry Bullinger,* trans. H. I., ed. Thomas Harding. Parker Society, xxxv. Cambridge, 1849.

Calvin, John. *Institutes of the Christian Religion,* trans. Ford Lewis Battles, ed. John T. McNeill. 1961.

Castiglione, Baldassare. *The Book of the Courtier,* trans. Sir Thomas Hoby. 1966.

Chaucer, Geoffrey. *The Works of Geoffrey Chaucer,* ed. F. N. Robinson. 1957.

Clifford, Lady Anne. *The Diary of Lady Anne Clifford,* ed. V. Sackville-West. 1923.

Colie, Rosalie L. *Paradoxica Epidemica: The Renaissance Tradition of Paradox.* Princeton, 1966.

Collinson, Patrick. *The Elizabethan Puritan Movement.* 1967.

——. 'The Role of Women in the English Reformation illustrated by the Life and Friendships of Anne Locke'. *Studies in*

Church History, ed. G. J. Cumming, II. 1965.

Copland, Robert. *The Seven Sorowes that Women Have When theyr Husbandes Be Deade.* [1525].

Coulton, G. G. *Five Centuries of Religion.* IV: *The Last Days of Medieval Monachism.* Cambridge, 1950.

Davies, W. Robertson. *Shakespeare's Boy Actors.* New York, 1939.

Defoe, Daniel. *Moll Flanders.* 1965.

Dod, John, and Cleaver, Robert. *A Godly Forme of Houshold Government.* 2nd ed., 1630.

Donne, John. *Complete Poetry and Selected Prose*, ed. John Hayward. Nonesuch, 1955.

——. *The Sermons of John Donne*, ed. George R. Potter and Evelyn M. Simpson. Berkeley and Los Angeles, 1953.

E., T. *The Lawes Resolutions of Womens Rights.* 1632.

Eliot, George. *Essays of George Eliot*, ed. Thomas Pinney. 1963.

Erasmus, Desiderius. *All the Familiar Colloquies of Desiderius Erasmus*, trans. N. Bailey. 1725.

——. *The Education of a Christian Prince*, trans. Lester K. Born. New York, 1965.

——. *In Laude and Prayse of Matrymony*, trans. R. Tavernour. [1532].

——. *A Mery Dialogue, declaringe the Propertye of Shrowde Shrewes, and Honest Wyves*, trans. [Antony Kytson]. 1557.

——. *The Praise of Folie*, trans. Sir Thomas Chaloner, ed. Janet E. Ashbee. 1901.

Ewbank, Inga-Stina. *Their Proper Sphere: A Study of the Brontë Sisters as Early-Victorian Female Novelists.* 1966.

Faucit, Helena, Lady Martin. *On Some of Shakespeare's Female Characters.* Edinburgh and London, 1887.

Foakes, R. A. 'Tragedy of the Children's Theatres after 1600: A Challenge to the Adult Stage'. *The Elizabethan Theatre II*, ed. David Galloway. 1970.

Freeburg, Victor Oscar. *Disguise Plots in Elizabethan Drama.* New York, 1965.

Gataker, Thomas. *A Good Wife Gods Gift.* 1624.

George, Charles H. and Katherine. *The Protestant Mind of the English Reformation 1570–1640.* Princeton, 1961.

Gibson, Anthony. *A Womans Woorth, defended against All the Men in the World.* 1599.

Golding, Arthur. *Shakespeare's Ovid: Being Arthur Golding's Translation of the Metamorphoses*, ed. W. H. D. Rouse. 1904.

Gosynhyll, Edward. *The Schole House of Women*. 1560.

Gouge, William. *Of Domesticall Duties*. 1634.

Haec-Vir: or The Womanish-Man: Being an Answere to a Late Booke intituled Hic-Mulier. 1620.

Hall, Basil. 'Puritanism: The Problem of Definition'. *Studies in Church History*, ed. G. J. Cumming, II. 1965.

Haight, Gordon S. *George Eliot: A Biography*. Oxford, 1968.

Haller, William, and Haller, Malleville. 'The Puritan Art of Love'. *Huntington Library Quarterly*, v (1942) no. 2, 235–72.

Harbage, Alfred. *Cavalier Drama*. New York, 1964.

———. *Shakespeare's Audience*. New York, 1941.

———. *Shakespeare and the Rival Traditions*. New York, 1952.

Harley, Lady Brilliana. *Letters of the Lady Brilliana Harley*. Camden Society. 1854.

Harrison, William. *The Description of England*, ed. Georges Edelen. Ithaca, New York, 1968.

Hic Mulier: or The Man-Woman: Being a Medicine to Cure the Coltish Disease of the Staggers in the Masculine-Feminines of our Times. 1620.

Hill, Christopher. 'Clarissa Harlowe and her Times'. *Essays in Criticism*, v (1955) no. 4, 315–40.

Hillebrand, Harold Newcomb. *The Child Actors*. New York, 1964.

Hoby, Lady Margaret. *Diary of Lady Margaret Hoby 1599–1605*, ed. Dorothy M. Meads. 1930.

Homilies, Book of. Sermons or Homilies appointed to Be Read in Churches in the Time of Queen Elizabeth. 1817.

Hunter, G. K. *John Lyly*. 1962.

Hutchinson, Lucy. *The Life of Mrs. Lucy Hutchinson*, written by herself. *Memoirs of the Life of Colonel Hutchinson*, by his widow Lucy, ed. Julius Hutchinson and C. H. Firth. 1906.

King James the First, *Daemonologie*, ed. G. B. Harrison. 1924.

Jameson, Anna. *Shakespeare's Heroines*. 1913.

Johnson, James T. 'The Covenant Idea and the Puritan View of Marriage'. *Journal of the History of Ideas*, XXXII (1971) no. 1, 107–18.

Johnson, Samuel. *Samuel Johnson on Shakespeare*, ed. W. K. Wimsatt, Jr. 1960.

Kahin, Helen Andrews. 'Jane Anger and John Lyly'. *Modern Language Quarterly*, VIII (1947), no. 1, 31–5.

Kautsky, Karl. *Thomas More and his Utopia*. New York, 1959.

Kitto, H. D. F. *The Greeks*. 1951.

Knights, L. C. *Drama & Society in the Age of Jonson*. 1937.

Knox, John. *The Works of John Knox*, ed. David Laing. Edinburgh, 1895.

Laver, James. *Dress: How and Why Fashions in Men's and Women's Clothes Have Changed during the Past Two Hundred Years*. 1950.

Lanyer, Æmilia. *Salve Deus Rex Iudaeorum: Containing the Passion of Christ*. 1611.

Lecky, W. E. H. *History of European Morals from Augustus to Charlemagne*. New York, 1955.

Lewis, C. S. *The Allegory of Love*. 1958.

Luther, Martin. *Luther's Works*, gen. eds. Jaroslav Pelikan and Helmut T. Lehmann. Saint Louis and Philadelphia, 1958.

McConica, James Kelsey. *English Humanists and Reformation Politics under Henry VIII and Edward VI*. Oxford, 1965.

Machiavelli, Niccolò. *The Prince*, trans. Luigi Ricci. 1935.

Meredith, George. 'An Essay on Comedy'. *The Idea of Comedy*, ed. W. K. Wimsatt. Englewood Cliffs, New Jersey, 1969.

Mill, John Stuart. *The Subjection of Women*. 1970.

Milton, John. *Complete Prose Works of John Milton*. New Haven, 1959.

Montaigne. *The Essayes of Michael Lord of Montaigne*, trans. John Florio. 1928.

More, Edward. *The Defence of Women, and Especially of Englyshe Women, made against The Schole Howse of Women*. 1560.

More, Thomas. *The Complete Works of St. Thomas More*, IV, ed. Edward Surtz and J. H. Hexter. New Haven and London, 1965.

——. *The Latin Epigrams of Thomas More*, ed. Leicester Bradner and Charles Arthur Lynch. Chicago, 1953.

Mulde Sacke: or The Apologie of Hic Mulier: to the Late Declamation against Her. 1620.

Munda, Constantia (pseud.). *The Worming of a Mad Dogge: or A Soppe for Cerberus the Jaylor of Hell*. 1617.

Oman, Carola. *Henrietta Maria*. 1936.

Orgel, Stephen. *The Jonsonian Masque*. Cambridge, Mass., 1965.

Osborne, Dorothy. *The Letters of Dorothy Osborne to William Temple*, ed. G. C. Moore Smith. Oxford, 1928.

Owst, G. R. *Literature and Pulpit in Medieval England*. Oxford, 1961.

Palmer, D. J. '*The Merchant of Venice*, or the Importance of Being Earnest'. *Shakespearian Comedy*, Stratford-Upon-Avon Studies, *14*.

Parker, R. B. 'Middleton's Experiments with Comedy and Judgement'. *Jacobean Theatre*, Stratford-Upon-Avon Studies, *1*.

Perkins, William. *Christian Oeconomie*, trans. Thomas Pickering. 1609.

Plutarch. *Shakespeare's Plutarch*, ed. C. F. Tucker Brooke. 1909.

Powell, Chilton Latham. *English Domestic Relations 1487–1653*. New York, 1917.

Rabelais, François. *Gargantua and Pantagruel*, trans. Sir Thomas Urquhart. 1940.

Rich, Barnaby. *The Excellency of Good Women*. 1613.

——. *The Honestie of This Age*. Percy Society. 1844.

Richardson, Lula McDowell. *The Forerunners of Feminism in French Literature of the Renaissance*. Baltimore, Maryland, 1929.

Righter, Anne. *Shakespeare and the Idea of the Play*. 1962.

Rye, William Brenchley. *England as Seen by Foreigners: in the Days of Elizabeth and James the First*. 1865.

Screech, M. A. *The Rabelaisian Marriage*. 1958.

Shapiro, Michael. 'Children's Troupes: Dramatic Illusion and Acting Style'. *Comparative Drama*, III (1967) 42–53.

Sidney, Sir Philip. *An Apologie for Poetrie*, ed. J. Churton Collins. Oxford, 1947.

Smith, D. Nichol, *Shakespeare Criticism: A Selection*. 1964.

Smith, Henry. *A Preparative to Mariage*. 1591.

Smith, Irwin. *Shakespeare's Blackfriars Playhouse*. New York, 1964.

Sowernam, Ester (pseud.). *Ester Hath Hang'd Haman: or An Answere to a Lewd Pamphlet, entituled, The Araignment of Women*. 1617.

Speght, Rachel. *A Mouzell for Melastomus: The Cynicall Bayter of, and Foule Mouthed Barker against Evahs Sex.* 1617.

Spenser, Edmund. *Complete Works of Edmund Spenser*, ed. R. Morris. 1873.

Stenton, Doris Mary. *The English Woman in History.* 1957.

Stone, Lawrence. *The Crisis of the Aristocracy 1558–1641.* Oxford, 1965.

Stubbes, Philip. *Philip Stubbes's Anatomy of the Abuses in England in Shakspere's Youth A.D. 1583*, ed. Frederick J. Furnivall. New Shakspere Society. 1877–79.

Swetnam the Woman-Hater Arraigned by Women, ed. A. B. Grosart. Manchester, 1880.

Swetnam, Joseph. See Tel-Troth, Thomas.

Tacitus. *On Britain and Germany*, trans. H. Mattingly. 1951.

Tel-Troth, Thomas [Joseph Swetnam]. *The Araignment of Lewde, Froward, and Unconstant Women.* 1615.

Thomas, Keith. 'The Double Standard'. *Journal of the History of Ideas*, XX (1959) no. 2, 195–216.

——. 'Women and the Civil War Sects'. *Past and Present*, XIII (1958) 42–62.

Thompson, Elbert N. S. *The Controversy between the Puritans and the Stage.* New York, 1966.

Tolstoy, Leo. *Anna Karenina*, trans. Louise and Aylmer Maude. 1918.

Trickett, Rachel. *The Honest Muse.* Oxford, 1967.

Utley, Francis Lee. *The Crooked Rib: An Analytical Index to the Argument about Women in English and Scots Literature to the End of the Year 1568.* Columbus, 1944.

Vives, Joannes Ludovicus. *The Instruction of a Christian Woman: De Institutione Foeminae Christianae*, trans. Richard Hyrde. *Vives and the Renascence Education of Women*, ed. Foster Watson. 1912.

——. *The Office and Duetie of an Husband*, trans. Thomas Paynell. 1550.

Wilson, F. P. *Elizabethan and Jacobean.* Oxford, 1945.

Wilson, John Dover. *Life in Shakespeare's England.* Cambridge, 1911.

Wollstonecraft, Mary. *The Rights of Woman.* 1970.

Woodhouse, A. S. P. (ed.). *Puritanism and Liberty.* 1938.

Woodward, William Harrison. *Desiderius Erasmus: concerning the Aim and Method of Education.* Cambridge, 1904.

Woolf, Virginia. *Collected Essays,* ed. Leonard Woolf. 1966.

———. *Orlando.* 1942.

———. *A Room of One's Own.* 1945.

Wright, Louis B. *Middle-Class Culture in Elizabethan England.* Chapel Hill, 1935.

Index